Making Meaning, Making Sense: Children's Early Language Learning

Terry Piper
Barry University

Bridgepoint Education, Inc.

Terry Piper
Making Meaning, Making Sense: Children's Early Language Learning
Bridgepoint Education, Inc.

VP of Learning Resources: Beth Aguiar

Editor-in-Chief/AVP: Steve Wainwright

Director of Editorial Technology: Peter Galuardi

Sponsoring Editor: Mireille Yanow

Development Editor: Carrie Brandt

Assistant Editor: Kristle Maglunob

Editorial Assistant: Nicole Sanchez-Sullivan

Editorial Intern: Lindsey Messner

Production Editor: Kim Purcell

Printing Services: Bordeaux

Composition/Illustration: Lachina Publishing Services

Cover Image: Flikr/Getty Images

ISBN-10: 1621780392

ISBN-13: 978-1-62178-039-7

Published by Bridgepoint Education, Inc., 13500 Evening Creek Drive North, Suite 600, San Diego, CA 92128

www.bridgepointeducation.com I content.ashford.edu

Contents

Chapter 3
Learning Language: How Children Do It   *53*

Chapter 4
Learning a Second Language   *81*

Chapter 5
Language and Cognitive Growth   *111*

Chapter 6
Developmental Milestones   *147*

Chapter 8
Bumps in the Road: Communication Disorders *209*

Chapter 9
Language for Learning *237*

Chapter 10
Making Meaning, Making Sense: Putting It All Together *267*

About the Author

Terry Piper has been a teacher or a teacher educator for more than 40 years. With a doctorate in linguistics from the University of Alberta (Canada) and a B.A. and M.A. in English from the University of New Hampshire, she has worked in both the United States and Canada, and is currently dean of the Adrian Dominican School of Education at Barry University. Throughout her career, she has focused on language and language education, particularly in early childhood. She has published dozens of scholarly and professional articles, and *Making Meaning, Making Sense* is her 11th book. When she is not working or writing, Dr. Piper is an avid reader and a chef-wannabe. The mother of two grown sons and grandmother of two girls, she lives in Miami and spends summers in Canada.

Acknowledgments

I am grateful to Estela Azevedo, my assistant, who managed my calendar to give me the time to write this book, for her loyalty and support. To my research assistant, Linda Schaffzin, I am indebted for editing of early drafts and for helping with research. Carrie Brandt and Ann Greenberger at Bridgepoint Education have also been invaluable to the process of creating this book. I am especially grateful to my granddaughters, Isabelle and Sarah, for providing some of the more delightful examples of language learning in progress.

The editorial team and author would like to thank the following peer reviewers for their feedback and guidance:

Pilar Carroll, Ashford University

Amy J. Heineke, Loyola University–Chicago

Tammy R. Hutchinson-Harosky, Ashford University

Preface

Language is complex; learning it is not. At least, it's not if you are a child. That is the conclusion I have reached as a linguist and an educator. Over the past four decades, as I've watched my own children and then my grandchildren learn to speak and to read and write, helped out in kindergartens and preschools, or observed student interns work with preschool and elementary school children, I have seen firsthand how children learn language as they go about their daily routines. I have also seen how good teachers can guide them to expand their language experiences in ways that help them to develop cognitively and to succeed academically. In this book, you will meet many of those children. Many I have known personally; some are the pupils, children, or grandchildren of my graduate students or friends. Each one has helped to shape my views about language learning and will, I hope, help to form yours.

My theoretical perspective, which stems not only from my training as a psycholinguist but from my experience as an educator, a mother, and grandmother, is innatist—I believe that children are born with a biological predisposition to acquire language and that they do so within a community of language users. It is a perspective and not a *bias* or *prejudice* because it is based on decades of solid research as well as personal observation of the conditions under which children learn language. You may reach a different conclusion. That's okay. As long as these chapters have helped you in some way to develop your own perspective on children's language learning and, more importantly, served to inform your practice as an educator of young children, I have achieved my purpose.

For half a century, I have been enchanted by language. I marvel still at its beauty, its structure, its diversity, and what it becomes in the hands of gifted writers, but what still leaves me with a sense of wonder is how tiny children learn it with so little effort. I hope that this book leaves you with some of that same sense of wonder.

Terry Piper

Miami, 2012

1

The Nature of Language

Learning Objectives

By the end of this chapter, you will be able to accomplish the following objectives:

- Define language and describe the difference between language and communication.
- Explain the four attributes of language.
- Describe how cognition relates to language.
- Explain the difference between language and dialect and the connection between culture and language.
- Explain why language acquisition is a natural process that can be difficult to teach.

Introduction

Jacob spends more than half of each 24-hour day sleeping. When he is awake, he is often content to sit on the kitchen floor trying to fit lids onto plastic containers, with only limited success much of the time. When he fails, he will sometimes throw the objects or cry out in frustration. He is incapable of dressing himself, although he will extend his arm in an effort to assist—sometimes. He pulls himself up by holding onto the leg of the kitchen table, and if he walks, it is only when he can hold onto something—a hand, a piece of furniture, or an oversized toy. Even then, his steps are unsteady. Sometimes Jacob curls up on the living room floor and falls asleep cuddling a soft furry stuffed animal. Other times, he flatly refuses to sleep at all. Jacob is 14 months old, and he is typical of other children his age. He has come a long way from the newborn who slept between 16 and 18 hours a day and couldn't turn over much less walk, didn't yet know his name or the name for anything else in his world, and whose only vocalization was crying. Today, he certainly knows his name and a great deal more. He responds to much of what is spoken to him. He can point to his body parts when they are named. He understands when his mother tells him it is time for a nap or lunch; and when the phone rings, he will say "Dada," having learned that it is likely his father checking in. He has at least four other identifiable words of his own—*mama, teddy, nana,* and *truck,* although his pronunciations of *teddy* and *truck* are imperfect.

In just six months' time, he will be running as much as he is walking, holding onto nothing or nobody, and his interests will have expanded to include almost everything in his environment. Animals, trees, cars, and puzzles will fascinate him. Linguistically, he will have been very busy, indeed. His **productive vocabulary**, or those words he is heard to speak, will be close to 100 words, articulated well enough that most people can understand him, and he will be used to making complete sentences. It's true that most of those sentences will have only two words, but to the toddler Jacob, they will constitute full sentences. He will be fairly effective at communicating his meaning, and when he can't, he may show signs of frustration. His **receptive vocabulary**, or those words he understands but does not necessarily produce, will be much larger. As a language learner, he is making giant strides, but he is by no means finished.

By the time Jacob blows out six candles on his birthday cake, he will have learned, on average, five new words per day, giving him a receptive vocabulary between 10,000 and 20,000 words (Rhodes, D'Amato, & Rothlisberg, 2010). He will be able to use most of those words in complex sentences that seem to run on forever. He will make mistakes occasionally, but those mistakes are likely to be evidence that he has over-learned a rule or two. For example, he might say, "I didn't broughted that," marking the verb *bring* for past tense not once, but two times. He will be able to recite the alphabet, identify a number of written words, and write his name.

Jacob's is a remarkable accomplishment, yet there is nothing remarkable about him at all. He is a typical human child growing up in circumstances and an environment that are not at all unusual. That is exactly what is so fascinating about human language. It is complex and difficult, yet children learn it largely without purposeful intervention by other humans.

Language is so much a part of the human experience that Steven Pinker calls it an instinct. Moreover, it is this instinct that has made possible much of human accomplishment: "A common language connects the members of a community into an information-sharing network with formidable collective powers. Anyone can benefit from the strokes of genius, lucky accidents, and trial-and-error wisdom accumulated by anyone else, present or past" (Pinker, 2010, p. 3).

In this chapter, we introduce the aspects of language and language learning that will be covered in greater detail throughout the remainder of the book. Beginning with a definition of language, we go on to describe the attributes of language that set it apart from other forms of communication including its unique association with thought and cognition and the many varieties of language that exist.

Pre-Test

1. The primary means by which humans communicate is
   a. texting.
   b. facial cues.
   c. language.
   d. body movements.

2. Representing ideas or symbols with words is
   a. semanticity.
   b. representation.
   c. pictograph.
   d. syntax.

3. Language
   a. is unrelated to thought.
   b. follows thought, but does not lead it.
   c. is strongly linked to thought.
   d. leads thought, but does not follow it.

4. "Standard" dialect
   a. is free of jargon and slang usage.
   b. uses popular slang of the time.
   c. includes grammatical inaccuracies.
   d. consists of the most correct dialect.

5. The story of Helen Keller demonstrates that
   a. people can overcome obstacles to learn languages.
   b. sign language uses different cognitive structures than does spoken language.
   c. even those who lack an innate desire to learn develop language skills.
   d. children do not need stimulation to learn a language.

Answers

1. **c.** Language. *The answer can be found in Section 1.1.*
2. **a.** Semanticity. *The answer can be found in Section 1.2.*
3. **c.** Is strongly linked to thought. *The answer can be found in Section 1.3.*
4. **a.** Is free of jargon and slang usage. *The answer can be found in Section 1.4.*
5. **a.** People can overcome obstacles to learn languages. *The answer can be found in Section 1.5.*

1.1 What Is Language?

Before we can discuss language and how children learn to function effectively with it, it is necessary to consider just what language is. We know it when we hear it and we know when we are using it, but defining it proves a little more difficult. That is because language is a complex system that humans all over the world learn in its many varieties. Basically, it is a mode of communication, or the means by which messages are transmitted, and it has, as we shall see, certain unique properties. Closely connected to cognition and thought, language is part of what sets us apart from the rest of the animal kingdom. To appreciate the unique complexity of the human brain that created language as well as the complexity of language itself, and, most importantly, to begin to appreciate the enormity of children's accomplishment in acquiring language, it is important to understand just how special human language is.

Defining Language

Language is the principal means by which humans communicate, but not the only one. **Communication** is the activity of a sender conveying a message, usually with meaningful information, to a recipient, and the communication may occur across space and time. Figure 1.1 illustrates the interactive nature of communication, which is complete when the recipient has received and understood the intended message.

Figure 1.1: Interactive model of communication

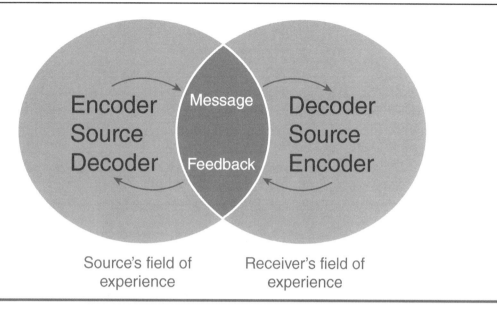

This graphic represents the interactive model of communication in which both encoder and decoder are human participants.

Source: Adapted from Wood, J.T. (2009). Communication in our lives (4th edition). Belmont, CA: Thompson-Wadsworth.

In humans, language is the usual medium for communication, but crying, screaming, gestures, bodily movement (as in pantomime), and facial expressions can also be used to communicate, either on their own or supplemental to spoken language. Communication as a means for transmitting information is not unique to humans—many other animals have means to communicate, but as we shall see, these differ in fundamental ways from human language.

Human Language vs. Animal Communication

Many species of animals can communicate, and some species do so with more complex systems than others—dolphins and whales, for example, use systems that more closely resemble human language than birds or bees, although each is capable of communicating what its species needs to communicate. Even the most complex of these systems, however, pales in comparison to what a 2-year-old child is able to do. Many pet owners do not agree. Mrs. K. is a case in point.

Mrs. K. was a widow who lived alone with her dog, Calvin. She insisted that Calvin not only responded to her commands or requests but that he initiated some kind of exchange, that he could, in her view, "talk." Calvin could sit, fetch, or lie down in response to the appropriate verb or gesture, just as any well-trained dog will do. He fetched his leash when she went to the closet for her coat or boots. He clearly understood some of what she said, and he was able to signal his wishes.

Mrs. K. insisted that the dog didn't just respond to her, but sometimes initiated "conversations." For example, he would retrieve and bring her his leash when he wanted to go for a walk, and she maintained that his bark when he wanted to go out was different from his bark warning her of an approaching car.

Mrs. K.'s neighbor wasn't convinced and asked, "What does he do when he's hungry?" Mrs. K. responded that he would go to his food dish and either wait or emit a short bark to remind her.

Could Calvin communicate? Yes. But is this language? No.

This dog communicates with his owner by bringing her his leash when he wants go out. How is this *not* a representation of language?

Exactostock/SuperStock

Humans are not alone in their ability to communicate. Bees are able to exchange information with other bees about the location of tasty pollen and about potential dangers. Not only are humans not alone in their ability to communicate, they are not the only animals to vocalize. Bird songs, for example, appear to have some degree of structural complexity that might bear some resemblance to natural language. Velvet monkeys use calls to warn of predators, using distinctive calls to distinguish one predator from another—a different call to warn of a snake than to warn of a leopard or other four-footed creature, for example. So what is the difference between animal communication and human language? The distinction between the systems animals use to communicate and the language that humans use rests primarily in the complexity of human language in comparison to other systems. In Chapter 2, we will see how human language is characterized by layer upon layer of complexity, but there are four attributes of language that essentially define its uniqueness.

1.2 Four Attributes of Language

There are four attributes of language that set it apart from other systems of communication: **arbitrariness**, **semanticity**, **productivity** and **displacement**. Before examining these attributes more closely, we should note that our emphasis here is on spoken language, or *oral-aural*. It is important to note, however, that there are modes of language other than the oral-aural. Some human languages are visual-gestural, meaning that they are perceived visually and transmitted via gesture. American Sign Language is an example of a visual-gestural language. These languages, like spoken languages, have internal structure; they are not the same as pantomime, which is a way of acting out or drawing pictures with the hands, without the use of words. Visual-gestural languages do have words. In fact, except for the way they are transmitted and received, visual-gestural languages have the same four attributes as spoken languages.

Arbitrariness: Form and Meaning Are Unrelated

First, and foremost, language is completely arbitrary. It is one of the unique design features of language that a word's meaning is not predictable from its form, or vice versa.

With the possible exception of a few onomatopoetic words (i.e., words that sound like what they mean, usually representations of animal sounds such as *baa*), there is nothing in the way a word sounds or looks that makes its meaning clear. *Water, agua, l'eau*, or *nước* all stand for the same thing, depending on the language, but there is nothing that makes one of them a better representation of H_2O than any other. In contrast, the waggle dance of the bee is not characterized by such arbitrariness—it is iconic in that its form directly represents its meaning. Universal signs for No-Smoking and the sign shown in the following image are two examples.

This sign illustrates both arbitrary and iconic forms of communication. Which is language?

Belinda Images/SuperStock

Semanticity: Ideas Are Represented With Words

Semanticity in language refers to its capacity for representing ideas, objects, or events with symbols. A case might be made for semanticity in bees' communication, because in their movements they represent an object (pollen or nectar) or possibly an event (danger lurking). Semanticity in human language, however, refers to the unique relationship between an arbitrary symbol and something in the real world. The noun *car* to represent a vehicle with wheels and some kind of an engine, the verb *walk* to indicate the action of moving one foot ahead of the other in progression, the adjective *red* to describe the color of a stop sign or a fire engine (in some places!)—these are wholly arbitrary designations agreed upon by speakers of English. French has different words to represent the same tangible objects, actions, or attributes, as do Italian, Spanish, Japanese, and so on.

Productivity: Infinite Sounds, Words, and Arrangements

Productivity in language refers to the capacity of speakers to produce an infinite number of distinct utterances. Productivity is possible because language is discrete (i.e., it consists of separate elements that can be rearranged and recombined to form new and unique utterances). This is true at all levels of description—the three distinct sounds in *cat* can be reordered to produce *tack* (remember that we're talking about sounds not letters). At the word level, it is easy to demonstrate how productive language is. Even if we could identify the number of possible verbs that could be paired with all the nouns in English, there would still be adjectives, adverbs, pronouns, and so forth that could be added to the sentences. Then, even if we could, using some complex mathematical formula, compute the number of all possible one-, two-, three-, four-, or five-word sentences in the language, the language still possesses the ability to add an *and* or a *but* or an *or* and keep that sentence going. This property is called **recursion** and is one important aspect of productivity.

Another aspect of productivity is the capacity of the language to add words and to change or add meanings to existing words. Many words have entered the lexicon in recent history. Modern English is approximately 500 years old, so "recent" may refer to any time in the past few decades. *Daycare* and *airbag* are recent additions, as are a great many words associated with space travel and wireless technology. The word *processor* has taken on new meanings in the computer age (as, indeed, has *computer*), and while *cell* has long existed in English, its use to refer to a small wireless telephone is much newer. Indeed, human language is created by humans and serves the changing needs of humans.

Displacement involves the ability to talk about things not in the immediate environment. By talking with someone who is not present, this child is demonstrating another aspect of displacement.

Photodisc/Thinkstock

Displacement: Discussing Things That Happened Last Week

Displacement, the fourth attribute that sets human language apart from animal communication systems, refers to its capacity to generate meaningful utterances not tied to the immediate environment. Language gives us the ability to talk about what happened last week, last year, or, indeed, about things that never happened at all. Not even the staunchest believer in animal language claims that they can talk about the superiority of the daisy pollen last season or speculate about how the drought in Florida will affect honey futures on the New York Stock Exchange. While many animals, possibly all, have some form of communication system, none, not even the most sophisticated of these meets the four basic criteria of arbitrariness, semanticity, productivity, and displacement that define human language. Humans are able from a very early age to communicate imaginatively, as illustrated in *A 5-Year-Old's Language Use*, because human language is inextricably linked to human cognition (i.e., to thought).

A 5-Year-Old's Language Use

Claudine, who is 5 years old, was 3 when her sister Monique was born. With a Francophone mother and an Anglophone father, both Claudine and Monique have been acquiring two languages since birth. Understanding a child just learning to talk is often a challenge, so often Claudine would be asked to "translate" Monique's speech that was incomprehensible to adults, because Claudine appeared to understand her sister. On one occasion when Monique had just turned 2, the following dialogue occurred:

Grandmother: Claudine, can you tell me what Monique is saying?

Claudine: She wants to play in the water.

Grandmother: What language was she speaking?

Claudine: I don't know.

Grandmother: Then how do you know she wants to play in the water?

Claudine: Because she always wants to play in the water.

Grandmother: So you were guessing?

Claudine: Yep. [Speaking to Monique] Do you want to play in the water?

Monique: Yes.

Grandmother: Can you ask her in French?

Claudine: Why? She already told me. She wants to play in the water.

Reflection Questions:

What does this dialogue tell you about the role of context in Claudine's language? How does this dialogue illustrate semanticity, productivity, and displacement? What does it tell you about Claudine's awareness of language?

1.3 Language and Cognition

Definitions of cognition differ slightly, depending on the dictionary, medical professional, psychologist, or educator one consults. All agree, however, that **cognition** refers broadly to the mental process of knowing, which involves awareness, perception, reasoning, memory, and conceptualization. We will examine these aspects of cognition in greater detail in Chapter 5 where we also look at how brain development relates to language and cognition. To begin understanding the interrelatedness of language and cognition, it is useful to look at an example provided by Isabelle learning to make pancakes.

By the time she was 30 months old, Isabelle knew the recipe for pancakes. She learned it by helping her grandmother make them. Her grandmother, allowing Isabelle to participate as much as possible, would also talk them through the task. "First, we crack the eggs and put them into the bowl. How many eggs?" Isabelle would always answer "two." "Then we add the oil," and they would continue. It was clear that Isabelle couldn't have learned and remembered how to make pancakes *either* as an exclusively kinetic process—by watching and doing—or as an exclusively verbal one. At that age and for another year or so, if she had been asked to recount the recipe on the phone, she would have had difficulty doing so. Unlike Martha Stewart or Wolfgang Puck, she could not have said to beat two eggs, add one tablespoon of oil and six ounces of milk, and so forth. But in the kitchen, she would go to the refrigerator, get out the eggs and lay aside two for her grandmother to crack. She knew that the milk was mixed with the eggs and oil before the dry ingredients were added, and although she didn't know in formal terms how much baking powder to use, she would demonstrate "this much" in the palm of her little hand. If her grandmother left out a step, such as spraying the griddle with a nonstick spray, Isabelle would tell her to do it. Moreover, when she assisted with the making of the pancakes, she invariably "talked her way through it," saying as she had heard her grandmother say, "First we break the eggs into the bowl, and then . . ." right to the point that the pancakes were ready to turn. "You have to watch for the bubbles," she would say every morning, "and then it's time to turn them over." Yet, when she tried to recite the recipe in the absence of the real objects (i.e., outside the situation), she did so very imperfectly. By the time she was 5, however, she could recite the recipe with a high degree of accuracy without being in pancake-making mode. Her cognitive development had reached the stage at which she could remember and retell a fairly complex process without the kinetic assistance she had needed earlier. In learning how to make pancakes, Isabelle was using language to shape, store, and recall the experience of making pancakes—strong evidence that language and memory develop in tandem.

Isabelle shows us what we know, almost intuitively: There is a strong link between language and thought. Without thought, there can be no language, and although thought is clearly possible without language, language development and cognitive development are so intricately related that some psychologists and educators believe that they run along a parallel and predictable course in children. Opinions about the exact nature of the relationship between linguistic and cognitive development are wide ranging, and intellectuals from many different disciplines—from philosophy to physics—weigh in. We will examine some of those views in far more detail in Chapters 5, 6, 7, and 9. For now, what we need to remember is that language, particularly talk, helps to shape thought. As teachers, we know that language is not just critical to but likely lays the foundation for conceptualization in all the other subjects in school. We know that all academic success depends on reading ability, but what we should also appreciate is that oral language development is essential to success in reading as well as to cognitive growth. In fact, children's reading and writing can only be built upon a foundation of oral language, so we must pay particular attention to the tandem nature of linguistic and cognitive development.

As she makes cookies with her granddaughter, this grandmother is helping her to develop cognitively and linguistically.

Blend Images/Corbis

1.4 Varieties of Human Language

Animal communication systems seem to be fairly consistent across the entire species, but human language has many varieties. Linguists use the term **language variety** to refer to different languages (e.g., Mandarin, English, and Portuguese) as well as to the way a specific group of speakers within a language speak (e.g., Appalachian English or New England English) and sometimes to differences among individuals, which they refer to as **idiolects**. We will concentrate here on the first two.

How many distinct languages are there? That is impossible to answer. One answer is "fewer than last year," because languages are becoming extinct at a rapid rate. It is not only language loss that makes the tally difficult, though. No one is sure how many distinct languages exist in Africa among tribal populations, and sometimes there is disagreement about what constitutes a distinct language and what is simply a dialect. Still, the Linguistic Society of America estimates put the number at somewhere between 6,500 and 7,000 languages (Anderson, n.d.).

Even in the United States, where English is the only language spoken by more than 285 million people, many other languages are spoken. In fact, Hispanics make up an estimated 19% of the U.S. population according to 2010 U.S. Census data, and as high as 35–45% in some states. The 2010 U.S. Census reports that more than 35 million people speak Spanish or Spanish Creole (the "mixed language" that occurs when speakers of two languages are in close contact). The next most popular language in the United States is Chinese with an estimated 2.6 million speakers, with Tagalog, French, Vietnamese, and German following closely behind (see Table 1.1). With this kind of diversity, it is unlikely that any teachers will know all of the languages spoken in their classrooms.

Table 1.1: Languages spoken by speakers over the age of 5 in the United States

Language	Number of Speakers
English only	285,797,345
Spanish or Spanish Creole	35,468,501
Chinese (Mandarin and Cantonese)	2,600,150
Tagalog	1,513,734
French	1,305,503
Vietnamese	1,251,460
German	1,109,216
Korean	1,039,021

Source: United States Census Bureau, 2010.

Within distinct languages there is also variation, the principal one of which is **dialect**. A dialect is a variety of language defined by either geographical factors or social factors such as class, religion, and ethnicity. So while most Americans speak English, they speak many varieties of it.

Dialects

Among native speakers of English, most dialectal variety is associated with geographical regions (see Figure 1.2). Such variation initially occurs because of geographic isolation, and then further change occurs over time as new people join the community and their language influences the local language. The difference between American and British English provides a good example. Broadly, we speak of them as separate dialects, and they are, but both have evolved many dialects of their own. The dialect of British English spoken by the original British settlers influenced the dialect spoken by people living along the East Coast of the United States, and that depended on where in England they came from.

As those settlers moved away from the East coast and became geographically isolated, their language evolved in different ways, was influenced by settlers from other countries, and thus developed its own character. As people joined the community, they learned but also brought their own flavor to the local dialect. The people of southeastern Pennsylvania, for example, speak a dialect of English influenced by the German language. This is *not* to say that everyone speaking the dialect of that region is of German heritage, but rather that they have adopted the local way of speaking. Similarly, the dialect of English spoken in some Miami neighborhoods is heavily influenced by Haitian Creole and Spanish, although many of the people in the community are from neither a Haitian nor a Spanish-language culture.

Figure 1.2: Regional dialects of the United States

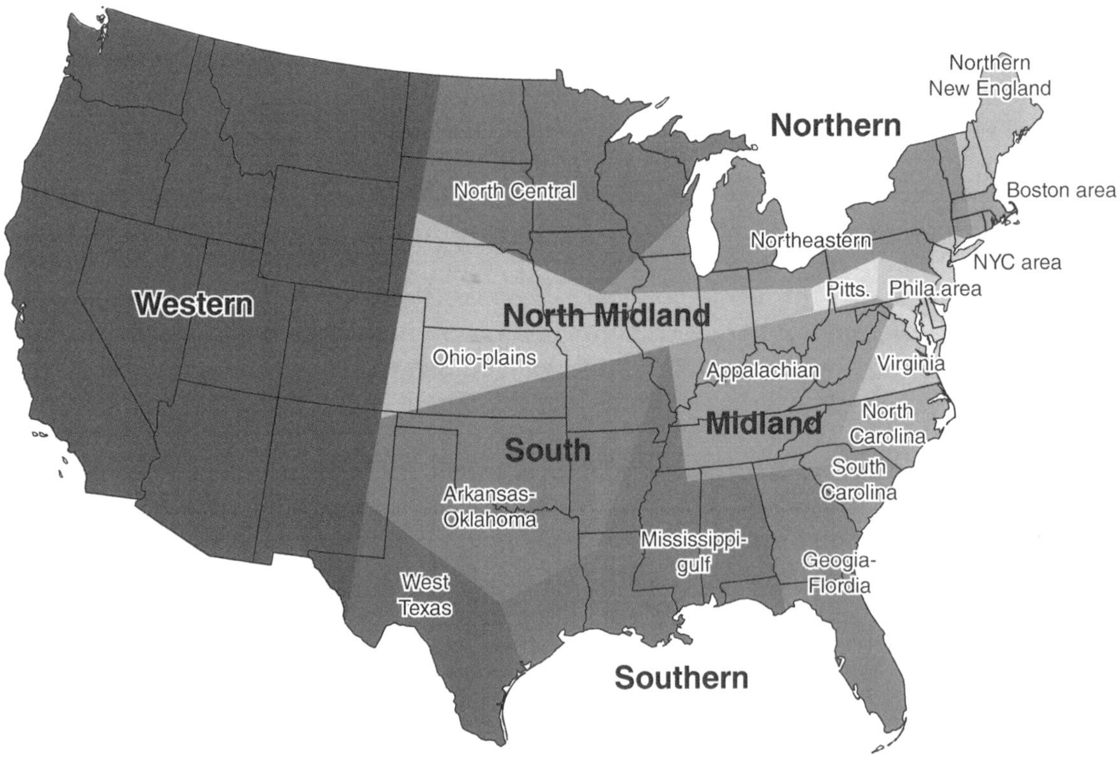

This map shows the main dialect regions of the continental United States.

Source: Dr. C. George Boeree, 2004. Dialects of English.

How Dialects Differ

Most people think about differences in dialect as affecting the sound of the language—the "accent" one uses when speaking. Certainly, sound is the easiest aspect of a dialect to identify. Where I live in Florida, for example, I regularly recognize New Yorkers from the cadence of their speech. If I lived in New York, I'd probably be able to differentiate Brooklyn from the Bronx or Queens in terms of accent. Many Northerners don't hear the difference between North Carolina and Georgia accents, but put them instead into the category of "Southern" along with Mississippi, Virginia, West Virginia, Alabama, Louisiana, South Carolina, and Texas. To those who live in these areas, however, a Virginia accent is as different from a Louisiana accent as it is from a New Jersey accent. The different geographical accents are remarkably resilient and have generally resisted the influence of the media. If television had had the effect it is sometimes assumed to have, for example, after the more than six decades it has been in American homes, we would expect it to have eradicated most accents. It has not.

But dialect affects other parts of the language as well. When I left my Ozark home and moved to New England, I lost my Ozark accent very rapidly. I made a conscious effort to "fit in" with my college classmates, and by Christmas I had lost the elongated syllables that characterized my original dialect. (I used to joke that when my mother said *dance*, it had three syllables.) Once I lost the accent, I was never identified with any particular region because I had not replaced the Ozark sound with a particular New England one, but something more generic. In New Hampshire or Maine, people usually assumed I was from Connecticut or somewhere else in New England. What marked me as a non-New Englander was not the way I "sounded" but the words I used. It was a lexical difference that gave me away. One day in the faculty lounge of the high school where I was teaching English, I referred to the container for my lunch as a "paper sack" instead of a "brown bag," which is what all my peers carried. Interestingly, it is at the word level that the mass media have had a marked influence. Situation comedies, cartoons, and even political commentary have introduced new words, or more commonly, new uses for existing words into the national lexicon. Until recently, the word *demagogue* was rarely used as a verb. During the last presidential campaign, however, politicians began to accuse one another of "demagoguing" issues, whether Social Security or Medicare. *Tweeting, retweeting, sexting*, and *LOL* may not be in the *Oxford English Dictionary* this year, but in 10 years they may well be, and if they are, it will be the result of their frequent use by younger people for whom they are already in common usage.

Any discussion of dialect eventually leads to the question of whether or not there is a **standard dialect**. While the term usually refers to the variety of language used by the media, by political leaders, and the one taught in school, it is also associated with "prestige" language.

Standard Dialect

If there is a standard dialect in the United States, it is the one used in the mainstream print media and, principally, in the publishing industry, particularly textbooks. The standard dialect is the "grammatically correct" one that most teachers demand in students' written work. It is generally devoid of **jargon** (language associated with a particular occupation, hobby, or sport) and **slang** (language used in informal settings, often indicative of the relationship between the speakers). (See *Jargon and Slang* for more on the distinction.)

The spoken language, however, is a different matter. A few decades ago, so-called "East Coast Broadcast English" was considered the standard. Following the same strict rules of usage and as accent-free as possible, broadcast English was supposed to be geographically neutral. In recent years, however, broadcast media have become more tolerant of regional accents, and anyone who surfs through the many channels available on satellite radio knows that there is a broader acceptance of what would be considered nonstandard grammar as well.

Jargon and Slang

Although the terms jargon and slang are sometimes used interchangeably, they are not the same. Both differ from standard usage mainly at the word level, but jargon refers to language associated with a particular field of study, job, sport, or hobby. Terms such as audible, crackback block, and balanced line, for example, have particular meanings associated with football. Jargon is intelligible to its users but may leave outsiders scratching their heads. Professional jargon is sometimes used to impress those outside the profession. "Rhinitis sounds a lot more serious than 'a runny nose.' Rhinoplasty sounds a lot more serious and professional than a 'nose job'" (Mihalicek & Wilson, 2011, p. 412).

Slang, on the other hand, is far less formal. While jargon might be appropriately used in résumés or letters of reference, slang would not. Slang also tends to be a less permanent feature of a dialect or language, although some slang vocabulary finds its way into the standard dialect—fan, originally a shortened form of fanatic, has entered the mainstream as have websites and TV (instead of television). There are two kinds of slang. One is common slang, the neutral, informal usage that will be understood by virtually any speaker of the language. The other is in-group slang, which Mihalicek and Wilson define as the informal language that

> . . . can be used to keep insiders together and to exclude outsiders. . . . Slang responds to a need in people to be creative in their language use and to show group membership (often unconsciously). These observations liken slang to some feature in the nature of being human and of interacting with humans. For these reasons, slang is found in all languages (even in Ancient Greek of 2500 years ago, for instance). (2011, p. 412)

Reflection Questions:

Look at the following terms. Identify those that are jargon and the field from which they come. Identify those that are slang and whether they have common or in-group usage. Do any have multiple meanings depending on the group using them? Do any of the terms qualify as both slang and jargon?

Torte
Dust-up
Fed-up
Vitals
ASAP
FAQs
Mirandize
Shrink
STAT
Backup
Clean Skin
AWOL

Just as speakers around the world function in two languages, many people function in more than one dialect. In the university where I work, for example, a significant number of students speak a variety of English that is heavily influenced by Haitian Creole. However, when they are in class interacting with their professors, they switch to a much more standard English, the same language expected of them in their writing. Any language variety that does not conform substantially to the standard is considered a **nonstandard dialect**. Both *standard* and *nonstandard* imply value judgments that we must try to avoid. It is simply not the case that one dialect is superior to any other. Nor is one more "correct" than the other. As teachers, whether our students are in kindergarten or graduate school, we have a responsibility to honor the language they bring with them, whether it be a different distinct language or a different dialect. We have the right to insist that they learn the standard dialect for writing—eventually—but we have to find ways of respecting and honoring dialectical variation at the same time. Sometimes it requires a little extra effort on the part of the teacher who may be unfamiliar with some of the dialects children bring to the classroom, but we need to think of the standard dialect as one that is being added to rather than replacing the child's own dialect. It is important to respect those differences rather than try to change them, a topic to which we will return in Chapter 7 and again in Chapter 10.

Language and Culture

Language evolves to meet the needs of the people who speak it. A people who live in a fishing economy develop the vocabulary they need to talk about catching and selling fish. People who live on a tropical island create, over time, the language appropriate for talking about heat, sand, and hurricanes. To a significant degree, then, language is culturally determined because different cultures have different perceptions, different beliefs, and different communicative needs that their languages must serve.

Within cultures, there are subcultures, or cultural groups that exist within a larger cultural community. Subcultures have particular interests, and they often develop ways of using the dominant language that serves their needs but may be unintelligible to those outside the group, demonstrating again how language is culturally determined. For example, people who surf the waves use words and expressions that are relevant to surfing but have little meaning to those who have no interest in the activity and which bear little resemblance to the vocabulary used by people who surf the Internet. The hip-hop subculture is another that has developed a rich dialect, which is used in lyrics and to talk about the music. It has also influenced mainstream English. Each group has shaped the language to fit its particular needs and to identify itself as a member of the subculture.

We do not have to look to subcultures, however, to find examples of how language use evolves. Children born in this century have learned words such as *computer, remote control, cell phone* or even *iPhone* at a much younger age than their parents or grandparents simply because those words are relevant to the world in which they were born. These are living examples of how flexible and expansive language is, of how it is created by and modified to meet the needs of the people who use it.

People who fish a lot may form a subculture with its own language. They may have language for talking about fishing that people who live away from the water may not know.

BananaStock/Thinkstock

Culture shapes language, but is the reverse true? Does the language a people speak influence how they perceive the world? There have been theorists who believe this to be the case. Benjamin Whorf, for example, held a rather extreme view that perception was limited by language; most linguists in the latter half of the 20th and in the 21st centuries have found his evidence suspect. Still, there is no doubt that an inextricable relationship between language and culture exists (Swoyer, 2010).

For our purposes, what is important to remember is that many bilingual children are also bicultural, comfortable in both the minority and the dominant culture. On the other hand, those children who begin school as beginners in English are likely to be acquiring both a new language and a new culture. As they acquire the language of their community, children are also acquiring the community's customs as well. Cross-cultural communication thus presents great potential for misunderstandings or miscommunication; since language is culturally bound, no exact translation is ever possible, so until learners understand the culture of a new language, it is likely they will make mistakes in communicating in that language. Even among people who speak the same language, customs and thus the language used, can vary. Anyone who has ever listened to teenagers talk at the mall knows this to be true! The teenage boy heard to say, "Dang, Girl, I ain't seen you for a minute!" actually means that it has been a long time since he has seen the girl. The girl who tells a friend to watch out for the 5-0 is warning about the presence of police. *Slanguage*, as language use of this kind is called, is only one kind of dialectic variation. Geography also accounts for differences, such that a teacher who has grown up and been educated in the rural Midwest has the potential for miscommunication with her students in urban Chicago or New York City.

The Structure of Language

Students who pursue graduate degrees in linguistics often spend many hours working out the intricate "rules" that govern the structure of different languages. In **phonology** classes, they might spend weeks writing accurate descriptions of the sounds that are meaningful and how they can be combined in Finnish or Aleut. In **syntax** classes, they might work for an entire semester writing the "rules" for word order in Old English or modern day Urdu. Can they speak all or, indeed, any of these languages? Usually not. But most students of linguistics are fascinated by the intricacies of language structure. Although not everyone has such an intense level of interest in the structural properties of language and would rather have a root canal than spend two hours in a traditional "grammar" class, most of us do possess some curiosity about how the language we speak is put together.

Each language, and to some degree each dialect, is structured differently. We tend to think of the differences between languages as differences in the words, but the differences between languages occur not just at the word level. Most of us know that Spanish uses the word casa to refer to what English speakers call a house or home. There is also a difference in word order. In English, for example, adjectives usually come before the noun they modify (as in the big, old, blue car), but Spanish is a little more complicated. Some adjectives come before the noun (mucho tiempo or "much time"), but others come after the noun. So the same sentence would be rendered *El gran coche azul de edad*, or literally, "the big car blue of age." In Chapter 2 we will look at some of the properties of English syntax and other aspects of language structure that children ultimately learn so that we will have a common basis and vocabulary for discussing and understanding the process of language development in children.

Some animal communication may possess structure. Scientists who study bird song, for example, believe that there is structure to the song of birds. Perhaps there is, as it might be possible to identify structure in the movement of bees. None, however, is as complex as the structure of human language. Usually, when we think about language structure, we think about sentence structure. Linguists refer to this as syntax. In fact, language is intricately structured at every level, from individual sounds, to **syllables**, **morphemes**, or minimal units of meaning, and **words**. It would take an entire book to describe, even in a rudimentary way, the structure of English at any one of these levels. We will nevertheless have a cursory look at how English is structured in the next chapter.

The complexity of human language mirrors the complexity of the human brain, but as complex as language is, children learn most of it without being taught. So why are we bothering to study language and language acquisition?

The simple answer is that early learning sets the stage for later learning, and teachers and early caregivers play an important role in that learning. The remaining chapters in this book provide information that helps to make clear why that is true. Following Chapter 2, which examines the enormity of the task in terms of structure, Chapter 3 examines the task from the meaning-centered perspective of the child. For example, both language environment and innateness play significant roles in language learning, but the relative importance of each depends to some degree on the theoretical perspective one adopts. Chapter 4 considers some of the same issues in second language learners, both **simultaneous bilinguals**, which refers to children who acquire two languages from birth, and **successive** (or **consecutive**) **bilinguals**, which refers to children who learn a single language at home and add a second language later, usually in school (Lightbown & Spada, 2006; Meisel, 2011). In Chapters 5 and 6 we see how language and cognition develop in tandem and look at the developmental milestones that help teachers to know when a child is on track and when a special intervention might be required.

Language involves much more than learning to articulate clearly and produce well-formed sentences. Chapter 7 explores the different functions that language plays in children's lives and looks at how they learn the conventions of conversation and how to tell stories. In acquiring the structures and functions of language, some children face greater challenges than others, and in Chapter 8 we identify some of those challenges and gain some insights on how to distinguish a slight developmental difference from a possible disorder.

As teachers, our ultimate goal is to provide children with the best education possible. Because language and cognition are interdependent processes, as we shall see in Chapter 9, so are language and the development of academic skills. Helping children to develop those skills requires that we understand how home language and school language differ, whether that difference be in function—children use language to achieve different outcomes at home and at school—or in culture. Chapter 10 examines how teachers can build on the language of the home to set children on the path to success in school.

Early childhood educators help children to continue growing in oral language and early reading skills.

Tetra Images/Corbis

1.5 Language Is Easy to Learn (but Hard to Teach)

Children the world over learn language—often two or three languages at a time—and while some parents are of the mistaken belief that they somehow "teach" their children to talk, the truth of the matter is that children don't need to be taught. The evidence is compelling: The order and speed of language acquisition (i.e., the speed and order in which parts of a particular language are learned) is very similar in all children who acquire that language despite the environment in which they acquire it. If parents were responsible for the feat, it would mean that they had followed a common curriculum, either for parenting or language teaching. We know, of course, that this is not the case. Parents and caregivers vary greatly in the amount of talk they direct to their children and in the amount and kind of talk to which children are exposed. We can chart language development broadly but with a great deal of accuracy precisely because children are predisposed to learn language. In fact, if parents did have to teach their children to talk, the task would be daunting, and most would fail. What they *do* need to do is to talk with their children. Even though children would likely learn some language just from hearing it and figuring out meaning from context, the most effective way—what constitutes "exposure"—is purposeful, meaningful talk.

Although some scholars might quibble with the assertion that language is "natural," at least in the same way that biological processes such as cell differentiation or cell aging are,

18

Helen Keller is an extreme example of the human ability to acquire language. Despite being blind and deaf, Keller developed a form of language that enabled her to communicate with others.

Science Faction/SuperStock

there is no doubt that the human brain is designed to acquire language. True, children are not born talking—language is a learned behavior—but all that children with normal or near-normal physical and mental abilities need to accomplish that learning is exposure. A language-rich environment (i.e., one in which the child is exposed to a great deal of talk about many subjects and to books from a young age) is ideal, but even children from linguistically impoverished environments learn language. Most of the English-speaking world is aware of the story of Helen Keller and the extreme circumstances she overcame to acquire a form of language. Certainly, much of her accomplishment is attributable to her teacher, Anne Sullivan, but without an innate need to communicate, she would not have been able to gain such impressive capabilities. Many less-extreme cases exist that demonstrate the human capacity to learn language. In my book, *Language and Learning: The Home and School Years* (Piper, 2007), I tell the story of Grace who acquired normal spoken English in a home where both her parents were nonhearing and communicated only through sign language. Children can and do overcome major obstacles to acquire language, and in Chapter 8 we will meet some children who, like Grace, do just that.

As teachers, we have particular reasons for caring about language and language learning. Over the years as I have studied children's language learning, both as a linguist and as a parent and grandparent, I have continued to marvel at the enormity of the young child's accomplishment in learning the language. As I have talked and written about how children are predisposed to acquire language, students have often posed the question, "If language is so natural and easily learned, what is there to teach?" Answering that will take the remainder of this book, but basically, these are the reasons:

- If by "language teaching" we mean drilling parts of speech or teaching 5 year olds to parse sentences into nouns, verbs, and modifiers, then we absolutely should not teach it.
- However, if we take "language teaching" to mean creating a rich verbal environment that exposes children to a variety of language—new words, different functions, an array of structures and usage—then understanding how language is acquired becomes very important to a teacher.
- Language is the medium by which children learn everything in the curriculum.
- Children build literacy on the foundation of oral language.
- Language development is inextricably linked to cognitive development. Growing language fosters cognitive growth as well.

Conclusion

L anguage is uniquely human, and children are born with the necessary "equipment" to learn it. Other animals use rudimentary systems of communication, but language differs in the intricacy of its structure and its capacity for complex communication. This chapter defined language in terms of arbitrariness, semanticity, displacement, and productivity, properties that distinguish it from other communication systems. The fact that human cognitive and linguistic development are so intricately bound together, that human language does not exist independent of culture, that it has many varieties and is as complex as the human brain itself—all these set human language well above other systems of communication. While children do not need to be taught language, teachers need to pay attention to language development, because it is closely linked to cognitive development and foundational to all future learning.

Post-Test

1. Which of the following species uses language that most closely resembles human language?

   a. Dogs
   b. Whales
   c. Bees
   d. Snakes

2. "Buzz," "croak," "bark," and "wham" are all examples of

   a. synonyms.
   b. palindromes.
   c. semantics.
   d. onomatopoeia.

3. The broad mental process of knowing, including memory and perception, defines

   a. metacognition.
   b. cognition.
   c. processing.
   d. language.

4. Subcultures are
   a. subversive cultures.
   b. cultures embedded within cultures.
   c. the lowest form of culture.
   d. cultures that borrow aspects from several other cultures.

5. In language learning,

     a. children must be explicitly taught the rules and use.
     b. parents follow similar methods for teaching.
     c. there is no evidence for a predisposition for learning.
     d. the order and speed of learning tends to be the same in all children.

Answers

1. **b.** Whales. *The answer can be found in Section 1.1.*
2. **d.** Onomatopoeia. *The answer can be found in Section 1.2.*
3. **b.** Cognition. *The answer can be found in Section 1.3.*
4. **b.** Cultures embedded within cultures. *The answer can be found in Section 1.4.*
5. **d.** The order and speed of learning tends to be the same in all children. *The answer can be found in Section 1.5.*

Key Ideas

- Communications systems exist in many species of animals.
- Language is the uniquely human system of communication.
- Language is an arbitrary system characterized by its semanticity, displacement (or the ability to talk about abstract ideas or things not present), and productivity (or the ability to create an infinite number of new utterances).
- Language is intricately related to human cognition.
- Human language does not to be taught; children will acquire it given adequate exposure.
- Humans are born with the *capacity* for language but not language itself.
- Language and culture are inextricably linked.

Critical Thinking Questions

1. What are some new words or new uses of words that have entered the language because of television or the Internet during your lifetime?
2. Bees, in communicating the location of nectar, cannot deceive other bees—they cannot lie. What does the fact that humans have the ability to lie say about the difference between human language and animal communication systems?
3. What evidence can you provide for the statement, "Thought is clearly possible without a language"?
4. Language is often the medium for human communication. What are other means of communication that humans use, and to what degree do they meet the criteria for language?
5. Spend some time in a preschool class and identify how the teacher's interactions with the children help them to expand their language.
6. Children's receptive vocabulary is always larger than their productive vocabulary. Why must this be true?

Key Terms

arbitrariness One of the four attributes of human language, referring to the fact that words are not predictable from their meanings. The animal known in English as *pig* is represented by other words in other languages.

cognition The mental process of knowing, which involves awareness, perception, reasoning, memory, and conceptualization.

communication The activity of a sender conveying a message to a listener.

dialect A variety of language defined by either geographical factors or social factors, such as class, religion, and ethnicity.

displacement An attribute of human language, referring to the fact that language is capable of generating meaningful utterances not tied to the immediate environment.

idiolect The idiosyncratic speech of individuals.

jargon Language associated with a particular occupation, hobby, or sport.

language variety A term linguists use to refer to different languages (e.g., Mandarin and English) as well as to the way a specific group of speakers within a language speak (e.g., Appalachian English or Boston English) and sometimes to differences among individuals.

morpheme The smallest unit of language that carries meaning.

nonstandard dialect Any language variety that does not conform substantially to the standard.

phonology The branch of linguistics concerned with the description of the sound system.

productive vocabulary The words that a child speaks, as opposed to those he understands but may not be heard to speak.

productivity An attribute of human language, referring to the capacity of language to create an infinite number of new and unique utterances.

receptive vocabulary The words a child understands but may not necessarily produce in speech.

recursion An aspect of language productivity that allows a speaker to add infinitely to a sentence.

semanticity One of the four attributes of human language, referring to the capacity of language to represent ideas, objects, or events with symbols.

simultaneous bilinguals Children who learn two languages from birth or before the age of 2 to 3 years.

slang Language used in informal settings, often indicative of the relationship between the speakers.

standard dialect A term used to refer to the variety of language used by the media, by political leaders, and the one taught in school, and sometimes considered to be the "prestige" variation of a language.

successive (or consecutive) bilinguals Those who add a second language after the first is largely established.

syllable A unit of pronunciation consisting of a single vowel and any consonants that cluster around it.

syntax The branch of linguistics concerned with sentence structure.

word A unit of language consisting of one or more spoken sounds, or their written representation, that is a principal carrier of meaning. A word must contain at least one morpheme but may have more.

Weblinks

Although animal communication is not the subject of this chapter or this book, many find the topic fascinating. This website offers further information on dolphin communication.
http://www.dolphins.org/marineed_communication.php

This site provides a thorough discussion about how language and communication differ.
http://www.psych.ualberta.ca/~chrisw/Psych357/L28Animals.pdf

A concise description of language and how it differs from speech is available on the American Speech-Language Hearing Association site:
http://www.asha.org/public/speech/development/language_speech.htm

Visit this site for an interesting perspective on the uniqueness of human language and on how languages are related:
http://sciencenetlinks.com/science-news/science-updates/human-language/

For an account of the Whorfian hypothesis of linguistic relativity:
http://plato.stanford.edu/entries/relativism/supplement2.html

For a description of how American dialects differ and a dialect map of the continental United States:
http://www.ling.upenn.edu/phono_atlas/NationalMap/NationalMap.html

2

Associated Press

How It's Built:
The Structure of Language

Learning Objectives

By the end of this chapter, you will be able to accomplish the following objectives:

- Describe how consonants and vowels sounds are organized in English and how we know which are important.

- Define *morpheme* and explain the difference between lexical and function morphemes.

- Identify the main constituents of a sentence, and explain the importance of word order in English.

- Define and explain the difference between semantics and pragmatics.

Introduction

After her first day of preschool at age 29 months, Isabelle and her father had the following conversation about the rabbit named Bela who shared the classroom with Isabelle and nine other children:

Isabelle: Papa, Bela bite Jason.

Papa: Who is Jason?

Isabelle: At my school.

Papa: Oh, and Bela bit him.

Isabelle: Yes. Bela bitted him.

Even though her language was still a work in progress, Isabelle had already, without being aware of it, mastered much of the language structure that will be described in this chapter.

In Chapter 1, we began to see how impressive a feat this is. In 29 months, Isabelle had grown from an infant who did not yet know her name and whose only vocalization was crying, to a little girl who could make herself understood talking about something that had happened in the past. True, some of her forms were imperfect, but she was already well on her way to being a proficient language user.

In order to understand and appreciate what she and children the world over accomplish in the first few years and how teachers can build on that accomplishment in the school setting, it is useful to understand how language is organized. Many people consider themselves experts on language by virtue of the fact that they have been using it successfully for a number of years and may have become quite proficient in it. Attaining proficiency does not require speakers to have a conscious knowledge of the formal structure of language—and certainly most children do not—but it takes a linguist to understand and explain the underlying mechanics of language that we all take for granted (Bauer & Trudgill, 1998). Actually, it would take many linguists and several volumes because there are so many aspects of language to be described. Here, we will take only an introductory look at how language is structured in order to begin to appreciate the magnitude of children's accomplishment.

Children learn language in order to express meaning and to communicate with people around them. The miracle of the infant brain is its capacity to acquire all of the structures of any language spoken on earth. Children do not learn the components of language separately or in isolation. They don't master the sound system and then move on to learning words and then sentences. Nor do they learn the structures of the language as a cognitive exercise. In order to learn to communicate effectively, children master the complex structures of their language. Watching them do so is fascinating. In Chapter 3 we take a closer look at how children acquire the structures of language. For now, let's look at how the English language is structured.

Language has several components—sounds (phonology), words (morphology), and sentences (syntax). These are descriptors that adults use. Children, at least at the beginning, are happily unaware of either the structure of language or the need to learn it.

Languages differ in many other ways. Have you ever tried to master the sounds of French, the syntax of German, or the tones of Mandarin? Mandarin speakers also struggle with the sounds of English, finding the l/r/w distinctions especially confusing. Speakers of Arabic have trouble mastering English prepositions because there are only about 20 prepositions in Arabic but 57 in English. Beginning learners often try to understand a new language in terms of their first language. Arab speakers of English cannot readily translate and have difficulty getting the troublesome little English words right. Indeed, almost all non-native speakers struggle to some degree with English prepositions.

All languages can be described using the same categories and the same descriptors. Phonology is the branch of linguistics concerned with the description of the sound system. **Morphology** is the branch concerned with word structure, and syntax refers to sentence structure. **Semantics** refers to meaning, and **pragmatics** refers to the functional use of language in real-life settings.

Pre-Test

1. In comparison to consonants, vowels

    a. use less air obstruction in their production.
    b. are more often the reason children are referred for speech therapy.
    c. exist in greater numbers in the English alphabet.
    d. are produced with more impediments in air stream.

2. Inflectional morphemes are types of

    a. function morphemes.
    b. lexical morphemes.
    c. content morphemes.
    d. function words.

3. The two major considerations of syntactic learning are

    a. the order of words and the relationships among aspects of sentences.
    b. to whom the speaker is speaking and the time frame of the information.
    c. the number of words needed and the time needed to communicate.
    d. the tense of the verbs and the number of objects.

4. Which of the following is true of semantics?

    a. Semantics can differ within the same language.
    b. Words in some languages do not mean the same thing in others.
    c. Individual and cultural variations do not affect language.
    d. Language has fairly rigid conventions for communication.

Phonology
morphology
syntax

Answers

1. **a.** use less air obstruction in their production. *The answer can be found in Section 2.1.*
2. **a.** function morphemes. *The answer can be found in Section 2.2.*
3. **a.** The order of words and the relationships among aspects of sentences. *The answer can be found in Section 2.3.*
4. **b.** Words in some languages do not mean the same thing in others. *The answer can be found in Section 2.4.*

2.1 The Sounds of English: Phonology

At age 3, Isabelle's pronunciation of *yellow* was "lalo." She couldn't manage the initial "y" sound, nor did she get the first vowel quite right. It wasn't that she was unable to produce the "y" sound or the correct vowel—the word *yes*, for example, with the same vowel and initial consonant, gave her no problem at all. But in the word *yellow*, she couldn't quite get all the sounds right. The reason is that the process of learning the sound structure of English is not just a matter of learning individual sounds, it is learning the system—all of the sounds and how they are combined and pronounced in various environments. For a child, the "environment" of a two-syllable word is very different from that of a single syllable, and she simplified the pronunciation according to certain predictable processes. In this section, we will look at the sounds of English, which ones are distinctive and which are not, and some of the rules for combining them. We will also look briefly at stress, or the force with which a syllable is articulated, and intonation, or the rhythm of the language, and the role they play in English.

Linguists who study the sounds of a language are called *phonologists*. In general terms, phonology is concerned with the physical, or acoustic, properties of speech sounds and the rules that govern how those sounds are combined in speech. From the child's point of view, the business of phonology is figuring out how to produce those sounds that are necessary for making meaning. When children are very young, it is unlikely that they can focus on any unit smaller than the word, at least not directly. As soon as they understand that *cat* and *hat* are different words conveying very different meanings, however, they have unknowingly recognized that the /k/ sound is different from the /h/ sound. This is a good example of a **minimal pair**, or two words that differ by only one sound, which is an important concept in determining which sounds are separate **phonemes**, or sounds that native speakers perceive to be different, in English.

 Sounds and letters are different. There is a somewhat predictable relationship between the sounds of English and the letters used to represent them in print. For the most part, the sound /m/ is represented by the letter "m," and we can usually count on the letter "b" to represent the sound /b/. But the sound-symbol correspondence in English is far from perfect, as any second language learner or anyone who struggles with English spelling can testify. The sound /f/, for example, can be spelled in four different ways, as illustrated by *fame, tough, phone,* and *puff*. Moreover, the word *of* has the letter "f" but the pronunciation is /v/. For now, we are concerned with the sounds of English with only passing reference to the alphabet.

How Speech Sounds Are Formed

Human speech can be described in acoustic terms, or the nature of the disturbance to the airwaves that occurs when we speak. Each vowel and consonant sound has distinctive acoustic properties that can be measured on a sound spectrogram. How and why do speech sounds differ from each other? Here is an example from a grade-school science class. If we take two identical, glass soft-drink bottles and pour 4 inches of water into one, leave the other empty, and then blow into them, as if blowing a flute or piccolo, the sound produced by each will be different. The sound produced by the bottle with liquid will be of a higher pitch than the sound produced by the one without liquid. That is because the resonator (i.e., the soft-drink bottle) has changed with the addition of liquid; vibration occurs above the level of the water only. The water has effectively shortened the resonator and caused the sound to have a pitch. The human head is also a resonator, and because we are all a little different from each other, our voices and speech sounds tend to be unique. But there is enough similarity that we can understand each other because we produce the speech sounds of our language in more or less the same way. Each speech sound is distinguished from the others by the shape of the resonator (i.e., the vocal apparatus) during speech.

When we speak, the airstream—the same one used in breathing—is modulated, or changed, by the articulators as it moves from the lungs upward to exit through the oral or nasal cavity (or both). The articulators, as shown in Figure 2.1, are of two types. Passive articulators, which include the teeth, alveolar ridge, hard palate, velum, uvula, and pharynx (or pharyngeal wall) remain static during speech. Active articulators move to create different speech sounds. The tongue is the most important of these, but the glottis and the lips, particularly the lower lip, also play roles in speech production.

Figure 2.1: Articulators involved in speech

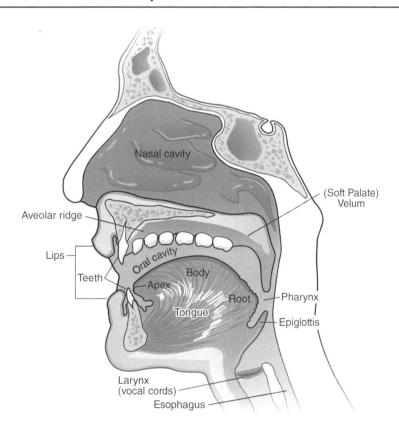

This figure shows the parts used to form verbal speech patterns.

How We Know Which Sounds Matter

The human vocal apparatus is capable of creating an almost infinite variety of sounds. Every child born with normal hearing and speech organs is born with the capacity to learn the sounds of any language. Anyone who has heard an infant babble will have heard sounds that may be difficult for an adult to reproduce and which may bear little resemblance to the speech sounds that adults use. A child's job in the first years of life is to figure out which sounds of language are meaningful and how to produce them. Children are not linguists, but in order to understand what they accomplish, it is useful to look at how adult speakers know which sounds are meaningful in a language. How is it that we come to recognize the two broad categories of speech sounds known as consonants and vowels?

Blowing into these bottles would create a different sound for each because of their different shapes. This is similar to what happens when we move our tongue or jaw during speech.

Hemera/Thinkstock

Generally speaking, **consonants** are sounds that are produced with more obstruction of the air somewhere in the vocal tract than **vowels**, which are produced with a relatively unimpeded airstream. English has many more consonants than vowels, and they are harder for children to learn than vowels. When children are referred for speech therapy, it is often because an adult has identified a problem with how some of the consonant sounds are produced.

Unlike consonants, vowels are produced with very little obstruction of the vocal apparatus but simply by changing the shape of the resonator. Vowels get their distinct character from the placement of the tongue in the mouth during articulation and whether or not the lips are rounded. Vowels are highly resonant, making them easier to hear and to distinguish from one another. When Sarah, at 27 months, pronounced *butterfly* as "fuhfly," she showed perfect control of the vowels, although she left out the middle syllable, but simplified the consonants to two, "f"and "l."

For a representation of how the change in tongue placement produces actual vowel sounds, see the Weblinks at the end of the chapter for a video.

The Consonants and Vowels of English

Infants are capable of producing the sounds of any human language. Gradually, they learn which ones are relevant to the language they are learning and which are not. As adult speakers of English, we already know which sounds are meaningful, but children have to figure out what to pay attention to and what can be ignored. If children were linguists, they would look for minimal pairs. Consider these words: *cat, hat, bat, sat, mat, fat, gnat, pat, rat, tat, vat.* Ten words, all with different meanings, tell us that English has at least 10 consonants, because as we change the first sound of each word, we also change the meaning. If we were to consider the words *bat*, *bit*, *bet*, *beat*, *boat*, *boot*, *bought*, and *but*, we would readily see that English has at least eight different vowel sounds, because that is what distinguishes one word from the other. Continuing to act as linguists, if we were given the words *trite* and *trout* (or *light* and *lout*), we would have evidence for two more English sounds. These are also vowels, but they are called **diphthongs** because they are created by one vowel gliding quickly into another.

While children are not little linguists, as they learn the meanings of words and understand that *hat*, *cat*, and *bat* all have different meanings, they sort out the relevant sounds of English. Table 2.1 shows the consonant sounds of standard American English, and Table 2.2 shows the vowels with the phonemic symbols linguists use to identify them.

Table 2.1: English consonant phonemes and common spellings

Phoneme (symbol)	Common spellings	Exemplar words
/p/	p, pp	pit, tipple, sip
/b/	b, bb	bib, kibble, stub
/t/	t, tt, th	time, little, thyme
/d/	d, dd	dust, puddle
/s/	s, ss	sister, miss
/z/	z, zz, s	zap, jazz, houses
/tʃ/	ch, tch	check, which, witch
/dʒ/	j, dg, g	jelly, grudge, gel
/ʃ/	sh, ss, t(i),ch(e)	shell, session, nation, panache
/ʒ/	z, s, g	azure, lesion, beige
/f/	f, ff, ph, gh	father, waffle, phone, rough
/v/	v, f	vote, evolve, of
/θ/	th	thick, thin, myth
/ð/	th	this, that, lather
/k/	k, ck, c, ch , q	kit, pick, cat, ache, quick /kwlk/
/g/	g, gg, gue	wig, wiggle, fatigue
/w/	w, wh	win, wile, while
/l/	l, ll	laugh, alive, doll
/r/	r, rr	range, arrange, far
/y/	y	yes
/m/	m, mm, mn	mix, summer, rhythm
/n/	n, nn	nine, penny
/ŋ/	ng	long, singer
/h/	h	high, ahem

Table 2.2: English vowel phonemes and common spellings

Phoneme (symbol)	Common spellings	Exemplar words
/ɪ/	i	kit, sit, quit
/i/	ee, ea, ey, ie, ei, e	keep, leaf, key, lien, receive, decide
/ə/	e, ea	set, led, tell, threat, lead (as in "lead pencil")
/eɪ/	a, ay, ai, ei	made, may, maid, weigh
/æ/	a, ai	sad, matter, plaid
/ə/	u, ou, e	cut, bubble, trouble, double, the
/ɔ/	ou, au, o	caught, cause, thought
/a/	o	cot, shot, got
/ow/	o, ow, oa	comb, shown, coat
/uw/	oo, u, ew	moo, prune, strewn
/ʊ/	u, oo	put, foot
/ɔj/	oy, oi	boy, boil
/aj/	ie, ai, i, uy	tie, Thai, time, guy
/aw/	ow, ou	cow, bough

Some readers will not be able to hear the difference between the vowels in *caught* and *cot*. There is no need to have a hearing test, though, since these vowels are the same in some dialects of American English.

Whether a child is learning English, Portuguese, or Mandarin, the task is the same—figuring out which sounds are meaningful and learning how to produce them. That is not the only task; part of learning the sound system is learning the stress and intonation patterns of that language.

Stress and Intonation

Stress refers to the force with which a syllable is articulated. In fact, stressed syllables are not only louder, they also have a slightly higher pitch and are longer in duration than nonstressed syllables. Sometimes, stress is distinctive. Consider the two pronunciations of the word *convict*. The noun, as in *The convict was released from prison*, has stress on the first syllable. The verb, however, as in *The jury took only two hours to convict the defendant*, is stressed on the second syllable. In this way, stress is phonemic because it contributes to the meaning. Stress in these examples occurs at the word level. The stress pattern of each word is part of its identity, just as its phonemes are. So the word *bluebell* is always stressed on the first syllable, and specifically, on the first vowel of the syllable. That is because syllables, by definition, must have a vowel (and only one vowel), and it is the vowel that carries the stress.

Learning the stress pattern of a word is part of learning that word, and it is an aspect of phonological learning that causes young children less difficulty than mastering each of the individual sounds. In fact, very early on, at the babbling stage, children "create" words that are nonsensical but somehow sound like the language of the adults around them. They are able to do so, in part, because they have picked up the stress patterns of the words they have heard. As evidence, children attend to stressed syllables more than to unstressed ones. Consider again Sarah's pronunciation of *butterfly* as *fuhfly*. She reduced a three-syllable word to two, and the syllable she left out was the middle, unstressed one. At the same time, her correct pronunciation of the French equivalent, *papillon* showed that she was capable of producing three syllable words. In the case of the French word, however, the middle syllable carries more stress than the middle syllable of *butterfly*, so she was not as likely to leave out the syllable.

Although English words spoken in isolation have syllabic stress, there is also a level of stress associated with the rhythm of continuous speech. **Intonation**, sometimes called prosodic stress, refers to the rhythm of the language as it is spoken or read—the rising and falling pitch that occurs in connected speech. Although explaining the rules for assigning English stress in sentences is difficult, learning them appears not to be difficult at all. Even at the babbling stage, before they have sorted out the individual phonemes and before they can articulate words, children babble in streams that have many of the prosodic qualities of the adult form of the language they are learning.

Syllables

How many syllables does the word *chocolate* have? In most American English dialects, it has two, although many people would say that it has three because they are aware of the written form and think it *should* have. If asked to read the word in isolation, many people will carefully produce that middle syllable. If asked to read a sentence such as "Do you want chocolate or vanilla ice cream?" most people will pronounce only two syllables. So what is this thing called the syllable?

In English, syllables have several different "shapes," or structures, depending on the configuration of vowels (V) and consonants (C). The one thing every English syllable must have is a nucleus, usually a vowel but sometimes /r/, /m/ or /ŋ/, or /l/ (as in the second syllable of *little*). English syllables need not have any consonants. The word *amazing*, for example, has three syllables, and the first one consists only of a vowel. The other two illustrate two additional syllable shapes in English: vowel-consonant-vowel (VCV) and vowel-consonant (VC). There are eight other possibilities in English, as shown in Table 2.3.

Table 2.3: Possible English syllable structures

V	VC	VCC	CV	CCV	CVC	CCVC	CCVCC	CCCV	CCCVC	CCCVCC
eye, oh	am, eyes	apt, ilk	me, woe	play, sty	did, make	plaid, stall	plaids, brains	splay, straw	splayed, straws	straps, screams

Syllable structures vary from language to language—the only universal is that every syllable must contain a nucleus. Beyond that, languages differ widely. In Mandarin, the usual syllable structure is CV. When Mandarin-speaking adults are learning English, they tend to "drop" the final consonant in words such as *cat* because that is the syllable form that is most familiar to them.

Children with normal hearing tend to be aware of syllable structure and reproduce it fairly accurately, even at a very young age. Evidence can be found in their ability to produce rhymes, which usually require them to create new forms with the same number of syllables, if not the exact same structure. A child's ability to rhyme *bad* with *sad* and *mad* shows that she can exchange the initial consonant, and when pronouncing *glad*, the child provides strong evidence that it is the syllable that is the salient unit, and not the individual sounds. In fact, nearly all preschool children can produce rhymes, even nonsensical ones, but if asked how many sounds in a word, they often falter.

The components of the sound system—sounds, syllables, stress, and intonation—are not learned in isolation. They are learned in the contexts of words, and words are made up of morphemes.

2.2 The Building Blocks of Words: Morphology

A mother, asked if her infant is talking yet, might well respond, "Yes, she has three words already!" To most people, at least those who are neither English teachers nor linguists, the smallest unit of language that has meaning is the word. Certainly, words are essential building blocks of language, and it is true that the word is the smallest unit that can stand alone in speech or writing. The smallest unit of meaning, however, is not the word but the morpheme, and the study of how morphemes are categorized and combined is morphology. English morphology is fairly complex—perhaps even more complex than the sound system. But it is also easier to understand because morphemes are more easily recognized than individual sounds. Most of us know a great deal about the different kinds of morphemes and how they are combined into words. It is the language for talking about them that gets a little complicated. Nevertheless, in order to appreciate what children accomplish in learning to make and use words, it is necessary to understand something about the morphology of English.

Identifying Morphemes

First, morphemes and words differ, although a word can be a single morpheme. The word *of*, for example, is a single morpheme, but it is still a word. Often, however, a word consists of more than one morpheme. Words such as *helpful, eyeball,* and *toys* consist of two morphemes while *helpfully* and *eyeballs* consist of three. How do we know? With *of*, we know because we cannot break it down further and be left with anything that makes sense. With *eyeball*, on the other hand, we can clearly see that there are two parts to the word that have meaning: *eye* and *ball*. Then, adding a plural suffix, -s, we add a third element of meaning and thus have three morphemes. Similarly, *toys* has two meaning elements: *toy* and the plural suffix.

What the adult knows about morphology, however, is not what the child knows. Returning to the word *eyeball*, for example, a 3-year-old who knows the meaning of the word and uses it will not be aware that it has two components, nor does she need to. For her, it is a single word, a single morpheme, and it has one specific meaning. For this reason, when linguists or teachers study children's language in terms of MLU (mean length of utterance), they normally consider compound words such as *eyeball*, *baseball*, or *cupcake* as a single entity.

English words can consist of many morphemes. The word *predictability*, for example, has four: *pre-* (a prefix meaning "before"), *-dict-* (meaning "to say"), *-able* (meaning "capable of"), and *-ity* (making the word a noun). Notice that these four morphemes have different kinds of meaning. That is because not all morphemes are created equal. Some carry a great deal of meaning, and others are merely grammatical conventions; still others fall somewhere in the middle.

Different Kinds of Morphemes

Broadly speaking, there are two types of morphemes: content, or **lexical morphemes**, and **functional morphemes**. To distinguish between them, let's return for a moment to the word *eyeballs*. As noted, it consists of three morphemes. Most of the meaning is borne by *eye* and *ball*. We see both morphemes in many other English words such as *baseball, ballgame, birds-eye*, and *eyeglasses*. Because they have meaning that can be understood independently of any other morpheme, they are called lexical morphemes. The remaining morpheme is of a different type. It indicates that the noun is plural and is thus called an **inflectional morpheme**, and is one kind of functional morpheme as shown in Figure 2.2. The **function words** and the inflectional morphemes are the little workhorses of the language. They do not carry a great deal of dictionary-type meaning, but their presence is necessary for constructing meaningful sentences. They essentially carry out grammatical functions. Function words stand alone as words, but unlike other words in the language, they cannot usually have other morphemes attached. The exception is with the personal pronouns, which can have number or case indicators as in *he, him, his, you, your, yours*, etc. and certain prepositions that can be combined, such as *into* and *within*. All the others stand alone; there is no suffix or prefix that can be added to *the* or *of*.

Inflectional morphemes serve similar purposes to function words in English sentences; they carry grammatical information. In English, most inflections are suffixes but some require an internal change—the plural of

When this child produces his first word, it will be a lexical morpheme. Why do you think this is true?

Exactostock/SuperStock

mouse, for example. Inflectional suffixes are added to lexical morphemes to indicate more information and include familiar forms such as the past tense marker (usually spelled as -ed) and the plural marker (usually an -s or -es). The most common English inflections are shown in Table 2.4.

Table 2.4: Examples of grammatical inflections in English

Tense	Aspect	Number	Possessive Case	Comparative	Superlative
• s/-es (walks, talks, fixes) -d/-ed (walked, talked, fixed) • Vowel change (write/ wrote; bring/ brought; sing/sang, shoot/shot)	• ed, with a form of *have* (have walked, has talked, had fixed) • No change (have brought; has shot)/ Vowel change (has / sung) • en (with an auxiliary have or be) (written, driven) • ing (with a form of *be*) (is writing, was singing)	• s/-es (cats, fits, horses, boxes) • Vowel change (mouse/ mice; goose/ geese) • en (Oxen) • um (singular in words such as medium datum) • a (plural in words such as media, data)	• s (Bob's, children's)	• er (funnier, meaner)	• est (strongest, liveliest)

Inflections are not the only suffixes in English. English also has a number of morphemes with sufficient content meaning to be considered lexical but which cannot stand alone. These include prefixes such as *bio-, morpho-, phono-,* and *multi-* and suffixes such as *-logy,* i, and *-ful.* Because they cannot stand alone but must be "bound" to other morphemes, they are thus considered bound lexical morphemes (see Figure 2.2). English, then, has a number of different ways of forming words: by adding prefixes and suffixes—whether lexical or inflectional—and by compounding (combining lexical morphemes). Other languages, however, have different processes.

Figure 2.2: How morphemes are categorized

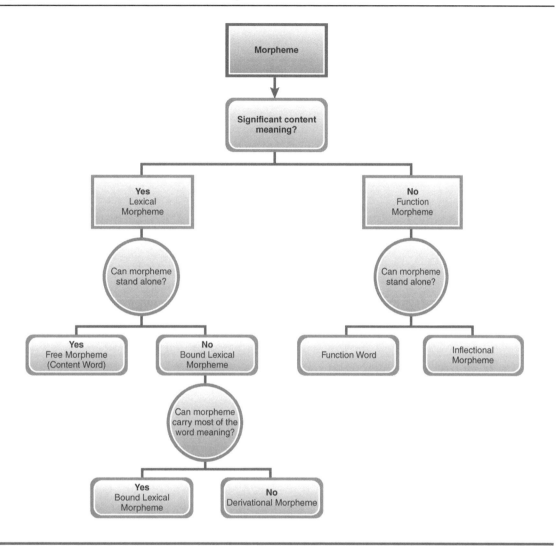

This diagram shows the criteria used for categorizing morphemes.

Morphology in English and Other Languages

In terms of how they combine morphemes to form words, the world's languages fall along a continuum with **analytic languages** at one end and **synthetic languages** at the other. A strictly analytic language would have one morpheme per word while a strictly synthetic language would combine all the morphemes needed to make the meaning of a sentence. Although there are no strictly analytic nor strictly synthetic languages, Mandarin and Vietnamese are highly analytic while Turkish and Russian are highly synthetic. English is usually categorized as an analytical language, although with its inflectional affixes and compounding, it too has certain synthetic properties.

English is the way it is because of its history. Every country that ever invaded the British Isles left behind some of its language. Three Germanic tribes—the Angles, the Jutes, and the

Saxons—arrived in less than friendly fashion around 450 CE and left behind the Germanic foundation of the English language, Anglo-Saxon. Words surviving into modern English include *earth*, *dirt*, *sheep*, and *tree*, along with many of the 100 most commonly used words in English today as well as most of the words that our mothers tried to keep us from using. The next major influence on English, still felt today, came with the Norman Invasion in 1066. In other words, the Latin influence came through the French language spoken by the invaders.

Every language that influenced English had a different way of forming words, and English somehow accommodated most of them, much to the frustration of adult learners of the language. Fortunately, children have no expectations about this, and for the most part, they figure out how morphemes fit together without difficulty. They do experience some confusion. Carter, at age 5, will say, "I forgotted that," adding the regular past tense form to a verb that already has the irregular form. In all likelihood, he does this because he learned *forgot* before *forget* and has yet to make the connection between the two forms. In time, he will sort it out just as he will figure out that the past tense of *bring* isn't "bringed," and the plural of *goose* is *geese*.

How would you help Carter tell his story about the geese flying over him?

iStockphoto/Thinkstock

Carter and other children his age are not terribly concerned about the correctness of the form. He is far more interested in talking about the geese that he saw flying in formation across the sky than with the fact that the word *goose* comes from Anglo-Saxon along with its plural form, largely unchanged. To tell his story about the geese, he needs more than individual words; he needs to be able to combine them into sentences, the next level of language structure.

2.3 How Sentences Are Made: Syntax

In everyday conversation, we sometimes speak in sentences and often speak in fragments. But even when we speak in shortened or truncated forms, we tend to mentally "fill in" the missing parts. In elementary school, most of us were taught that a sentence must have a subject and a verb or, depending on the precision of our teacher, a subject and a predicate. That is true—not terribly helpful, but true. It is just the beginning of the story. English sentence structure, or syntax, is about word order. More precisely, English sentence structure is about how morphemes are combined to form meaningful utterances.

Basic Sentence Structure

All human languages were created by humans as a way to express meaning, and there are many experiences that all humans have in common. Thus, it is not surprising that all languages share certain structural properties. They all use sentence structures with a subject, a verb, and an object, but the order in which those elements appear differs from language to language. In some languages, word order is flexible because the role the word plays in the sentence is indicated by an affix—a morpheme indicating whether a noun serves as a subject or an object, for instance. Most of the languages of the world, however, are either subject-verb-object (SVO) or subject-object-verb (SOV) languages. SOV is the most common word order in terms of the number of distinct languages that employ it (Mihalicek & Wilson, 2011). Japanese, Korean, and Turkish are all SOV languages. SVO is the most common word order in terms of the number of people who speak a language, since it is employed by English, all of the Romance languages, and Mandarin. Not all SVO languages have exactly the same structure, but the major constituents tend to be ordered in the same way.

Humans use language to communicate meaning. As diverse as we are, our languages share certain structural aspects. Why do you think this is?

Alex Treadway/National Geographic Stock

There is far more to sentence structure and syntax than the ordering of the major constituents. Look at the following sentences. Can you explain the kinds of differences apparent in them?

a. Sarah builds sandcastles.
b. Isabelle builds sandcastles.
c. Sarah built sandcastles.

For the moment, let's ignore the likelihood that Sarah, at age 2, is more apt to sit down in the middle of her sister's sandcastle than to build one. Think about the differences between sentences (a) and (b) and between (a) and (c). Sentences (a) and (b) have exactly the same structure but profoundly different meanings: It is Sarah who is building the sandcastle in (a) but Isabelle in (b). The two sentences have different subjects. Sentences (a) and (c) have a syntactic difference that changes the meaning. The morphemes in sentence (a) can be described as follows:

- *Sarah* (a lexical morpheme)
- *build* (a lexical morpheme)
- the present tense inflection, *-s*, indicating habitual or current activity
- three additional morphemes: the nouns *sand* and *castle*, which form a compound word and the plural inflection, *-s*.

Sentence (c) has the same major constituents as (a), but instead of the present tense marker, there is a past tense morpheme changing *build* to *built*. The difference here is syntactic.

The difference between sentences (a) and (b) is easier for children to understand than the difference between sentences (a) and (c). The "players" are different—it is a lexical difference that has a great deal of meaning. With (a) and (c), the difference is grammatical, a change in tense. Because tense is related to time, the difference is one that adults readily understand, but it takes a while for children to learn it. It takes longer to learn not only because it is a very subtle change in form (*build* to *built* is not even easy to hear) but because very young children have a shaky notion of past time.

There are, then, basically two kinds of syntactic learning that children must accomplish: the order in which words are put together to form sentences and the relationships that exist among the different constituents. In sentences, not all words are of the same magnitude of importance. Consider this sentence from Isabelle at age 5:

Papa winned the race.

Even though Isabelle regularized the past tense of *win* to make it sound like other regular verbs such as *talks* and *runs*, she had all the elements of a perfectly formed sentence. I have used a bracketing convention that linguists sometimes use to show the major constituents, subject and predicate:

[[winned the race]]

We learned that English is an SVO language, so we will break down the predicate further. From this point, it is easier to see the syntactic constituents of Isabelle's sentence using a tree diagram, although the tree and brackets convey the same information. Figure 2.3 represents the basic SVO constituent structure of the sentence.

Figure 2.3: Basic sentence structure

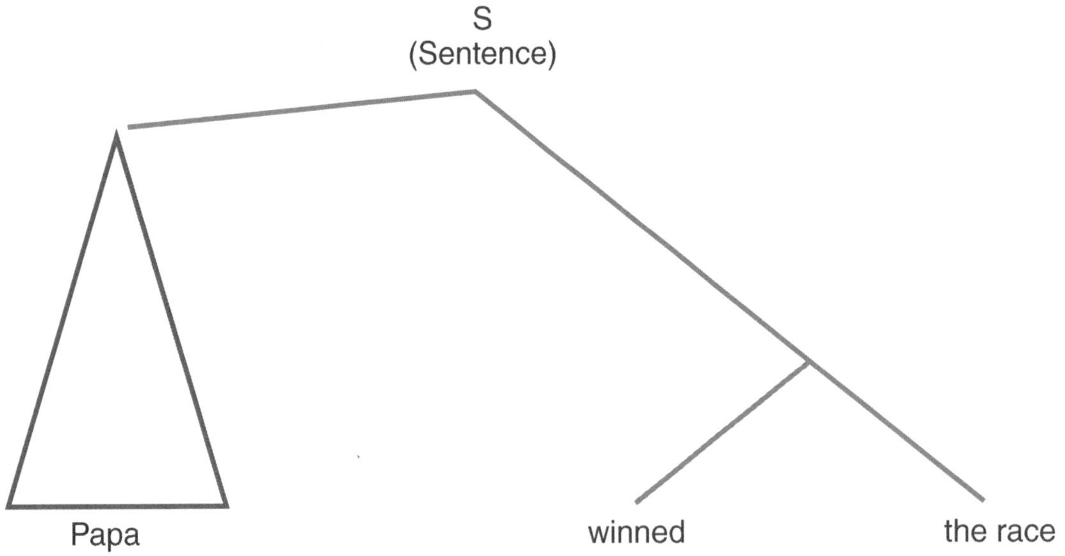

Basic sentence constituents for *Papa winned the race.*

If Isabelle were asked when her Papa won the race and she answered in a full sentence, the same structure would be expanded as in Figure 2.4, which shows all the morphemes in the sentence and their relationship to each other.

Figure 2.4: Constituent sentence structure

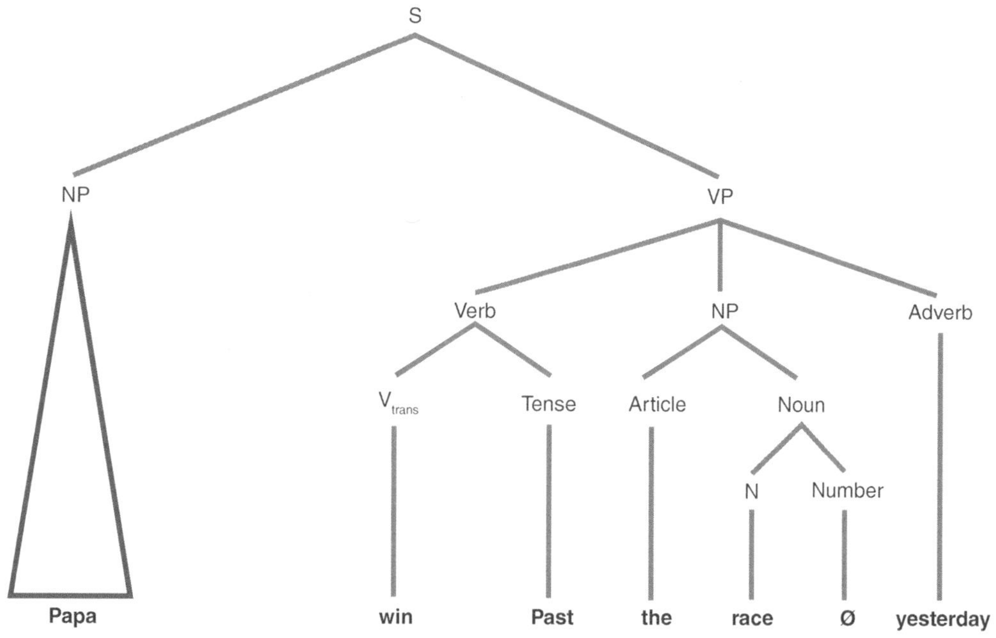

Constituent structure of *Papa winned the race yesterday.*

Learning Sentence Structure

The task of learning sentence structure involves learning the conventions for word order and constituent structure or, from the child's perspective, which bits of meaning fit together and how. Until children learn at least rudimentary syntactic rules, they cannot make themselves understood, but it is learning that begins very early. When a child barely able to walk says, "Want cookie," she is already demonstrating SVO word order. Although she has left out the subject noun, it is clearly understood to be "I." From this point on, syntactic learning progresses very quickly. Graham, at age 2 years 10 months, produced the following sentences:

   a. *Calley hit me 'cause it hurt.*

   b. *Mama give me time-out 'cause I bit Melissa.*

Both sentences are complex, meaning that they have two clauses—two units, each with a subject and a verb. In sentence (a), he gets the word order within each of the two clauses right but the order of the two clauses themselves wrong, likely because he has an imperfect understanding of the meaning of *because*. In sentence (b), he gets everything right in terms of word order. At this age, Graham was also able to produce negatives and questions:

   a. *I don't like yellow Jell-O!*

   b. *Melissa won't give me the clock.*

   c. *Mama, can Melissa have a cookie?*

Graham has already learned a great deal about English word order, but there is still much more to learn. One kind of structure, the passive voice, will continue to be a problem for several years (we will look more closely at the progression of syntactic learning in Chapter 6). As mentioned earlier, English is an SVO language. This is one of the first realities of English syntax that children internalize. When Graham was 4 years old, his mother conducted an experiment to test his understanding of the passive structure. She used the two sentences:

The dog bit the cat.

The cat was bitten by the dog.

When asked to demonstrate the second scenario (The cat was bitten by the dog.) using stuffed animals, Graham showed the cat biting the dog. Why do you think he is struggling with the passive form?

Clover/SuperStock

Using stuffed animals, Graham's mother asked him to demonstrate the action when she said each sentence. His responses demonstrated that word order was far more significant than the bothersome little grammatical morphemes, *by* and *so*. While he correctly demonstrated the dog biting the cat in response to the first sentence, when it came to the second, he was convinced that the cat bit the dog. Graham will start to figure it out when he is 6 or so, and that learning will likely continue until he is 9 or 10. Fortunately, it isn't a problem that will often arise before then because the passive form is more often used in writing than in speech, and adults rarely use it with children. Still, Graham's struggle with the passive structure provides a good illustration of how significant word order is to young children learning to understand the language around them. Meaning is also important, as children's understanding of the truncated passive shows. Truncated passives are those sentences in which the "doer" of the action is not expressed. Sentences such as *the ball was stolen* or *the doll was broken* are usually easier for children to understand. Upon hearing such a sentence, a child of 4 or older might even ask, "Who stole the ball?" thus revealing that in the world of children, meaning always trumps structure.

Learning to combine words according to the rules of syntax, children learn to understand and to produce new and unique sentences (i.e., sentences that they have not heard or produced before). Learning the rules of syntax is essential to language learning, but it is only part of the business of meaningful communication.

2.4 Semantics and Pragmatics: Making Meaning, Making Sense

The study of meaning in language is called **semiotics**. Although all the levels of language work together to achieve meaning, most linguists consider the study of semiotics to include three levels of language: syntax (which we already examined in brief), semantics, and pragmatics. Semantics refers to the relationship between linguistic signs (whether words or sentences or larger units of discourse) and the real world. Pragmatics refers to the study of the relationship between language signs and language users. Certainly, all three are essential to understanding how meaning is created. Syntax cannot do the job alone. Linguists are fond of using sentences such as the following to exemplify how syntactic rules can generate perfectly formed but meaningless sentences:

If you can't hear me, please hold up your hand.

Syntactically, there is nothing wrong with the sentence. All the words have meaning and are properly sequenced, the subjects and verbs agree—it is perfectly formed. A syntactician wouldn't be much interested in the sentence, but a semanticist, interested in how meaning is constructed, might be interested in explaining why the sentence fails to generate the intended meaning, why it actually expresses an impossibility in the real world. The pragmatist, however, concerned with the relationship between speakers and listeners and utterances, would be positively salivating at the opportunity to analyze it. To understand why, let's take a closer look at semantics and pragmatics.

Constructing Meaning: Semantics

To study any aspect of language without taking meaning into consideration is impossible. We don't go around (most of us, usually) babbling nonsense syllables. Meaning is, after all, the business of language. Semantics is concerned with word meanings as well as the meaning that results from combining words in various ways and with how language represents real-world meaning—in brief, meaning as it resides in and is constructed with language. Formally, semantics is a little more resistant to formal description than is phonology, morphology, or syntax. The reason is that in order for people to communicate, language has to have certain fairly rigid conventions—if words didn't have more or less the same meanings from speaker to speaker, it would be impossible to communicate. Similarly, if English sentence structure were a matter of random ordering of words, the result would be miscommunication or, indeed, no communication at all. Linguistic descriptions of phonology, morphology, and syntax are possible only because there is considerable agreement on what the rules are—there is standardization. When it comes to meaning, or specifically, how people view and represent reality, the "rules" are harder to formulate. The reason is that reality is defined, to a significant degree, by individual and cultural experience. In English, unless we are talking about rain, we use the word *water* to refer to the chemically defined substance H_2O. In Japanese, however, there are different words for hot water and cold water, and it is not possible to talk about water without specifying one or the other—there is not a generic term.

Even among speakers of the same language, there can be differences. Although there has to be a commonly agreed upon "dictionary" in order for any communication to happen, it is surprising how much variation is possible. For example, there is a difference between Canadian and American English in the meaning and usage of the word *quite*. In general, Americans use the word to indicate a significant amount or degree. To say that someone is "quite beautiful" usually means that the person possesses an extraordinary beauty. In Canada, however, the term may indicate reservations. To say that someone works "quite hard" may actually mean that the person works somewhat hard or even imply that the person doesn't work all that much.

In England, this would be called a *zebra crossing*. An American child hearing this term might look for large, striped animals.

iStockphoto/Thinkstock

Cultural variation is only one thing that frustrates linguists attempting to describe semantic structure in any way that comes close to the precision with which they are able to describe the other levels of the language. The major problem is that meaning doesn't reside in one place. Because meaning is the purpose and the product of language, it resides in every level from the sound through the sentence and to even larger units of discourse. The generative and case grammar models are of relevance to teachers for the simple reason that understanding or even describing children's language learning is difficult without also understanding that the levels of language interact with one another.

Making Sense: Pragmatics

The distinction between semantics and pragmatics is easily demonstrated with a true anecdote, courtesy of my granddaughter Isabelle, when she was about two and a half. Isabelle is bilingual; her mother speaks only French to her, and her father speaks only English. She lives with her family in Canada. Twice a year, the family comes to Florida where I live in a condominium where most residents are retirees. Nevertheless, residents are accustomed to children and enjoy having them around. Usually. One day we were all at the swimming pool. An octogenarian named Julia saw Isabelle, who is very petite, in the pool, and as soon as she came out asked her, "Child, are you potty trained?" Isabelle did not understand the question and turned to her mother who repeated the question in French, using terms more familiar to the child. Isabelle turned to Julia and said, in perfect French, *Oui, Madam, et vous?* ("Yes, Madam, and you?") Syntacticians would find nothing of interest in this sentence; semanticists would have to concede that the meaning was clear. To a pragmatist, however, the conversation is fodder for analysis and discussion. Certainly, Isabelle made sense, and from her perspective there was nothing inappropriate about the utterance. But the fact that it is amusing tells us that there is some kind of mismatch between the child's understanding of real-world language use and the adult's.

In constructing rules for English sentences, syntacticians focus on "grammatical" and fully formed sentences. Their work is highly theoretical, more about the language that people think they speak than the language they use. Real language used in everyday conversation is filled with fragments, false starts, and wrong words. For linguists studying pragmatics, it is the language used by real people to communicate in real time that provides the data for their study.

Stylistics is a form of pragmatics. Earlier in this chapter, we looked at syntactic paraphrase. For purposes of describing sentence structure, the meanings are considered to be identical, but in actual usage, they seldom are. Consider the following paraphrases:

   a. The duchess wore the diamond well.
   b. The diamond was worn well by the duchess.
   c. It was the duchess who wore the diamond well.

Each sentence consists of exactly the same propositions, and they would all have the same underlying syntactic structure. But for native speakers, each sentence conveys slightly different information, and it has to do with focus. In sentence (a), a simple declarative statement, there is no particular emphasis on either the duchess or the diamond. In sentence (b), the diamond is the focus of the sentence by virtue of its placement at the beginning of the sentence. Similarly, the addition of *it was* at the beginning of sentence (c) emphasizes the duchess (as opposed to other potential wearers of the diamond). Word order, then, conveys more than just the syntactic role words may play in a sentence. If we consider the meaning difference between *the blue house* and the *house that is blue*, we see once more the subtle differences conveyed by word order. When an adjective comes before a noun, as in *the blue house*, it defines or characterizes the house. When it comes in a relative clause following the noun, as in *the house that is blue*, the modifier serves to distinguish it from other houses. The distinction is in emphasis and the conditions under which each would be used. English has conventions for arranging words to achieve particular meanings, and while they are somewhat difficult to formalize, speakers of the language eventually come to understand what they are and to apply them. For example, it would be rare to hear a native speaker say, "the blue old house," even though it is perfectly grammatical.

Manipulation of Language

Another aspect of pragmatics relates to how language is used to manipulate situations or people for specific purposes. Two such uses are fairly common: the language of propaganda and language related to gender and sexism.

Propaganda

Propaganda presents a classic example of language used to manipulate. Whether in wartime or in everyday political life, people (often politicians) use language to influence or persuade, not through a thorough presentation of all sides or all information available, but through highly selected and sometimes inflammatory language. Today, the term *propaganda* carries largely a negative connotation, but it has an honorable past. It originally referred to any language used to persuade. Today it refers to biased language used to manipulate opinion or behavior (Hoyt, 2008). When politicians started to refer to rich people as "job creators," the point was to influence how people thought about the wealthy. It was easy to see, whether one agreed with the politicians or not, that the change was motivated by a desire to keep tax rates low for wealthy people. By relabeling rich people as *job creators*, politicians tried to make the idea of taxing them less more appealing to the general public. Not only political talk is designed to manipulate. Some would argue that the language of commercial advertising verges on propaganda. In the sense that it is intended to persuade or manipulate us into buying something, that is true, and advertisers are often very clever in their use of language to ensure that they speak the truth—selectively—while simultaneously seducing us into their worlds.

Advertisers often use propaganda to influence consumers to prefer their product. How might bright colors and cartoon characters appeal to children?

Associated Press

Sexist Language

Sexist language is another excellent example of how language can be used to manipulate. The fact that there are far more pejorative terms for talking about females than males is not only a consequence of women's secondary status in society for many centuries; it arguably serves to shape perceptions of women and perpetuate that status. Even supposedly equivalent terms such as *master* and *mistress* are not equivalent in certain contexts. Saying that "Bruce is Betsy's master" conveys a very different kind of power arrangement than "Betsy is Bruce's mistress." Throughout the English language, there are examples of language that diminish females. Even the fact that style manuals normally insist on *he* as the so-called neutral pronoun in English is evidence that females are historically of less significance in the society, and arguably, this has a role on how children perceive themselves. There is, in fact, evidence that young children do not perceive the so-called gender neutral *he* as neutral at all. Throughout the 1970s and 1980s, researchers, educators, linguists, and those in the women's movement all paid a great deal of attention to sexist language (Cincotta, 1978; Gaff, 1978). As a result, there has been a real attempt in recent decades to ensure that children's books are more gender-neutral than they were in the past. The issue has not disappeared, however. As a colleague of mine recently noted, "The Three Bears are still boy bears." Perhaps the best evidence that gender bias is still an issue in language may be the number of books, articles, blogs, and Web pages still devoted to the subject of gender bias in language.

Another matter in language and gender that occupies the time of sociolinguists, anthropological linguists, and others interested in linguistic pragmatics is the differences between male and female language use. What is particularly interesting is not structural differences per se, although some of these may

A professor at Georgetown University, Deborah Tannen has written both popular and scholarly books and articles about the differences in how males and females use language.

Associated Press

exist, but differences in how language is used for communication. One of the foremost scholars on this subject is Deborah Tannen who makes the case that men and women use talk for different purposes. Men, she claims, are more likely to use talk to establish or exhibit status while women are more likely to use it to build solidarity (Tannen, 2001; 2011). Hence, men are generally more talkative in public than in private, and the reverse is true for women. Women are more likely to engage in talk about their troubles to establish solidarity while men tend to avoid such talk. In general, women establish and maintain eye contact more than men, and while both men and women will engage in linguistic sparring, men are far more likely to do it "for fun," than are women.

Conclusion

This chapter begins to explain the complexity of language so that we can appreciate what children—infants, really—accomplish as they learn to communicate through language. There is much to do. There is a sound system to learn, and words to learn and to string together into sentences that make sense in all kinds of situations. In the first months and years of life, children lay the foundation for the language that will take them to school. This foundation will continue to grow throughout their lives. Anyone who has been a parent or who has spent enough time with young children stands in awe at the speed of their learning. Now that we have a basic understanding of what children accomplish, in the next chapter, we take a closer look at how children acquire language.

Post-Test

1. A diphthong occurs when

    a. a change in one consonant sound changes the meaning of a word.
    b. two vowel sounds glide quickly together.
    c. a word is spelled the same forward and backward.
    d. the use of a word changes its meaning.

2. Morphemes are

    a. the same as words.
    b. fairly basic to understand in English.
    c. difficult to use in English.
    d. the smallest units of meaning in a word.

3. Of the following, generally the most complex structure for English-speaking children to use is

    a. questions.
    b. multiple clauses.
    c. passive.
    d. SVO.

4. Using "he" as a term for both males and females

    a. has increased since the 1970s.
    b. is perceived by most children as gender neutral.
    c. is the style recommended by some writing manuals.
    d. provides evidence that females are generally considered to be superior.

Answers

1. **b.** Two vowel sounds glide quickly together. *The answer can be found in Section 2.1.*
2. **d.** The smallest units of meaning in a word. *The answer can be found in Section 2.2.*
3. **c.** Passive. *The answer can be found in Section 2.3.*
4. **c.** Is the style recommended by some writing manuals. *The answer can be found in Section 2.4.*

Key Ideas

*   The English language has four distinct "levels" of structure: phonology, morphology, syntax, and meaning, including semantics and pragmatics.
*   All languages have all these levels of structure and each language is unique.
*   The human brain is able to learn any human language.
*   Before they reach school age, children have learned a great deal of language structure; they have not done so intentionally or consciously but rather in the process of learning to communicate.

Critical Thinking Questions

1. English has 25 distinctive consonant sounds and 19 distinctive vowel sounds. Most dialects of Spanish have only 16 consonant sounds and 5 vowels. Does this mean that Spanish-speaking children learn their sound system faster than English-speaking children? Defend your answer. You will be asked to reassess it after reading Chapters 3 and 4.

2. Some people insist that there is a distinction between the initial sound in the words *which* and *witch*. Do you hear one? If so, what are the distinct phonemes that distinguish the two?

3. When you go to the doctor and she wants to look at your throat, which vowel does she ask you to say and why? (Why not /i/ or /u/, for example?)

4. How many morphemes are in *unsystematically*? List and provide the meaning or function of each.

5. Look at the auxiliary verbs in Table 2.5. Why do you think the auxiliary verbs *had*, *has*, and *was* are not included in the list? Is it simply that they were left out of the sample, or is there another explanation?

Table 2.5: Auxiliary verbs

Prepositions	Articles	Conjunctions	Pronouns	Auxiliary verbs
to	the	and	I	be
for	a	or	you, your	have
of	an	nor	he, him, his	may, might
in		but	she, her	shall, should
into		neither	It	can, could
on		either	who	will, would
onto		yet	some	must
from		because	one	ought to

6. In which category would *more* and *most* (as in *more likely* and *most productive*) fall in Figure 2.1?

7. Look at the following three sentences and suggest a context that would be more appropriate for each sentence. In other words, what question might each be answering?
   a. Mommy ate the cookies.
   b. It was Mommy who ate the cookies.
   c. The cookies were eaten by Mommy.

8. Find three examples of magazine or newspaper advertisements that use language to manipulate you into buying a product.

Key Terms

analytic language A strictly analytic language would have one morpheme per word.

consonant A speech sound produced by impeding the airflow in the vocal tract.

diphthong A vowel sound created by one vowel "gliding" into another as in the word *eye*.

functional morpheme A morpheme, either a word or an inflection, that has minimal content meaning but serves a grammatical purpose in the sentence.

function words Stand alone as words, but unlike other words in the language, they cannot usually have other morphemes attached.

inflectional morphemes Types of function morphemes; they carry grammatical information.

intonation The rise and fall and rhythm, or cadence, of language.

lexical morpheme A morpheme with substantive content meaning.

minimal pair Two words that differ by only one sound.

morphology The branch of linguistics concerned with how words are structured.

phoneme The smallest unit of sound that has meaning to a native speaker.

pragmatics The study of language as it is used in real-life context.

semantics The branch of linguistics concerned with the study of meaning.

semiotics The study of signs and symbols and how they are used or interpreted.

stress The force with which a syllable is articulated.

synthetic languages A strictly synthetic language would combine all the morphemes needed to make the meaning of a sentence.

vowel A highly resonant speech sound made when air passes through the vocal tract with little obstruction.

Weblinks

For charts illustrating the different conventions for representing vowel sounds as well as the audio representation of each sound:
http://faculty.washington.edu/dillon/PhonResources/newstart.html

http://www.clsp.jhu.edu/ws2000/presentations/preliminary/victor_zue/Zue-lecture2.pdf

http://www.indiana.edu/~hlw/PhonUnits/vowels.html

For a complete description and discussion of syllable structure, see *The World Atlas of Language Structures Online* at
http://wals.info/chapter/12

Deborah Tannen also puts interfamilial talk under the microscope in her *I Only Say This Because I Love You: How the Way We Talk Can Make or Break Family Relationships Throughout Our Lives*. (2001, New York: Random House). For further writings by Deborah Tannen, see her homepage at
http://www9.georgetown.edu/faculty/tannend/

For an interesting study on gender differences in written text, see
http://homepage.psy.utexas.edu/homepage/faculty/pennebaker/reprints/Newman SexDif2007.pdf

For an excellent video and opportunity to assess your understanding of persuasive and manipulative language, see
http://www.mindset.co.za/learn/node/44968

There are many good videos of babies babbling on YouTube and other sites:
http://www.youtube.com/watch?v=bPGekZreJLc

http://blog.sfgate.com/sfmoms/2011/04/03/babbling-twins-video-goes-viral/

3

Learning Language: How Children Do It

Learning Objectives

By the end of this chapter, you will be able to accomplish the following objectives:

- Cite the evidence for the view that children are "prewired" to learn language.
- Describe the role environment plays in language acquisition.
- Differentiate among the four major theories of language acquisition and the evidence for and against each.
- Explain what is meant by *developmental forms* and how they differ from errors.

Introduction

Sarah doesn't yet know how to tie her shoes. In fact, even Velcro fastenings present a challenge for her, and even if they didn't, she rarely gets her shoes on the correct feet. Right/left is a distinction she is still a couple of years from acquiring. She can count, but anything above the number two is pretty much a guess. She likes to play, but her attention to any one toy or activity is limited to a few minutes. Although she knows that she needs to hold the paper down when she is coloring, what she draws consists mainly of scribbles. She can't yet draw a stick figure or stay within the lines in a coloring book. She knows her body parts; she knows that she is a girl and not a boy. But she doesn't know when to use *she* or *her* instead of *he* or *him*, and probably doesn't see any compelling reason to.

Cognitively and intellectually, Sarah has a long way to grow. This 25-pound child who is less than 3-feet tall, plays alongside other children but not with them yet. She hasn't quite mastered potty training, building sand castles, or the rules of tag, but this 2-year-old is already a very competent language learner.

In this chapter, we describe what Sarah and children like her accomplish in acquiring the first language, and the environmental factors that affect that learning. We also examine some theories about how they do it. We conclude the chapter by examining some of the "mistakes" children make as they learn language and what these mistakes tell us about what they are learning.

Pre-Test

1. Acquisition of language seems to be

    a. exclusively due to environmental influences.
    b. based on inherent structures.
    c. time varied due to cultural differences.
    d. an unnatural and lengthy process.

2. Critical periods are

    a. times in which individuals are more sensitive to environmental influences.
    b. prenatal for language acquisition.
    c. generally during adolescence.
    d. intervals during which individuals may lose skills acquired earlier in life.

3. Arguments against behaviorism as the best explanation for children's language learning include all of the following EXCEPT that

    a. adults tend to focus on the meaning as opposed to syntax of children's speech.
    b. children are not exposed to all of the words that they use.
    c. children imitate and use the speech that they hear.
    d. making corrections to syntax rarely effect changes in speech.

4. Developmental forms are

   a. the papers that pediatricians fill out about milestones.
   b. the mismatch between adults' and children's use of language.
   c. the correct use of language by children.
   d. methods for measuring a child's language development.

Answers

1. **b.** Based on inherent structures. *The answer can be found in Section 3.1.*
2. **a.** Times in which individuals are more sensitive to environmental influences. *The answer can be found in Section 3.2.*
3. **c.** Children imitate and use the speech that they hear. *The answer can be found in Section 3.3.*
4. **b.** The mismatch between adults' and children's use of language. *The answer can be found in Section 3.4.*

3.1 Born to Talk

At age 2, Sarah speaks clearly enough to be understood, although there are still many sound distinctions she cannot make—the word *piggy* sounds more like *kee-kee*, for instance, which sounds pretty much the same as *kitty*. She has already acquired a substantial vocabulary, and she combines words into two- and three-word sentences in both her languages. At 20 months, she said clearly, "Want go down," to tell her grandmother that she wanted to go downstairs to the playroom. Sarah was not sure she was making herself clear, since her grandmother hadn't yet acceded to her request. So Sarah reiterated, "Ah-ah go down" (Ah-ah is her pronunciation of her own name). At age 2, Sarah's vocabulary is growing at a rate that is almost too fast to count. Conservatively, her productive vocabulary, or the words she has spoken, is between 40 and 50 words. Her receptive vocabulary, or those words she understands, is much larger, certainly in the hundreds. As a language learner, Sarah is a work in progress, but she has made a very impressive start. The sum total of all her physical, cognitive, and linguistic development in 24 short months constitutes compelling evidence that babies are born with brains "prewired" to acquire language, and that language is "the product of a well-engineered biological instinct" (Pinker, 2010, p. 6).

Renowned linguist professor Steven Pinker believes that children possess a strong biological instinct to acquire language.

Associated Press

To say that Sarah's language learning is instinctual in no way diminishes her achievement. Quite the contrary. Human children accomplish something as complex as language at a time when they struggle with learning things that, to the adult way of thinking, are much less complicated, such as figuring out how a smart phone or a computer game works.

The Complexity of the Task

As we know from the hundreds of thousands of volumes written on the subject, language is complex. Any adult who has tried to learn a new language has an appreciation for what children accomplish in acquiring their first language. Although adult learners of a new language have certain advantages (Chapter 4), because already knowing one language makes learning a second easier. Human languages are alike in significant ways, and adults take advantage of the similarities. Adult learners, unlike infants, have advanced cognitive abilities and better memory, but still the task is daunting. What infants and children accomplish in learning a language is truly remarkable. Long before they can draw a recognizable flower or even a stick figure, children can understand the talk surrounding them and have begun to use language in meaningful ways to accomplish many purposes. Some children even manage to overcome major physical, environmental, and cognitive challenges to do so, as we shall see a little later.

This boy knows the names of the colors he is using and the family members he is drawing. Understanding this is just part of the task of learning language.

Digital Vision/GettyImages

Now that Sarah has celebrated her second birthday, it seems to her parents that she was born talking. She wasn't, but the work did start on that first day. Actually, it began before birth as her brain formed with its particular propensity to learn language. We'll talk more about the brain later in Chapter 5.

The Nature of the Task

Some people naively assume, as an entire branch of psychology once did, that a child's task in learning language is to repeat parrot-like the language she hears around her. The theory is that children rely on memorization and mimicking, gradually refining their own speech until it eventually matches the adult models around them. This theory makes the process sound very easy. It would, however, be very difficult to learn language in this way because of the huge amounts of language children would have to memorize. This explanation might be feasible at the word level—which requires remembering that the word *horse*, as opposed to *duck* or *cat*, refers to a large four-footed creature with a mane and possibly a saddle. At the sentence level this theory of language learning is not very feasible. If children had to hang around waiting for an adult to utter the very sentence needed to express all of the meaning they might ever need to make, they wouldn't do much talking at all in their early years. What children need to talk about is fundamentally different from most adult conversation. Moreover, as Meisel points out,

> One of the most important insights of language acquisition research during the past decades is the finding that grammatical development proceeds through invariant developmental sequences, that is, that the acquisition of crucial grammatical properties follows an order which is largely the same across individuals. (Meisel, 2011, p. 241)

This finding, along with the sheer speed with which children learn sentence structure, argues strongly for the existence of an innate language learning mechanism. Other kinds of evidence come from the uniqueness of children's utterances—children say things that they have never heard from an adult. A question that Chloe, age 3, asked her father illustrates the point:

> *Daddy, are we going to your Ami today?*

For several days before Chloe asked this question, her parents had been talking about an upcoming trip to visit Chloe's grandmother, who lives in Miami. Chloe had parsed what she heard as "going to my ami." In this sentence, she not only turned a statement into a question, she used the pronoun (*your*) appropriate to what she assumed the meaning to be. What Chloe showed us here is that language learning involves learning not random words and phrases, but the vastly complicated rule system that governs language. If language were random and not rule-governed, it would be impossible to learn. Although language does have rules, children do not pay much attention to learning structure—the way that language is organized, which we learned about in Chapter 2. For them, the sole business of language is to make meaning—meaning that accomplishes something they seek to accomplish. For adults trying to understand the process, however, it is easier to talk about how children learn the different components of language in terms of structure.

How Children Accomplish the Task

At the most basic levels, what is involved in the task of learning a language? Children need to figure out how to make sense of the continuous stream of sounds (those things that we, as adults, recognize as words and sentences). While it is our perception that there are spaces between words, that is only because we know the words. When we are listening to a foreign language, it is not easy to know where the word boundaries are. Infants listening to adults speak have much the same problem. They have to figure out which of those sounds can stand alone as words. In the previous example, Chloe shows us that children do not always get this right.

Identifying the words of the language is only part of the puzzle. Children also have to learn which sounds matter and which do not. In any language, there is only a finite number of meaningfully distinct speech sounds (the phonemes described in Chapter 2). However, in actual speech each of these sounds has a variety of pronunciations. It is not easy to figure out which are important and which are not. For example, the phoneme /k/ has different pronunciations depending on the vowel that follows it. If the vowel is the one in *kit* or *key*, the /k/ is pronounced further forward, right at the hard palate. If the vowel is the one in *cat*, the /k/ sound is articulated a little further back, but not as far back as it is articulated in the pronunciation of *comma* or *cause*. For adult speakers, the differences aren't noticeable, but children do not yet know what we know. In the process of learning the sound system, children sort out whether the differences between the pronunciations of /k/ are more or less significant than the difference between the pronunciation of /k/ and /g/ or /t/. At the same time that children are sorting out these differences, they are learning to produce the distinctions themselves. As their control over their vocal apparatus improves, they come closer and closer to the adult pronunciation. Consider how Chloe progressed from *wahwoo* to *yellow:*

This boy may know that the umbrella he is holding is yellow, but saying the name of the color presents more of a challenge at this age.

amanaimages/Corbis

> *wahwoo* (/wæwu/ (24 months)
>
> *lalo* (/lelo/) (34 months)
>
> *lalo/yewo* (/lelo/, /yɛwo/) (40 months)
>
> *yellow* (yɛlo/) (49 months)

Notice that at 40 months, she alternated between her younger form and a new one that was even closer to the adult pronunciation, providing clear evidence that she was making progress.

Chloe did not expend all her language-learning efforts mastering the pronunciation of *yellow*. In fact, she was perfectly happy with her own version at each stage, although she would object if an adult said *lalo* for *yellow*. She was able to hear the distinction before she could produce it. At the same time, she was busy learning how to combine sounds into syllables, morphemes, and words, and expanding her vocabulary at an impressive rate. By the time they are 2 years old, most children have begun to produce two- and three-word sentences, usually with the correct word order, showing that they are well on their way to learning the complex rules of syntax. Consider these early sentences from Sarah:

Ah-Ah nana. (19 months)

Want go down. (20 months)

No go in. (24 months)

Each utterance represents a different syntactic structure conveying the meaning that Sarah intended. In the first, the adult equivalent would be *Sarah wants a banana*. Note that she had mastered the basics of subject-verb-object (SVO) word order, although the verb was not present yet. She did not yet have the personal pronoun or the article, but these are arguably "frills"—using her own name and the name of the object she wanted accomplished the communicative intent. Just one month later, however, her *Want go down* with its adult equivalent of *I want to go down*, illustrated more complexity. At this stage of development, she could not produce sentences longer than three words, but once more, she got in the essentials. The subject, or who wants to go, was perfectly predictable in the context, so she concentrated on the verb, *want go* (*to* is another of those frills she needn't bother with), and the place, *down*.

At 24 months, Sarah's three-word sentence revealed even more complex structure, but still she reduced it to the minimal structure required for her meaning. The adult equivalent *I don't want to go in* is perfectly rendered within the situational context in *No go in* even though she omitted the subject and much of the verb. None of her utterances indicated verb tense, but again, the situations made it unnecessary. What is impressive in these utterances was that Sarah found exactly the right words for expressing her meanings. She got them in the right order, and she made herself understood. She also demonstrated that she was well on her way to mastering sentence structure.

Mastering the complex rules of the language seems a daunting task from the adult perspective (see *Learning the Present Tense: A Linguist's Perspective* for an example from a linguist's point of view). From the child's perspective, however, great concern with language structure is highly unlikely. For the child, language is all about meaning and communication. Learning the components and the rules for combining them merely gives children the tools to accomplish the real purpose of language. Children also have to learn how and what to communicate to the different people in their lives. They have to learn all the conventions of conversation—turn-taking, staying on topic, how to shift topics, meaning confirmation, and so forth. They also have to learn what kinds of talk are appropriate in various settings—why screaming "No way!" might be acceptable with a playmate or sibling but probably not with a preschool teacher or grandfather.

Learning the Present Tense: A Linguist's Perspective

Children by the age of three or three and a half have largely mastered the present tense inflection, producing runs, walks, eats, etc. correctly. Linguist Steven Pinker has pointed out that this inflection is actually a remnant in modern English—something that may be of historical significance but has little relevance in Modern English. He notes that "if it were to disappear, we would not miss it, any more than we miss the similar -est suffix in Thou sayest. Even though that little -s is a grammatical frill, children have to know and keep track of quite a lot of detail to produce it correctly. They have to know

- whether the subject is one that requires an -s ending or not (i.e., whether it is in the third person—he, she, or it—as opposed to I or you;
- whether the subject is singular or plural;
- whether the action is present tense or not; and
- whether the action indicated by the verb is happening at the moment of speech or is habitual (She runs for president every four years vs. She is running for president).

All this presupposes that they already know the suffix. In order to learn it in the first place, a child must

- notice that verbs end in -s in some sentences but not others;
- start to try to figure out the relevant causes of this variation (i.e., figure out the grammatical "why"); and
- not rest until all the grammatical factors—"tense, aspect, and the number and person of the subject—have been sifted out of the ocean of conceivable but irrelevant factors (like the number of syllables of the final word in the sentence, whether the object of a preposition is natural or manmade, and how warm it is when the sentence is uttered)."

The question is, why do young children bother?

Source: Adapted from Pinker, 2010, pp. 32–33

Despite all there is to learn, children do so with astonishing speed, and they begin at birth. Research has shown that even newborns are more attentive to speech sounds than to other sounds, pay more attention to people than to objects, and are able to identify relevant sound distinctions in their native language within the first three months of life (Eimas, Siqueland, Jusczyk, & Vigorito, 1971; Plunkett & Schafer, 1999). How do they do it? Linguists and child psychologists do not have definitive answers, but more than a century of research has provided us some reasonable theories. Before examining these theories, let us look at the different environments in which children learn language.

3.2 Environmental Influences

There is no single environment in which children learn language. Nor is there a "best" environment for language learning, although there are some that are less than ideal. First-born children born to quiet, studious parents; children born into a large family of "talkers"; children who are confined to a medical facility at birth because of health problems; or even children who are emotionally or physically traumatized—they all learn to talk. That children persevere and learn language, sometimes in severely abnormal circumstances, constitutes compelling evidence that they have a genetic predisposition to do so (i.e., that at least some portion of language acquisition is innate). In the following sections, we examine the accomplishments of children in some of those environments. Then we examine some of the theories that attempt to account for those accomplishments.

Abnormal or Impoverished Environments

First, a caveat: The terms *abnormal* and *impoverished* refer only to the environment from the perspective of language acquisition, meaning that children in such environments are not exposed to normal oral language use during the early years of life. None of these terms refers in any way to socioeconomic, cultural, geographic, physical, or any other conditions not directly and significantly related to exposure and opportunity to use language. Some of the most dramatic cases of impoverished environments come from accounts of **feral children**, or human children who have lived in relative isolation, apart from or only marginally exposed to human society. While it is unlikely that any of us will encounter a feral child, the examples that follow are useful for understanding the relative importance of environment and children's predisposition to learn language. The cases of Isabelle and Grace represent two points on a continuum from extreme linguistic deprivation to a relatively normal communicative situation.

Isabelle was discovered in 1937. Some reports place her age at around 5 and others at 6 and a half. Isabelle's nonspeaking mother had been deaf since the age of 2, and both mother and child had been kept in isolation by the child's grandfather. There is no evidence that Isabelle had been mistreated in other ways. Shortly after she was discovered, Isabelle was tested and found to have the mental age of a 19-month-old child. Her oral language consisted of croaking. After working with experts at The Ohio State University for two years, her intelligence and language ability were judged to be completely normal for a child her age. She could tell stories and recite nursery rhymes and had an estimated vocabulary of between 1500 and 2000 words (Mihalicek & Wilson, 2011, p. 315).

Piper (2007) provides an account of Grace, a child raised in a healthy but relatively isolated environment by two deaf, nonspeaking parents. The nearest neighbors were almost a mile away, and Grace remembered having only limited contact with them. She recalled going with her mother to deliver home-grown vegetables and the occasional pie or cake to them, and she remembered them speaking to her. She also recalled aunts and uncles who visited once every summer, and she learned a few words from them. Her main source of spoken English, however, was her brother George, who was three years older. So from the age of approximately three, she had one speech model, on a regular basis, in her brother. Still, she was very clear in her recollection of the language she learned; her first language was sign language, and her second, oral English, was limited until she began attending school in first grade. Once there, she rapidly developed oral and written English abilities. According to her own report, 50 years later, she struggled through the first few months, but by the end of the year, she had no problems keeping up with her class. She went on to complete elementary school and attended two years of high school before dropping out to work in a factory during the Second World War. She was adamant that she liked school and was good at it. The report cards she happily offered as evidence attest to the fact that she was an able student.

Both Grace and Isabelle were able to acquire normal language ability in a relatively brief time, although their circumstances were quite different. Isabelle had very little exposure to speech, but she did have interaction with her mother who had developed a rudimentary method of communicating with gestures. Grace, while having little exposure to spoken language, had a fully developed communication system and enough exposure to oral language to develop normal pronunciation. These two cases, taken together, illustrate a great deal about the importance of environment and provide some insights into the degree to which language acquisition is innate. One of the most compelling cases for innateness, however, comes from a group of children in Nicaragua who created for themselves a linguistic form of communication, specifically a kind of sign language, initially outside a linguistic environment.

Until the 1970s, there were no formal education programs for deaf students in Nicaragua. In fact, deaf people were isolated from the general population and developed idiosyncratic systems for signing at home. Called **homesigns**, these systems tend to be very rudimentary. Typically, they do not have a syntactic system and consist only of a limited lexicon for indicating common objects and activities. Then, in 1980, a school for deaf adolescents was opened in Managua. Initially, staff at the school emphasized spoken Spanish and lip-reading, and sign language was limited to finger spelling. This approach resulted in little success in the classroom. What happened on the playground, streets, and buses, however, was a different matter. Outside the classroom, the children developed a system of communication combining gestures with elements of whatever homesigning systems they knew. What emerged was a **pidgin**, a simplified language with elements taken from local languages, used for communication between people who do not share a common language. Subsequent children at the school developed the pidgin further into a **creole**, a language with more of the properties of natural language that has its origins in a pidgin:

These deaf Nicaraguan children are signing using Nicaraguan Sign Language. What do you think the development of this language means to language acquisition theories?

Reuters/Corbis

> After the pidgin was created by the first students at the school, younger children came and were exposed to the pidgin. Without instruction, and based only on their exposure to the pidgin used by their older peers, these younger children created Idioma de Signos Nicaragennse (ISN), which is a full-fledged language with a complex system of grammatical rules." (Mihalicek and Wilson, 2011, p. 316)

These children effectively invented their own language, something that was discovered when staff, believing that the children's gesturing was mime and represented a failure to acquire Spanish, asked for outside help. The Nicaraguan Ministry of Education contacted researchers from MIT who analyzed the language and uncovered the complexity of the invented grammar. Linguists have differing interpretations of what the existence of Nicaraguan Sign Language (NSL) means for theories of language acquisition, but Steven Pinker asserts that it is a unique event in human history that provides strong evidence that the human brain is hard-wired to acquire language (Pinker, 2010).

Hard-wired, yes, but these cases all provide evidence that there might be a limit on what children in impoverished linguistic environments can attain and that this limit is largely influenced by the age at which acquisition begins. In other words, children are born with the capacity to acquire language, but there is a time stamp on that capacity in the sense that the ability atrophies if it is not used by a certain time. In tandem with the **innateness hypothesis** (Chomsky, 2006) that humans are predisposed to learn language, then, is the **critical period hypothesis**. With regard to human language learning, the age span, or critical period, is usually described as lasting from birth to the onset of puberty, the argument being that it is easier to acquire language before puberty, and that after that, there are limitations on what can be learned. The assumption is that if children do not have exposure to language during this critical period, their brains do not create the necessary structures to develop native-speaker competency in a language. Looking at the examples cited earlier, we see what could be interpreted as evidence for such a hypothesis. Isabelle and Grace were exposed to normal language well before the onset of puberty, and by the age of 8, both acquired language to the same level of proficiency as their peers.

It is the Nicaraguan children, however, who provide the most interesting and compelling data for the critical period hypothesis. When the first generation came together to attend the school, they were adolescents, and while they did acquire some language, they did not acquire a fully formed language. The next generations of children, though, were younger, and in two generations, they had created a complete new language, a fully formed creole with all the structural properties of a natural language. The most compelling evidence for the critical period hypothesis comes from the fact that the first generation of deaf students never fully acquired the newly invented language even though they were exposed to it. In adulthood, their language use retained the simplified characteristics of a pidgin. Successive generations, in contrast, were younger when they were exposed to the new language and acquired it fully. We will return to the critical period hypothesis in Chapter 4 in our discussion of second language acquisition.

"Normal" and Enriched Environments

What constitutes a normal environment? Most of us would answer by describing our own experiences, and that is entirely appropriate since "normal" admits of degrees. Some caregivers pay a great deal of attention to their children's language by reading to them, expanding their abbreviated utterances, or asking questions that elicit more language. Some mothers read Shakespeare and Dickens aloud to their infants. Other parents may do nothing special beyond the communication involved in day-to-day care. Is one environment better than the other? That is hard to say because of the many children who have thrived in less-than-ideal circumstances. What we do know is that, in general, children who have experienced language used in a variety of contexts and, in particular, those who have had stories and books read to them, attain greater proficiency in language. We also know that language proficiency helps to determine children's success in school. Educators have known this for years and have touted the benefits of an "enriched" linguistic environment. Enrichment, fortunately, does not require any special materials or even additional time. If adults repeat and expand their children's utterances, for example, they provide an extra measure of linguistic modeling that helps the child to learn. When Sarah said, *"Nana outside,"* her grandmother responded, *"You want to go outside?"* Thus, her grandmother not only confirmed Sarah's meaning but also provided her with a fully formed, grammatical sentence that could be used to convey that meaning.

Another way of enriching the linguistic environment is to read to children. Television, computers, smart phones, and iPads might seem more attractive—and certainly they command children's attention—but in terms of linguistic stimulation, children love stories. Telling stories to children helps them to develop "the mind's eye" (i.e., to envision events and characters outside the here-and-now). Reading serves a similar function; it not only broadens their experience of language, it helps them to become better readers later on. In the 1990s and the first decade of this century, it became fashionable to teach children sign language before they were capable of forming real words. Based on research show-

ing that nonhearing children acquired a vocabulary of signs much larger than the vocabulary attained by hearing children of the same age, parents began to teach American Sign Language, or, in some cases, homesigns, to their infants. Usually, they introduced signing at around 7 to 9 months. Whether early signing had any benefits for oral language or literacy development is unclear, but it certainly did no harm and arguably gave rise to better communication between caregivers and their infants.

This child is learning American Sign Language to help him communicate despite his inability to talk. Do you know anyone who uses signs with their prespeech children?

Blend Images/SuperStock

It might seem that if we believe in innateness, we need not concern ourselves with environmental influence—if language is instinctive, then children will learn it no matter what. But we should not be lulled into thinking that the fact that language seems so effortless means that it is. As Pinker puts it, "The effortlessness, the transparency, the automaticity are illusions, masking a system of great richness and beauty" (2010, p. 21). Moreover, although there is widespread agreement about the magnificence of the feat, there remains controversy about how it is accomplished, about the precise nature of the relationship between nature (or instinct) and environment. These issues have led psychologists and linguists to pose numerous theories about how language is learned.

3.3 Theoretical Perspectives

Theorists at one extreme of the issue contend that language is a learned behavior and that language learning is no different from any other kind of human learning. Theorists at the other extreme take the position that not much learning is required, that language is wholly instinctive. Neither extreme is reasonable, but in between the two are a number of competing theories about how it is that a preschool child has a tacit understanding of how the grammar of his language works that would take a linguist hundreds of pages to describe.

We cannot describe all the theories that have evolved or the cases that have been made for them, but we will examine four broad categories of theory related to language that have had a major influence. They are behaviorist, active construction of a grammar, neural connectionism, and social interaction.

Behaviorist Theories

As appealing as behaviorism was in the early part of the 20th century, it has little credence as a theory of language acquisition. Basically, behaviorist theories take the position that children learn through imitation. They listen to the speech around them, imitate what they hear, and then through a system of reinforcement (i.e., being praised or rewarded for correct utterances and having errors ignored or corrected), they learn to discard their imperfect imitations. The problems with applying this theory to real children learning language are obvious. First, children produce utterances they have never heard and, second, adults rarely respond to the form of the utterance. No theory of imitation can account for this and similar utterances. See *Chomsky's Case Against Behaviorism* for more on this topic.

Chomsky's Case Against Behaviorism

Noam Chomsky pointed out the many problems with behaviorism in his 1959 review of Skinner's *Verbal Behavior*. Although Chomsky's criticism spoke to first language acquisition, the argument holds for second. Chomsky argued that behaviorism cannot account for the various facts of language acquisition, namely:

- Young children acquire language at a remarkable speed.
- Children are largely impervious to correction of form.
- By the time most children are 4 or 5, they have an almost limitless capacity to understand and produce sentences they have never heard before.
- The notion that reinforcement accounts for learning runs counter to experience—a child does not utter the word dog over and over in the presence of adults who reinforce that behavior.

Noam Chomsky is an American philosopher, political activist, and linguist. In the 1960s and 1970s, he made an influential case for the existence of a language instinct.

Associated Press

Chomsky speculated that the abilities that account for all of these facts are largely innate, part of the cognitive endowment children have at birth.

Chomsky, N. (1959). Review of verbal behavior. *Language, 35, pp. 26–58.*
Skinner, B. F. (1957). Verbal behavior. *New York: Appleton-Century-Crofts.*

The most serious flaw of imitation as a theory is that it cannot account for how children come to produce or understand novel utterances, whether in the way they pronounce words or in the way they inflect them, or in the sentences they produce. Pronunciation errors are generally attributed to children's immature articulators (i.e., their physical inability to produce an exact replica of the adult form). Chloe's *lalo* for *yellow* would be assumed to be caused by her articulators not being sufficiently well developed to produce two distinct consonants and two distinct vowels in the same word.

Other kinds of errors are more problematic. It is highly unlikely that Chloe ever heard anyone say, "Nana, you forgotted." Yet she and all children her age regularly produce sentences they could not have heard from anyone else. Even if behaviorism could account for how these forms are created, the theory stumbles on the notion of reinforcement. There is overwhelming evidence that, in general, adults neither negatively reinforce flawed utterances nor positively reinforce correct ones. When I responded to Chloe with, "Yes, I suppose I did forget," although I modeled the correct form, my response was to her meaning, not her imperfect syntax. This type of response is typical of adult-child interactions: Adults focus on the meaning that the child is trying to make, and any correction is geared toward helping to make that meaning clear rather than to correct the form. More importantly, even if I had (foolishly!) tried to correct Chloe's syntax, and if she had understood what I was trying to do, it would not have effected any change in her language. Children attend to meaning.

Another compelling kind of evidence against behaviorism is the observation that children learning the same language tend to do so in remarkably similar ways. There is strong evidence, for example, that children acquire certain of the grammatical morphemes of English in a largely invariant order, as we see in *Learning Grammatical Morphemes.*

Learning Grammatical Morphemes

In a longitudinal study of three children, Roger Brown (1973) revealed compelling data showing that the order in which children acquired grammatical morphemes in English was very consistent. Even allowing for slight individual variations, the results showed that children acquired 14 common morphemes in the following order:

1. Present progressive *-ing*
2. Preposition *in*
3. Preposition *on*
4. Plural *-s*
5. Irregular past, e.g., *went*
6. Possessive *-'s*
7. Uncontractible copula *be*
8. Articles *a, the*
9. Regular past *-ed*
10. 3rd person regular *-s*
11. 3rd person irregular, e.g., *has*
12. Uncontractible auxiliary *be*
13. Contractible copula *be* (*It's Mommy*)
14. Contractible auxiliary *be* (*He's eating.*)

Later, de Villiers and de Villiers replicated the study with 21 English-speaking children, and the order they obtained correlated very highly with the children in Brown's study:

> There is a consensus that this research has uncovered a crucial property of first language development, namely that the acquisition of a number of grammatical features follows an order that is largely the same across individuals. A plausible inference from this insight is that the underlying mechanisms determining this developmental order are identical across individuals and largely unaffected by external influences. (Meisel, 2011, p. 64)

The Active Construction of a Grammar Theory

Active construction of a grammar theory contends that children use the speech they hear around them to construct the rules of the language by listening for and discovering patterns, hypothesizing about the rules that create those patterns, and then testing those rules in their own usage. They are, in a way, "little linguists." Certainly, there are data which would appear to support such a theory. In the sentence *Nana, you forgotted,* Chloe had clearly detected that past tense is formed by adding an -ed. Other words that she used at this time give strong indication of the rule that she had created:

Sarah holded my doll.

She gived it to me.

I ated all my lunch.

(Chloe 4 years, 6 months)

With *forgotted* and *ated*, she had doubled up on her past tense, probably because she did not realize that the verbs were already in the past tense, or perhaps because she had heard the past tenses more often than the present. Eventually, she will discover that her forms do not match the language used by others around her, and she will refine her rules and try again. Chloe's utterances were governed by her own grammar, which differs in significant ways but also shares important characteristics with adult grammar. Through the testing, modification, and editing of her rules, she will progress gradually, as a linguist does when constructing the rules of an unfamiliar language, until she achieves the same set of rules underlying adult speech.

Children's language errors present no difficulty for the active construction of a grammar theory. In fact, those who hold this theory do not even see the imperfect forms as errors, but rather as **developmental forms**, those language forms, differing notably from adult forms, that children produce as they learn the language. They are seen as evidence that children's learning is rule governed, as exemplars of rules in progress rather than as errors to be eradicated.

Connectionist Theories

Connectionist theories hold that children learn language through neural connections in the brain, developing these connections by being exposed to and using languages.

Proponents of connectionist theories would concede that rules are useful for describing the language forms that children produce during the acquisition process, but they would also argue that children play no active role in actually creating those forms. These theorists recognize that children bring some significant degree of innate capacity to the task of language learning and would also concede that eventually children's language is rule governed. Connectionists argue, however, that in the process of acquisition, children are not little linguists working out rules in their heads, but are more like little statisticians, computing probabilities and building neural connections in the brain based on their exposure to and use of language. With increased exposure, the connections are strengthened. (See Figure 3.1.)

Figure 3.1: A neuron

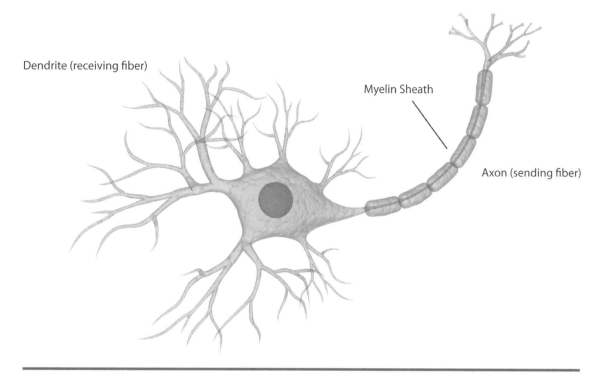

Dendrite (receiving fiber)

Myelin Sheath

Axon (sending fiber)

Each brain cell, or neuron, has a sending fiber or axon (right), which is coated in myelin, and a receiving fiber, or dendrite (left). These neuron connections are the basis for connectionist theory.

Source: Hemera/Thinkstock

Two kinds of language learning are often cited in support of connectionist theories. One is how children learn what a word is. The second is their learning of the past tense. How does a connectionist believe a child learns what a word is? In a continuous stream of speech in which there are no overt demarcations between words, how is it that children learn where the word boundaries are? More specifically, how do children, hearing, "Once upon a time in a land far away, a little boy and a little girl lived in a cottage at the edge of the woods," come to know which parts of that string constitute words? Over time, they will hear parts of that utterance in other contexts—perhaps in a sentence such as, "What is that little boy doing?" or "She couldn't find her little boy anywhere." Based on the evidence, they might conclude that *littleboy* is a word, but hearing *little* and *boy* separately in other contexts over time, they eventually create a mental representation for *little* and *boy* separately. Remember Chloe's question, "Are we going to your ami today?" She had segmented Miami as *my* and *ami*, and according to this theory, she would have done so based on the statistical probability that whatever came after *my* was another word. In this instance, she was wrong, but connectionists hold that this was not because she had formed the right rule and applied it in the wrong context but that she had not yet had enough experience with *Miami* in other contexts to form the correct representation (i.e., the place where her nana lived).

Connectionists also use children's acquisition of the past tense to explain their theory of language acquisition. When children produce *blowed* as the past tense of *blow*, these theorists argue it is because they have calculated it to be the most likely past tense based on other words the child has heard, such as *mowed, flowed,* and *glowed.* The connectionists may be right, but how do they account for the fact that some children will produce *bringed* as the past tense of *bring* while others will produce *brang*? If children are actively constructing rules, the theory would predict that they would produce *bringed* and later learn that there is an exception, *brought.* If, however, they are working from a probability or statistical basis, the theory would predict that they might produce either form—*brang,* analogous with *rang* and *sang,* or *bringed* because they had heard other regular past tense forms. In other words, connectionism would predict that some children will get it right and others get it wrong, and this appears to be the case, at least at first. Chloe's *forgotted* might be evidence that exposure, or frequency of occurrence, plays a role. She had heard *forgot* often enough to internalize it as a verb form but had not yet recognized it as a past tense, so she added a regular verb ending because that is the form she had heard on so many other verbs. In fact, it would fit the pattern of *spot/spotted, dot/dotted,* or *plot/plotted.* Before any of these rules can be learned, children must first learn words. Let us consider how Sarah learned *baby* from this theoretical perspective.

One of Sarah's first words was *baby.* How did she learn it? According to this theory, she would have heard people using the word *baby* in several different contexts—female infants, male infants, infants wearing snowsuits, pictures of infants, dolls, and even in reference to herself. Through multiple exposures to the word, she formed neural connections of various kinds—to the word itself, to a mother holding an infant, to pictures, dolls, or possibly just the letter /b/ or people without much hair. Eventually, these connections would coalesce into her mental representation of the word *baby.* These connections are not all of the same strength, or so the theory goes. If she heard the word *baby* used more frequently in reference to a doll than to a human baby or other referents, then the connection between *baby* and *doll* would be stronger than the connection between *baby* and any other possible referent. If, however, she had heard the word used more often with reference to a human baby, she might well develop a neural connection between *baby* and human infants (see Figure 3.2).

Figure 3.2: Example of connectionist theory

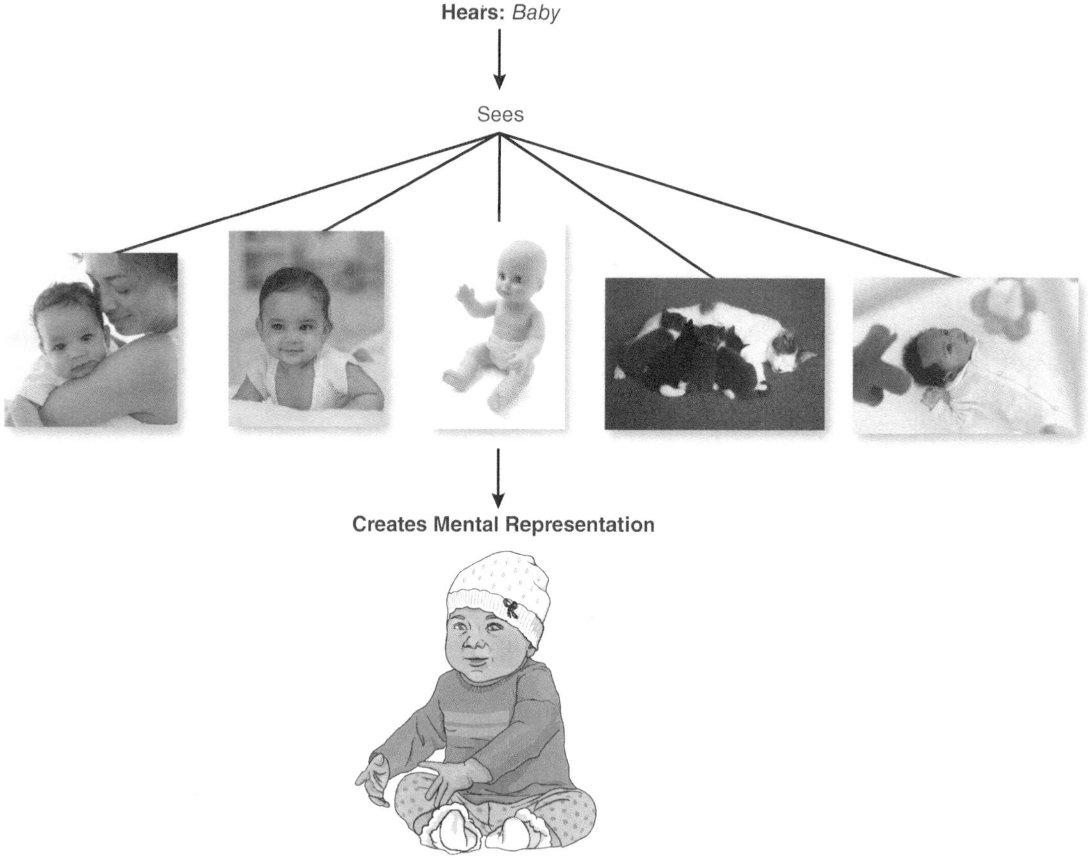

According to connectionist theory, this is how Sarah would learn the word *baby*.

Source: Thinkstock

Social Interaction Theory

Social interaction theory purports that children have an innate predisposition to acquire language and that they develop their own rules. This belief is shared with the active construction of a grammar theory. These theorists also believe that children acquire language as a result of interaction with more mature speakers of the language (i.e., older children and adults). On the face of it, this would seem to be obvious and self-explanatory. In fact, these theorists believe that children take a very active role by cuing "their parents to supply them with the appropriate language they need" (Wilson & Mihalicek, 2011, p. 320). This is a truly interactive theory. On the one hand, children need the social environment to improve their linguistic and social skills, and on the other, the language-rich environment exists in large part because it is prompted by children. Social interactionists have observed that the speech older speakers use with children is specifically created to be more learnable. They may have a point. Consider the following pair of utterances:

> a. *See the choo-choo? Look at how big it is! It's going really fast, isn't it?*
>
> b. *There is in our immediate vicinity a locomotive, which, despite its impressive size, is traveling at great speed.*

Few, if any, adults would use sentence (b) when speaking with an infant. Most people instinctively adjust their speech to what they perceive to be an appropriate level for a young child to understand. This adaptation is called **child-directed speech (CDS)**. CDS has distinct characteristics:

- Different rhythm and pitch. The speech typically has a sing-song quality, and the speaker's pitch is usually higher.
- Simplified vocabulary. Rarely would we use *choo-choo*, *doggie*, or *potty* with adult speakers.
- Shorter sentences. The difference between utterances (a) and (b) illustrate this distinction well.
- Simplified structure. Shorter sentences usually have simpler structure than long ones. Again, the difference between (a) and (b) demonstrates this principle.
- Particularly helpful responses. Adults are more tolerant of and likely to respond to infantile utterances that are barely comprehensible, if at all. For example, when Sarah referred to herself as Ah-Ah, simplifying the sound structure, adults did not say, "Who?" or "Whom are you talking about?" Nor did they try to explain to her that she really should be using "I" to refer to herself and not the third person. Instead, they acknowledged the meaning of her utterance and even began to refer to her in the same way.

Apparently, adults use CDS for two reasons, neither of which is that they are consciously attempting to teach their children language. One is to maximize the likelihood of meaningful communication, and the other is to express affection, which might explain why people tend to use similar speech when talking to their pets (Apel & Masterson, 2009).

There are three problems with social interaction theory: The first is that nobody is certain about how long children need to be exposed to CDS. The second is that they do eventually understand and use complicated sentences such as the one in the previous example; and the third is that CDS may be a cultural phenomenon—we do not know whether it is universal, although there is evidence from German, Mandarin, Russian,

All kinds of social interaction help children to learn language. This coach adapts her language to help her young players understand.

and Swedish (The Talaris Institute, 2005, cited in Williamson, 2011). On the other hand, Shirley Brice Heath has provided evidence that there are cultures in which adults make no special adaptations to the language they use with children. In such cultures, children who want to participate in the conversation have to interrupt and do so to the best of their ability (Heath, 1983, 1986). We also know that some parents consciously attempt *not* to use CDS, yet there is no evidence that their children's language learning is impaired or that they advance faster than other children.

On Choosing a Theory

Faced with so many theories, students often ask, "Which one is right?" The answer is none of the above. Theories are not facts but hypotheses crafted to fit the facts as they are known. There are aspects of each one of the theories that fit the facts. Although there is no compelling evidence that child-directed speech is necessary for language acquisition, nobody would argue that *some* degree of social interaction is necessary for learning to occur, and therefore some aspects of that theory are consistent with both connectionist and active construction of a grammar theories. Moreover, since it is likely that a child can construct rules only when the necessary neural connections are made, those two theories may not be mutually exclusive. In fact, in many ways they are fully compatible. While behaviorism is largely discounted these days for its inability to account for the facts of language acquisition as we know them, even imitation— that cornerstone of behaviorism—plays a role in children's earliest utterances, providing babies with a "starting place" on which to build their language. The active construction of a grammar theory may best fit the data. But social interaction is also important, and there is no doubt that neurological factors also play a role.

When this toddler says, "I hided from you," connectionist theorists would maintain that he is forming the past tense on the basis of other past tenses he has heard.

Digital Vision/Thinkstock

3.4 Mistakes in Language: Errors or Developmental Forms?

Except for the behaviorists, who would consider children's imperfect forms as errors, the consensus is that the mismatch between children's forms and adult forms are not mistakes but developmental forms, or the imperfect renderings of children in the process of learning language. The social interactionist and active construction of a grammar theorists would see errors as evidence of rules-in-progress, or under construction, while the connectionists would see them as evidence that the mental representation is incomplete. Whatever the cause, children's developmental forms are interesting, particularly when we consider the progression. Let's look at the data for a child, Marcos, from age 15 months to 48 months (Table 3.1).

Table 3.1: Marcos's development of the production and use of *pancake*

Age	Utterance
15 months	Cancake?
18 months	Want cancake
24 months	I want cancake
36 months	Can we have pancakes, Nana?
48 months	Can we have lion and bear pancakes, Nana?

From the time of his earliest utterances, Marcos was focused on meaning and made that meaning clear. Between the ages of 15 and 48 months, he made tremendous strides toward adult forms of language. Notice how, at 15 months, he let the noun bear the syntactic burden alone, relying on context to clarify any potential ambiguity. Just three months later, he added a verb to produce the sentence structure, VO. By the time he was 2, Marcos had produced an SVO sentence (*I want cancake*), and when he was 3, he was able to produce a fully formed question. Also, by age 3, he had mastered the pronunciation of *pancakes*, and by age 4, his phonology was mostly complete. He also made tremendous strides in syntax (Table 3.1).

At every stage of learning, the inconsistencies between the forms produced by children in the process of language acquisition and the target adult forms tell us that children are active participants in their learning. While they may start by mimicking the language sounds they hear, they figure out very quickly that there is purpose and form to language. We know this is true because their mismatches or "errors" are not random but systematic. At the time when Marcos was producing cancake for *pancake,* for example, he also produced forms such as kickin for *chicken* and gucky for *ducky.* This was compelling evidence that he was operating on an assimilation rule that simplified the pronunciation by harmonizing the consonants. It is undeniable that language, even for a child under the age of 2, is a rule-governed undertaking. *Learning the Sound System: A Work in Progress* shows that children simplify their language in predictable ways as they move toward the adult form.

Learning the Sound System: A Work in Progress

These data come from Juan at age 3.

Adult word	Juan's pronunciation
sit	(sit) [sɪt]
snack	(nack) [næk]
soup	(soop) [sup]
sun	(sun) [sʌn]
stop	(top) [tap]
spoon	(poon) [pun]

Concentrating only on the initial consonants, provide the rule that explains Juan's pronunciations. How do you think he would pronounce the following words?

snake

spin

scoot

sock

still

Over the course of a child's first 10 years, the phonological rules will move closer and closer to the adult norm through a process called **successive approximation**, which refers to how children move progressively closer to the adult forms in certain aspects of their language learning. There is little doubt, however, that the most impressive development occurs in the first five years. We can see just how impressive in the following conversation between 5-year-old Marcos and his grandmother:

Nana: So, Marcos, who is your teacher this year?

Marcos: I have two teachers. Miss X teaches us in the morning, but Miss Y comes and teaches us in the afternoon.

Nana: What does Miss Y teach you?

(Marcos shrugs.)

Nana: You don't know what she teaches you?

Marcos: I know, Nana, but I don't know what you call it in English. I can tell you in Spanish.

Nana: Ah, I see. Try to tell me in English, but if you need to use some Spanish words, that's okay.

Marcos: You understand Spanish?

Nana: Poco.

Marcos: (Laughing) No, more than that. Miss Y shows us pictures (He hesitates.). Oh, I know, maps! Like on Dora, and the maps have different shapes and words on them. Did you know the big blue spots are water?

Nana: Real water?

Marcos: No, Nana, that's silly. Not real water.

Nana: Right. I think I remember that, yes.

At age 5, Marcos has a solid grounding in all aspects of language. Yes, there is much left to learn—more vocabulary in both his languages, as well as the more subtle nuances of semantics and pragmatics that will make him a fully competent communicator. But, as we shall see in Chapter 6, when we take a closer look at each period of his learning, the foundation is firmly in place, and Marcos is not unique.

Conclusion

How children learn the intricacies of language remains, to some degree, a compelling puzzle although there are a number of theories that attempt to account for all the facts. What we know for certain is that children are born with the innate capacity to learn language and that the main requirement for doing so is exposure to language and opportunities to use it. We also know that although they are able to overcome physical and environmental challenges to learn language, there appears to be a critical period during which language learning is optimal, and that period ends around the onset of puberty. By the age of 5 or 6, the foundations of language are largely in place, but much learning of new vocabulary, sentence structure, and how to use language will occur over the next few years. We know that caregivers and teachers play an important role in this learning from birth throughout the school years.

Post-Test

1. By 3 months, most infants do NOT
   a. pay more attention to people than objects.
   b. imitate sounds made in their environment.
   c. attend more to speech sounds than other sounds.
   d. identify relevant sounds made in their native language.

2. In comparison to hearing children, nonhearing children
   a. take longer to learn forms of communication.
   b. learn forms of communication faster.
   c. have a larger vocabulary at the same age.
   d. have a smaller vocabulary at the same age.

3. The active construction of language theory explains language acquisition as a process of

    a. reinforcements and punishments for right and wrong language use.
    b. using language and learning the rules simultaneously.
    c. speaking the language prior to understanding the rules of language.
    d. learning the rules of language prior to using the language.

4. The assimilation rule claims that children

    a. simplify pronunciation by harmonizing consonants.
    b. distinguish among the morphemes in their language.
    c. accommodate new language in their schemas.
    d. learn the language that they hear.

Answers

1. **b.** Imitate sounds made in their environment. *The answer can be found in Section 3.1.*
2. **c.** Have a larger vocabulary at the same age. *The answer can be found in Section 3.2.*
3. **b.** Using language and learning the rules simultaneously. *The answer can be found in Section 3.3.*
4. **a.** Simplify pronunciation by harmonizing consonants. *The answer can be found in Section 3.4.*

Key Ideas

- Children are born with an innate capacity to acquire language.
- This capacity needs to be activated during the first five years of life in order for them to acquire normal language proficiency. This time is referred to as the critical period for language learning.
- All that is required for language acquisition is normal exposure to language through social interaction.
- Child-directed speech helps children to understand the purposes of language and to work out meaning.
- Children's ability to understand precedes their ability to produce language.
- Children have a larger receptive vocabulary than productive vocabulary.
- No perfect theory of language acquisition exists.
- Language acquisition theories that focus on the importance of social interaction and the child's cognitive abilities are most useful for language teachers.

Critical Thinking Questions

1. List three classroom age-appropriate activities for a child in prekindergarten (age 4) that would help to develop conversational skills.

2. Why would the receptive vocabulary of a 2-year-old child be difficult to measure?

3. How does reading aloud to infants foster language development? Be as specific as possible in identifying components of language learning that will benefit.

4. Why is it impossible to learn to communicate in sentences through memorization?

5. What is the "good news" about language learning in the following forms?
   a. *I seed him do it!* (36 months)
   b. *She didn't ate her food.* (48 months)
   c. *Cat bite me 'cause it hurt.* (40 months)

6. What is the theoretical perspective underlying the following quotation?

   "In nature's talent show we are simply a species of primate with our own act, a knack for communicating information about who did what to whom by modulating the sounds we make when we exhale."

7. The following sentences are from Janie, a few weeks before her third birthday. Look at the past tense inflection she used in each sentence:
   a. *I heared Daddy (pronouncing heard to rhyme with feared).*
   b. *Mommy bringed the cupcakes.*
   c. *Mommy didn't bringed the cupcakes.*
   d. *I singed that song at church.*

   Looking at sentences (a) through (d), what rule for past tense formation would you assume that Janie was using? Why do you think she would have formed this rule?

   At the same time, Janie spoke this sentence:

   e. *Mama sanged the wrong words.*

   Does *sanged* cause you to change your answers? If so, how?

   Now, read the following sentences from Janie.

   f. *Jessica hitted me!*
   g. *Sarah bit me!*
   h. *Molly bited me.*
   i. *Papa drived his car in the ditch.*

   Based on these sentences, what general statements can you make about what Janie has learned about forming the past tense?

8. If language is a product of instinct, what is the point to studying theories of how it is acquired?

Key Terms

active construction of a grammar theory
A theory that contends that children use the speech they hear around them to construct the rules of the language by listening for and discovering patterns, hypothesizing about the rules that create those patterns, and then testing those rules in their own usage.

child-directed speech (CDS) Language that adults use in talking with a young child, adapted to the child's level of comprehension and featuring simplified structure and changes in pitch and rate of speech.

creole A language with more of the properties of natural language that has its origins in a pidgin; sometimes referred to as "second-generation" pidgin.

critical period hypothesis With regard to the first language, the first 5 years or so of life during which the child's brain is most receptive to language learning.

developmental forms Imperfect forms (i.e., pronunciations, past-tenses, etc.) that young children produce during the process of learning a language.

feral children Children who have lived in relative isolation, apart from or only marginally exposed to human society.

homesigns A rudimentary sign language that nonhearing people develop themselves to communicate within their own communities.

innateness hypothesis The belief, first put forth by Noam Chomsky, that humans are predisposed to learn language.

pidgin A simplified language with elements taken from local languages, used for communication between people who do not share a common language.

successive approximation The process by which children move progressively closer to the adult forms in certain aspects of their language learning. For example, a child learning the past tense of sing might progress from singed to sanged to sang.

Weblinks

Visit this website to watch and listen to Steven Pinker speak.
http://www.ted.com/speakers/steven_pinker.html

This website offers a brief overview of many of the issues discussed in this chapter.
http://www.slideshare.net/zmiers/feral-children-presentation-presentation

This website includes more information about Isabelle and other feral children.
http://www.audiblox2000.com/book7.htm

This website provides additional information on Nicaraguan Sign Language (NSL).
http://www.youtube.com/watch?v=pjtioIFuNf8

This website links to a description of connectionist theory and how it differs from active construction of a grammar theory (Elman, 2001).
http://crl.ucsd.edu/courses/commdis/pdf/elman-chapter.pdf

This website has an easy-to-read description of the simplified talk that adults use with children (and pets!). See Graham Williamson's (2011) article "Child-Directed Speech."
http://www.speech-therapy-information-and-resources.com/child-directed-speech.html

4

Learning a Second Language

Learning Objectives

By the end of this chapter, you will be able to accomplish the following objectives:

- Define simultaneous bilingualism and explain how it resembles first language acquisition.

- Describe how children learn a new language in the preschool or kindergarten setting, and describe the different programs available to foster bilingualism.

- Identify the cognitive benefits of bilingualism.

- Articulate principles for creating a language-rich classroom environment that will benefit all children.

- Discuss the similarities between first and second language learning in young children, and describe the major theoretical issues in second language learning.

Introduction

A typical day for Roberto begins when he tumbles out of bed and pads barefoot to his grandmother's room. He climbs into her bed and begins to chatter about what he wants for breakfast—in *her* native language, Portuguese. She tells him to go get dressed, and he carries his jeans, a tee shirt, and mismatched sneakers in search of his father, whom he finds already in the kitchen. He tells his father that his grandmother is going to make breakfast after he's dressed, and this he communicates in his father's language, Spanish. Roberto's mother comes into the kitchen and asks him, in Portuguese, which of the two colors of sneakers he wants to wear because he is going to school today, and he shouldn't go with one black and one green shoe. When he gets to school, he will speak the language of the school, English. Roberto lives in Phoenix, and at age 4, he is fully trilingual. He is not alone among the children of Arizona, or of the United States, for that matter. But relative to the entire population of 4 year olds, he is rare—even though a significant proportion of the U.S. population speaks a language other than English, monolingualism is still the norm. That, however, is changing.

According to the 2010 U.S. Census, 20% of U.S. residents over the age of 5 speak a language other than English in the home. Current projections are that the number will grow to 40% during the next two decades; in some states, it already has. Most teachers will encounter children who speak a language other than English and who arrive in school with little or no English language ability. These children may require special attention since they have to accomplish two things at once: acquire all the skills and concepts appropriate to their age and grade level while simultaneously acquiring the English language. The good news for teachers is that second language learning in children bears a strong resemblance to first language learning. In other words, much of what we discussed in Chapter 3 will be applicable here as we learn more about young children who are learning more than one language.

Globally, bilingualism is the rule rather than the exception. Most European and Asian children learn two or more languages and do so at a young age. It is thus somewhat surprising that, in the early years of the 21st century and given the Census data mentioned earlier, bilingual schooling is still relatively rare in the United States. But since bilingualism is the global norm, the wealth of research available on second language learning, both at home and at school helps us to understand the similarities and the differences between first and subsequent language acquisition

In Chapter 3, we looked at the influence of environment on first language acquisition and discovered that while environment is important, children overcome major obstacles to acquire language. We also learned that there appears to be a biologically based critical period during which language learning is optimized. These are themes to which we will return in this chapter, focusing on the broadest of environmental differences in second language learning, the home and the school. We begin by attempting to define bilingualism.

Pre-Test

1. Bilingualism

    a. has a common definition.
    b. involves functionality in at least two languages.
    c. can be easy to clearly identify.
    d. applies to speaking at least two dialects.

2. Which of the following is not characteristic of two-way immersion programs?

    a. They promote a positive view of the minority language by the English speaker.
    b. They began in the 1990s.
    c. They enable children to learn from one another.
    d. The majority are Spanish-English programs.

3. Gray matter is NOT

    a. responsible for intellectual activity.
    b. most apparent on the right side of the brain.
    c. denser in bilingual children younger than age 5.
    d. made up of brain cells.

4. Teachers should

    a. focus on abstract and future situations.
    b. model and expand on correct language.
    c. correct language forms.
    d. explicitly teach language.

5. For most people, the easiest time to learn a second language tends to be

    a. before age 5.
    b. during middle and late childhood.
    c. during adolescence.
    d. after puberty.

Answers

1. **b.** Involves functionality in at least two languages. *The answer can be found in Section 4.1.*
2. **b.** They began in the 1990s. *The answer can be found in Section 4.2.*
3. **b.** Most apparent on the right side of the brain. *The answer can be found in Section 4.3.*
4. **b.** Model and expand on correct language. *The answer can be found in Section 4.4.*
5. **a.** Before age 5. *The answer can be found in Section 4.5.*

4.1 What Is a Bilingual?

First, let's look at definitions of some important terms. What is bilingualism? Bilingualism refers to the ability to speak two languages, and bilinguals are those who do so. This definition raises important questions. How much language ability is enough? If you know how to speak in French, but cannot read French, are you bilingual? In other words, would we consider any of the following to be bilingual?

a. someone who is able to read French but speaks only English;
b. a person who can read Italian and translate Italian text to English but cannot understand or produce oral Italian;
c. the child who comes to English-language preschool not speaking any English but is obviously able to understand most of what is spoken to him.
d. the child who grows up in a home where more than one language is spoken and who learns to communicate in both languages from birth.
e. the child born to a Mandarin-speaking mother and a Portuguese-speaking father, who also has an English-speaking caregiver from birth, and who is able to communicate with each of these people.

Except for the child in (d), who would be considered a bilingual under any definition, there are no clear answers in these hypothetical cases, given the definition provided. So let us consider a more useful definition. For our purposes, a good working definition of **bilingualism** is the ability to function in an age-appropriate manner in more than one language. Those people described in (a) and (b) are not, therefore, bilinguals, while the child in (c) is. Even though that child may not have yet demonstrated speaking ability, he is functioning in an English language environment in a manner appropriate to his age. The child in (e) is also a bilingual by virtue of being a trilingual—in other words, we use the term *bilingual* to refer to anyone able to function in more than one language.

These parents speak two languages with their baby. By the time he gets to preschool, he will be able to function in both English and Spanish.

Radius/SuperStock

Throughout the chapter, the terms *second language learning* and *second language acquisition* are used interchangeably. Some theorists make a distinction, labeling as *acquisition* the learning that happens in very young children who acquire a second language in the same way they acquire the first. These same theorists argue that language *learning* requires a conscious attempt to learn patterns or rules and is more typical of what older children and adults do in a formal setting (Krashen, 1981; Lightbown & Spada, 2006). For our purposes, it is more useful to talk about the environments in which children become bilingual. We will begin with children who acquire two languages at home.

Many children learn two or more languages at home. Consider Min, the child of a bilingual mother and a monolingual father. Min was exposed to both Mandarin and English from birth. Her first 20 words or so were pretty much evenly divided between Mandarin and English. A truly simultaneous bilingual, Min is essentially acquiring two first languages. If Min were growing up in China or Europe, her accomplishment would not be unusual or remarkable. In North America, although she is not unique, she is exceptional. Children such as Carlo present the more typical kind of simultaneous bilingualism. Carlo's parents both speak English, but his mother is the daughter of Italian immigrants and his father's family came from Argentina. For the first three years of his life, his Italian-speaking maternal grandmother cared for him three days a week while his mother worked. She spoke Italian to him almost exclusively since she was uncomfortable with her ability to speak English. His paternal grandmother, who spoke Italian and occasionally Spanish with him, cared for him two days a week. When he began preschool at age 4, Carlo's English was judged to be native-like in fluency, and his vocabulary appeared to be typical of any child his age. He was also comfortable in Italian, although after a few weeks in an English-language preschool, he started to favor English.

For more than a century, researchers have been interested in how children like Min and Carlo become bilingual. A very early study by French linguist Jules Ronjat detailed the language learning of his son, Louis. From birth, Louis was exposed to his father's native French and his mother's German. Although both parents were bilingual (i.e., each spoke the other's language), they each addressed Louis in their native tongue only. They were careful to keep the languages separated, so that the child would associate one language with one parent. According to Ronjat (1913), by the time Louis was 3 years and 5 months old, he was able to produce the phonemes of both languages correctly. He also learned the vocabulary and syntax of both languages without confusing the two languages. Other researchers in the century since Louis was a child have made similar observations: When the languages are kept separate, the child associates one language with one person and learns both equally well. The occasional mixing of vocabulary (e.g., using a French word in an English sentence) likely occurs because the child had no opportunity to learn it in the other language; it is not evidence of language confusion.

Children such as Min and Carlo require no special assistance in preschool. Because they have essentially acquired two first languages, they are not generally distinguishable from monolinguals. Some simultaneous bilinguals may not know some common vocabulary in English, having learned the equivalent words in their other language. But it is also true that some monolingual children will be unfamiliar with certain words used by teachers. Both groups will pick up the terminology quickly and without intervention, but teachers still need to know about simultaneous and successive bilingualism, because as we will see in Chapter 5, some researchers believe that bilingualism imparts certain cognitive advantages.

4.2 Learning a New Language at School

Not all bilinguals have had the same experience as Min or Carlo. Many early childhood educators encounter children whose language background is a mirror image to Carlo's (i.e., their parents speak a language other than English, and they encounter English in daycare or playing with neighborhood children). If they are very young and if they are functioning comfortably in English by the time they begin prekindergarten at age 4, these children may also be considered simultaneous bilinguals. Prekindergarten teachers do not need to do anything other than provide a language-rich environment in order for these children to continue to acquire English.

Because there are many paths that lead to bilingualism, children will arrive at school with different levels of competence in each language (Bialystok, 2001). The children who are of most concern to teachers of young children are those at one end of this spectrum: those who will be successively (or consecutively) bilingual (i.e., who have a firmly established first language when they come to school but little or no communicative ability in English). Although they may still be very young, these children face the task of adding a language outside the environment of the home.

Many parents see the benefits of bilingualism and enroll their children in dual-language education programs.

Associated Press

The Learners

For our purposes, *school* refers to preschool as well as kindergarten and later years—any organized setting, including government-sanctioned home schooling. Children who learn a language before the onset of puberty are generally referred to in terms of **early second language acquisition** as opposed to the more general **second language acquisition (SLA)**.

Early SLA is similar to simultaneous language acquisition, but there are differences. Having only one language to rely on, when children are thrust into an unfamiliar language environment, they quickly figure out that the first language won't serve their needs. Typically, this stage lasts for a very short time and is followed in many children by a silent period, when they say little but are actively processing the language around them. Although they will have little to say, they will be learning the new names for objects and activities and how to talk about them.

Simultaneous bilinguals do not normally have the same experience. Having no other language to rely on, they jump right in and start talking. But early second language learners often need time to absorb the language around them before starting to vocalize. Following the silent period, most of these children will acquire a few formulaic or "ready-made" phrases to use whenever they can. They may learn to say, "Yes, please," or "No, thank you," when asked if they want a snack or help with tying their shoes. They will sometimes use them incorrectly. For example, the child who answers the teacher's polite request, "Will you please sit down?" with "No, thank you," hasn't quite mastered the pragmatics of the utterance.

Finally, children will begin productive use of the language, and at this stage the developmental errors may start to appear. The child who says *shut the lights* analogous with "shut the door" is demonstrating a rather common developmental error. The new language won't be fully acquired at this point, but as time goes on and young learners gain more exposure to and experience in the new language, the developmental errors either disappear or change to resemble those made by native speakers of the same age. A 5-year-old second language learner who says, "I bringed it from home," is making the same assumption about how past tense is formed as a native English speaker of the same age.

An important distinction between simultaneous and early bilinguals is the role of environment. The language of the home, where the child has already acquired one language, is largely rooted in the here and now. There are plenty of contextual clues to meaning. Children learn to talk as a way to participate in the family, and they typically want to talk about what is important to them—they learn the words for food, the names of their parents and their favorite toys, or to signal hunger or discomfort. They learn these very early because those are the meanings they need to make. For preschool children, language functions to get things done, to satisfy needs, to talk about themselves, to discover and to learn, to engage in make-believe, and, to some degree, to communicate information to others.

As they learn to function with language at home, children usually have a resident tutor; there is someone, an adult and sometimes an older sibling, to provide feedback. Even when an adult cannot understand a child, the feedback, "I don't understand" or "Do you want this?" assists them to clarify meaning. A sibling, being closer in age and stage of development, provides a good model for talking about the things that children want to talk about. So what happens when they get to school? That depends largely on the kind of program the school offers.

School-Based Programs for Bilingual Learners

In general, the options available to assist children in becoming bilingual, some more successful than others, include immersion, two-way immersion, bilingual programs, sheltered English, submersion, and pull-out programs.

Many factors lead school districts to experiment with and change the types of bilingual programs they offer—the shifting demography of the country; the reduction in school budgets; the availability of bilingual teachers. Also, even though there are broad categories of programs described in the following sections, variations exist across the country in how these are actually implemented and for how long.

Immersion

For the past several decades, the Canadian government has sponsored a national program to educate children to speak both English and French. **Immersion programs** are those in which children are taught school subjects in an unfamiliar language for half the school day or more. What set immersion apart from other kinds of second language instruction was the exclusive use of French as the medium of instruction even though the children typically knew no French when they began. Teachers had to be bilingual because at first the children spoke only English. The teachers, however, always responded in French—unless there was a concern for safety—and had been specially trained to make their meaning clear using gestures, physical objects, and any environmental context available to them. Their French was greatly simplified and appropriate to the age of the children in their classes. For children who began immersion in kindergarten, English was usually introduced in third, or fourth grade in some programs, and the amount of English was gradually increased until English was used for approximately 60% of instruction in high school.

The Canadian government sponsored a national program to encourage all Canadians to be bilingual. All signage in Canada must be provided in both English and French.

Associated Press

As might be expected, Canadian researchers have studied immersion students extensively. The students who began in the first five years of the program have now completed University, and they have been found to acquire a higher level of competence in French than those who studied French in any other type of program. Student attitudes toward French-Canadians are generally more favorable than their nonimmersion peers. Despite these generally positive outcomes, the program has not been an unqualified success, because their French language proficiency has not been "native-like." That may be because their exposure to French has been almost entirely in a school setting.

Immersion programs in the United States are almost all intended for teaching a foreign language. According to the Center for Applied Linguistics, there are 239 such programs in the United States, more than 45% of which are offered in Spanish. Twenty-one other languages are also offered, with French, Mandarin, Hawaiian, and Japanese being the next four most popular (Center for Applied Linguistics [CAL], 2011).

Immersion is not a practical choice for ESL (English as a Second Language) settings because there are too many differences in the conditions. The main difference is that the dominant community in immersion is not the language of instruction, whereas in programs designed for ESL learners in the United States, the language of the school and the language of the community are the same. The following are other differences in the conditions of ESL teaching:

- Immersion is both elective and selective. Parents are allowed to choose whether to educate their children in French, and the choice not to do so has no particular educational consequences other than the fact that the children will remain monolingual.
- There is competition for places in immersion programs across Canada because it is expensive—teachers have to be specially trained and fluent in both languages.
- All children in an immersion class are new to the language of instruction.

Recognizing these differences, some U.S. educators have adopted the structured immersion approach. This approach features English-only instruction in the content areas for two to three years before children transition into mainstream classes. The structured immersion program requires teachers to be bilingual or at least to have strong receptive skills in the children's native language. Obviously, this approach will work only when all the children are from the same language background or if the teacher happens to know many languages. There are important lessons to be taken from immersion programs. Research shows that kindergarten children in immersion classes tend to focus on adapting to and understanding the schooling process and treat language learning as a secondary process (Tardif & Weber, 1987). In other words, they tend to mimic the first language process in a significant way.

Two-Way Immersion

Two-way immersion programs integrate English-speaking children with language-minority children—usually Spanish—in an effort to promote academic achievement in both languages. Two-way immersion programs are also called two-way bilingual or developmental bilingual programs. Normally, students are integrated for 50–60% of the day at all grade levels, and there is a concerted effort to ensure that both content and literacy instruction are provided to both groups of students in both languages (Howard & Sugarman, 2001). In practice, there is a fair amount of variability in how these programs are structured. The ratio of minority to English-language speakers varies in programs across the country, as does the language used for initial literacy instruction.

Two-way immersion programs began in the early 1960s, and there were only a very limited number of these programs until the 1990s. They have become popular because they are viewed as an effective way of maintaining and supporting the minority language while simultaneously building competence in English. Two-way immersion programs allow children to learn from one another, thus addressing the problem encountered in immersion of students being proficient in "academic" rather than more informal language use. Like immersion, two-way immersion helps in creating more positive attitudes in English speakers toward speakers of the minority language.

What immersion and two-way immersion have in common is the protection of two languages, and to some extent, two cultures. In the case of immersion, the dominant language is spoken outside the school day, and in two-way immersion, both languages are spoken during the school day. Two-way immersion programs are still fairly rare and exist mainly in Spanish and English. There are also a few programs (six or fewer) for Mandarin, Korean, French, and Japanese-English bilinguals. According to the Center for Applied Linguistics, only 10 of these programs nationwide are offered from kindergarten through twelfth grade (CAL, 2011).

Considering that the 2010 United States Census recognizes more than 14,000 public school districts in the United States, the number of two-way immersion programs—fewer than 400—is very small. There are many reasons, including demographics, cost, and the availability of bilingual teachers. More common, but similar to two-way immersion, are bilingual or dual-language programs.

Bilingual or Dual-Language Programs

Like two-way immersion, **bilingual programs** are intended to maintain children's first language while adding English. The loss of the first language is a matter of great concern to many cultural groups and to parents. They have cause to worry; the introduction of English at school, together with the extreme dominance of English in the environment outside the school, does cause some children to lose proficiency in their home language. Loss of proficiency will be a particular problem if the parents do not make a special effort to maintain the first language in the home. Yet many do not because they believe that it is detrimental to the child not to have maximal exposure to English. Many school districts have instituted bilingual programs to help maintain the first language while simultaneously providing an easier transition into English in the school. These programs fall into two basic categories—maintenance programs and transitional programs.

Maintenance bilingual programs are intended to protect the native language while introducing English as the primary language of instruction. While they superficially resemble two-way immersion, maintenance programs are intended only for speakers of the minority language, while two-way immersion is intended for learners from both the majority and minority language. Maintenance bilingual programs are not widely available in the United States. Slightly more common and widely used in other countries is the transitional bilingual program, which is intended to provide a smooth transition into English. Usually, the child's home language is used during the early years of schooling and then the new language is gradually introduced—the exact opposite to practice in immersion.

This boy is studying in a bilingual Vietnamese/English class. This program will help him gain academic proficiency in Vietnamese while he also gains proficiency in English.

In the United States, there are two models of transitional programs: the early-exit and the late exit. In early-exit bilingual programs, the goal is to help children attain the language skills needed to function in an

English-only classroom and to do so fairly quickly. Normally, such programs "provide some initial instruction in the students' first language, primarily for the introduction of reading, but also for clarification" (Rennie, 1993). Instruction in the children's first language is rapidly phased out, usually by the end of second grade if not earlier. In late exit programs, on the other hand, the first language is a medium of instruction for a longer time, usually through the end of elementary school. Even when children have attained a high level of proficiency in English, the first language may be the language of instruction for as much as 40% of the time (Rennie, 1993). In this case, the program resembles two-way immersion, the difference being in the languages of the students participating. In immersion, students from both the minority and the majority, or target language, participate. In transitional bilingual programs, on the other hand, all the students are non-English speakers.

Sheltered English Programs

Also called content-based programs, **sheltered English programs** may have students from a single language background or, depending on the demography of the school, may group together students from different language backgrounds. The focus in sheltered English is on content, so the teaching methods resemble those used in immersion. Such programs do not require bilingual teachers but do require that teachers be trained in special methods using gestures, visual aids, and simplified language to make meaning clear so that children simultaneously learn language and content. There are no hard data on the number of sheltered programs in the United States, but they are far more common than two-way immersion or bilingual programs. They are also very common for older children and adult learners.

Submersion

Submersion is not a formal program but rather the "default" when educators do nothing but place second language learners in mainstream classes without providing any supplemental instruction. It is the sink-or-swim approach, and in some cases it may work. In others, it is disastrous, leading to frustration, dislike of school, and low academic achievement, although most children will eventually learn English. Sometimes, it is successful with very young children who are able to adapt some of their first language acquisition abilities to acquiring the new language. Or it may work in an environment where there are other bilingual children who can help out. It is a high-risk strategy, however, and not recommended. If a district does not have the sufficient resources, or if the number of non-English speakers is too low to warrant the district offering one of the other types of bilingual programs, then a pull-out program may be the best option.

Pull-Out Programs

The **pull-out program** is, as the name suggests, designed to keep second language learners in mainstream classrooms and then to withdraw them to specialized English language classes for part of the day. Ideally, students who are pulled out of their classes for ESL receive instruction that is supplemental to the content they are learning in the mainstream classroom. ESL teachers coordinate their instructional planning with classroom teachers to ensure that students receive the appropriate language support they need to function in the classroom. Most schools in urban centers will have one or more ESL teachers, but in smaller schools or communities with smaller immigrant populations, ESL teachers may

In some schools, children spend part of the day away from their regular class to work with the ESL teacher on learning English words for colors, numbers, and other concepts.

Comstock/Thinkstock

travel from school to school. Some schools have an **ESL resource center**, a drop-in center where second language learners can go for language materials or other supplemental assistance in English.

Knowing which program is right for which learner depends on many factors, some of them related to the characteristics of the student, as outlined in *Choosing the Right Program: Student Characteristics*, and some related to the resources of the school and district, as outlined in *Choosing the Right Program: School Resources*.

Choosing the Right Program: Student Characteristics

What is the best way to educate children whose first language is not English? Educators will have to consider the characteristics of the students.

What are the ages of the children?

It may be possible to integrate children from preschool through second grade into mainstream classes with only slight modifications to the instructional environment. Older children will require additional kinds of assistance, depending on other factors.

How strong is their previous academic preparation?

Some older children arrive with little or interrupted formal schooling, due to cultural or economic conditions in their home countries, while others arrive with a very high level of schooling. The former group will require special care. For example, if an 8-year-old arrives without having attended school and with no English, she cannot be placed in a kindergarten or first grade class, even though it might seem appropriate for her educational level. She will need individualized intervention.

Are the children true beginners, or have they had some prior exposure to English?

Children who have been exposed to some English will generally find it easier to pick up the language than those who are true beginners.

Do all the children speak the same language?

If the children all speak Mandarin, for example, a bilingual or a two-way immersion program might be best, if the school district's resources permit. If they come from different language backgrounds, the bilingual program would not be an option for all of them. Both groups, however, would benefit from a sheltered program.

Choosing the Right Program: School Resources

Which program is best for children with limited English ability? This will also depend on the school's financial and personnel resources. Resources vary greatly across the United States and depend to some extent on the size of a community's immigrant population.

Does the district have bilingual teachers?

Even in Miami with its significant Spanish-speaking population, there are not enough Spanish-English bilingual teachers to offer two-way immersion or bilingual programs.

Does the school district have experience with non-English speakers?

In the major urban centers, most schools have long dealt with the needs of bilingual learners. Others are in the learning process.

Do the teachers have an ESL certificate or endorsement?

Many states, including Florida, now require that certified elementary teachers have an ESL or bilingual endorsement, which usually involves specialized courses in ESL or bilingual education. In other states, such specialized professional development is available as an optional part of the initial teacher education preparation or as an add-on, usually a certificate.

Is the school able to dedicate classroom space for ESL programs?

If the school is suffering from declining enrollment, it may be possible to create a magnet program to draw students from other schools in the district for a transitional bilingual or sheltered program. On the other hand, if the school is overcrowded, school personnel will either have to find other programs in the area or create helpful environments within existing mainstream classes. Following the latter course will require that teachers have specialized training.

4.3 Bilingualism and Cognitive Development

One of the hurdles second language learners encounter when they begin school in a monolingual setting is the mistaken belief on the part of some educators that bilingualism is an impediment. Such an attitude is apparent in the story of *Ivan, the Trilingual*, about a child who is currently enrolled in a fifth-grade class for gifted children.

Ivan, the Trilingual

Ivan is a gifted student in the fifth grade. His teacher is convinced that Ivan does not belong in her class because he is "hampered by" his trilingualism. She believes that he needs to be moved to another program in another school.

Ivan is the son of Russian parents who moved the family to the United States when Ivan was 3. They have continued to speak Russian at home even though they live in Miami, where English and Spanish are the dominant languages. Ivan has also attended Hebrew school and is functioning in that language.

According to the teacher's assessment, the child does not have an adequate vocabulary in English because his family persists in speaking Russian at home. The teacher was certain of her "facts" when she stated that there is only a finite number of words a child can learn or know at any given age, and that if space is being taken up in the child's brain with Russian words, there won't be space for the number of words in English that a fifth-grade child should know.

Ivan may or may not be experiencing difficulty with English vocabulary. If he is, it is difficult to ascertain the reasons without having more information about the child and all the environments in which he functions. If there are problems, however, the reasons are almost certainly temporary and they have nothing to do with brain capacity. As we will see in the next chapter, the human brain has far more capacity for all kinds of learning than most people ever use.

Having two, three, or more languages does not mean that the brain has less space for any one of them. Psychologist Dr. Paul Reber makes an interesting comparison to the digital video recorder (DVR), basing his analogy on the number of neurons in the brain and the number of connections that each neuron is capable of making. For comparison, if your brain worked like a digital video recorder in a television, 2.5 petabytes would be enough to hold 3 million hours of TV shows. You would have to leave the TV running continuously for more than 300 years to use up all that storage (Reber, 2010). The brain can certainly cope with several languages at once.

More than a century of research supports the positive benefits of bilingualism. Developmental psychologists, for example, have found "convincing evidence that bilingualism can have positive effects on abilities that are related to academic success" (Lightbown & Spada, 2006, p. 26). In particular, bilingual children acquire what is called **metalinguistic awareness**, which refers to a person's ability to reflect on and ponder over language (i.e., to objectify it). A child who "knows" the word *ball* in the sense that she associates it with a spherical object used in play, has learned a word. But if she says that *ball* starts with the same sound as *bottle*, that *ball* has three sounds in it, or that *ball* rhymes with *doll*, she has demonstrated an awareness of language *as* language rather than just as a symbolic representation of a real world object. Simply put, bilingual children are more sensitive to language and aware of what it can accomplish, and this heightened sensitivity is an important skill for learning to read and write as well as acquiring additional languages.

There is also evidence that bilingual children possess a kind of cognitive flexibility that is rarer in monolingual children. Specifically, there is some evidence that they are generally better at **convergent thinking**, which refers to the ability to bring together different kinds of information to arrive at a solution to a problem. There is also evidence that bilingual children excel at **divergent thinking**, which refers to an individual's ability to come up with multiple solutions to problems. Both convergent and divergent thinking are associated with creativity. Divergent thinking yields a variety of options to a given problem, while convergent thinking leads the individual to analyze and choose the best or most workable one.

Another cognitive advantage to bilingualism that has special relevance to academic success involves **selective attention**, or the ability to focus on a particular aspect of a task and ignore others. Bilingual children are better than monolinguals at ignoring irrelevant or extraneous information (Bialystok, 2001).

> Selective attention is controlled by a mental process called "executive function." "Executive function" refers to the general ability to coordinate the many distinct activities that must be integrated in order to carry out any goal-oriented task. It is thought to develop between two and five years of age and to continue improving through adolescence and young adulthood, but then it declines with age. (Pearson, 2008, p. 26)

Actual physical evidence exists to help explain why bilingualism has cognitive benefits. Specifically, bilingualism changes the brain. Brain imaging has shown that bilinguals have more and denser gray matter than do monolinguals. Gray matter consists of brain cells that are associated with intellect, particularly language, memory, and attention. The denser gray matter is most visible in children who acquire two languages before the age of 5, and it is most apparent on the left side of the brain, the one associated with language, although the difference is also apparent in the right brain (Hitti, 2004; Pearson, 2008).

The cognitive advantages of bilingualism appear to manifest themselves in reading ability, which is, in turn, the best predictor of academic success. Researchers at the University of Miami demonstrated that bilingual children who learned to read in two languages scored better in second grade than their monolingual peers or bilingual peers who had learned to read only one language. In other words, children who learned to read in both Spanish and English performed better in English reading tests than either of the other two groups. Moreover, the apparent advantage was still evident in fifth grade (Pearson, 2008).

This boy is learning to read in one of his two languages. Bilingual children who learn to read in both languages tend to do better academically than bilinguals who read in only one language.

Beau Lark/Corbis

Returning for a moment to Ivan, his teacher can relax. She may be right, and Ivan's English vocabulary may be a little smaller than his English peers since he has also learned two other languages. It is not, however, because his brain has only limited capacity. Besides, he will catch up very quickly, as most children do, almost always by puberty (Mihalicek & Wilson, 2011). Still, it may be the case that Ivan is experiencing some difficulty with English, and it would be a mistake to assume that acquiring a second language in the school setting is effortless and does not require teachers to make accommodations.

4.4 Creating an Environment for Success

Pearson (2008) envisions the simultaneous bilingual child in terms of two trees growing side-by-side in a forest. Both trees are rooted in the same soil, they have independent roots and branches, but there can be some intermingling of roots and branches. Sarah, for example, has always used the French word *couche* for *diaper* even when speaking English to her father, probably because her Francophone mother was usually the diaper changer. She would use *gateau* and *cake* interchangeably, mixing her languages in *I want gateau*. She used *please* before *s'il vous plait* or *s'il tu plait* whether she was speaking to her mother or her father. Other than these exceptions, though, Sarah seemed to keep her languages separate.

To continue Pearson's analogy of the adjacent trees growing in the forest, it is important to note that in order for children's two languages to be considered *bilingual first language acquisition* (Pearson's term for simultaneous bilingualism), the two languages must be "planted" at the same time, at or near the time of birth (p. 81). She sees early second language acquisition as analogous to botanical grafting. The original tree is rooted in the soil, and then onto it another species of tree is grafted. Thus, the trunk and the roots are from the original tree, but the newly added second tree will share them, and the branches of the new tree will be intertwined with the original. According to Pearson, "The grafting image more neatly parallels the situation of second language learning in a school setting. The roots and trunk are clearly from the first language, and an outside agent—not the tree itself—initiates the learning" (2008, pp. 82–83). The challenge facing preschool and elementary teachers is creating an environment that allows the grafted tree to flourish.

When they begin school, all children are likely to encounter unfamiliar words and phrases. Whether they are monolingual children, simultaneous bilinguals, or just beginning their second language learning, they will also find that language functions differently in the school environment. At home, children's thinking and language are directed toward the present: toward the real, concrete world. At school, there is a movement toward more abstract, academic language. Teachers spend more time talking intangibles—ideas and things that happened in the past. School language is used more for interpreting—rather than just informing—and for expressing logical relations. This will present additional challenges to children who are new to English. That is why environment is so important and why teachers have to pay special attention to their needs.

When planning language activities for young children, teachers should remember how children learned their first language. There is much in the environment that can be replicated or modified to create a productive environment for learning the new language. Although we will examine particular strategies for teachers in Chapter 10, the following are some general guidelines that relate to what we have learned in this chapter about the environments in which bilinguals are created.

- *Don't correct form.* Children use language to create meaning, and that is their focus. Second language learners will make mistakes—they will use the wrong plural form or they will struggle with subject-verb agreement. These are developmentally normal. But remember that first language learners do the same thing, and they eventually get it right without intervention. Unless the mistake affects the meaning or the child's ability to communicate, leave it alone. Concentrating on the mistakes may cause the child to become frustrated and stop trying.
- *Model and expand.* If children hear the correct forms often enough, they will learn them. It isn't effective to correct a 5-year-old's, "I seed dogs," but it is effective to model and expand by saying, "Oh, you saw the dogs playing? They were having a lot of fun, weren't they?"
- *Focus on the here and now.* One of the reasons that immersion works so well is that teachers are well trained to use contextual clues including a great deal of object manipulation to make themselves understood. Objects, pictures, gestures, movement, and acting out verb meanings—all of these help to ground the language in the here and now and make learning easier for learners of all ages.

- *To the degree possible, make language learning invisible.* Again, to borrow from the lessons of immersion, the focus is on the content, not on the form of the language. Immersion teachers teach content using simplified language, and while it is inevitable that children are aware that they don't speak or have only limited knowledge of the language, their attention is not drawn to the forms they hear, but to trying to solve the puzzle of meaning.

Rather than correcting her students' mistakes, this teacher models and expands in order to create a successful learning environment in her Creole, Spanish, and French classroom.

Associated Press

- *Silence may be good, or not.* Don't assume that a child's silence means that she understands. She may, but it is always best to rephrase and try again to elicit the response. On the other hand, it is not uncommon for beginning learners to go through a silent period during which they are listening and processing. Eventually, they will speak.

These are very general guidelines, and they are based both on prior experience with second language learners and on what we know about first language learners. Most teachers of young children will have a variety of children in their classrooms—monolingual English speakers, bilingual children with different levels of competence in English, and some children who are true beginners in English. All of these learners have one thing in common: They have acquired a first language. Therefore, we conclude this chapter by examining the similarities and differences between first and second language learning

4.5 First and Second Language Learning Compared

With simultaneous bilinguals, both languages are acquired in the same way. There are, as we have seen, cognitive differences that exist in bilingual children *because of* bilingualism, but the processes they use in acquiring their two languages are the same—the same as each other and the same as those used by monolinguals. In successive bilinguals, however, there may be differences, and most of these are associated with the age of the learner. The age of the learner is highly relevant for the following reasons:

- The experience of learning a first language means that second language learners know more about what language is about and how it is structured. They are experienced in finding patterns in what they hear. Older children might experience some temporary interference from the first language, but generally, the experienced learner is more efficient than the inexperienced and cognitively less well-developed first language learner.
- Babies are born with more acute hearing than adults (Pearson, 2008, p. 103). Over time, their hearing acuity attenuates to adult levels. Superior hearing is part of the reason why younger children are better able to discriminate between individual language sounds and why they are superior mimics of the sound system. Second language learners will acquire the pronunciation of the new language faster and more accurately than children who begin after the onset of puberty.
- Babies go through a babbling stage during which they practice the sounds of their language without either the pressure or the ability to produce perfectly formed words. Older learners do not have this practice period, and their hearing will be less acute than infants. Nevertheless, their improved cognitive processing abilities will compensate.
- The "input" is different. For school-aged children, the first exposure to a new language may be at school. The language of the school differs in content and in purpose from the language of the home, and the older the learner, the greater the difference.
- The older the learner, the more experience he or she has in learning. Even after the first language is essentially established, children continue to learn, and all prior experience in learning is potentially beneficial. For educators, the issue is how best to take advantage of it.

At the heart of the issue of age is the critical period hypothesis (see Chapter 3). Is there a critical period for language learning, as some believe? Popular wisdom that holds that where language learning is concerned, younger is better, would appear to be true. But is it? For a first language, yes, it does appear that there is an "expire" date on the brain's ability to acquire language. But the preponderance of bilinguals in the world, many of whom learned the two languages sequentially, is a compelling argument against a critical period for second language learning.

The Critical Period and Second Language Learning

Toddlers appear to acquire their language—one, two, or more—with relative ease and seemingly without effort. Older learners, however, appear to struggle, and even when they become highly proficient, many do not acquire a perfect, native-like accent. Others stumble and falter and never manage to learn much of the second language at all. At first blush, it might seem that we can simply call upon the critical period hypothesis to explain why children under the age of 5 are so adept at learning another language, children before the age of puberty require more assistance but can become extremely proficient, and adults often struggle. But the fact that many adults do learn one or more new languages later in life suggests that the matter is far more complicated. Language teachers and researchers alike increasingly suspect "that whatever enables the child to acquire the mother tongue might not be lost forever, rather that it could be hidden somewhere among or underneath our other cognitive faculties" (Meisel, 2011, p. 1). If this is the case, then several questions arise:

- Why are some learners better able to access this capacity than others?
- What is the role of language instruction, and what kind of instruction will stimulate this capacity?
- What other "cognitive faculties" are involved in language learning?
- How is the language acquisition capacity influenced by these other cognitive faculties?

Because we cannot answer any of these questions with any certainty, formulating a coherent and adequate theory of second language acquisition is even more complicated than formulating one for first language. Although the environments may vary widely, with first language acquisition, we are talking about learners who are all the same age. The theoretical issue is to explain how and under what conditions the innate language capacity is activated. Second language learners, in contrast, are more diverse, impacted by the following:

- *Age*. We saw that some children effectively acquire two first languages, some are early simultaneous bilinguals, and some add a language much later. Many language learners are adults, so age and all the attendant life experience it brings with it is a major factor.
- *Reasons for learning*. Children acquire their first language or their second language, when it is the language of their community, with relative ease. But people have different reasons for learning another language, and these can impact not only the speed of their learning but what they ultimately learn.
- *Place*. Children surrounded by a new language in school pick it up easily. Learning a "foreign" language, however, in a classroom setting when the language of the

community is a different one—as it would be for an English speaker learning Finnish in Cleveland, for example—brings with it another set of issues, all of which will impact the learner's success.

- *Method of instruction.* As learners get older and have more experience of formal instruction, they respond differently to the ways they are taught. Some may be resistant to unfamiliar methods, and this, too, will affect their language learning.

When it comes to second language learning, young children *do* appear to have certain advantages. First, they have less to learn at a time when their brains are working hardest. Pearson (2008) notes that young children's brains "are working twice as hard as adults'. The level of glucose they use rises until age two and then stays twice as high as adults' until around age nine" (p. 102). The younger the child, the less there is to learn to reach age-appropriate proficiency. As an example, on average, a 4-year-old child has a productive vocabulary of around 800 words (Beauchat, Blamey, & Walpole, 2010, p. 18) and a much larger receptive vocabulary. While it has taken her four years to acquire those words, older students can learn that many words in a matter of weeks. But the goal of a 10-year-old language learner is not to sound like a 4-year-old. Second, the younger learner is less skilled in avoidance and less prone to worry about failure. Older learners, particularly adults, are very good at finding ways to avoid using an unfamiliar language, partly out of concern that they will get it wrong. Young children are less skilled at avoidance and are more likely to jump right in and use the new language, although there is often a silent period at the beginning of the process. Given the added advantage of the more-recent first language experience, younger learners would seem to have an advantage. It would be a mistake to conclude, however, that the ability to learn a new language is lost with age. Indeed, as we have seen, there are certain advantages to age, the chief one of which is that experienced learners are better at learning. What is important for educators is to create the educational environments that are most likely to lead to success.

So are there any theoretical underpinnings on which we can base our approach to teaching a second language to young children? The answer is a qualified yes. Remembering that theories are not facts but represent an attempt to account for all the facts that we have about language acquisition, let us look at the main contenders.

There are different challenges that come with teaching older language learners. These high school Spanish students will be more skilled at avoidance than younger learners.

Associated Press

Theoretical Perspectives on Bilingualism

Let us begin with a short history lesson. Before the 1960s, researchers assumed that first and second language acquisition were completely distinct processes. That assumption was not based on any empirical data, and researchers studying the two kinds of acquisition paid little attention to what those in the other camp were doing. It simply hadn't occurred to them that there might be some similarities. Until the 1960s, both linguistics and psychology were disciplines whose research agendas were largely grounded in behaviorist learning theory, as described in Chapter 3.

> Only after the constraints and restrictions of behaviourist psychology had been shaken off could the language sciences begin to understand language learning as a mental activity happening in the cognitive system of the individual. Chomsky's (1959) famous and influential review of Skinner's (1957) book "Verbal Behavior" is a milestone to the "cognitive turn." (Meisel, 2011, p. 3)

The term *cognitive turn* refers to the shift in thinking that occurred as researchers began to view language as a cognitive event and the study of language acquisition as involving the study of the mind rather than behavior per se. This change in focus had a tremendous and liberating impact on the study of first language acquisition and, eventually, on second language acquisition, which was slower to shake the influences of behaviorist thinking. Meisel observes that behaviorism lingered in SLA because for many years, research had been dominated by *foreign* language learning in classroom settings as opposed to second language learning in more natural settings. Most foreign language teachers were using techniques based in behaviorism, and so there was little counter-evidence on which to build a new theory,

From a behaviorist perspective, the task of SLA would be to replace one set of habits (i.e., the first language) with a new set of habits, the language to be learned. The first language was seen as relevant only because it interfered with the second. Instructional techniques, thus, were designed as drills to instill the new forms and eradicate any imperfect ones that might be created. Learners were given passages of text to memorize to perfection, and relatively little attention was paid to meaning. Generations of learners learned sentences for which they would never have any use. Generations of learners completed majors in foreign languages without gaining fluency or conversational competence.

Following Chomsky's review of Skinner's *Verbal Behavior* (see Chapter 3), researchers began to place more emphasis on cognition, and eventually SLA researchers began to look at their data from the perspective that the human mind might well use the same processes that had been effective in learning the first language in learning the second. Once they began to view language data from that perspective, the central question that they asked was different, and a new set of issues emerged, making the matter of theory construction a great deal more difficult. The central question that has guided SLA research for the past four decades has been what kinds of knowledge the second language learner brings to the task and whether and to what degree he has access to that same innate capacity (called a language acquisition device, or LAD, by Chomsky) as the young child. Instead of focusing exclusively on differences between first and second language learning, researchers, starting in the 1970s, began to look at similarities. One of the most influential series of studies showed that the order in which second language learners acquired English grammatical morphemes closely resembled the order in which first language children acquired them (See *Morpheme Acquisition Order in Second Language Learners*.).

Morpheme Acquisition Order in Second Language Learners

As early as 1967, Pit Corder suggested that the errors that second language learners make bear a striking resemblance to those made by children learning their first language. Over the next several years, researchers began to formulate hypotheses based on this notion.

In the early 1970s, researchers began to work from the hypothesis that the first and second language acquisition processes were essentially the same. These researchers went on to propose the creative construction hypothesis, that learners do not merely imitate what they have heard but actively construct their own rules, based on internal knowledge. They postulated that if children were learning a second language in the way that behaviorists claimed, then most of the errors they made could be predicted on the basis of their first language (i.e., interference errors). On the other hand, if they were using innate mechanisms, their errors would more closely resemble those made by first language learners.

The researchers studied the errors in the speech of 145 Spanish-speaking children between 5 and 8 years of age, using a measure designed to elicit particular grammatical morphemes such as past tense, plural, present progressive, and so forth. They found that only 3% of the children's errors could be predicted based on Spanish, 12% were unique to the child, and an overwhelming 85% were developmental, meaning that they were the same ones English-speaking children make.

A year later, they replicated the study with 250 Chinese- and Spanish-speaking children of the same age, and this time they were able to establish an acquisition order for each of the two language groups and for the combined group. They concluded that the order of acquisition was virtually identical for the Chinese- and the Spanish-speaking children. Following is the order they found:

1. pronoun case
2. articles
3. present progressive
4. copula
5. plural -s
6. auxiliary
7. past regular
8. past irregular
9. long plural (e.g., -es as in *breezes* rather than -s as in *cats*)
10. possessive
11. third person regular

Nine of these were the same ones studied by Brown and by DeVilliers and DeVilliers (See *Learning Grammatical Morphemes* in Chapter 3). While the order was not exactly the same for the first language speakers and the second language speakers, what is compelling about these data is that second language learners seem to follow the same order, and that order is independent of their first language. These results and others using similar methods led Steven Krashen (1977, 1981) to formulate a natural order hypothesis, stating that second language learners acquire certain language structures in a predictable order.

When the underlying assumptions changed and both researchers and teachers began to view the second language learning process as not unlike the first, the task of theorists changed as well. Now, their job was to discover the nature and characteristics of the human language capacity and how they are activated, reactivated, and constrained throughout life. In all likelihood, theorists will be working on these issues for many decades, assisted by research on brain and cognitive function as well as learning theorists. Because our primary interest here is learners in early childhood, we are able to view second language acquisition from the same theoretical perspectives addressed in Chapter 3. More specifically, theories of second language acquisition that focus on the cognitive dimension as well as the sociocultural context in which all language is learned offer the best hope for accounting for what learners of all ages accomplish (Atkinson, 2011).

Teachers must be aware that they are not only instructing but also creating an environment conducive for language learning.

Associated Press

A Note for Teachers

If teachers had to wait for theorists to explain how language learning—or any learning—happens, then little would be accomplished in the classroom. Theory develops over time, and it gets added to as research methodology improves and, as we have seen, as the underlying assumptions change. But teachers needn't wait for the "final word," on theory and not just because it will never happen; theory is not fact, after all. As Ellis has observed, "Teaching involves curriculum planning, designing lessons and then implementing and evaluating them. This is shaped less by teachers' technical knowledge than by their practical knowledge of what is likely to work in their specific contexts" (2012, Chapter 11, para. 17). Teachers of young children have observed that the following methods are effective:

- creating a language-rich environment that includes language used for many purposes;
- using age-appropriate language;
- using simplified language, gestures, and many concrete objects;
- not teaching language per se, but providing many opportunities for language learning and use; and
- being attentive to any specific needs that may arise because of unfamiliarity to the language.

For most early childhood educators, these principles are just common-sense guidelines that they use with monolingual as well as bilingual children. Fortunately, they are also consistent with what theory is currently telling us (Meisel, 2011; Atkinson, 2011; Ellis, 2012).

Conclusion

While there are many advantages to bilingualism and few if any disadvantages, it would be a mistake to interpret the material presented in this chapter to mean that bilingual children are always smarter or more creative than monolingual children. Bilingual children in American schools often struggle, not because of their bilingualism per se, but because not all schools and teachers are prepared to deal with their needs. Learning a new language and, for some children, a new culture, can be hard, even for young children. A central purpose of this chapter has been to make the point that educators must look beyond what may appear to be a deficit in language to the benefits that having two languages will confer and to understand that creating positive language environments will greatly assist all learners.

Post-Test

1. Which of the following would be considered bilingual?

   a. An adult who speaks only Spanish but can read both English and Spanish.
   b. A child who can communicate with her French-speaking father and her ASL-speaking mother.
   c. An adult who grew up in a French and German-speaking household who speaks only English but can understand all three languages.
   d. An English-speaking adult who is enrolled in beginner Arabic classes.

2. The two types of transitional bilingual programs are

   a. early-exit and late-exit.
   b. aggressive and passive.
   c. partial and total.
   d. independent and dependent.

3. Which of the following is not discussed as a possible benefit of bilingualism?

   a. Improved convergent and divergent thought.
   b. The ability to focus on extraneous information.
   c. Greater selective attention ability.
   d. The ability to objectify language.

4. Pearson's (2008) use of bilingual first language acquisition is the same as

   a. simultaneous bilingualism.
   b. serial bilingualism.
   c. sequential bilingualism.
   d. severe bilingualism.

5. Babies' early-language babbling

   a. hinders their ability to learn two languages.
   b. is similar to what we do in babbling later in life.
   c. allows them to practice the sounds of their language.
   d. includes pressure to perfect their phonemes.

Answers

1. **b.** A child who can communicate with her French-speaking father and her ASL-speaking mother. *The answer can be found in Section 4.1.*
2. **a.** Early-exit and late-exit. *The answer can be found in Section 4.2.*
3. **b.** The ability to focus on extraneous information. *The answer can be found in Section 4.3.*
4. **a.** Simultaneous bilingualism. *The answer can be found in Section 4.4.*
5. **c.** Allows them to practice the sounds of their language. *The answer can be found in Section 4.5.*

Key Ideas

- Children who acquire two languages simultaneously are essentially acquiring two first languages.
- There is strong evidence that the innate language acquisition device continues to function until the onset of puberty, but it is most effective before the age of 5.
- There are more similarities than differences between first and second language learning in children under the age of 5.
- Children can learn a new language at any age.
- Bilinguals have been shown to have greater cognitive flexibility, and there is evidence that their brains differ from monolinguals'.
- All children learn language in a language-rich environment.
- Building a theory of second language acquisition is complicated by the many variables associated with the learner—age, prior experience, other languages, reasons for learning, etc.

Critical Thinking Questions

1. Read the following dialogue between Claudette and her first-grade teacher. Which of the tree analogies appears to fit her best? (Does she appear to have acquired two first languages, or is she an early second language learner?)

   Teacher: [Seeing Claudette in tears] What's the matter, Claudette?

   Claudette: Ça fait mal. Fall off swing.

   Teacher: Where does it hurt?

   Claudette: [Pointing to her knee] Ici.

   Teacher: Your knee hurts?

   Claudette: Oui, my knee me fait mal.

   Teacher: Okay, let's get you to the nurse. Do you want me to help you?

   Claudette: No, thank you.

2. People who are divergent thinkers draw ideas from various sources to come up with multiple creative solutions to a problem. Often, the solutions are very different from each other. Divergent thinking is not, however, a monolithic cognitive process. Rather, it has four dimensions:

    • Fluency refers to the number of different ideas one can produce.
    • Flexibility refers to the variety of ideas one produces.
    • Originality refers to how unusual are the ideas one produces.
• Elaboration refers to richness of detail in the ideas one produces (Prieto et al., 2006).

Although research generally supports the notion that bilinguals outperform monolinguals in tests of divergent thinking (Ricciardelli, 1992), it also seems to be the case that much depends upon how proficient one is in the second language, the degree to which one is also bicultural, as well as the age at which the second language was attained.

Consider the following task:

Figure 4.1

Look at this picture in Figure 4.1. Now, write down all the things this might be a picture of.

What kinds of responses would provide evidence for fluency? Flexibility? Originality? Elaboration?

3. Two children, both age 7, are given a list of object names and asked to come up with as many uses for each object as possible within a limited period of time. Consider the following responses:

Child A

    Cup   drinking milk, holding flowers, putting pencils in, Daddy's coffee

    Hat   keep head warm, keep head dry, wear to church

    Horse   ride, pet, run race, pull wagon

    Fork   eat food, move food, punch holes in stuff, dig in ground

    Headband   wearing on head, wearing like a necklace, keep a package closed, decorate a Christmas tree

Child B

    Cup   drink milk, eat soup

    Hat   wear outside, look pretty

    Horse   ride, pet

    Fork   eat, stick holes

    Headband   wear on head, hold hair back

Which do you think is the bilingual child and why?

4. What would you say to a parent who worried that speaking Russian at home with her child might impede his progress in English in kindergarten?

5. Locate and interview a bilingual speaker in your class or in your community and engage in a conversation for five to ten minutes. Try to find out the following:

a. At what age did the person begin to learn English?
b. How does the speaker rate his or her own proficiency in English?
c. Do you hear any "foreign" accent?
d. Do you detect differences in word choice or sentence structure?
e. How do you rate his or her general comprehension?

6. At the end of Chapter 2, you were asked the following question:
English has 25 distinctive consonant sounds and 19 distinctive vowel sounds. Most dialects of Spanish have only 16 consonant sounds and 5 vowels. Does this mean that Spanish-speaking children learn their sound system faster than English-speaking children? Defend your answer.

Having read Chapters 3 and 4, has your answer changed? How?

7. Sarah, the child of a French-speaking mother and an English-speaking father, has been exposed to both languages since birth. She speaks only French with her mother and only English with her father. They live in an English-speaking community. The following are examples of her language at age 3:

I don't like dress green.

I can't see. I'll get my tabouret (stool).

I big girl. No couche (diaper).

What evidence of language mixing do you see? (Keep in mind that in French, the adjective often follows the noun.) What do these examples tell you about simultaneous language acquisition?

Key Terms

bilingualism The ability to function in an age-appropriate manner in more than one language.

bilingual programs Language programs designed to maintain children's first language while adding a second language, usually English in the United States. There are two types: maintenance programs are intended to preserve children's first language in the school setting, and transitional programs are intended to assist them in coping with English as a medium of instruction.

convergent thinking The ability to bring together different kinds of information to arrive at a solution to a problem.

divergent thinking Ability to come up with multiple solutions to problems.

ESL resource center A drop-in center in a school where second language learners can go for language materials or other supplemental assistance in English.

early second language acquisition Used to describe children who acquire a second language before the onset of puberty.

immersion A carefully planned instructional approach for children to learn a language that is not the dominant one of the community. Children are taught school subjects in an unfamiliar language for half the school day or more. (Compare to *submersion*.)

metalinguistic awareness Refers to a person's ability to reflect on and ponder over language (i.e., to objectify it).

pull-out program Language program in which second language learners attend mainstream classes but are withdrawn for specialized English language classes for part of the day.

second language acquisition (SLA) The more general term referring to all second language acquisition, but particularly that which occurs after the onset of puberty.

selective attention The ability to focus on a particular aspect of a task and ignore others.

sheltered English programs Language programs that may have students from a single language background or may group together students from different language backgrounds and focus on content, with teaching methods resembling those used in immersion.

submersion A "sink or swim" approach, essentially doing nothing. Submersion is not a formal program but rather the default when educators do nothing but place second-language learners in mainstream classes without providing any supplemental instruction. (Compare to *immersion*.)

two-way immersion Language programs that integrate English-speaking children with language-minority children in an effort to promote academic achievement in both languages.

Weblinks

For a directory of language immersion programs in U.S. schools, visit:
http://www.cal.org/resources/Immersion/

This site offers a directory of two-way bilingual immersion programs in the United States:
http://www.cal.org/twi/directory

5

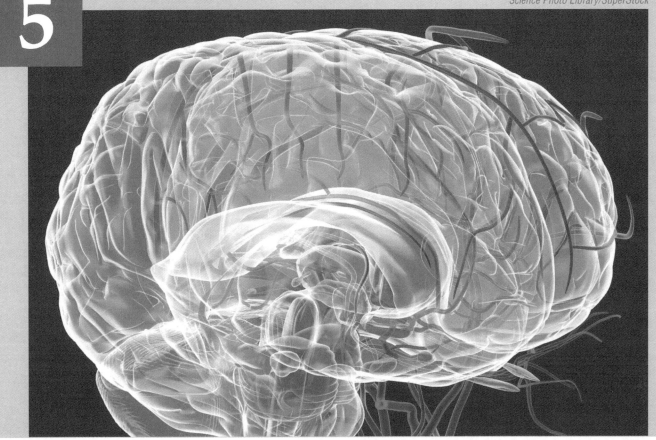

Language and Cognitive Growth

Learning Objectives

By the end of this chapter, you will be able to accomplish the following objectives:

- Describe the basic stages of brain development, and explain how it affects language development.

- Describe the role of language in the formation of concepts and categories.

- Explain the role of language in memory growth.

- Explain how language development affects learning, and identify characteristics of children's early learning.

Introduction

By the time Katya's mother, Martine, knew that she was pregnant, Katya's brain was already starting to develop. When Katya was born, her brain weighed approximately 2 pounds, or a quarter of her birth weight. While her brain had all the capacity to develop into an organ of near-infinite learning, her environment would greatly influence the course of that development. Martine and Katya's father, Jeffrey, were not focused on brain development per se, but everything they did for their newborn served to build the neural pathways essential to brain growth. Healthy food, sleep in a quiet environment, and a home filled with music, games, and brightly colored objects—all served to stimulate the brain growth necessary for cognitive development. This chapter describes how the infant brain develops, beginning before birth, and its role in cognitive and linguistic development in infants and toddlers. After examining the interrelationship between language and cognitive development, we go on to identify six characteristics of children's preschool learning that serve as guidelines for planning curriculum for early childhood education.

Cognitive development refers to the way in which thought processes develop in the brain. Long before they begin to speak or even appear to understand language, children have begun to develop cognitively. Cognitive growth and linguistic growth are tandem processes—some would even say "codependent" or "interdependent" processes. As children gain experience of the world around them, they begin to develop a larger memory capacity and to organize their world into categories that will eventually become concepts. Words and concepts are closely related. When a child learns the word *dog*, the name of an object, she has a tool for learning what things are included or excluded from the category *dog*. If she uses *dog* to refer to a cat, someone will correct her, and she will have one more piece of information for building her concept. So it is with all word learning. From the time children begin to acquire language, their ability to conceptualize is enhanced, as is their memory capacity. Words, and language in general, provide convenient tags that allow young children to store and retrieve information. Being able to conceptualize and to store and recall those concepts are essential to learning.

Before we can talk sensibly about cognition, though, it is necessary to consider the development of the organ that makes it possible—the brain.

Pre-Test

1. The plasticity of the young brain

   a. makes it less susceptible to environmental influences.
   b. requires that young children have particular genetic markers.
   c. occurs within a critical period of development.
   d. is a controversial theory.

2. A concept differs from a category in that a concept

   a. is a group of entities.
   b. is a single entity.
   c. is a cognitive organizer.
   d. combines related elements.

3. Which of the following is NOT a reason for developmental improvement in memory?

   a. gains in memory capacity
   b. better focus on which material to remember
   c. improvement in use of strategies
   d. increases in amount of material to remember

4. Which of the following is a characteristic of early learning?

   a. Learning precedes in a predictable way.
   b. Genetics heavily influence learning.
   c. Learning is rooted in socialization.
   d. Adults are responsible for children's learning.

Answers

1. **c.** Occurs within a critical period of development. *The answer can be found in Section 5.1.*
2. **b.** Is a single entity. *The answer can be found in Section 5.2.*
3. **d.** Increases in amount of material to remember. *The answer can be found in Section 5.3.*
4. **c.** Learning is rooted in socialization. *The answer can be found in Section 5.4.*

5.1 Brain Development

At birth, the infant brain is about 25% of its eventual adult weight. It has already grown *in utero* from a tiny plate, which by the fourth week after conception has closed into a neural tube to form the brain and the spinal cord. First to form are the brain stem structures that will control reflexes and basic motor coordination—the eventual ability to crawl and to stand, for example (See *Sequence of Brain Development*). At this point, the brain is forming brain cells, or **neurons**, at the rate of 250,000 per minute. At 5 weeks gestation, the two lobes have formed, and the brain continues to form neurons. By the time a child is born, most of the neurons are already in place. Brain development, however, also requires the creation of neural connectors, or **synapses**, and most of these are formed after birth. At birth, there are approximately 2,500 synapses per neuron, but by the age of 2 or 3, it is around 15,000 per neuron, more than the brain will ever use. Therefore, another aspect of brain development is the pruning of unneeded synapses and cells. *Pruning* refers to the discarding of unused cells and continues to some degree throughout life.

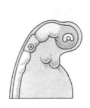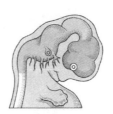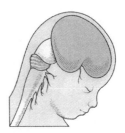

This illustration shows the three major stages of brain development in a fetus.

Dorling Kindersley RF/Thinkstock

Sequence of Brain Development

The human brain develops from bottom to top—from brainstem (1), which develops in utero, to the midbrain at the top of the brain stem (2), followed by the limbic brain, which is the inner central portion of the brain (3). Finally, the outer layer of the brain, the cortex (4), develops. These areas are identified in Figure 5.1.

The least complex functions—breathing, most reflexes, and most sensory capabilities—are the responsibility of the brain stem. The cortex is responsible for the higher cognitive functions. Much of human brain development occurs after birth over the course of many years. This longer period of development means that the cortex has many years to grow, hence its greater volume. The cortex can also be influenced by more environmental factors.

Figure 5.1: The structure and functions of the human brain

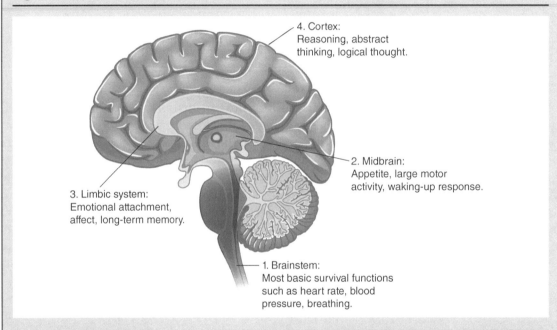

4. Cortex:
Reasoning, abstract
thinking, logical thought.

2. Midbrain:
Appetite, large motor
activity, waking-up response.

3. Limbic system:
Emotional attachment,
affect, long-term memory.

1. Brainstem:
Most basic survival functions
such as heart rate, blood
pressure, breathing.

This figure shows all of the major areas of the brain and their functions. Which ones do you think contribute to language development?

The Critical Period

Although brain development continues through adulthood, the major difference between brain development in a child and an adult is a matter of degree. The child's brain is far more impressionable, or "plastic," in early life than in adulthood. This **plasticity** means that young children's brains are far more susceptible to enriching influences and to learning than are adults', but it also means that they are more vulnerable to the influences of unfavorable circumstances—poor nutrition, lack of sleep, or lack of mental stimulation and emotional security. This time when the brain is most impressionable, before the plasticity ends, is often referred to as the **critical period** for brain development. In fact, it would be more accurate to refer to critical periods or windows of opportunity since different areas and functions of the brain appear to develop at different times. For example, there is a critical period for the development of normal vision. From the time they are born, infants need normal visual input in order to develop acuity, or the perception of fine detail, and binocular vision, or the coordinated use of both eyes, which is necessary to develop depth perception. If a child is born with a strabismus, more commonly known as "lazy" eye, or with crossed eyes and the condition is not corrected early, the ability to develop depth perception is threatened.

There is little doubt that environment is extremely important during the first year of life. A British team studying Romanian children adopted into English families before the age of 4 concluded that they showed significant intellectual gains after adoption, although those who showed the most improvement were adopted before the age of 6 months (Rutter et al., 1998). Not all researchers have reported such encouraging results, but all have shown improvement once children were adopted out of the impoverished environment.

A long-term study done at the University of North Carolina adds further evidence that the infant brain is extremely susceptible to environmental influences. Researchers demonstrated that early intervention with children deemed at-risk, as defined by the mothers' low income and education levels, could have a measurable impact on the IQ of these children. The five-year intervention began in the first few months after birth. The experimental group received a program of full-day year-round childcare, nutrition counseling, and parent involvement activities. The control group received only formula and diapers. After 3 years, the impact of the researchers measured the IQ of both groups. The results were startling: The average IQ score of children who had received the additional stimulation through greater parent involvement was 105 while the average IQ of the children who had received only formula and diapers was 85. What is more significant is that the higher IQ held over time—at age 21 the experimental group still displayed a significant intellectual advantage over the control group (Ramey, Campbell, & Blair, 1998). Long-term effects are less obvious when the intervention starts at age 4, but it may also be that the long-term effects are difficult to assess because such precise data are unavailable for government-supported programs such as Head Start. What data are available do suggest some benefit, however, and since we know

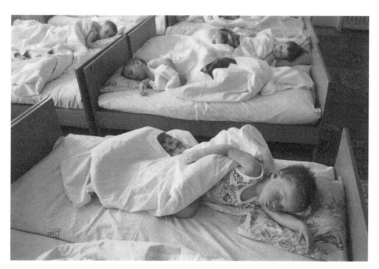

Children who have spent time in orphanages may experience slower cognitive development, although good care can help to overcome early deficits.

Gideon Mendel/Corbis

that the young brain remains highly receptive until age 5 or so, we cannot dismiss the importance of environmental enrichment and stimulation up to that age and beyond.

We learned in Chapter 3 that the critical period for language development likely extends to puberty, although some capacities are diminished after the age of 5. Because language and cognitive development are so closely related, as we find out later in the chapter, some impairment is likely to result if a child is not exposed to language before the age of 5. Children are born with the capacity to acquire language—the human brain is prewired, so to speak. At 3 months old, a baby can distinguish several hundred different sounds, far more than are required to learn any one native language. At this point, the brain is capable of acquiring any human language at all. But over the next several months, the infant's brain adapts to the sounds of the language, or languages, spoken around him and ignores and loses those that are not. Young children's brains retain the plasticity needed to relearn any of those earlier sounds, but that ability begins to atrophy at around age 5, and after the onset of puberty, the ability to acquire the sounds of another language is greatly reduced. Hence people who learn a new language before puberty are more likely to sound like native speakers than those who learn it later.

There is also strong evidence that the development of social skills and emotional well-being depend on positive, nurturing attachments being formed during the first year of life, and that emotional security is necessary for intellectual development as well. Child psychologists know very well that there is a straightforward relationship between emotional well-being and brain development. Babies cry when they need something, whether food, sleep, a dry diaper, or another blanket. During the first months of life, babies are busily assessing the effectiveness of their crying. If someone responds to the cries and provides what is needed, babies will be more likely to develop a sense of security and safety with that person. When they no longer have to concern themselves with

safety, their brains can focus on the objects and activities that surround them. On the other hand, if their cries do not bring what they need, then that sense of safety does not develop, and their focus is on ensuring that their basic needs are met (Hawley, 2000; Lieberman & Zeanah, 1995).

Over the past two decades, research literature and the popular media have reported much anecdotal data from children reared in Romanian government-run orphanages. A Canadian study of Romanian adoptees showed that these children experienced severe attachment problems (Chisolm, 1995). Experience of adoptive parents

Positive interactions with adults that include casual conversation and a variety of experiences help young children to develop both cognitively and linguistically.

116

and experts who have studied these children supports what to most of us is common sense: Infants need nurturing to grow emotionally strong and able to learn.

What happens in the first three years is especially critical to which neural connections get strengthened and which are discarded. The first three years are thus critical to the brain's development and to children's ability to learn.

Growing a Healthy Brain

Many educators of young children ask, what can we do to help children to develop into well-adjusted, successful learners? Most early childhood educators do not encounter their young pupils until they are well past the 6-month stage. That 6-month stage is critical to developing strong emotional attachments and security.

But there is still much brain development that occurs after this point, and so there is much that we can do. The popular media have reported many stories in recent years about the extraordinary measures that some parents have put into place for stimulating brain growth—playing opera or classical music for the growing fetus, teaching sign language to infants under a year old, purchasing video and audio stimulation kits intended to provide brain stimulation activities that will lead to advanced brain development. Despite the popularity of these interventions, there is no scientific evidence that such measures are any more effective than a normal environment that includes interaction with other people, affection, adequate nutrition and sleep, as well as audio and visual stimulation that comes as a part of regular daily activities. Providing well-fed babies with a variety of things to look at, different voices, and different songs during the waking hours will get most children off to a good start.

Let's take a closer look at the environment and activities that foster brain development in the first five years and that ensure children are ready for learning in school. Preschool children need the following things for optimal brain development:

- *Adequate nutrition and sleep.* Especially in the first year when the brain is actively creating neural connections, or synapses, children require adequate amounts of protein, fats, and vitamins in their diets. They also need adequate sleep. Both good nutrition and sleep help to create these synapses.
- *Loving interactions with caring adults.* Young children need a sense of security so that they can turn their focus away from acquiring what they need to the task of learning. When basic needs are met, then interactions with caring adults "strongly stimulate a child's brain, causing synapses to grow and existing connections to get stronger. Connections that are used become permanent. If a child receives little stimulation early on, the synapses will not develop, and the brain will make fewer connections" (Graham, 2001, revised by Forstadt, 2011).
- *Exposure to casual conversations, rhymes, songs, reading, and stories.* Many of the synapses being formed are those that will soon make language possible. Young children need to hear language and experience language in a variety of contexts so that they will make the neural connections needed for using language appropriately in those contexts.

- *Visual stimulation.* Young children need a variety of visual stimuli, not only to aid in the development of vision but in order to stimulate brain growth in general. Colorful objects of different sizes and shapes are especially important because they catch the baby's attention, and caregivers need to pay attention to how well the baby's eyes are focusing and tracking moving objects.
- *A variety of experiences.* If neural connections are not used or are rarely used, they will atrophy. We learned in Chapter 3 how language learning was impaired when a child was not exposed to language during the first years of life. It is therefore very important to encourage children to explore and to play in safe environments.
- *Routines.* Children need a variety of experiences, but they also need routines and repeated experiences in order to preserve the neural connections they form in the first year. Routines keep the neural pathways open for all future learning.

The absence of any of these factors can lead to stress, which, if prolonged, can have a damaging effect on brain development (see *The Effect of Stress on Brain Development*). The majority of brain development that occurs after birth is in the cortex, the outer layer of the brain responsible for most cognitive functioning and language. In the sections that follow, we will look briefly at the areas of the brain involved in language. Then, we consider how cognition and language are intertwined, particularly in the development of memory and conceptual development.

The Effect of Stress on Brain Development

Traumatic life experiences such as neglect, abuse, or poverty can be toxic to a child's brain development, especially if there is no caring, supportive adult to provide balance. A caring adult who supports the child's experiences and finds ways of decreasing the stresses can make the stress tolerable and reduce the impact on brain development. For example, a child can tolerate the stressors such as the death of a loved one or a serious illness when there is a caring adult to help him adapt.

Not all stress has a negative effect; in fact, some smaller amounts of stress such as the kinds that occur when a playmate breaks a playdate or a favorite toy goes missing cause no long-term damage. In these cases, the system returns to a calm state fairly quickly. But more serious stress, such as physical or emotional stress or trauma, causes the hormone cortisol to be released.

> High levels of cortisol can cause brain cells to die and reduces the connections between the cells in certain areas of the brain, harming the vital brain circuits. The connections in the brain can be severely damaged or miswired if a child is exposed to repeated and longtime stress without the assistance of a caring adult. Babies with strong, positive emotional bonds to their caregivers show consistently lower levels of cortisol in their brains. (Graham & Forstadt, 2000, 2011)

Graham, J., & Forstadt, L. A. (2000, 2011). Children and brain development: What we know about how children learn. University of Maine: Cooperative Extension Publications #4356. Retrieved from http://umaine.edu/publications/4356e/

The Brain and Language

Researchers are a long way from understanding how language is organized in the cortex. For many years, scientists believed that language was a function of the left hemisphere (in right-handed people, but reversed in left-handers). That belief is now seen as simplistic if not erroneous. In fact, there is evidence that the right hemisphere does play a role in language processing and that it even takes over the functioning of the left hemisphere in patients who have damage to the left hemisphere before the age of 5.

To some degree, it is possible to identify areas of the brain that are primarily associated with language. We know, for example, that in roughly 98% of right-handed people, the language processing center is located in the left hemisphere, but the ability to understand the emotional intent of language is located in the right (Stennes, Burch, Sen, & Bauer, 2005; Segalowitz, 1983; Mihalicek & Wilson, 2011). We also know that specific areas of the brain accomplish particular tasks in language. Wernicke's area, or that region in the upper back part of the temporal lobe, is the area responsible for comprehension while Broca's area, located in the lower back part of the frontal lobe is responsible for oral fluency (more about this in Chapter 7). Surgeons, however, operating on patients with brain tumors cannot work on such general descriptions. When they are removing brain tumors, they must do so with no or minimal damage to the patient's language functioning. To achieve the goal, they require a precise "map" of the brain, showing where language functions reside in each patient.

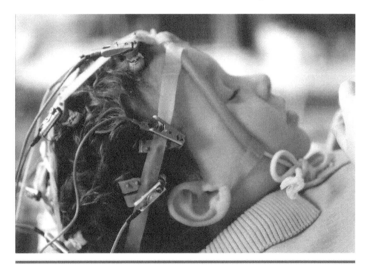

Scientists are using an electroencephalograph to gather data needed to construct a map of this child's brain.

Phanie/SuperStock

In recent years, surgeons have mapped the language areas of the brain through "negative" mapping, or by finding out which areas of the brain had no language functioning. In this way, they established that language functions are less centralized in the brain than was once believed. There are many areas of the brain involved in language, and the good news about what surgeons and therapists have learned is that if one language area of the brain is damaged or removed, another undamaged area can often learn the "job" of the other area. As educators, our principal concern is not with brain development per se but with the product of that development: the child's growing mind, especially language and cognition. Let's turn to the role language plays in memory development and in early conceptualization.

5.2 Language and Conceptual Development

If the mind were to treat each object and experience as unique and store it as such, it would be a very cluttered place. What really happens as children see, touch, and hear the objects and events in their lives is that they try to make sense of it all, and the way they do that is to discover links between similar experiences and to group them together. That is the way a **concept**, a general idea that is produced by combining several separate elements or attributes into a single entity, is formed. In order to form concepts, children have to be able to identify the similarities between experiences, and that is the task of categorization. A **category** is a grouping of similar attributes—things that fly, words that begin with b, fruits with rinds, and so forth. Concepts rely on categories being formed, but they are not exactly the same. Take the concept of flying: To understand what the concept entails, it is necessary to know some of the things that fly as well as some of the things that do not, but the concept is more abstract than the category. The ability to find commonalities and establish categories is foundational to conceptualization, so both categories and concepts are the essential building blocks of cognitive development. We are able to make sense of the world because we possess an extensive and varied system of categories.

How Children Form Categories and Concepts

As adults, when we encounter a new object or event, we can usually turn to a companion and ask, "What's that?" Two-year-olds do that, too. It is the quickest way to learn, but it is not quite that simple. What do they do with the answer? If, for example, a 2-year-old sees a cruise ship docked in the harbor and asks, "What's that?" a helpful adult says, "That is a ship." The child likely repeats "ship," but where does she store it? Initially, it is a unique occurrence, a category with a membership of one. Later, she sees the ship sailing into open water. She might ask for confirmation, "Ship?" When the adult says yes, the child has two important pieces of information: Ships move and they travel on water. She has also stored some of the visual characteristics of ships.

But what about the infant who does not have the words to ask or to use as "tags" or "labels" for things? How does she gather the information she needs to begin to organize her world into categories and concepts? There is evidence that very young infants group things together and form mental representations of categories well before they have words to help them do so, and that they group things together based on the perceptual features of the object. Perceptual categories are based on the visual attributes of objects, such as shape and color. As they grow older, infants refine their groupings, using less obvious features of objects to determine their category membership. These features will be more abstract and may include the function of the object, and the categories could be "things that move on wheels," "things to play with," or "things with four legs that do not move." This more abstract categorization is necessary for forming concepts. Conceptual categories can also include information that comes from other people, such as the names for objects or descriptions of what they do. This is where we begin to see the interaction between learning words and learning concepts. (See *How do Infants Categorize?*)

How Do Infants Categorize?

Researchers have developed techniques for determining that infants as young as 3 to 4 months are able to categorize (Arterberry & Bornstein, 2001; Bomba & Siqueland, 1983; Fantz, 1963). These techniques commonly involve three stages:

Stage 1: Infant is shown a set of stimuli on a computer monitor, one after the other:

Figure 5.2: First set of stimuli

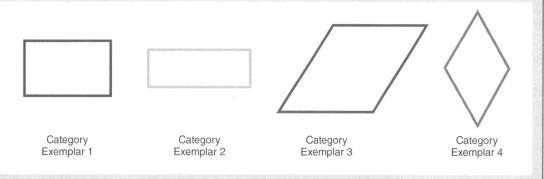

Category Exemplar 1   Category Exemplar 2   Category Exemplar 3   Category Exemplar 4

Stage 2: Infant is shown two additional stimuli:

Figure 5.3: Second set of stimuli

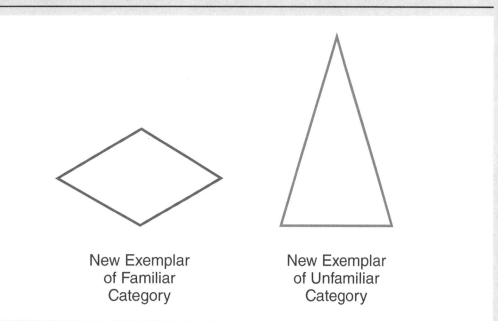

New Exemplar of Familiar Category   New Exemplar of Unfamiliar Category

Stage 3: Researcher measures length of time infant stares at each of the new exemplars.

Which exemplar would you expect the infant to stare at longest? What does this tell you about how the infant is categorizing the shapes? (Remember that infants are generally more interested in things they haven't seen before, and in this case, they haven't seen either shape before.)

How Do Infants Categorize? *(continued)*

Experiments such as these confirm that infants are processing two kinds of information: (1) They treat the four-sided figure as a member of the same category they have previously seen even though they have never seen that particular figure before. They have, thus, internalized a category and recognized a member of it, even though they haven't seen it before; and (2) they recognize that the triangle does not belong to this category.

Word Learning Versus Concept Formation

When we examine the relationship between word learning and concept formation, it is the same as exploring the relationship between categorization and early language development. Young infants create a rich store of categories before they are able to speak (Quinn & Oates, 2004). When a child begins to use the word *bottle* or *wheel*, she must have a mental representation of a bottle, for example, in order to use it appropriately—the child has "matched" the real-world object with some mental representation that has been given the label, *bottle* or *wheel*. If this is the case, there should be a correspondence between spurts of vocabulary growth (see Figure 5.4) and high levels of ability to categorize. Experiments have borne out this relationship (Quinn & Oates, 2004, pp. 54–55). In other words, children need to form categories in order to begin to learn words, but once that learning begins, they can use the information gained in the process of learning words to form increasingly additional accurate category representations. Does the **vocabulary spurt** cause the improvement in conceptualization? Or does the greater ability to form more abstract conceptual categories fuel the growth spurt? Scientists do not know the answer to these questions, but it is clear that the two processes are somehow symbiotic and interactive.

Figure 5.4: Growth in vocabulary comprehension in boys and girls

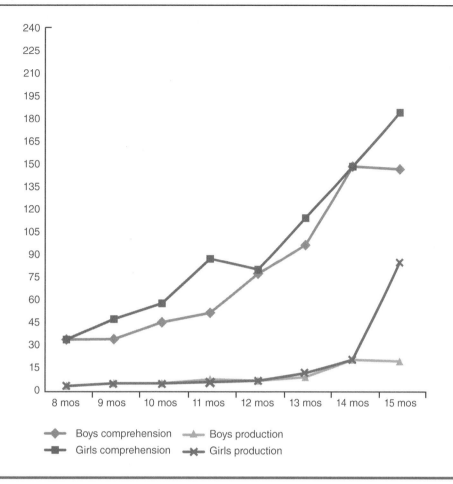

What factors contribute to the increase in girls' ability to acquire language quicker than boys?

Source: Adapted from data from Burman et al. (2008); Galsworthy et al. (2000); Goldfield et al. (1990); Heinrichs et al. (2010).

The data in Figure 5.4 raise important questions about gender differences in language acquisition. The graph does not show that the apparent advantage that girls have appears to extend to about the age of 7. While there may be social factors at play—adults tend to treat male and female children differently—what is also likely is that the differences in male and female brains mean that boys and girls process language differently. Some of these differences include the following:

- Language processing is more abstract in girls and more sensory in boys.
- Areas of the left brain associated with language work harder in girls during language use than they do in boys.
- In reading or being read to, the visual and auditory areas of the brain are more active in boys than in girls.
- Boys show more aggressive development in the right hemisphere development, which governs large motor activities and spatial reasoning, while girls show

Children's first words are grounded in their immediate experience. This boy has learned the names and colors for the toys he plays with, and he understands even more than he produces.

Gulf Images/SuperStock

more aggressive development in the left, which directs most language and fine motor skills. (Burman, Bitan, & Booth, 2008)

The differences in how male and female brains process language account for some developmental differences but generally do not affect the sequence of language learning. In word learning, for example, boys and girls will proceed through the same stages, although possibly at a different rate.

When parents talk about their children's word learning, they usually refer to the number or the kinds of words they use. There is a great deal of variation in the particular words infants learn first, and there are also individual differences in the rate at which words are learned. What is less variable, however, is the progression, or stages, involved in word learning. These stages may vary in length, but the order is consistent across cultures—comprehension always precedes production, for example.

Comprehension

The first stage in word learning is comprehension. Comprehension precedes word production (speech) because a baby has to draw on a greater number of abilities—controlling the musculature of the lower jaw as well as the tongue and vocal tract—to create an intelligible representation of a word. It isn't just that the infant hasn't learned to use the vocal apparatus to make words though. The infant vocal tract is not a miniature of the adult's. Until the age of 3 months or so, the larynx is positioned higher and the tongue is proportionally larger in the infant's mouth than the adult's, which is why an infant is much better at comprehending words in the first year than speaking them.

The earliest stages of word learning, therefore, involve comprehension. The first task is to figure out what constitutes a word. As we learned in Chapters 2 and 3, there is not actually any silence between words in normal speech, so an infant has to figure out where the boundaries are. Babies are especially sensitive to the prosodic qualities of speech—the rhythm and the rise and fall in speech, and can distinguish between two languages on this basis alone (Harris, 2004). It is likely, then, that they rely on stress patterns and other prosodic features of speech (Johnson & Jusczyk, 2001). They may also rely on certain properties of individual sounds. In Chapter 2, for example, we learned that the sounds /p, t, and k/ are aspirated, meaning that there is a small puff of air that accompanies them when they occur at the beginning of a word. This is a subtle clue, but it is the kind of thing that infants use to determine where the word boundary is. A third cue comes from the context and the frequency they hear adults use the word. For example, children hear adults using the word *dog* in sentences such as

There's the dog.

Where's the dog?

That dog needs a bath!

After hearing *dog* in these different contexts, children eventually conclude that *dog* is a word, and they also have a good idea what it means, particularly if the parents have provided an additional clue by pointing. Word comprehension begins around 7 months and progresses slowly at first.

Word Production

The second stage is early word production. In most infants, the first sounds are *ma, ba, da,* and sometimes *ga*, which usually appear in their first words at between 10 and 13 months. Some children do not produce words with reliable meanings until closer to age 2 years, and as long as their hearing is normal and they exhibit ability to comprehend, this is not usually indicative of a problem. While children will always understand more words than they produce, in most children there is a predictable relationship between the two. Notice in Figure 5.4 that except for a time around 11 months when there is rapid growth in comprehension, for girls, the lines showing growth in comprehension and production are almost parallel.

Many of children's early words are **context-specific**; that is, when they first appear, they refer only to a particular person, object, or action. Some children, for example, use the word *blankie* or *bankie* to refer only to a particular blanket or quilt used at naptime. In general, more than half of the words that children use before the vocabulary spurt (Figure 5.4) are object names. Not all early words are context-specific, however. Researchers have found that among children's earliest words are many that are **contextually flexible**, meaning that children used them in more than one situation (Bates, Bretherton, & Snyder, 1988, cited in Harris, 2004). Two very common contextually flexible words that children use at a very young age are *more* and *no*. In their first 50 words, children demonstrate a great deal of variety not only in the rate at which they add new words to their vocabularies but also in the content of these words.

Many children adopt a **referential strategy**, meaning that their early words refer mostly to objects; others adopt an expressive style, meaning that they use more action words and people's names. Girls are slightly more likely to adopt the referential strategy, and boys are slightly more likely to adopt an **expressive strategy**. These early words are largely dependent on children's experiences, in the sense that children have heard them many times before using them. As they get older, they are able to add words that they have heard less often. They are able to do so because their ability to categorize has improved and their memory capacity has also improved.

5.3 Language and Memory

We know that as children grow, they become better at remembering. How does this happen and what role does language play? Sometimes, it plays very little—we navigate the rooms in our house and reach for things in our kitchen cupboards without using words, either mentally or out loud. But for much of the cognitive activity in which we engage, we routinely use language to facilitate recall. Imagine a grocery shopping list without words. Conversely, it is impossible to engage in a conversation without being able to remember what has been said. Language provides us with both a means of encoding experience and with a means of recalling that experience. An experiment conducted many decades ago demonstrated clearly how important language is:

> A simple experiment reported by Carmichael, Hogan, and Walter (1932) demonstrated how inextricably linked they can be. In reproducing line drawings they had been asked to remember, subjects in the study routinely distorted them in a way consistent with additional verbal information they had received. (Piper, 2007, p. 242)

What this means is that the language the subjects heard altered their recall of the object shapes they had seen.

Simply put, as children grow, their memories improve. There are several possible explanations for how this happens:

1. Their basic capacity increases; in other words, the physical and physiological mechanisms needed for memory expand—the connections that form between brain cells grow and become stronger.

2. Their memory strategies improve. Through practice, they simply get better at storage and retrieval of information.

3. They learn more about how memory works, and they use this information to manage their own memory.

4. As they grow older, they know more about the content they need to remember, so they have a better basis for remembering new material (Piper, 2007).

In all likelihood, memory growth involves all four explanations, and language is involved in each.

Language and Basic Memory Capacity

The basic capacities of memory include recognition, association, storage, and retrieval, and these are governed in large part by the neural connections, or synapses, which you will learn more about in Chapter 6. What is important here is how language is involved in the development of each.

126

Recognition is at the heart of memory and all cognition. This phenomenon is very well developed at birth. Newborns are remarkably good at visual and auditory recognition. They are able to recognize their mother's voice, and by one month are capable of recognizing differences between speech sounds such as /p/ and /b/, suggesting that there is some innate mechanism at work (remember our discussions in Chapter 3). Around 6 months, infants can distinguish between phonetic sounds in their own language or other languages they happen to hear. Researchers discovered, however,

> by 10 to 12 months, . . . monolingual babies were no longer detecting sounds in the second language, only in the language they usually heard. . . . The researchers suggested that this represents a process of 'neural commitment' in which the infant brain wires itself to understand one language and its sounds." (Klass, 2011)

Bilingual babies followed a different course of brain development. Unlike the monolingual infants, at between 6 and 9 months, they were unable to detect phonetic sounds in either of the languages to which they were exposed. At 10 to 12 months, however, "they were able to discriminate sounds in both" (Klass, 2011). Research, summarized in Table 5.1, offers evidence that the fact that bilingual babies are exposed to more linguistic diversity means that their perception of linguistic sounds does not narrow as early as that of monolingual children. It offers powerful support for the notion that experience helps to shape the brain.

Table 5.1: Monolingual and bilingual brain development

Age	Skill or ability	Monolingual infants	Bilingual infants
In utero	Distinguish rhythms of speech from other rhythms	Yes	Yes
At birth	Show preference for the language(s) they have heard before.	Yes	Yes
	Able to distinguish between their two languages		Yes
4 months	Distinguish different languages visually (i.e., by watching a silent video of speakers switching languages)	Yes	Yes
6 months (up to 9 months)	Distinguish between phonetic sounds in any language they hear	Yes	No
8 months	Distinguish different languages visually (i.e., by watching a silent video of speakers switching languages)	No	Yes
10–12 months	Distinguish between phonetic sounds in either language they hear	No	Yes

Sources: Byers-Heinlein, Burns, & Werker (2010); Weikum et al. (2007); Garcia-Sierra et al. (2011); Bialystok (2001).

Association, or the ability to link certain stimuli with certain responses, is also present at birth, to some degree. For example, if a rattle is placed in an infant's hand, he quickly learns that moving that hand causes the rattle to make noise. As they get older and acquire language, children are able to make an entirely new set of associations, and with these verbal associations, their memory and learning capacity increase.

In terms of storage and retrieval, the role of language is even clearer. The phenomenon of *infant amnesia,* or the inability of adults to recall what happened in the first few months of their lives is likely related to the lack of language at that age. The length of time that has passed cannot account for this inability because we are able to recall events that happened many years earlier, often in great detail. What is more likely is that we remember best those events that are also encoded with language. We see this as adults—we verbally "rehearse" the directions to a location even though we may have driven there many times. It is entirely possible that our failure to remember what happened when we were 4 or 5 months old is because we are trying to recall with words things that were never stored as words. This mismatch between the way an event was stored and the way we try to retrieve it points us to the importance of language in building memory capacity: As children grow older, they have language as part of their experience and thus available as a means for encoding that experience while infants do not.

This grandmother is telling her granddaughter family stories associated with the quilt. When the granddaughter retells the story, she will rely on her memory of the stories rather than the events themselves.

Radius/SuperStock

Language and Memory Strategies

Memory strategies include those conscious activities we employ in the hope of improving our chances of remembering. Occurring at some time between the event we want to remember and the attempt to recall it, memory strategies include rehearsal, organization, and elaboration. In the previous section, we saw how rehearsal works. Organization is another key memory strategy. Read the following list of words and then cover up the list so that you can't see it. How many words from this list can you remember?

dog

computer

robin

desk

radish

watermelon

printer

telephone

steak

cat

bookshelf

horse

pencil

mustard

Now, look at the reorganized list:

dog

cat

robin

horse

computer

desk

printer

telephone

bookshelf

pencil

radish

watermelon

steak

mustard

Does it make it easier to remember the 14 items once you see them as a list of four living creatures, six items of office equipment, and four edibles? The ability to categorize is greatly simplified by having language and is a highly effective memory strategy.

Finally, elaboration is another strategy assisted by language. Elaboration also involves making connections between items or events, but it can occur even when there is no categorization involved. Using *mnemonics* is a commonly used elaboration strategy for remembering. For example, phrases such as, "Rhythm helps your two hips move," may help you recall the spelling of *rhythm*. Clearly, the existence of language makes this kind of elaboration possible and thus creates another memory strategy.

Memory and Bilingualism

If language is critical to the development of memory strategies, what is the impact of having two languages? Kormi-Nouri and associates (2003) studied the effect of bilingualism on memory in children between the ages of 7.9 and 13.3. They examined their recall for specific events (episodic memory) as well as their memory for general information and facts (semantic memory). Comparing 60 monolingual and 60 bilingual children, the researchers found that the bilinguals did better. Another positive benefit of bilingualism where memory is concerned occurs later in life. Researchers have recently discovered that the onset of Alzheimer's and other forms of dementia occurs, on average, four years later in bilinguals than in monolinguals, if the bilingual continues to speak (as opposed to read and write) two languages later in life (Craik, Bialystok, & Freedman, 2010; Bialystok, Craik, & Freedman, 2007). While children do not have to be concerned about dementia, the fact that bilingualism appears to confer some protection against memory loss argues for the relevance of language acquisition to brain development.

Language and Metamemory

Metamemory refers to the knowledge or awareness that we have *about* how memory works that assists us in improving our ability to remember. Suppose that you are in a lecture and at the same time texting your friend about plans for after class. For the most part, you are successful at both tasks, but then suddenly you realize that what the lecturer is saying does not make sense to you, that you have missed something crucial. What you will likely do is to stop texting and listen more attentively, trying to find clues to what you have missed. It is the decision to employ this strategy (stop texting, listen, find clues to what you missed) that constitutes metamemory. As children grow older, they gradually learn that there are limitations on their ability to remember. This awareness leads them to develop a sense of what is hard to remember and to begin to monitor their own ability and create strategies for remembering.

People make shopping lists because they know the limitation of memory. This awareness of how memory works (or doesn't) constitutes metamemory.

age fotostock/SuperStock

The relationship between metamemory and language is through self-monitoring. From the time they are 2 years old, children are able to correct many of their own language errors. The fact that they can do so means that they are able to compare their utterances with some mental representation of what they know about language. They monitor pronunciation, word choice, and to some extent grammar. They are also able to monitor what they hear. Consider the following exchange:

Quy: Dat fuhfly.

Mother: Yes, that's a fuhfly.

Quy: No! Dat fuhfly.

Mother: Oh, a butterfly?

Quy: Yes.

Quy has rejected his mother's infantile pronunciation because it does not match what he knows the word should sound like, even though he is unable to pronounce it correctly himself. Later, when children begin to read, they develop the ability to monitor their reading, eventually developing the ability to monitor their own comprehension and intervene, by re-reading or asking a question, when it is lacking. This ability to monitor one's own comprehension marks a significant difference between good and poor readers. **Self-monitoring** begins with language, and as language ability improves, so does memory.

Content knowledge is another factor in the parallel development of language and memory because it affects how much information is stored and how it is recalled. Consider the experience of two women attending a cooking demonstration. Clara is an experienced cook and avid connoisseur of gourmet magazines and television shows. Margaret heats frozen dinners in the microwave and makes dinner reservations. After the cooking demonstration, Margaret explained that she watched a man make thin pancakes and fill them with shrimp and sauce. Clara explained that the chef demonstrated how to make whole wheat crepes, which he filled with shellfish that had been poached in wine and then stirred into a sherry-flavored béchamel. Clara's knowledge of cooking and the language for talking about it have obviously influenced what she recalled and the amount of detail. This is similar with children: The more they know about the world, the easier it is for them to categorize their experiences; the more language they know, the easier it is to label those categories, and as we have seen, the ability to form categories is critical to concept formation.

What are children actually *doing* while the basic capacities, memory strategies, and metamemory develop? How do their activities contribute? Generally speaking, they are interacting with the adults in their lives, possibly with other siblings, engaging in a variety of language activities. Long before they can speak, they hear and attend to language being addressed to them, and in that way they learn that language is purposeful, communicative, and meaningful, and, we hope, associated with pleasurable events. As children learn the labels for objects, they are not worried about increasing their memory capacity or vocabulary size—they are merely consumed by an eager and lively curiosity that they are trying to satisfy. Whether babbling or producing rhymes or telling stories, they engage in language because it is fun. Children don't realize that they are also developing elaboration strategies to help with memory, yet they are very much in charge of their own learning. They can be prompted through social interactions, but the speed and the sequence in which they learn is up to them. Other than providing a rich language environment, adults do not control the pace of development. What they *do* control is the environment, and here they play a critical role. Language is central to the growth of memory, which is, in turn, central to children's overall cognitive development, and it is a principal means by which

131

children come to understand and to organize their experience. It is, therefore, incumbent on adults to provide a variety of play and other opportunities for language and thus cognition to grow and to thrive.

Although from the perspective of young children, their "job" during the first few years of life is to figure out how their world is organized and how they relate to others in it, what is happening largely without their awareness is that they are preparing for schooling. They are getting ready, with help, to read and to write as the basis for everything else they need to learn in school. In the final section of the chapter, we examine the role of language in the development of early academic skills.

5.4 Language and Early Academic Learning

Although we tend to think of children's academic thinking ability as developing during the school years, the fact is that the foundations are laid much earlier. Researchers have estimated that at least a third of children's academic skills are acquired before the age of 6 years (Yardley, 1973; Piper, 2007). That means that it is especially important that early childhood educators understand the role that language plays in creating these early skills. Before going deeper into this topic, it is necessary to make one thing clear: The kind of language that helps children to learn is not necessarily the adult telling them how to do something. That kind of intervention often deprives children of the opportunity to learn something on their own. In the process of learning on their own, children also learn more about how to learn. The language that is helpful is the kind that prompts children or subtly directs them toward finding the solution themselves. Fortunately, there are abundant opportunities in the early years for children to learn and to develop strategies for learning more (see *Learning in Preschool*). Much of this learning will help them with the subjects they will later encounter in school because their parents have actively taught them— the ABC song, for example, or how to count to 10, or they have watched educational television or videos, or they have found their own resources for learning, perhaps by observing older children. The three areas that we will examine here are reading, writing, and arithmetic, generally considered to be the building blocks of a good education.

This father and daughter are reading a book about the alphabet, thereby laying the foundation for academic learning when she goes to school.

Blend Images/SuperStock

Learning in Preschool

The learning that occurs in the first five years happens at home and, for many children, in preschool and daycare settings. Wherever it occurs, it is important because research has shown that the quality of preschool experience has a measurable effect on children's later cognitive performance.

Researchers observing 4-year-olds in preschool classrooms in 10 countries found compelling evidence that the children's scores on tests at age 7 were positively influenced by their preschool experience. In particular, they found that cognitive performance was associated with their having spent more time in small-group activities and having a greater number and variety of toys and objects to play with. They found that language development was enhanced by having more activities that children chose for themselves rather than by the teacher and by having better educated teachers. In countries where the norm was for the children to spend most of their time working or playing individually, more interaction with teachers was linked to better language development.

On the other hand, in countries where teacher-centered classrooms were the norm, better language learning was associated with less interaction with teachers. These findings underscore "the importance of active exploration for young children's concept learning and the importance of active speaking for their language learning" (Bardige, 2009, p. 147).

Early Learning and Arithmetic

Most children know how to solve simple addition problems with sums smaller than 10 before they enter first grade. One of the strategies they use to do this is to choose the larger of the two numbers to be added and then count upward from it the number of times indicated by the smaller number. Sometimes, fingers are involved! So a child adding two and four will begin with four and count up two—five, six—to arrive at the right answer. Language and memory are required for this simple task; a child has to be able to remember the strategy to use and keep in mind the starting place and the number of places to count ahead. Most 5-year-olds can do this, many 4-year-olds can, but it is still beyond the ability of a 2- or even most 3-year-olds. Children apply the same strategy in reverse for subtraction, counting backward. This is not the only strategy children employ to figure out the answers to arithmetic problems. Whether they are counting forward or counting backward, children cannot count at all without language.

During the early childhood years, there are abundant opportunities for children to learn numeracy. From the time that a baby notices that all the bananas have been eaten and says, "All gone," and then follows up with a request, "More," we can see that the foundations for numeracy are in place. Later, as a child plays with blocks or finger puppets or small cars, she begins to count them, add and take away, the opportunity arises for parents or teachers to encourage the child by probing with questions such as, "And now how many are there?" and perhaps counting along with the child. In such a way, they assist children to learn not only basic arithmetic but the language for doing it.

Mathematics and Bilinguals

Researchers have further demonstrated the close relationship between language and mathematics skills by studying bilingual children. A team of British researchers analyzed primary school children using two languages in mathematics and English lessons. They found that having two languages was not at all confusing but appeared to deepen their understanding of key concepts. It appeared, for example, that children who were allowed to use their mother tongue as well as English grasped division and multiplication more easily than monolinguals (British Broadcasting Corporation [BBC] News, 2007).

Early Learning and Reading

The earliest learning associated with reading occurs when children develop concepts about books. In other words, they figure out what a book does or what it is for. As they are read to, or as they observe others reading, they begin to attend to print. They learn that there is a connection between those marks on the page and oral language and that they have meaning to the person reading them. By the time they get to kindergarten, some children will already have learned to read, meaning that they can not only identify a number of words correctly but that they are able to read printed text and understand its meaning, whether that text be a sign, a book, or a billboard. In simple terms, what happens is that children hear stories being read to them, they show an interest in "decoding" the printed text by pointing to text and asking, "What's that?" by watching children's educational television or video, or through more direct intervention such as a parent showing them flashcards or writing down words for them. Early readers excel at the decoding stage and quickly move on to more advanced strategies such as predicting, and they are able to do so because they have had a great deal of exposure to reading and stories. In short, they know that the task of text is to tell a story or convey a message, and they set themselves the task of figuring out how to extract that meaning.

Among children who do not learn to read before they get to school, most know a great deal about the reading process anyway. They have begun to learn that words are different from drawings and that not all squiggles and lines are the same. Making these distinctions is a complex perceptual task; it requires that children learn which curved, horizontal, vertical, and diagonal lines are meaningful and which are not. An interesting question arises here: Does learning to name the letters (e.g., recite the alphabet) help children learn to read? My older son, who was able to read simple children's stories by his 3rd birthday, saw no point to the exercise at all. When he was 4, he told his teacher that learning to say the ABCs was "silly because you just mix them all up anyway." On the one hand, there is some indication that children's ability to identify and name letters predicts their early reading achievement (deHirsch, Jansky, & Langford, 1966; Walsh, Price, & Gillingham, 1988; cited in Piper, 2007). It would be a mistake to assume, however, that simply teaching young children to name letters will improve reading ability, because the association may not be direct. What is more likely is that knowing the names of letters means that a child has been exposed to a stimulating print-rich environment that has not only allowed her to learn the names of letters but has helped her to a greater awareness of what reading entails and a rich set of oral language skills. While teaching young children the alphabet will probably be helpful, it is equally important to help children develop strong oral language skills.

In order to become proficient readers, children must acquire more than letter perception and identification skills. They also have to make the connection between letter and phoneme (Chapter 2) and learn to identify words. But ultimately, what they must do to become true readers is to re-create meaning from printed text. In other words, they must acquire comprehension skills. Reading comprehension is one of the most active and complex cognitive activities in which we engage, even as adults. It is also an important skill children must acquire to succeed in school and to develop and pursue a wide range of interests for the rest of their lives. A full description of what is involved in reading comprehension, or listening comprehension, is beyond the scope of this book. We can examine the process in general terms with the following example.

> *The high wind blew the chairs into the pool.*

What is involved in extracting the meaning from this sentence? The reader must accomplish the following:

- Have some kind of recognition and retrieval system to match the words on the printed page with the words in memory.
- Select the appropriate meaning for words with more than one meaning (e.g., *high* and *pool*).
- Discern all of the meaning propositions present in the sentence. In this sentence, those include the following:
  - There was a wind blowing.
  - The wind was strong (high).
  - There were chairs outside.
  - There was a pool.
  - The chairs were near the pool.
  - The chairs went into the pool.
- Integrate all of the meaning propositions into a single sentence to store in memory. When readers *integrate,* they combine all the propositions, and they do so according to the rules of English syntax.

Asked to recall this sentence several days later, a reader might remember *There was a high wind and it blew some chairs into the swimming pool.* This is not the sentence he read, but it does include all the meaning propositions and capture the writer's intent. This is the essence of reading comprehension—not memorizing what the words were, but remembering what was communicated.

One further skill that children need to develop if they are to become successful readers is to monitor their own comprehension. Readers of all ages are more proficient if they are able to monitor their understanding of the text they are reading and adopt strategies for dealing with any problems they encounter. Different kinds of texts require different strategies—most of us can read a novel in a busy airport or with music or television blaring. We probably would be less successful reading a graduate-level text on astrophysics in those environments. The reason is that the strategies we use for comprehending different kinds of text depend on our purpose, on how the material is structured, and the knowledge and experience we bring to the task. In the child's world, some texts will be easier to comprehend than others. Children who have heard many stories know how stories are structured

These girls do not yet know how to read, but because their mother reads to them regularly, they show an interest in reading and have learned how stories are structured.

Alaska Stock Images/National Geographic Stock

and, to some degree, what to expect. If they have not had those experiences, then they might experience a little more difficulty working out a reading strategy. In this case, teaching the child word-recognition skills won't help much. Certainly, that is a first step, but an even more important step is to build up the child's oral language experience with stories and narratives in which the child can participate. None of this would be possible, of course, without language and, specifically, without oral language. Oral language (or sign language in deaf children) is the foundation for *all* future reading and writing abilities.

Reading in Bilinguals

With bilinguals, progress toward literacy will depend on a number of factors including the language to which they are first introduced to print. In some instances, children are introduced to print in both their languages. With Isabelle, the bilingual French-English child we met in earlier chapters, her mother read to her in French and her father in English. Isabelle learned to read first in English—the language which she used more often—the summer before she began attending a French-language kindergarten. Her reading ability transferred easily to French, and now in first grade, she is able to read both languages at grade level. Isabelle had a strong oral basis in English, learned to read in English, and then transferred the reading skill to French. Not all bilingual children are in this situation. "The progress in acquiring literacy by bilingual children will depend in part on social, political and educational factors that define the child's environment at the time that literacy is introduced" (Bialystok, 2001; Chapter 6, para. 4). Sometimes, children have to learn to read in the majority language (English) even though their oral language skills are stronger in the minority language. This situation places an additional burden on bilingual children who have not yet acquired reading skills to transfer but who must first master the cognitive skills necessary for reading in a less-familiar language. But despite the many differences, "Children must ultimately learn how to read texts, and this is a cognitive problem" (Bialystok, 2001, Chapter 6, para. 8). They go through three stages as they move toward independent literacy:

1. Preliteracy. At this stage, children learn that print represents language and the basics of the writing system.

2. Early reading. At this stage, they learn the rules for matching the print symbols to language sounds.

3. Fluent reading. At this stage, the meaning of the text takes priority. Children begin to read and to write to get and to transmit ideas or information that they did not have before.

These are the same stages through which monolingual children progress and what precedes all of them is oral language.

Early Learning and Writing

Writing is the language skill that causes more problems for more people than any other. Everyone learns to speak and understand oral language, most people eventually learn to read, with varying degrees of proficiency. But even people who are extremely well read profess to having difficulty with writing. It would seem that reading and writing should involve the same processes in reverse, and if that were the case, proficiency in reading *should* lead to proficiency in writing. Certainly, most competent writers are also very competent readers, but many competent readers are only marginally successful writers. Why? We don't actually know why writing is so hard to remediate. We know a great deal more about what is involved in learning to speak and in both aural and written comprehension than we do about learning to write. What we do know about young children learning to write involves a complex network of interactive processes. The first task is organizing what it is that the writer wants to say. Many of us have faced the tyranny of the blank page and know that having a topic given to us is only slightly better than having to find one. But let's consider a 6-year-old faced with the challenge of writing a story. What is involved?

The obvious first step is having something to say. Sometimes, teachers consider that they are offering sufficient guidance when they ask children to "write a story." But that is difficult even for an adult. We do not—or should not—begin to write until we have something to say, so the experienced teacher knows to help children do some prewriting by talking through the story or the experience they will write. In order to do that, writers have to retrieve the information relevant to the topic from long-term memory. The next task is to organize it. Our memory of an event does not always provide us with the best structure for writing it down. This paragraph, written by a 7-year-old child, illustrates the problem:

> *The ocean was cold. We went to visit my uncle Josh. We went swimming. The water was salty and also cold and that's because Uncle Josh lives in Oregon. Oregon is colder than California.*

This child has simply put down everything he could recall about the trip to his uncle's. With guidance, though, this child could be talked through the story and re-create it chronologically. In order to do this, the writer has to formulate a plan for the story and keep it in mind long enough to write it down. Until late in the third-grade year or even the fourth-grade year, children have difficulty in this kind of mental advance planning. That is why oral language is such an important part of developing skills. The more familiar children are with hearing and telling stories, the easier it is to organize them in their minds and then on paper. To get the story on paper, the writer must manage the mechanics, whether with pencil, pen, or keyboard. Often, with 5- and 6-year olds, the physical demands of writing down their thoughts require so much of their attention that they have little to devote to organization. It is extremely helpful for teachers (or parents or older children) to serve as scribes, writing down the stories children tell (Bereiter & Scardamalia, 1982; Kirk, 1999). They will create better quality stories than they otherwise would, but more importantly, they have built a skill that will transfer when they are older and better able to cope with the physical demands of writing. Once again, we see the importance of oral language to children's learning of a skill that will not only be necessary in school but will serve them for the rest of their lives.

The process of learning to write begins at the same time as learning to read, although it takes a different course. In the preschool through primary years, the process involves four stages:

Although it appears that this boy simply puts scribbles on a page, he is actually showing signs of language awareness.

age fotostock/SuperStock

1. Beginning writing, which describes the stage at which children use their drawings to represent their meanings and pretend-read aloud the story they convey. Their writing at this stage may follow a left to right orientation and may consist of scribbles. They are essentially mimicking what they have seen older children and adults do.

2. Early emergent writing, which describes the stage during which children typically demonstrate their awareness that print represents sounds. For example, they may draw a picture and then write some of the letters associated with the picture.

3. Emergent writing, which describes the stage at which children begin to create more identifiable letters with spaces between them, may begin to use sequences of letters, and make letters over and over to practice the way they are formed. Children at this stage may begin to write their own names.

4. Early writing is the stage in which children demonstrate increased awareness of sound/symbol correspondence by creating their own spellings. They begin to use capital and lowercase letters and to space words more consistently. Many children at this stage practice by copying letters, words, or even sentences. (Adapted from Welton, 2010)

Six Characteristics of Early Learning

It is not an overstatement to say that almost all the learning we will do during a lifetime is based in language. True, there are certain mechanical acts that we learn independent of language before we have language, but once we acquire the ability to speak and to think in language, we use it to teach ourselves and to learn. This is true of children in the preschool years, a time in which their learning has certain identifiable characteristics, six of which are especially important to preschool teachers.

Learning Proceeds According to Degree of Readiness

Language itself is a good example of how this is true. It does no good to try to teach a 2-month old baby to say *Mama* or *milk* or any other word. Physically and cognitively, the baby is not yet able to do so. In a few months, he will be able to do that, but even when he's 8 months old, he won't be able to produce meaningful three-word sentences. When I asked my granddaughter Isabelle what she wanted for her 5th birthday, she told me, "Nana, I really, really want to learn to read." I had tried to interest her in the task a few months earlier, noting her intense interest in books, but I failed. After her birthday, we spent a month on the task, and Isabelle became a reader.

Children Are in Charge of Their Own Learning

They might not know they are in charge, but they are. Their decisions are governed in large part by maturity but also by their curiosity about the world around them. Sometimes it happens that children's wish to learn something is in advance of their ability to do so, and this can be very powerful. Alberto could put together simple wooden puzzles intended for 3–4 year olds before his second birthday. He appeared to be motivated by a desire to see the completed picture, but it was also the case that he had watched older children do it and wanted to be able to do it himself. His younger brother Juan had no interest in puzzles, but he wanted to learn to count and would practice counting with anything he could find to count. Juan eventually learned to do puzzles, and Alberto learned to count, but in each case, the brothers determined, what, when, and how they would learn.

Play is serious business for children; it helps them to develop cognitively, linguistically, and socially. Here, Isabelle plays and learns with her potato head toys.

Stephanie Hull

Much Learning Happens While Children Play

Play is the work of childhood. It serves to foster motor and cognitive development, and its importance cannot be underestimated. Playing on swings, monkey bars, or just running after a dog or a ball will help them to acquire gross motor skills. Playing with puzzles and building blocks will help to develop fine motor skills, and when they play rhyming games or play games counting red cars and blue cars on a road trip, they are not only learning but they are learning *how* to learn.

The Role of Adults Is to Facilitate Rather Than to Teach

It follows that if children are really in charge of their own learning and that if play is central to that learning, that adults should not worry about teaching as much as providing opportunities for learning. For parents, perhaps the most important role they play is to be partners in daily interaction. Whether they are engaged in routines such as the washing of hands or getting ready for bed, or in special activities such as decorating a gingerbread house at Christmas or dressing up for a birthday party, the dialogues that occur between parents and children are the means through which children learn. In school, it is very similar. Teachers talk children through the routines of the classroom and special events, they demonstrate when necessary, and they provide an environment that is rich with learning opportunities. At home and at school, conversation between adults and children should be a collaborative event with the adult adapting speech as necessary to children's maturity level. Parents and teachers who understand that their own knowledge cannot be transmitted directly also understand that their job is to guide gently.

Learning Is Essential to Children's Language Acquisition

We have seen through these five chapters that language is not something children learn as a mental exercise but in order to communicate, to engage in meaningful interaction with the people who surround them. We don't have to teach children to talk, but we do have to provide them with the opportunities to do so, and not just to talk, but to listen, to experience language used for many purposes, and eventually to read and to write. It begins with birth. An infant cannot understand what his mother is saying or singing, but the fact that she does so is critical to the infant developing a sense of security, a knowledge of what language does, and cognitive skills. When a father takes the time to explain to his 3-year-old son what he is doing as he changes the oil in his car, the father knows that some of the language and concepts are beyond his son's ability to understand. But the dialogue is important because the boy will understand some of it, he will likely learn some new vocabulary, and his interest will be piqued—in language and possibly in cars and how they work. The child's understandings at this point will be imperfect, but the seeds are there and, with attention, will grow.

Dialogues between adults and children provide opportunities for learning, but the dialogue has to be real, that is, the adult has to learn to listen to the child. It isn't always easy—young children do not always have the language they need to express what they want to say, or they may say it differently. Adults, and especially teachers, need to pay attention to what is being said and ask questions or offer interpretations to help them out. An absent-minded, "Oh, good," or even "Wow" in response to a child's utterance doesn't count as dialogue. Children catch on very quickly if the adult is not paying attention or is only partly attending. If that happens often, the child may conclude that there's no point to trying to make him or herself understood.

Learning Is Embedded in the Process of Socialization

The life of a preschooler is an integrated whole of experiences. The day does not even slightly resemble a school curriculum. The day is not divided into blocks of time—a half hour for hygiene, an hour for motor development, an hour for cognitive learning, half an hour for socialization, and so forth. The experiences all relate in some way to the process of attaining full membership in the family and the larger society in which the family lives. Children's early learning is directed toward achieving membership in a group—family, extended family, neighborhood, et cetera. They don't learn words because their biological clocks say it is time to do so (although they can't learn them before that) but because they are trying to connect with other people. From our perspective as educators, we see the abundance of learning that takes place during the preschool years—children learn thousands of words, develop concepts, and acquire the foundations for all the academic learning that will follow. That is not, however, the perspective of preschool children— what they are doing is learning to become like the people around them. They are learning to belong.

Conclusion

During the years before children reach school age, they are building the foundations for a lifetime of learning. The brain is much more "plastic" during these years, making this a time during which environmental influences have a tremendous impact.

There are several critical periods for learning, depending on what is being learned. The window of opportunity for acquiring native-speaker-like control of language, for example, begins to close around the age of 5 and is almost entirely diminished by the onset of puberty. Cognitive development occurs in tandem with language development. Word learning is inextricably linked with the ability to categorize and conceptualize, and language plays an important role in the development of memory.

We also explored the relationship between language and early learning of arithmetic and literacy skills. To a large extent, children are the architects of their own learning. Nevertheless, most children follow the same developmental sequence, as we will discover in Chapter 6.

Post-Test

1. Synapses in the brain

   a. are mostly formed before birth.
   b. connect the brain lobes.
   c. number about 2,500 per neuron at age 2.
   d. are pruned throughout the life span.

2. Vocabulary comprehension for boys and girls

   a. develops at equal levels.
   b. occurs in spurts.
   c. has little to do with differing brain development.
   d. is equal to their word production.

3. The 1932 study by Carmichael, Hogan, and Walter found that

    a. memory can be distorted by verbal information provided.
    b. all memories have some verbal component.
    c. the deterioration of memory starts with verbal information.
    d. verbal information is stored in memory differently than visual information.

4. The typical sequence of gaining reading skills is

    a. preliteracy → early reading → fluent reading → oral language.
    b. early reading → preliteracy → oral language → fluent reading.
    c. oral language → preliteracy → early reading → fluent reading.
    d. early reading → oral language → preliteracy → fluent reading.

Answers

1. **d.** Are pruned throughout the life span. *The answer can be found in Section 5.1.*
2. **b.** occurs in spurts. *The answer can be found in Section 5.2.*
3. **a.** Memory can be distorted by verbal information provided. *The answer can be found in Section 5.3.*
4. **c.** Oral language → preliteracy → early reading → fluent reading. *The answer can be found in Section 5.4.*

Key Ideas

- Although some cognitive development occurs before children acquire language, once they begin to learn language, cognition and language grow in tandem.
- In the first two years after birth, brain development consists of creating synapses and, subsequently, of pruning them to the ones most frequently used.
- Although brain development continues into adulthood, the young brain is much more susceptible to both positive and negative environmental influences.
- Although the language center of the brain is typically thought to be located in the left hemisphere (in right-handed people), there is growing evidence that other areas of the brain are also involved.
- An environment rich in visual and aural stimuli assists in brain development and, thus, in linguistic and cognitive development.
- Word learning and conceptual development are closely linked.
- Language is involved in almost all aspects of memory development.
- Although a great deal of children's academic thinking ability develops during the school years, researchers estimate that a third or more is acquired before the age of 6.
- Reading and writing abilities are built upon a solid foundation of oral language, which in turn is embedded in the process of socialization.

Critical Thinking Questions

1. Why do you think the words *more* and *no* are usually learned early? Why do you think they are likely to be "contextually flexible"?

2. Why does comprehension always precede production in word learning?

3. Given that children's earliest word learning is grounded in the "here and now," which of the following probably has the most influence on their first words? Why?

   a. the child's gender (whether the child is a boy or girl)
   b. the language that the child's mother or other caregiver used in normal interactions
   c. the language of children's books and stories

4. What is the difference between categories and concepts?

5. Margaret Harris and her colleagues compared word learning in children who were developing normally and children who were language delayed. They found that 78% of the speech of mothers of the typically developing infants was directed to objects on which the child was focusing attention. Mothers of language-delayed children, however, directed only 25% of their utterances to objects the child was attending to. They were also more likely to use general names such as *thing* or *one* when referring to objects (Harris, Jones, & Grant, 1983, cited in Harris 2004). Based on the information in the chapter, what are two possible explanations for these findings?

6. The author lists four known differences in how girls' and boys' brains process language. Do any of these differences account for the vocabulary differences shown in Figure 5.4?

7. Look at the labeled shapes in Figure 5.5 for seven seconds and then cover the figure. Leave it covered as you answer the following questions.

   a. Write down the colors you saw in the circles.
   b. Try to describe HOW you stored the information and how you recalled it.
   c. Was there anything confusing about the task? What?

   Now uncover the figure. How accurate were you? What role did language play in the task? What does this tell you about the relationship between language and memory?

Figure 5.5

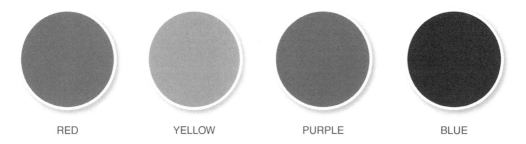

RED   YELLOW   PURPLE   BLUE

8. Suppose your friend's cell phone number is 555-135-9753 and you did not have your phone or paper to record it. What memory strategies would you use to remember it?

Key Terms

category Essential to the formation of concepts, a grouping of similar attributes—things with wheels, words that begin with *r*, vegetables that grow underground, etc.

cognitive development The process of acquiring intelligence and increasingly advanced thought and problem-solving ability from infancy to adulthood.

concept A general idea derived or inferred from specific instances or occurrences.

context-specific words In first words, those that refer only to a particular person, object, or action.

contextually flexible words In first words, those that are used generically or with several referents.

critical period (for brain development): The period before plasticity ends and the brain is at its most opportune time for development.

expressive strategy The approach used by children whose first words are action words or people's names.

memory strategies Those conscious activities we employ in the hope of improving our chances of remembering.

metamemory The knowledge or awareness we have *about* how memory works that assists us in improving our ability to remember.

neurons Brain cells.

plasticity Refers to the ability of the human brain to change in response to environmental experiences.

referential strategy The approach used by children whose first words refer mostly to objects.

self-monitoring Children's ability to compare their utterances with some mental representation of what they know about language.

synapse The junction between two nerve cells, consisting of a minute gap across which impulses pass.

vocabulary spurt Sudden surge in the number of words a child knows and uses, typically occurring a little later in boys than in girls.

Weblinks

More information about how the infant brain develops can be found at
http://www.zerotothree.org/child-development/brain-development/
http://www.pbs.org/wnet/brain/episode1/index.html
http://umaine.edu/publications/4356e/

An interesting summary of the benefits of the government-sponsored Head Start program can be found at
http://home.uchicago.edu/~ludwigj/papers/NYAS-LudwigPhillips-HeadStart-2008.pdf

For more on brain and gender, see
http://www.sciencedirect.com/science/article/pii/S0028393207004460

Accounts of the effects of deprivation on early attachment can be found at
http://childsrighttothrive.org/topics/socioemotional-development/what-are-effects-early-severe-deprivation-attachment

For further information on language centers and the brain, see
http://www.sciencedaily.com/releases/2008/01/080102222904.htm

For further research on the cognitive benefits of bilingualism, see *Being bilingual 'boosts brain power' at* http://www.bbc.co.uk/news/health-17892521

6

Developmental Milestones

Learning Objectives

By the end of this chapter, you will be able to accomplish the following objectives:

- Describe the major developmental milestones in the first 6 months of an infant's life, and explain the importance of early vocalizations to language development.

- Describe how the major developmental milestones of the 6-month to 1-year-old infant relate to language development.

- Describe the linguistic growth that occurs in the second year, especially the expansion of vocabulary, and explain the difference between *speech delay* and *language delay*.

- Explain how cognitive and physical changes influence language development in the third year as children leave infancy behind and become toddlers.

- Describe development between 3 and 4 in terms of what preschool teachers can expect children to be able to do.

- Explain the developmental changes that characterize children's transition from toddlers to pre-schoolers during the year between age 4 and 5, and describe the linguistic foundation that has been established.

Introduction

On his first day of kindergarten, Kai is afraid. He hasn't been to preschool, and he's lived in the United States for only a year. He doesn't know what will be expected of him, and he is nervous about being able to speak well enough to get by. Even though many children in the school he will attend speak his language, Mandarin, Kai doesn't yet know this. His parents are worried that they have not prepared him for his new life in an American school. His language skills are good; he can read and write his own name and those of his family members in both his languages, and he has already picked up a lot of English in the community. Still, they worry. What will the school expect of him? Will he understand? Will he succeed?

As long as Kai has had a relatively normal environment, there is no cause for concern. We learned in Chapter 5 that much of cognitive development occurs before children are able to use language. Once they begin to acquire language, that growth is accelerated because language and cognition are intricately linked. Although most of the academic skills children need to succeed in school are acquired during the school years, about a third of those skills are acquired before the age of 6. Understanding the course of that development is necessary so teachers can create appropriate learning activities based on children's developmental stages. Every child is unique, yet in the development of language, there are more similarities than differences between children. In infancy, most children babble by the time they are 6 months old (Chapter 3). The first identifiable words usually appear before the first birthday (Chapter 5). Continued development generally follows a predictable course as well, although it would be a mistake to assume any child will follow an exact schedule. It is important to note, however, that although children reach different stages at different times, the order in which they progress through the stages varies very little. This consistency is due to the biological "equipment" that children bring to the task of learning language and to the interrelationship between language and cognitive development.

In this chapter, we will look at developmental milestones in a child's life from birth until 5 years. With examples from Kai and other children, we look broadly at physical, cognitive, and language development during this period. The exact age for any particular developmental achievement is somewhat arbitrary. The ages used here represent general tendencies across all children rather than a calendar or schedule for development. In each period, we begin with a general overview of physical, cognitive, and linguistic development before examining linguistic development in more detail.

Pre-Test

1. An absence of language precursors suggests

    a. that the child cries too much.
    b. a lack of exposure to language in utero.
    c. auditory or cognitive problems.
    d. typical developmental markers.

2. The "dress rehearsal" for language is

    a. cooing.
    b. crying.
    c. gestures.
    d. babbling.

3. Which of the following does NOT typically occur between 12–18 months?

    a. Children's speech becomes more recognizable.
    b. Children refine the meanings of the words they use.
    c. Children overgeneralize word use less.
    d. Children utilize full sentences in speech.

4. One linguistic difference between 2 year olds and adults is that 2 year olds

    a. get the order wrong.
    b. are more self-focused.
    c. fail to include verbs in sentences.
    d. use fewer words in sentences.

5. Children are considered preschoolers at/between age(s)

    a. 1–2 years.
    b. 3–4 years.
    c. 5–6 years.
    d. 9 months.

6. The acquisition of what we call the "first" language(s) occurs before age

    a. 2 years.
    b. 4 years.
    c. 5 years.
    d. 7 years.

Answers

1. c. Auditory or cognitive problems. *The answer can be found in Section 6.1.*
2. d. Babbling. *The answer can be found in Section 6.2.*
3. d. Children utilize full sentences in speech. *The answer can be found in Section 6.3.*
4. d. Use fewer words in sentences. *The answer can be found in Section 6.4.*
5. b. 3–4 years. *The answer can be found in Section 6.5.*
6. b. 5 years. *The answer can be found in Section 6.6.*

6.1 From Birth to 6 Months

On the day he was born, Kai weighed 7 pounds, 4 ounces, and was 21 inches long. He cried loudly, without any tears, and although his parents showered him with attention, he appeared oblivious to their attempts to comfort him. Over the next few weeks, however, they began to notice that he attempted to focus on their faces when they talked to him, and his mother was certain that his crying differed as he attempted to express different needs. The development changes that occurred during Kai's first 6 months might have appeared to be minimal to a casual observer. But Kai was following the same course of development as every other normally developing human child. Changes occurring during the first 6 months of life aren't easily observed, but there are very significant developments:

- Infants develop binocular vision, meaning that their eyes begin to move together in unison. This is especially important for their ability to see and form visual perceptions.
- They will produce tears when crying (newborns typically cry without forming tears).
- The swallowing reflex, which moves food from the front to the back of the tongue, is still immature until the latter weeks of this period; the same tongue movements will be important for language later.
- The Landau reflex will appear at around 3 months. This reflex is an instinctive reaction in which infants held in a face-down position will lift their heads and fully extend their legs. It is useful to keep a baby from smothering when placed face down. It disappears once the child has developed sufficient muscular control to no longer need it, usually around the first birthday. This reflex helps the child to strengthen muscle tone and refine motor skills necessary for sitting, crawling, and walking. Without this reflex, a baby placed on a blanket would only be able to move her head from side to side. Unable to raise her head, she would have a limited field of vision and be unaware of anything occurring above the level of the blanket; thus, her range of perception would be greatly reduced.

Although cognitive development is difficult to observe or measure during this period, there are certain indicators of what is happening. For example, Kai loved to play peek-a-boo, as do most infants. It is a way for them to begin to learn object permanence (i.e., that an object does not cease to exist when it disappears from view), and most cultures have their version of peek-a-boo. In Japanese, for example, it is called *inai inai ba*. Between 4 and 6 months old, babies begin to realize that crying gets adult attention, and babies will begin to develop other ways of gaining attention—squealing or wiggling, for example. Some infants appear to know their names by 6 months, turning toward the person who says it. They also begin to differentiate between familiar faces and strangers. In terms of language, the behavior at this point is not linguistic per se, but infants do exhibit behaviors indicating important prerequisites to language learning. These are the precursory behaviors discussed next.

A game of peek-a-boo with Mom is not only fun but is helping this baby learn the concept of object permanence.

Brand X Pictures/Thinkstock

Precursors to Language

We tend to think of language acquisition as starting when the child clearly understands words—by pointing at an object named by an adult, for example. But language learning begins much earlier than that. Some researchers argue that language learning begins before birth (see *Precursory Language Behavior*), and to some degree this is true. As we learned in previous chapters, there is an innate predisposition to learn language, and that is formed in the brain before birth. Also, some evidence indicates that children become accustomed to the rhythms of their mothers' speech while in utero. Newborns' crying has been found to mimic the prosodic features of their own language (Cross, 2009). However, crying is not language per se, nor is babbling. Both are precursors to language, and they are important because they are prerequisites to language learning. Their absence could signal auditory or cognitive problems that should be assessed by a physician.

Precursory Language Behavior

The capacity to acquire language is innate, and evidence shows that language development begins in utero. The fetus hears the distinct cadences, intonations, and pitches of his mother's voice and, to some degree, other sounds in the environment. Evidence that fetal learning takes place includes the following:

- The newborn infant recognizes and shows a preference for the human voice above other sounds.
- The newborn will also show strong preference for the mother's voice over other female voices.

Researchers at the University of South Carolina studied the behavior of children of mothers who had been instructed to read Dr. Seuss out loud while pregnant. In particular, they tested to see whether infants recognized Dr. Seuss stories and whether they were able to recognize their mother's voice against other readers. Infants were able to do both, picking up on the vocal patterns they'd become familiar with in utero (DeCasper & Spence, 1986).

British researchers discovered that infants born to mothers who had routinely watched a particular soap opera during pregnancy were attentive to the theme music of the soap opera after birth while children whose mothers had not watched the program did not exhibit such behavior (Hepper, 1988).

What other kinds of behavior would you consider as evidence for fetal language learning?

Babies are born with brains primed to acquire language. They have the capacity to distinguish human speech from other sounds, to figure out which sounds are significant and which are not, where word boundaries are, and how words get strung together to make meaningful sentences. During the first few months of life, infants perceive and produce sounds. They also learn about events, objects, and relationships as they interact with the people around them. From birth, infants can hear the full spectrum of sounds produced around them. In terms of language learning, their task in the first months is to work out which ones are significant and which ones can be ignored. Eventually, they will learn to pay attention and to produce the distinctive ones—the phonemes—of the language or languages they hear (Chapter 2).

Babies do not lie silently in their cribs working out the sound system in silence, though. They cry when wet, tired, or hungry; they coo or smile when happy or amused; and these are forms of communication. These are **precursory language behaviors** which differ from language in two important ways. First, during these early vocalizations, they do not use any of the conventions of language in these communications. The second difference has to do with intent. During the first 6 to 10 months, infants' vocalizations reflect states of being—discomfort or pleasure. These early vocalizations are related to language learning and share characteristics of the language the children hear around them (Cross, 2009; Mampe, Friederici, Christophe, & Wermke, 2009). They represent **affect** (feelings or emotion) and changes in affect. Later with language, children begin to communicate intentionally (i.e., they are aware of and intend to communicate a particular meaning).

Although these newborns cannot yet speak or even babble, they can distinguish the human voice from other sounds. They can also communicate their needs vocally. Such vocalizations are a precursor to true language.

age fotostock/SuperStock

Early Vocalizations

Crying begins at the moment of birth and is the child's earliest vocalization. Crying is not language, but it is important to note that crying appears to be differentiated in a similar way that language is—different cries serve different purposes, even if the infant may not be aware of the distinction. Cooing begins at around 6 weeks of age, and it is at this time that the vowel sounds *ahh*, *ee*, and *oo* begin to appear. Cooing behavior serves as a rehearsal of the tongue movements that will later be necessary for speech. The earliest vocalizations—crying, cooing, and seemingly random acts of vocal noisemaking—can be thought of as warm-up sessions. At 2 to 3 months, the cooing and noisemaking appears to be random, but gradually this gives way to babbling with a more rhythmic or sing-song quality. By around 5 months, infants begin to make more complex and more organized sounds. They have begun to babble.

6.2 From 6 Months to 1 Year

This is a very active time in children's development; it is the "doing" stage in which many changes occur. Physically, they grow rapidly and begin to develop mobility. Typically, babies during this period will

- begin to roll over and crawl;
- sit up, first with support and then by themselves;
- pull themselves up to a standing position;
- walk while holding onto furniture or a person's hand;
- cut the first teeth;
- triple their birth weight (by the end of this period); and
- begin to assert self by resisting dressing or undressing and feeding.

Babies during this stage also exhibit behavior that demonstrates their cognitive growth. They begin to

- imitate sounds and actions;
- recognize words and simple phrases;
- attempt to say a few words;
- look for familiar objects that have disappeared from view;
- respond to their own names;
- point to familiar objects;
- enjoy stacking things and putting things into containers;
- show evidence that they remember familiar objects and people; and
- anticipate routines, thereby also exhibiting memory.

Crawling is an important developmental stage; it helps infants develop muscular strength and large motor skills. It also provides a way of expanding their experiences.

Pixland/Thinkstock

At birth, crying is the principal vocalization that babies engage in. Gradually, however, their vocalizations become more language-like.

Babbling

If the earliest vocalizations are the warm-up, babbling can be thought of as "dress rehearsal" for language (see *The Importance of Babbling*). "Although precisely how babbling relates to language development is not yet clearly understood, psychologists and linguists have suggested that babbling serves at least two functions: as practice for later speech and as a social reward" (Mihalicek & Wilson, 2011, p. 324). At first, infants' babbling may sound like random noises with only a few of the sounds resembling language, but gradually the noises start to take on the characteristics of the language or languages around them. In fact, over the next months and extending into the stage when first words appear, it is possible to see steady growth toward real words.

By the time they are 6 months old, babies begin to produce recognizable syllables such as *ba*, *ma*, and *da*. Within 2 months, most babies will begin to reduplicate these sounds, creating *baba*, *mama*, and *dada*. Many parents will hear these combinations of sounds as words, but it is unlikely at this point that babies intend any meaning. Rather, they are rehearsing the sounds they hear and are beginning to differentiate those that correspond to the language around them from those that do not. During the final stage of babbling, babies begin to create two-syllable utterances (some of which may be words) by adding one syllable to an entirely different one, thus producing forms such as *ma me*. In most children, this final stage of babbling occurs around 10 months and is coincident with first words.

The Importance of Babbling

Although it is hard to say with any precision exactly how babbling relates to later language development, much of what we know about babbling in infants constitutes evidence that it does play an important role. We know that

- babbling gives babies practice in using the articulatory system—especially the mouth, tongue, and lips—that they will eventually use to talk;
- early babbling sounds pretty much the same all over the world;
- children who are deaf do babble, but they tend to start a little later. If their parents sign to them, they may start to "babble" with gestures; and
- one of the first identifiable speech sounds is m, a sound that a contented baby can make while nursing.

To hear different kinds of babbling sounds, go to the Weblinks section at the end of the chapter and find the link under "Babbling."

First Words

Babbling is articulatory practice for producing real words, but using real words intentionally to express meaning is a result of the categorization and concept development that has been going on since birth, as we learned in Chapter 5. The age at which children begin to produce real, intentional words varies, but it is usually around 1 year, although there is no cause for concern if the first words do not appear until 16 or even 18 months. Some infants simply take a longer time with warm-up and rehearsal, and there is undoubtedly a great deal of categorization conceptualization going on as well, learning that is important to language acquisition but which is unobservable. Whatever language the child speaks, the first words will be concrete content words (*mama, cookie, doggy*). That is because children's first words tend to grow directly out of their experience.

Researcher Margaret Harris and colleagues (Harris, 2004) studied four children from the age of 6 months until 2 years old to determine how their first words were used and, in particular, the degree to which they reflected their mothers' use of the words. They asked parents to keep a word diary for each child, recording the use and context of each word. The researchers also filmed interactions between the mothers and children at 2-week intervals. Once they were sure that a child was using a word and not just babbling, they examined the mother's utterances over the previous month to discover how many times the mother had used the word and the context in which she had done so. Studying a total of 40 words, they discovered that in 33 instances, the child's use was identical to the

mother's, and in only 3 instances out of the 40 did the child's use bear no resemblance at all to the mother's. In an earlier study, Harris had concluded that "78 per cent of maternal utterances to 16-month-old infants referred to objects on which the child was currently focusing attention" (Harris, 2004). Therefore, it is not surprising that children's first words are so firmly rooted in their interaction with the world around them. These words are usually the names of familiar objects or persons—*mama*, *daddy*, *nana*, *cookie*, and *jump*. At this stage, the sounds of those words may be imperfect, as we saw in Chapter 3. Isabelle, for example, could articulate *mama* and *daddy* almost perfectly, but *nana* (for banana) left off the first syllable. *Cookie* was pronounced "kookoo" and *jump* was "yum."

When children begin to use a word, often they will use it only in a single context. Margaret Harris gives the example of a child named James who "initially used the word *mummy* only when he was handing a toy to his mother and *there* only when pointing up to a picture on a frieze" (Harris, 2004, p. 85). Not all early words are used in limited contexts, however. One of the most common examples is the word *more*, which children often use in a variety of contexts—to request another cookie, more milk, or the repeat of an activity.

Eager to learn to walk, this child gets some assistance from an adult. Walking and talking are similar in this way—a little assistance is useful but not required.

Blue Jean Images/SuperStock

6.3 From 1 to 2 Years

The second year of life is a period of rapid cognitive growth. Children love to play hide-the-object games, and at the beginning, they will always look in the same place. They learn to pass an object from one hand to the other when offered a second object, and this ability, called **crossing the midline**, is considered to be a significant neurological development. Perhaps the most impressive growth of all, however, comes in the toddler's developing language.

12 to 18 Months: Vocabulary Expansion

Language lies quietly in wait during the first twelve to eighteen months of a child's life. Though you can see only the merest hints of it in infancy, it grows like an air bubble submerged deep in the sea, rising and expanding until finally, somewhere in the middle of the second year, it explodes at the surface for all to hear. (Eliot, 1999, p. 168)

Language production and learning typically pick up during the 12–18 month stage, especially in girls.

Tetra Images/Corbis

From the first birthday onward, word learning proceeds rapidly in both boys and girls, although as we saw in Chapter 5, the growth spurt usually happens about 2 months earlier in girls. Girls seem to understand and to produce more words than boys and do it faster. In later years, the boys will catch up, and they are busy acquiring other kinds of cognitive advantages at the same time. Not all boys will exhibit slower word acquisition, nor will all girls excel; there is a wide range of normal.

At 16 months, Janet had a productive vocabulary of 24 words. By the time she was 18 months old, she could say more than 60. After that, her mother reports, Janet added words so fast that she gave up counting. During the 2 months in which she more than doubled her vocabulary, Janet was doing much more. Table 6.1 illustrates some of the changes that were occurring in Janet's language. At 16 months, she showed a strong preference for open syllables (consonant-vowel CV), and her principle means of producing two syllable words was reduplication (the repetition of a sound segment, particularly a syllable). We see that process in *bottle*, *Mummy*, *Daddy*, *bubbles*, and *cookie*, although not in *window*. By 18 months, however, this process almost entirely disappeared, and her pronunciation more closely resembled adult forms.

Table 6.1: Changes in Janet's use of selected words, 16–18 months

Word	Pronunciation at 16 months	Changes at 18 months
wheel	wee-oh	wee/wee-oh
bottle	ba-ba	ba -doh
gurgles (her teddy bear's name)	ga-ga	gur-goh
Mummy	mum-mum-mum	mum-mum
juice	doo	doos
no	no	no
daddy	da-da	daddy
bird	buh	buh
cat	da (/dæ/)	ka (/kæ/)
more	mo	more
go	doe	go
stop	bop/top	top
street	dee	teet
bubbles/water	buh-buh	buh-boo
window/door	wee-moo	win-oe (/wino/)
shoe	doo	soo
pie/cake/pudding	by	by
Janet	da (/dæ/)	shanet
cup	guh	gup
diaper	dye	dye-puh
cookie	koo-koo	cookie
Matthew (her brother)	du	ma-du

In this short 2-month period, Janet's overgeneralization of words such as *pie*, *bubbles*, and *window* had disappeared as she refined the concepts those words represented. Other changes occurred during this period: Her vocabulary more than doubled, and her pronunciation became less infantile. She added a number of verbs such as *jump*, *see*, and *go*, and her pronunciation of her brother's name changed from a single syllable to two, more closely approximating the adult pronunciation. At this point, it was possible to get an accurate measure of Janet's vocabulary because her mother kept complete records of the words she used and appeared to understand. See *How Adults Help Children Learn to Communicate* for a description of how vocabulary size is estimated in young children.

How Adults Help Children Learn to Communicate

Different kinds of interactions are useful at different stages in a child's development. Look at Table 6.2 and explain what each interaction helps the child learn.

Table 6.2: Children's interactions, 0–3 years

Age	Type of Interaction
0–6 months	• Respond to crying and other vocalization with language. • Talk face-to-face so that baby can see facial expressions. • Talk frequently during baby's waking hours, describing what is happening as the child is being fed and dressed. • Name and describe common objects. • Respond to the baby's expressions—laugh when the baby laughs and express concern when he cries. • Recite rhymes and sing songs. • Hang photographs where the infant can see them, and describe what is pictured. • Use both languages if either parent is bilingual.
6–18 months	• Continue to respond to nonverbal vocalizations with language. • Continue to talk frequently in a conversational tone. • Continue to talk face-to-face so that baby can see expression. • Continue to name common objects. • Identify actions with verbs—running, walking, etc. • Point out attributes of objects—the big blue truck or the ball is round. • Introduce the notion of same and different and the appropriate language—See, this cup is the same as this one. This Princess fork is different from the Mickey fork. • Label and discuss feelings—I know you feel sad because Nana went home; Are you sleepy? • Read short simple children's books at bedtime and other times, if possible. • Encourage baby to turn the pages of books being read to him. • Concentrate on rhyming stories and games. • Encourage child to play with building blocks and other small objects, thus helping to build hand-eye coordination and fine motor coordination needed later for writing. • Ask baby to point to real-world objects pictured in books, on cards, or in photographs. • Read the same story repeatedly. • Read aloud in an expressive manner. • Continue using two languages if bilingual. *(continued)*

How Adults Help Children Learn to Communicate *(continued)*

Table 6.2: Children's interactions, 0–3 years *(continued)*

Age	Type of Interaction
18 months–3 years	<ul><li>Continue to talk frequently in a conversational tone.</li><li>Continue to talk face-to-face so that baby can see expression.</li><li>Expand the names of objects that are identified—light switch, garage door, necklace, etc.</li><li>Continue to identify actions with verbs—running, walking, etc. and expand to include adverbs—running fast, walking slowly, jumping high.</li><li>Point out attributes of objects—the big blue truck or the ball is round—and expand the adjectives used—skinny dog, fluffy bear.</li><li>Ask child what the attributes are—is the bear big or little?</li><li>Deliberately use comparatives—Is this ball bigger than that one? or Which boy is taller?</li><li>Continue to label and discuss feelings—I know you feel sad because Nana went home; Are you sleepy?</li><li>Read children's books with rhymes or short memorable stories, and good colorful illustrations.</li><li>Use books with one or two sentences per page and continue to encourage child to turn the pages.</li><li>Continue to read favorite books and stories, but try to introduce a new one each week.</li><li>Encourage child to participate in reading process by asking, "What do you think the Princess will say?" or "And then what happens?" This also helps to develop memory.</li><li>Be attentive to what the child wants to talk about, listen and engage in conversation meaningful to him.</li></ul>

Janet's language development was typical of children her age, although it would be a mistake to assume that every child learns in exactly the same way. For example, most children prefer the CV syllable during this stage, but VC syllables are not uncommon. As shown in Table 6.1, children during the 16–18 month period begin to produce words that are more recognizable as they refine the sound system. They also begin to refine the meanings so that they, too, conform more closely to adult usage.

18 to 24 Months: More Words and Beginning Sentences

For most children, and especially girls, the period from 18 months to 2 years is marked by very rapid vocabulary expansion. The words they learn will more closely resemble adult pronunciations, although there will still be many developmental forms, or those imperfect pronunciations produced by children in the process of learning the sound system.

One of the most significant language developments of the 18–24 month stage is the emergence of sentences.

Exactostock/SuperStock

Perhaps the most notable change during this period, however, is the emergence of sentences. Janet, the child represented in Table 6.1, produced her first two-word sentence at 18 months when she said "no nap." In general, the sentences children create during this time are of five types, although not all children will produce all five types during this period:

1. agent performing an act
2. action affecting an object
3. location of object
4. person or object described
5. negative, plus action or object

Table 6.3 illustrates these five kinds of sentences with exemplars produced by Juan at 22 months.

Table 6.3: Juan's first sentences, 22 months

Agent performing an action	Action affecting an object	Location of object	Person or object described	Negative, plus action or object
Doggie eat.	Kick ball.	Cookie there.	Juan cold.	No go.
Mommy jump.	Hit ball.	Doggie there.	Doggie hungry.	No Cheerio.
Baby cry.	Get Teddy.	Daddy home.		
	Drink milk.			
	Read book.			

Although the first two-word utterances tend to be of the type shown in Table 6.3, some children will begin to use two-word noun phrases in expressions such as *bad doggie* or *big boom.*

Meaningful interactions with people that expose children to language—like story time—provide motivation for toddlers' earliest sentences.

Joel Sartore/National Geographic Stock

Usually, by 18 months, and almost always by the age of 2, most children will have a productive vocabulary of about 60 words, and many will have more. They will also have begun to combine them into sentences such as those in Tables 6.1 and 6.3. What about those who do not?

Language Delay

As discussed earlier in the chapter, Harris and her colleagues' research revealed the concrete nature of mothers' language with their children. In a follow-up study, the researchers compared mothers' speech with their children whose language was developing typically. These children's speech was compared with the speech used by mothers with 2-year-old children who appeared to be language-delayed. **Language delay** refers to language that is developing in the normal sequence but slower than expected. In a 2-year-old, language delay is assessed mostly on the basis of words produced, and is referred to as **speech delay** (see *Speech Versus Language Delay*). In mothers of children deemed to be developing normally, mothers' speech referred to concrete objects that the child was attending to 78% of the time. In contrast, in the speech of mothers of children deemed to be language delayed, less than 50% of their speech referred to objects to which their children were attending. When the researchers took a closer look at the way the mothers of children with typical language development referred to the objects, nearly half of the mothers' utterances contained at least one specific object name. Mothers of children with language delay, however, made specific object references only 25% of the time. Moreover, these mothers were more likely to refer to these objects using generic names such as *one* or *thing* rather than specific names such as *teddy* or *truck* (Harris, 2004; Harris et al., 1988). So is there a direct relationship between the mothers' speech and children's language development?

Speech Versus Language Delay

When a child is not speaking by the second birthday, parents may begin to worry that the toddler has a speech or language delay. If they have another child who had begun speaking earlier, they are especially concerned. At that point, they might not know which, if either is causing the child's failure to produce words. But there is a difference between a speech delay and a language delay.

Speech delay refers to a delay caused by a developmental problem with the speech mechanism—lungs, vocal cords, tongue, teeth, lips. Tracy, at age 4, could not accurately reproduce all the consonants of English. *Shoe* sounded like *Sue* but might also be confused with *zoo* or *juice*. In all other ways, though, she seemed normal. Her comprehension was excellent; she appeared to know a great many words and became frustrated when she was misunderstood or when people corrected her. When her parents took her for an evaluation, the speech therapist examined her mouth and determined that there was a simple physical reason for her pronunciation problems—the membrane under the tongue extended too far toward the tip of the tongue. A simple procedure called a tongue-clip remedied the situation, and after a few months of speech therapy, Tracy's speech was normal.

Language delay refers to the condition in which a child fails to develop language abilities more or less on the developmental timetable outlined in this chapter. It refers specifically to a delay in the development of the underlying knowledge of language. Children with language delays are also likely to have speech delays, since the underlying system has not yet formed. Language delays can affect the comprehension of language, the production of language, or both. It is a risk factor for other kinds of developmental delay. Both speech and language delay will be discussed further in Chapter 9.

It appears that the language-delayed children had a slower rate of word learning because they had less experience of the kind of concrete, object-centered speech than their peers. Why? One possibility is that there is a difference in language ability between the two groups of children, and the mothers adjusted their speech according to the responses they observed in their children. But a second possibility exists, namely that differences in maternal speech are responsible for the difference in language ability. Other researchers have confirmed that while children are greatly dependent on concrete language "input" as they learn their first words, they become less dependent on the nature of the input in later stages, presumably because later learning is more dependent upon internal cognitive development (Bloom, 1973; Dromi, 1987, 1993, 1999). We certainly cannot draw any conclusions about the causes of language delay from these data, but they do point to a strong connection between the language environment and children's early language learning. This connection likely diminishes over time but probably extends well into the school years.

6.4 From 2 to 3 Years

Between their second and third birthdays, children leave infancy behind. They have begun to develop a stronger sense of self and to separate more easily from parents. They are capable of expressing a wide range of emotions, and frequently do, without being able to control those emotions. They may object to changes in routine. They are highly mobile with rapidly developing large motor skills, and their play with other children seems to be more "parallel" than interactive. In other words, children of this age may play alongside each other, but until close to the third birthday, there is not much interaction between the children. During this time they

Parallel play—where children play near but not with one another—is common among children in the 2–3 year range.

Associated Press

- climb on playground equipment, furniture, and up stairs with ease;
- walk up and down stairs, at the beginning by placing both feet on each step and then by alternating feet and holding onto a rail, hand, or wall;
- run easily;
- pedal a tricycle; and
- maintain balance while bending over.

Their fine motor coordination has also improved, and during this year, they

- make vertical, horizontal, and circular strokes with a crayon or pencil;
- turn the pages of a book;
- build towers of six or more blocks; and
- turn rotating handles and screw and unscrew jar tops.

Cognitively, children between 2 and 3 years demonstrate a great deal of growth and proficiency as they play. They can

- match a real object with a picture in a book;
- engage in make-believe with toys, animals, and people (girls may be better at this than boys at this age);
- sort objects by color;
- complete puzzles with three or four pieces;
- understand the concept of "two";
- make most mechanical toys work (boys may be better at this than girls at this age);
- recognize and identify most common objects and pictures;

- know the difference between males and females; and
- understand physical relationships such as those expressed by *on, in, above*, and *under*.

At this stage, observing the relationship between cognitive and linguistic development is easy. The appearance of personal pronouns corresponds with the growing awareness of self versus other, and the appearance of prepositions indicates their growing awareness of physical and spatial relationships. In general, children between 2 and 3 understand most sentences, say their name, age, and sex; and as they approach their third birthday, they speak clearly enough for strangers to understand most of their words.

Morphological Development and Longer Sentences

In the third year of life, children are very busy language learners. They continue to work toward mastery of the sound system, their sentences become longer and more complex as they learn to express more complex meanings, and there is marked growth in morphological development. Suddenly, at around the age of 2, the negative, as well as the word *mine*, become very prominent parts of children's speech. Parents will hear both *no* or *not* appended to almost any word in their children's vocabulary as they become more assertive in expressing their views. *Mine!* demonstrates an awareness of self and asserts the child's ownership and individuality. The vocabulary children use during this period will increase to between 50 and 300 words, and as words are added, there will be evidence of more abstract cognitive development. For example, a child who goes to the closet, retrieves mittens and says, "Me go bye-bye," is not reporting on an action but expressing a wish, and the child who says, "No go bed," is not expressing a reality but an intention.

Growth in the Sound System

Phonological development proceeds rapidly during this period, although there is still much to be learned. Children begin to master more syllable shapes; although CV syllables still dominate, consonant-vowel-consonant (CVC) and vowel-consonant (VC) syllables are not uncommon. Certain infantile pronunciations will remain because children at this age are not yet cognitively mature enough, nor are their articulators mature enough, to reproduce the sounds of the language perfectly. Instead, they simplify adult sound sequences to those they can manage. These **simplification processes** are not random but are governed by three universal processes:

1. **Consonant reduction**. This refers to children reducing the number of consonants in a syllable. The preponderance of CV syllables occurs, in part, because children reduce consonant clusters or even syllable-final consonants, producing, for example, cool or coo for "school."
2. **Assimilation**. This refers to making a sound more like another one in a word. Assimilation is very common, especially in two-syllable words. When Janet pronounced doggie as gah-gee, she was making the first consonant more like the second one.
3. **Substitution**. This refers to replacing a difficult sound with one that is easier to articulate. An excellent example of this is the replacing of word-final /l/ with /o/ in words such as bubble (buh-bo) and little (lito).

These processes and the forms they produce are perfectly normal and, in most children, will disappear between 4 and 5 years of age if not before.

Growth in Syntax

Within a month or two of the second birthday, most children will produce three- and even four-word utterances. Children are able to produce many kinds of meaning with longer sentences. Typically, they include the semantic relationships shown in Table 6.4.

Table 6.4: Semantic relationships in children's sentences, 2–3 years

Semantic relationship	Exemplars
agent action object	Matthew eat cookie. Daddy chase doggie.
possessor possession place	My cookie there. Mommy's car here.
possessor possession attribute	My hands dirty. Mia's pool cold.
action attribute entity	Go big pool.
action entity place	See cake there. Bite me here.
negative agent action	Me no go!

As Table 6.4 illustrates, although there are missing words (relative to the adult form), word order is generally consistent with adult word order. One of the major indicators of syntactic growth to appear during this stage is the appearance of questions and negatives. *What this?* may be the question parents hear most often from their 2-year-olds, and it is indicative of their growing ability to elicit new information and new words; it is evidence of their active participation in language learning.

Growth in Morphology

Before the age of 2, most children's speech is devoid of grammatical morphemes (Chapter 2). We have seen how their vocabularies tend to be grounded in the here and now; and when their sentences consist of only two words, it is not surprising that grammatical information is left out. As they become more adept at creating longer sentences, however, they begin to show some grammatical awareness. One of the first grammatical morphemes to appear is the -ing, or progressive, morpheme followed closely by the first person possessive. It is not hard to imagine why these appear early. The progressive -ing morpheme is usually associated with action (Matthew jumping!), and the possessive is highly relevant to a toddler because it is used to assert ownership. Other grammatical morphemes may also appear in this period. Some children at this stage use the plural form on nouns, especially in words like *shoes*, possibly because the plural is heard more often than the singular. The only plural inflection Janet used was the -s on *shoes*, and she used the third person possessive ("Mummy's juice") when she was 2 years, 7 months old (Piper, 2007).

The first 3 years are a time of rapid language and cognitive growth. The quality of children's interactions with adults can have a very positive impact on their learning. *How Vocabulary is Measured* provides some examples of how adults help children learn during this period. It is important that they do so because the next year will bring another period of rapid growth as the toddler transforms into a preschooler whose world will continue to expand.

How Vocabulary Is Measured

Estimates of children's knowledge of vocabulary vary widely. Different researchers and psychologists report different numbers. Some of the difference is attributable to the confounding of productive and receptive vocabulary, but another cause is the different methods for estimating children's vocabulary.

To measure vocabulary in adults, methods usually involve sampling—a person is given a list of 100 or more words and asked to mark those he knows the meanings of. The sample is deemed to be representative of the entire lexicon, or dictionary, and the researcher computes the resulting score into a proportion of the whole dictionary. Such techniques do not work well with very young children. How *do* we determine a child's vocabulary? For the most part, researchers use parental reporting in one of two forms:

- Researchers use parental journals in which a parent keeps a record of everything an infant says and appears to understand. It becomes much more difficult to keep up as the child becomes more proficient.
- They also use parental report forms. These are similar to the sampling techniques used for adults, but with the parents doing the reporting. These tools include vocabulary estimators that require a parent to view a list of words and indicate which words the child knows. Depending on the measure being used, the list can be very short or very long. In general, the longer the list, the more accurate the estimate is considered to be. See Weblinks at end of this chapter for more on this.

During this year before their third birthday, children make huge strides toward becoming proficient language learners. They will be far from perfect, but their developmental errors illustrate that they are actively acquiring the words, sounds, and sentence structure of their language. Take Oliver, for example. He is playing outside with his mother, when the following exchange occurs:

> *Mother : That spider has only five feet!*

> *Oliver: Dat pider have fie feets!*

Figure 6.1 breaks down Oliver's language rules in progress.

Figure 6.1: Oliver's language rules in progress

Phonologically	**Morphologically**	**Syntactically**
• Replaces /th/ sound with /d/, which is easier to pronouce • Reduces cluster /sp/ to a single consonant /p/ • Changes the syllable structure of *five* from CVC to CV	• Ignores 3rd person form and produces *have* • Adds regular plural suffix to feet, which is already plural	• Produces perfectly ordered sentence

This figure shows that a very complex set of rules work together to enable Oliver to complete his sentence: *Dat pider have fie feets, or "That spider has five feet."*

6.5 From 3 to 4 Years

During this pivotal year, the toddler transforms into a preschooler. The "terrible twos," during which toddlers display frequent emotions, gradually subside, and children begin to show more control over emotions. The parallel play that younger toddlers engage in is replaced by a willingness and ability to play with others in small groups, and they begin to grasp the notion of turn-taking. Children of 3 to 4 have a greater sense of personal identity. In terms of their physical and motor development, they

- eat independently using utensils;
- put away their toys;
- undress themselves independently; and
- dress themselves with a little assistance, in part because their fine-motor skills have improved and they can snap, zip, and manage buttons with greater ease.

At the same time, their cognitive development is advancing quickly, and during this time, they

- understand and follow simple rules;
- follow simple requests or commands, usually with little resistance;
- recognize and name colors and shapes;
- name almost all their body parts;
- match sequences of three to six items;

Learning to get dressed is a pivotal accomplishment in this boy's development, marking both fine and gross motor coordination as well as increasing independence.

Exactostock/SuperStock

- count to 10 or higher;
- understand the concept of same and different;
- comprehend opposites—up and down, in and out, etc.
- sort items by color, shape or size; and
- categorize items according to function (shoe and sock, plate and spoon, ball and glove).

During this year, it becomes increasingly evident that cognitive and language development are interdependent. Table 6.5 (in the next section) shows the principle differences between a 3- and a 4-year-old in language ability. Remember that these milestones apply to most children, but every child will vary somewhat from these expectations.

Children show rapid growth in all aspects of language during the year between their third and fourth birthdays. They combine words into longer sentences, conveying more complex thoughts and relationships. They gain greater control over pronunciation, and they show signs of learning the rules of morphology—plurals, possessive and past tense, for example. But perhaps the greatest change is in the expanded functionality of language.

6.6 From 4 to 5 Years

By the time Kai, whom we met earlier in this chapter, celebrated his fifth birthday, he weighed 40 pounds and had achieved considerable cognitive and linguistic growth. Like all typical 5-year-olds, Kai's physical development included the following:

- 20/20 vision (unless otherwise impaired);
- improved coordination, especially apparent in skipping, hopping, and jumping;
- better balance, allowing him to balance while standing on one foot with eyes closed;
- increased skills with crayons, pencils, and simple tools;
- well-established handedness;
- ability to color within lines;
- ability to copy a triangle;
- ability to spread with a knife; and he
- may have begun to lose baby teeth by the end of this year.

Both the cognitive and linguistic development exhibited by a 5-year-old are profound; they are also difficult to separate given the tandem identity of cognition and language. We learned in Chapter 5 of the close link between cognition and language. In particular, memory capacity and memory strategies are closely related to the ability to learn language. At age 5, Kai was much better at remembering and retrieving information, thus all aspects of language seemed to expand. His language was typical of other children his age. Like other children his age, Kai's ability to learn new words and expressions seemed boundless during the year between 4 and 5.

Five-year-old children are becoming more social. They have friends outside the family, and they are better able to play with and integrate into small groups of children. Language learning continues, but from age 5 onward, it happens within a larger social sphere. With the structural building blocks in place, children begin to learn to use language appropriately in a wider variety of settings and for a broader range of purposes, as we will see in Chapter 7.

Bilingual Children

Before the age of 5, bilingual children have essentially acquired two first languages. This is not to say that all bilingual children will have achieved equal competence in both, but they have activated the same processes for learning them. To get an accurate measure of a bilingual child's language development, it is necessary to evaluate *both* languages. For example, Sarah, at age 3, had an English vocabulary of around 600 words, which would appear to lag behind the norm (Table 6.5). But Sarah is bilingual, and in French, she had 600 or more words. Therefore, her vocabulary size is 1,200 words. Similarly, while she appeared to be confused by *why* questions in English, at age 4, she handled similar questions much better in French.

These bilingual children may not have yet achieved equal competence in both their languages, but with proper instruction and some time they will catch up with their monolingual peers in English.

Associated Press

In most instances, it is not possible to get an accurate estimate of the development of a bilingual child's two languages. The number of variables makes it too difficult to estimate—all of the different ages at which learners begin the second language, the different languages and settings involved, and the different levels of proficiency achieved, but as we will see in Chapter 9, it is especially important to look at the bilingual's total accomplishment, especially if there is any suspicion of language or speech delay. What we need to remember too, is that bilingual children have a cognitive advantage, as we saw in Chapters 4 and 5. If they appear to lag behind, this advantage will help them to catch up in the dominant language when the time is right.

Table 6.5: Language abilities, 3–5 years

3-year-olds	4-year-olds	5-year-olds
Speak clearly enough for strangers to understand.		
Vocabulary of 1,000 words.	Vocabulary of up to 2,000 words.	Vocabulary of more than 4,000 words, growing to 6,000 words by end of this year.
Speak in sentences of three or four words.	Speak in sentences of five or six words.	Longer sentences with greater complexity.
Sing simple repetitive songs.	Remember and recite rhymes and simple songs.	Repeat more complicated songs and rhymes.
May experience some difficulty in turn-taking in conversation. May change topics abruptly.	Engage in conversational turn-taking and can sustain one topic longer.	Follow directions and can give simple directions (e.g., "put your books away").
Struggle with some word pronunciations, especially those with three or more syllables and with consonant clusters.	Have mastered most of the sound combinations of the language. May still have difficulty with consonant clusters.	Some consonant clusters and multisyllable words may cause some problems.
Ask questions with who, what, where and why but may not always be able to answer such questions.	Often able to answer who, what, and where questions, but may still have difficulty with why.	Can answer why questions. Ask more probing questions, addressing meaning and purpose.
Will overuse words such as because, but, and when.	Will still overuse because and show confusion in the use of because (e.g., "Mia hit me 'cause she hurt me!")	Increasingly self-correct.
May have some difficulty with appropriate use of before, after, and until.	Show better understanding of before, after, and until, but still have difficulty, especially with until.	Understand before, after, and until, and generally uses them correctly, but until age 6, may struggle with correct use of until.
Can do simple sentence combining to link ideas, mostly using and ("I eat my lunch and I eat it all.")	Try to communicate beyond what vocabulary allows, creating new words or extending meaning of existing words.	Can recite full name, address, and phone number if taught.
Will resist talking in front of groups.	Will talk in front of small groups, with some reluctance.	More willing to speak in front of groups.
Is able to retell a simple story but may confuse the order or forget the point of a story, concentrating on favorite parts.	Can accurately retell a story with a sequence of four to five events.	Can tell a story and engage more meaningfully in conversation (see Chapter 7). *(continued)*

Table 6.5: Language abilities, 3–5 years *(continued)*

3-year-olds	4-year-olds	5-year-olds
	Use more advanced sentence structures such as relative clauses ("Sheepy ate the pancakes that Nana made") and tag questions ("It's pretty, right, Mommy?")	
	Have mastered some basic rules of grammar.	Most of the rules of grammar are in place. Can understand and use some passive constructions ("Sheepy got hit!" "It was ruined.")
Show interest in written materials, especially books.	May be able to identify some written letters, and may ask what a written word says.	Often able to identify written letters and numbers.

Conclusion

Chapter 5 examined development from the perspective of cognition, but because language and cognitive ability develop in tandem, it was necessary to talk about language. In this chapter, we examined development more directly from the perspective of language, although it is always necessary to contextualize linguistic development within children's physical and cognitive development. In particular, this chapter examined the developmental milestones in young children's lives with emphasis on the language learning that occurs between birth and age 5. Beginning with the precursory language behavior of infants, we have seen how children grow their vocabularies, learn to form sentences, and gradually become more proficient in understanding and using language. Language development in bilingual children under the age of 5 will follow the same path as in monolingual children, but their development is more properly assessed by considering both their languages. As we will see in Chapter 7, as children become more proficient with the "mechanics" of language, they are better able to acquire the social aspects of language. They are gradually learning how to use language for conversational purposes and how to construct narrative. These skills are necessary for their success in school and for establishing effective social skills throughout life.

Post-Test

1. Precursors to language like cooing and smiling differ from language in that they

   a. do not involve sounds.
   b. do not express affect.
   c. are not intentional communications.
   d. are not methods of communication.

2. Which of the following skills does NOT typically develop between 6 months and the end of the first year of life?

   a. pull up to standing
   b. respond to their own names
   c. imitate simple sounds and behaviors
   d. say simple common phrases

3. Many children use assimilation with

   a. one syllable words.
   b. two syllable words.
   c. three syllable words.
   d. four syllable words.

4. Syllable simplification occurs when children

   a. reduce the number of syllables in words.
   b. eliminate consonants within syllables.
   c. ignore syllables that are tough to pronounce.
   d. use fewer words in sentences.

5. Socially, 5-year-old children

   a. integrate into small groups.
   b. tend to play alone.
   c. engage in parallel play with other children.
   d. play in large groups of same-sex children.

6. Bilingual children

   a. must be equally competent in both languages.
   b. have used the same processes for learning both languages.
   c. are measured in terms of vocabulary in only one language.
   d. can accurately be measured for competence.

Answers

1. c. Are not intentional communications. *The answer can be found in Section 6.1.*
2. d. Say simple common phrases. *The answer can be found in Section 6.2.*
3. b. Two syllable words. *The answer can be found in Section 6.3.*
4. b. Eliminate consonants within syllables. *The answer can be found in Section 6.4.*
5. a. Integrate into small groups. *The answer can be found in Section 6.5.*
6. b. Have used the same processes for learning both languages. *The answer can be found in Section 6.6.*

Key Ideas

- Precursory language behavior includes crying and cooing and is important because they help the child to learn the purposes of language and to practice using the articulators.
- Precursors to language represent feelings and emotions and are not intentional, while true language is both purposeful and intentional.
- Babbling is the intermediate stage between nonintentional vocalization and intentional language. It is the "dress rehearsal" for true language.
- First words grow out of a child's experience and are concrete and referential, usually the names of objects, actions, or people.
- Children simplify the sound system in regular ways—by reducing the number of consonants in a syllable, by making a sound more like another, and by replacing a difficult sound with one that is easier to pronounce.
- Interactions with adults are profoundly important to children's preschool language and cognitive development, especially in the first 3 years.
- Language development in bilingual children must take into consideration their knowledge of both languages.

Critical Thinking Questions

1. What is the difference between precursory language behavior and true language? Why is it important?
2. Why should a preschool teacher be concerned about the difference between speech delay and language delay?
3. Consider these two sentences from Michaela:
   a. Age 4 years: "I miss you, Nana!" (spoken over the phone to her grandmother who had returned home after a visit).
   b. Age 4 years, 6 months: "I'm going to miss you, Nana" (spoken in person to her grandmother who was preparing to leave Michaela 's house to return to her own home).
   What cognitive understandings lie behind Michaela's first utterance (a)? In other words, what kinds of things does she know and understand in order to produce this sentence appropriately? Now, look at the second utterance (b). What additional cognition is revealed? What kind of linguistic growth is evident?
4. According to the data in Table 6.5, a 3-year-old has trouble using words such as *before* and *after* appropriately. What can you conclude about the conceptual learning that needs to occur before those words can be used appropriately?
5. A 4-year-old is "often able to answer *who, what* and *where* questions but may still have difficulty with *why*" (see Table 6.5). What might be the reason a 4-year-old has difficulty with "why" despite the fact that, at age 2 and 3, "why" would have been the most common question the child asked?
6. Look at the following dialogue between Domas and his father. Based on what you have read in Chapters 5 and 6, do you think Domas is closer to age 2 or 4? Answer in terms of cognitive and linguistic development.

Domas: Want kookoo.

Father: You want what?

Domas: Kookoo. Want kookoo.

Father: [Hands him a stuffed toy] You want Kitty?

Domas: No! Kookoo.

Father: Show me.

Domas: [Goes to pantry and tries to open door] There.

Father: Oh, you want something in there?

Domas: Yep.

Father: [Opens pantry] Show me.

Domas: [Points toward a box] Dat!

Father: Oh, you want a cookie!

Domas: Yep. Kookoo.

7. If a bilingual 4-year-old uses *casa* in an English sentence and *doggie* in a Spanish sentence, is this cause for concern? What does it tell you about bilingual language acquisition?
8. What is the importance of interaction with adults for children's language development?

Key Terms

affect Feelings or emotion.

assimilation Making the sounds in a word more like each other (*yellow* becomes *lalo*).

consonant reduction Reducing the number of consonants in a syllable (*stop* becomes *top*).

crossing the midline The point at which an infant learns to pass an object from one hand to another, indicating a significant neurological development.

language delay Language that is developing in the normal sequence but slower than would be expected.

precursory language behavior Infant vocalization such as crying and cooing, more related to emotional state than to intention to communicate.

simplification processes The processes by which children simplify pronunciation to forms their immature articulators can manage. These include consonant reduction, assimilation, and substitution.

speech delay A delay caused by a developmental problem with the speech mechanism—lungs, vocal cords, tongue, teeth, lips.

substitution Replacing a difficult sound with an easier one (*juice* becomes *du* or *dus*).

Weblinks

For an overview of child development, see
http://www.albertahealthservices.ca/1874.asp
http://www.wvdhhr.org/birth23/milestones.asp
http://www.dimensionsfoundation.org/media/Develomental_Milestones_3to5.pdf

Forms of peek-a-boo are seen in many cultures around the globe. To see how it is played in Japan visit http://www.worldofjapan.net/2011/05/inai-inai-ba-peekaboo/

For an overview of the stages of language acquisition, see
http://www.lsadc.org/info/ling-faqs-lang_acq.cfm

More on estimating vocabulary size is available at
http://babylab.psy.ox.ac.uk/research/oxford-cdi/vocabulary-size-estimator-1

For more on speech and language delay and disorder, see
http://www.med.umich.edu/yourchild/topics/speech.htm

7

Learning to Use Language

Learning Objectives

By the end of this chapter, you will be able to accomplish the following objectives:

- Explain what is meant by a language function, and describe the basic functions of language in the life of a preschooler.

- Identify the components of conversational competence.

- Explain why learning to construct a narrative through storytelling is important to children's academic success.

- Describe some of the cultural differences in how narratives are structured and the impact they may have on second language children in school.

Introduction

Four-year-olds Kam and Ari are both newcomers to their community, a suburb of Portland, Oregon. They attend a combined prekindergarten program with nine other children. Seven of the nine are monolingual English speakers, and the other two are bilingual in English and Spanish. Newly arrived in the United States, neither Kam nor Ari is yet fluent in English, although they are learning quickly. They began to attend the prekindergarten class in September, and by December, both children are functioning well. Kam no longer uses his native Tagalog in school—nobody else speaks it, and he has quickly learned to make himself understood in English and with gestures. Ari does not use her native Hebrew at all, but instead uses a mixture of English and, occasionally, Spanish that she has learned by playing with the two Spanish-speaking children.

At age 4, these children are well within the critical period for language learning, and their English language skills will continue to grow as the year progresses. Their teacher, wisely, has not sought to "teach" them English formally. Instead, she has used objects and visuals to make her meaning clear and, most importantly, she has provided a rich environment that invites the children to participate in storytelling and conversation, that, in short, exposes them to English for many different uses. From their perspective, learning language is not about learning nouns, verbs, plural endings, verb agreement, or the other grammatical paraphernalia that concern adults. Rather, they are interested in learning English in order to play with the children in their class and to fit in with the new world in which they find themselves.

Kam and Ari are biologically equipped to acquire language, and the environment they are in will provide the motivation, the language models, and the practice they need to activate the process. Although the acquisition of language is closely related to brain and cognitive development, children do not learn language just because they are biologically predisposed to do so. They learn language to communicate, and they learn to communicate in order to participate in the family and the broader social community. In fact, one of the major tasks of learning a language, whether first, second, or fourteenth, is learning to use the language appropriately. To do so, children have to learn to use language for a variety of purposes and in an ever-widening social circle. For Kam and Ari, the circle begins to widen in the prekindergarten class where they will start learning the language they need to serve their academic and increasing social needs.

In this chapter, we will take a closer look at what Kam and Ari need to learn by examining the functions of language that children need and acquire in their first 6 years. We will also take a close look at how children learn to construct narratives through hearing and telling stories, and why it is important for their academic and social lives. Finally, we will also consider what children have to learn in order to become competent conversationalists.

Pre-Test

1. "This my best drawing, right?" would be an example of the social subfunction
   a. to assert by threatening.
   b. to seek approval.
   c. to assert through argument.
   d. to criticize.

2. Some common cues given to listeners to signal that it is their turn to speak include all of the following EXCEPT to
   a. change vocal intonation.
   b. tell them it's their turn.
   c. ask a question.
   d. make eye contact.

3. A personal narrative is best defined as a/an
   a. account of procedures or recurring events.
   b. set of events experienced by the speaker.
   c. story that a child creates about herself.
   d. monologue that a child uses in make-believe.

4. The order and rate of language acquisition tends to
   a. take longer in less-industrialized nations.
   b. be faster in areas with access to adequate nutrition.
   c. differ in terms of order, but at similar rates.
   d. be the same regardless of location or culture.

Answers

1. b. To seek approval. *The answer can be found in Section 7.1.*
2. b. Tell them it's their turn. *The answer can be found in Section 7.2.*
3. b. Set of events experienced by the speaker. *The answer can be found in Section 7.3.*
4. d. Be the same regardless of location or culture. *The answer can be found in Section 7.4.*

7.1 Language Functions in Early Childhood

When it comes to describing what children accomplish when they learn language, it is useful to talk about how they learn words, grammar, and pronunciation. "Learning a language is not simply a matter of learning a system of rules for linking sounds and meanings: it is learning how to use such a system for communication" (Clark, 2004, p. 430). Moreover, to focus exclusively on describing the "nuts and bolts" would greatly underestimate their accomplishment because such descriptions cannot account for what children are able to *do* with language. It completes the language-learning picture to think also about and to categorize language according to the various functions it can and does serve in children's lives.

It is useful, especially for teachers of young children, because it helps them to assess language from a very practical perspective by considering not only whether a child knows a particular structure or vocabulary item but also whether a child is able to accomplish what he needs to with language.

For preschool children, much of language learning involves learning the social functions of language. They learn many of these while engaging in cooperative activities.

Associated Press

The Growth of Language Functions

As they grow and their network of friends and acquaintances extends beyond the home, children become far more sophisticated and resourceful in their uses of language. They continue to use it to categorize, and, as we have seen, it continues to facilitate cognitive development, but children also develop a broader inventory of uses. In very general terms, language serves to inform, to direct or command, and to express feelings, emotions, or beliefs. In order to analyze children's growth in language during the preschool years, however, it is necessary to further refine these broad functional categories. Several schemes have been developed for analyzing language functions into more precise categories.

In 1975, M. A. K. Halliday rebelled against the structural analyses of language popular in previous decades, especially the work of Noam Chomsky. Contending that these analyses completely missed the point of language—to make meaning—he built on the work of Roman Jakobson (1960), one of the earliest linguists to describe language in terms of function, to analyze children's language learning in terms of their expanding ability to create the different meanings needed in order to function socially and academically. He published an important book in which he eschewed use of the term *acquisition* in any description or discussion of children's language, arguing that the term suggested that language is a static product when it is more rightly considered a dynamic process. Rather, he asserted, what the child develops is *meaning potential*. Learning language, in his view, is the process of *learning how to mean*, which was the name of his well-known book on children's language development. Halliday identified seven functions (see Table 7.1), which later researchers refined into categories that were more useful to educators because they were developed specifically to assist teachers in working with children to develop and expand their uses of language (Shafer, Staab, & Smith,1983; Painter, 2005; Piper, 2007). The descriptions of language functions in this chapter draw upon the work of all these writers.

Table 7.1: Halliday's functional analysis of language

Function	Definition	Example
Instrumental	Language used to express a child's needs.	When 2-year-old Sarah told her mother, "want cancake," or when 4-year-old Kam said, "Get coat," to indicate that he wanted his coat so he could go outside.
Regulatory	Language used to tell others what to do.	When Ari told Kam, on their first day of prekindergarten to "go away!" she was attempting to regulate Kam's behavior.
Interactional	Language used to make and maintain relationships with others requires the interactional function.	When Kam said to Ari, "Do you want to play with this?" (handing her a toy car). When children say, "I love you, Mommy."
Personal	Language used to express feelings, opinions, or individual identity.	Isabelle, at age 4, was in time-out for pinching her baby sister when she asserted, "I'm NOT bad!"
Heuristic	Language used to gain knowledge about one's environment.	When Kam asked, "What he doing?" in reference to a picture of a man hang gliding.
Imaginative	Language used to tell stories and jokes and to create an imaginary environment.	When Ari said, "I am the princess Ari, and you can be the prince."
Representational	Language used to convey fact or information.	"That's a tractor," Maria explained to Ari while the two children looked at pictures in a book.

Are Language Functions Culturally Dependent?

Before we take a closer look at how language functions develop in young children, it is important to consider the role of linguistic and cultural diversity. The five functions that we will examine in detail in upcoming sections are likely universal, although that is an impossible hypothesis to test. We know that all children learn to function in language in these five broad categories. What differs, depending on language and culture, is the way those functions are realized or observed. For example,

These Quechua Indian preschoolers probably come from a different cultural tradition than you do, but they will still develop similar functions of language. Why is this significant?

Michael & Jennifer Lewis/National Geographic Stock

"Inuit children are deemed to have acquired their native language when they demonstrate their understanding by doing as they are told" (Piper, 2007, p. 237). Some Asian cultures share this belief. This means that in some situations, Inuit children's actions will speak louder than words in terms of evaluating their repertoire of functions. Alternatively, they might use different expressions than English-speaking children for a common function, or they might use no language at all. We have to be very careful in assuming what children do or do not know based on our observations if we do not share the same culture, and especially careful of reaching conclusions based on what they do *not* say. The failure to observe a child using a function does not mean that it does not exist in a child's repertoire. With these warnings in mind, let's look more closely at the five functions of language that develop in a child's first 5 years.

The Social Function

The **social function of language** is the way in which children assert and maintain social needs. When Andy, at age 2, says, "Want juice!" he is asserting a need. When his sister picks up his teddy bear and Andy insists, "That mine!" he is asserting his right to that toy. This is a broad category of use with many subfunctions. Following are five of the most common subfunctions:

1. To assert by threatening. "I'm gonna tell!" When Ari tells Kam that she is going to tell the teacher that he is throwing sand outside the box, she is using language to assert herself by making a threat.
2. To assert through argument. "It's not fair!" When a child says this, she is also asserting herself by making an argument.
3. To criticize. When Ari told her mother that the sweater her mother picked out for her "looks like a baby's," she was using language to criticize. When Kam said, "You're doing it wrong," he was using the same function.
4. To assert positive views. Ari was working with two other children in her class on an art project. When one of the other girls added a sparkly star to the collage they were making, Ari observed, "That looks pretty." This is an example of a child using language to state a positive opinion.
5. To seek approval. "Do you like this one?" or "I made it pretty, right, Papa?" are examples of language being used for social purposes, in this case to seek approval.

The Projecting Function

Projecting language is the function of language that allows a child to "live" the experiences of others, to enter into fantasy worlds and roles. Also called the imaginative function, it is the use of language to engage in make-believe or pretend. Children as young as 2 can be heard playing with toys and changing their pitch as they take on the role of a doll or an animal. Even before the words are intelligible, the child is using her voice to project into the role. Later, we hear expressions such as, "Mommy, Sheepy doesn't like chocolate!" which illustrates the child's beginning to reach outside her own identity. The following dialogue reflects this function in two 4-year-old girls:

Connie: I'll be the teacher and you be you.

Marissa: No, I'll be the teacher and you can be me.

Connie: No, I'm the teacher. [Changing her pitch to sound more authoritative] You sit down right now! Get out your crayons.

Marissa: I can't get my crayons. Shelby (her sister) broke them!

There is some evidence that boys and girls may differ in the kinds of pretend play they engage in and thus in the kinds of language that emerge. Researchers have found, for example, that preschool girls are more likely to engage in cooperative pretend play focused on daily events and more readily accept different roles, even those requiring gender shifts. Boys, on the other hand, tend to engage more in fantasy play involving objects or machines and are reluctant to assume female roles (Garvey & Kramer, 1989; Black, 1989; Muthukrishna & Sokoya, 2008).

Often children "talk their way through" tasks. These two are using language to help guide their actions in building their village. What functions of language are involved?

Hemera/Thinkstock

The Controlling Function

Controlling language is the language children use for controlling the self and others. When children direct the actions of others or their own in expressions such as, "Give me that, now!" or "Stop that, Cora!" they are attempting to regulate the actions of others. In older speakers, this function may be realized through a direct command or order, or through an implied one. "Water the flowers" is direct while "I think the flowers could use some water," is implied. In preschool children, however, the implied command is rarely heard, and children often do not interpret it correctly. In the following monologue, a child is regulating his own behavior as he builds a tower with interlocking plastic blocks:

Cameron, age 4 years, 9 months: This one goes like this. Then I can put this one here. The red one goes on the top. Where can I put the green one?

This is an example of a child using the controlling function as he monitors his own actions. It is very similar to what adults do when they "talk through" a complex task. The monitoring function of language is a good illustration of the interrelationship of cognition and language. Many kindergarten and first-grade teachers have observed that children are suddenly able to tie their shoes once they are able to talk themselves through it. Once they have sufficient language to construct the narrative, they can use that narrative to guide their own actions.

The controlling function of language has an even more important purpose than providing a means for getting things done: it plays an important role in learning. When language is used to teach oneself or to direct others in ways that facilitate understanding, it is assisting children to make sense of and to organize the world around them. Therefore, it is an important tool for early cognitive development.

The Informative Function

Informative language covers a number of uses of language, all related to conveying information, whether to the self or others. It encompasses, for example, the following uses of language:

- Commenting on past and present events. When Ari said, "I saw a big monkey at Jungle Island" (past), or Kam observed, "There's a fire truck!" (present), they were both using the informative function to make a comment.
- Labeling. Children hear a great deal of informative language in their early years as helpful adults teach them the names of objects. When Ari told Kam, "That's not a radio, it's an iPod," she was using the informative function to label something that was unfamiliar to Kam.
- Talking about a sequence of events. "We went to see the princesses on ice, and they skated around. Then the prince came and there was a party." Whenever children recount events, more or less chronologically, they are using informative language.
- Talking about details. When Ari described the new sweater she got for her birthday, she was using the informative function to provide detail: "It's pink but not really pink. Kind of white but a little bit pink."
- Making comparisons. When a child says, "I'm faster than Marco," or "Marissa is bigger than I am," she is using informative language to make a comparison.
- Generalizing. This is an important subcategory of the informative function for academic purposes. Sentences such as "The clouds usually mean rain is coming," and "Papa went too fast and so he falled down," demonstrate that a child has learned something about cause and effect.
- Requesting information. This is another subcategory of the informative function that is important for academic learning. Seeking information is one significant way a child learns about the world. "When are we going to the party, Mommy?" and "Is it time to go?" illustrate how the child asks what he needs to know.

Children hear a great deal of language used to inform, and they develop the ability to use it very early. Although the examples just given are all fully formed sentences, children demonstrate ability to use the informative function when they begin to learn words. They begin by labeling the objects in their environment, and this is the informative function.

When a 2-year-old points to an object that his mother names, he is demonstrating the informative function. More importantly, he is using language to help him learn.

Children use the informative function to test whether things are as they believe them to be and to question and discover. It thus plays a critical role in cognitive development and helping children to succeed in school because it is one of the most commonly used in classrooms. Language for forecasting and reasoning is another function important in the school years, but it is also important for cognitive development in younger learners.

The Forecasting and Reasoning Function

Forecasting and reasoning language allows children to express their curiosity and allows them to find out about the world. A toddler who asks, "Why?" or "Why can't I?" is seeking information as well as trying to understand the reason or cause for an action. This function operates in three ways:

1. To request information. The kind of information requested differs from what is requested in the previous informative function. In this case, children are not just seeking names of objects or actions. "Why can't I go?" is a question asked by a child who seeks to understand a cause or a reason. Understanding that she can't go outside to play because it is raining helps her to develop understanding of cause-effect relationships.
2. To predict an event. A child who says, "I think it's going to snow" is using language to predict. If the sky is grey and the wind is blowing, it is obvious that the child has made the prediction based on past experience. In other words, she has learned something about how one event often leads to another.
3. To forecast and reason. On the other hand, if the sky is bright and the sun is shining, or if the child lives in South Florida, and the child says, "I think it's going to snow," the usual response from an adult is to question the child: "Why would you say that?" or "What makes you think it will snow?" In drawing out the child's reasoning, the adult then has an opportunity to engage further with the child, offering possible alternative conclusions along with the language for those conclusions so that the child will come to understand the relationship between the color of the sky and the likelihood of snow.

This function of language gives children an extremely useful tool for coming to understand the world and how it works. It also provides valuable insights into the reasoning abilities of children. The following dialogue takes place between Jack, a few months before his 5th birthday, and his older brother Mark, 12. Mark has just received a new baseball mitt for his birthday and is not happy because his brother has been playing with it and apparently got paint on it.

Mark: You got paint on my glove!

Jack: Did not!

Mark: Yes, you did. Look! There's blue paint on it. And there's blue paint on your hands, too.

Jack: Nope. I didn't.

Mark: There's nobody else here, and there is paint on my glove.

Jack: Maybe you . . .

Mark: Don't be silly. I wasn't painting, and you were. And now there's paint on my new glove.

Jack: Maybe it fell in the paint.

Mark: Jack, how would it fall?

Jack: Well. Maybe we can wash it off.

Mark: Go wash your hands and if it comes off, we can try washing it off the glove.

Jack: Okay. [He starts to cry.] Don't tell Mommy!

Mark: I won't tell. Don't cry. Maybe it will wash off. We'll try.

At first, Jack tries to deny causality despite the evidence. He even looks for another explanation, and the fact that he does, shows another kind of causal reasoning—the glove might have fallen into the paint. We also see strong evidence that he understands cause and effect when he asks whether Mark will tell their mother. Jack and the other children we have met in this chapter are active language learners, learning to cope with the parts that make up language, from sounds through sentences. They are learning to use language in ways that accomplishes what they need to accomplish and which also advances their cognitive development. Children do not acquire language functions in a strictly sequential manner—there is overlap—but they do acquire them in roughly the order shown in Figure 7.1.

Figure 7.1: Order in which language functions are acquired

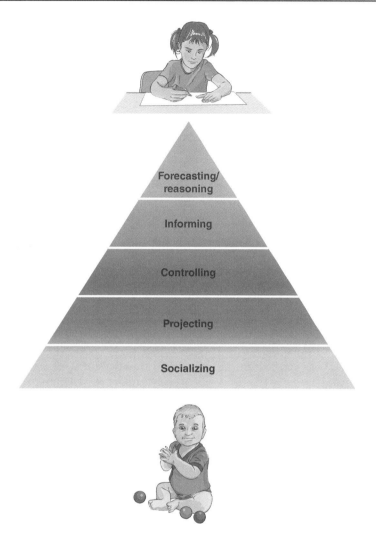

Children acquire language functions over time. The functions overlap one another but develop in the general order shown.

We have seen that learning a language involves learning the rules of that language and to use that language to carry out a variety of social and academic functions. Neither the rules nor the functions are learned in isolation. They are learned in social contexts, so learning a language means learning how to use language appropriately in a variety of social contexts. While they are still acquiring all of the building blocks we have been looking at, children must also acquire the skills needed for developing and maintaining social relationships. For preschool children, learning to match language use with social context involves acquiring two important skills—building conversational skills and learning to construct narrative. These skills begin to develop early, but most actively between the ages of 4 and 6.

7.2 Acquiring Conversational Competence

With a firm linguistic foundation in place and with rapidly advancing cognitive skills, children around the age of 4 begin to make very notable progress in the social uses of language. Their interactions with adults and other children reflect the progress they are making and what they have yet to learn. Much rides on the ability to use language appropriately, so we will take a closer look at how conversational and narrative skills are built.

What does learning conversational skills entail? Pioneers in automated telephone services have attempted to answer that question in order to improve the range of services an automated system can handle. Most of us have had the experience of trying to "converse" with a system that does not recognize or respond to more than very basic information gathering; it is unable to recognize anger or frustration. That is because it is difficult to program computers to recognize nuance, and yet a 6-year-old child must have mastered much of this nuance in order to get along with others That child will have to have acquired understandings about how conversations are structured. These elements of conversational competence include

In order to make his request to Santa, this boy will have to have acquired some level of conversational competence.

Cusp/SuperStock

- becoming sensitive to the listener's perspective;
- becoming skilled at taking turns;
- learning to make conversational repairs when there is a miscommunication;
- becoming sensitive to relevance;
- learning to interpret and to make indirect requests; and
- acquiring appropriate gender-based distinctions.

Understanding the Listener's Perspective

Sensitivity to a listener's perspective is a prerequisite for all conversation. It is also the skill on which all the other elements of conversational competence are built. Unless each participant in a conversation is aware of how much the other participants are paying attention or comprehending, it is impossible to structure his narrative or information appropriately.

A good indicator of whether or not children are aware of the listener's perspective can be found in the child's use of definite and indefinite articles. Look at the following pairs of sentences:

a. Pick up a toy and bring it to me.
b. Pick up the toy and bring it to me.

In (a), the speaker is introducing something unspecified, hence the use of the indefinite (meaning undefined) article, *a*. In (b), the speaker assumes that the listener knows the object referred to; in other words, it is assumed that the speaker and listener share the same referent for *toy*. In general, during the years between 4 and 6, children develop a fairly firm command of the definite and indefinite article, but they are not always reliable in using the indefinite article to introduce a new topic into a conversation. Consider the following conversation between Carmelita, age 4 years, 7 months, and her mother:

Carmelita: The boy gived me this [Holding up a sand shovel].

Mother: [Looking around] Which boy? What was his name?

Carmelita: I don't know. See, it's for digging up shells.

Mother: Can you show me which boy, so we can go thank him?

Carmelita: I don't know. One boy. I'm going to dig here.

This conversation isn't totally ineffective, but it does show how a 4-year-old may be referentially correct in the use of definite and indefinite articles but be conversationally confused. Had she begun "A boy . . ." instead of "The boy . . .," the focus would have been, as she intended, on the shovel.

Other indicators show that a speaker is unaware of or ignoring the listener's perspective. For example, some people habitually begin a narrative somewhere in the middle without providing sufficient information for the listener to know what the topic is. A friend of mine recently began a conversation like this: "I don't know what she was thinking of when she said that." It was a little like Carmelita in the previous example. I had no idea who "she" was or what she said. There were two options available to me. I could ask, or I could respond as though I knew. Most people would simply ask (assuming that they wanted to engage in this conversation). But some would respond, "I don't know either. What do you think happened?" hoping to pick up clues in the responses. Starting in the middle of the story is, thankfully, rarer in adults than in children, but in both cases, the cause is likely the same—the speaker has the information in her head and begins to speak aloud, starting to vocalize the narrative that has been running in her head without any real intent of engaging in conversation. It is more of a monologue than a dialogue. Whatever the reason, it shows little awareness of the listener and is not effective conversation.

Providing insufficient information for the listener is not the only kind of conversational malfunction. Sometimes speakers do just the opposite, providing excessive, redundant, or irrelevant information. Understanding the listener's perspective means being able to judge how much information a listener is likely to have and to need. It entails supplying sufficient information but not superfluous or redundant information. As children become more fluent in conversation, they learn to do **comprehension checks**. A comprehension check involves the speaker finding out whether the listener understands. Adults talking with young children do it routinely:

Grandmother: Would you go upstairs and get my phone?

Katrina: Okay. Where is it?

Grandmother: Go into my room. It is on the windowsill.

Katrina: Okay.

Grandmother: Do you know what the windowsill is? What part of the window?

Katrina: Like the shelf, under the window.

Grandmother: That's right.

Katrina, at 4 years and 6 months, has understood very well, but her grandmother checks anyway to make sure. Adults do this in different ways:

I was down at Buffy's by the Bay. You know, the rib place that used to be Shannon's? Right. So I was there on Saturday with my sister and her friend, Ruth . . .

Here, the speaker is aware that the listener might not know which restaurant she is talking about, and so she interrupts her story with a comprehension check, thus showing her sensitivity to the listener's perspective. One of the limitations on young children's ability to provide necessary information to a listener is the language required for doing so; it is impossible to provide the listener with information if the child's own understanding is lacking or she doesn't have the language for expressing it. As children gain more knowledge about the world, especially the world outside the home when they begin schooling, they gain the language they need to take the listener's perspective into account and make effective conversation. Being sensitive to the listener's perspective is closely related to another skill necessary for the development of conversational competence, turn-taking.

Turn-Taking

Turn-taking is necessary in advancing conversational skills for the simple reason that conversation is not a monologue. "Children need to get both the content and the timing of their turns right on each occasion, and this takes considerable skill. Each turn should be designed to add new information to what is already given" (Brown, 2003, p. 304). Children begin to learn turn-taking almost from birth. When parents respond to their babies' smiling, laughing, crying,

In class, it is easy to signal the wish to contribute to the conversation. In other situations, children must learn the more subtle rules for conversational turn-taking.

Associated Press

190

with language, they help to establish the patterns of turn-taking. Infants at the precursory stage of language development engage in a kind of turn-taking in their cooing interactions with their mothers or other caregivers. When they begin to babble, this turn-taking can also be observed when they stop and wait for a response. By the time children reach school age, they have become fairly adept at conversational turn-taking and even help to prompt it themselves.

There are two basic "rules" for conversation, both involving turn-taking. One is that only one person talks at a time, and the other is that there should be no prolonged silences. There are a number of ways in which turn-taking is accomplished in conversation. They include

- an "invitation" to comment, such as, "What do you think?" or "Don't you agree?" or "I can see you don't agree with me";
- asking a question such as, "Have you ever been there?";
- a change in intonation; and
- a direct gaze. Normally in conversation, people do not constantly look at each other, so a direct gaze invites a change of speaker.

Violations of turn-taking are more common in younger children. Children of 3 and 4 overlap or interrupt because they have trouble holding in memory what they want to say until there is an obvious turn-change opportunity. By the time they are 6, most children can hold their thought until an appropriate entry into the conversation appears. During this period, they also become increasingly adept at repairing turn-taking violations. A common repair is to stop, wait, and then repeat the last part of what they were saying before the interruption. Again, cognitive maturity makes it easier to remember where they were before being interrupted. A less effective repair, used more often by 3- and 4-year-olds than 6-year-olds, is simply to talk louder.

Making Conversational Repairs

Conversational repairs can occur only if the speakers are sufficiently aware of the other's perspective (i.e., that there has been a miscommunication). Consider these conversations:

Christian, age 3, and Sammy, age 5, are cousins. They are playing on their grandmother's porch. There is a basket of fruit on a table. Christian wanders over, picks up an apricot and shows it to Sammy.

Christian: This is peach. Little peach.

Sammy: No, it's not. It's called apricot.

Christian: [Looking carefully at it] Nope. Peach. Baby peach.

Sammy: No, it's not! It's called apricot. Grandma has a tree that grows them.

Christian: Grandma gots peach trees!

Sammy: Yep, but that's an apricot!

Christian: No, it's a peach, and you're stupid!

Sammy: You're more stupid!

In just a few months' time, Sammy will be able to accept the correction, but until then, more conversations will end in this way.

A child may not yet be able to say, "No, that's not what I meant," when an adult misunderstands their intent, but they do realize that a miscommunication has taken place and attempt to correct it. Consider the following dialogue between Carmelita, age 3 years, 10 months, and her mother:

Mother: [Holding up two sweaters] Which sweater do you want?

Carmelita: Don't want any sweater!

Mother: You have to have a sweater. It's cold outside.

Carmelita: But I don't like any sweater!

Mother: Okay, so let's go outside without a sweater.

Carmelita: But I'll be cold!

Mother: Yes, but you don't want to wear a sweater.

Carmelita: Yes, I do!

Mother: Well, here then.

Carmelita: No! I want a different sweater.

In this dialogue, Carmelita understands that a miscommunication has taken place before her mother does. The cause of the miscommunication appears to be her misuse of *any*—an older learner would say *either* or *either one*. More importantly, Carmelita repairs the conversation and makes her intentions clearer. At age 3, Carmelita would not have been able to advance the conversation but would have resorted to repetition to try to make herself understood. But here, at almost 4, she is able to change tactics. This ability represents a giant step toward conversational effectiveness. This corresponds with the increasing ability of a 4-year-old child to engage in cooperative play. During that cooperative play, children will also begin to develop their awareness of conversational relevance.

Sensitivity to Relevance

Relevance, broadly speaking, is the ability to stay on topic and contribute useful commentary. Learning topic relevance begins to develop around age 5 and continues well into the school years. In school, children learn that older children will be more likely to include them in their conversations if they introduce interesting and relevant topics, and if their contributions to conversations initiated by others are pertinent or useful. Topic relevance is a skill that some people never fully master. We all know people who begin to talk about anything that pops into their head without considering whether or not listeners will be interested.

The ability to contribute useful commentary is necessary for moving conversations forward. As with most language, this aspect of conversational competence is something that a child learns without being taught. Part of acquiring this ability is coming to realize that the child is not the only arbiter of what is relevant. Preschool children can often be heard engaging in parallel monologues, in part because they have not yet mastered the concept of topic relevance. Consider the following between two 4-year-olds:

> *James: I don't want to play dolls.*

> *Delia: I don't want to play trucks.*

> *James: Dolls are silly.*

> *Delia: Trucks are boring.*

> *James: Mom won't let me go outside today.*

> *Delia: My mom had to take her car to the garage.*

> *James: It's not fair.*

> *Delia: But it's broken!*

> *James: No it's not. See? [He holds up his toy truck.]*

Neither child is paying much attention to what the other is saying, so this extreme case of topic irrelevance can be thought of as dual- or parallel-monologues rather than as dialogue or conversation. In addition to being able to make relevant contributions to a conversation, children have to learn some of the more subtle ways in which others, particularly adults, communicate. The indirect request is a good example.

Understanding Indirect Requests

Understanding indirect requests is an aspect of conversational competence that makes one seem less authoritarian. Sitting in a cold room with a window open and wishing someone else to close that window, a young child will say, "Close the window," while an adult will usually say, "It's a little cold in here, don't you think?" Either way, the window will likely get closed, but the adult's form using the indirect request makes her seem less bossy. It is considered more polite. The indirect request has several forms, and some take longer to learn than others. Children as young as 3 or 4 tend to learn the declarative form, as in "The light is a little dim for reading" earlier than, "Would you mind sitting down?" which the child is more likely to take literally and might answer verbally. It is, however, somewhat difficult to determine how much or exactly what a child understands of such a request. If she sits down, it may be that she ignored everything except "sitting down," and made a good guess. By the time they are 5, most children are able to interpret "It's 8 o'clock" as a request to go to bed, if they know that to be their usual bedtime. Although they understand many forms of indirect requests before they are 6, most children do not use the form until sometime after the 6th or 7th birthday.

Acquiring Appropriate Gender-Based Distinctions

Understanding gender-based distinctions is an important component of acquiring sociolinguistic competence. Males and females differ in the vocabulary they use and in their style of speech, and there is little doubt that this difference is a result of socialization that begins at home and continues in school. Researchers have found, for example, that males are more assertive in their social interactions than are females (Cook, Fritz, McCormack, & Visperas, 1985). If there were not more similarities than differences in the speech used by males and females, communication between them would be more fraught with misunderstanding than it is already. Still, there are differences that appear very early. Girls tend to use language to negotiate closeness or establish a sense of belonging to a group, while boys are more likely to use it to negotiate status within the group. By the time they are 5 or 6, most children are using gender-appropriate language, and from the time they are about 4, their talk reflects the same kinds of difference in interest reflected in adult speech. Anyone who has tried to engage a 4-year-old boy in talk about princesses or a 5-year-old girl in the rules of football will have noted this early distinction. Not that it always holds true; children differ in their interests.

The conversation these children engage in might be thwarted by different interests as well as gender-based differences in conversational style. What other challenges might they encounter?

Associated Press

Conversation is only one of the sociolinguistic skills that children must acquire. The ability to construct a narrative, that is, to tell a coherent story, is important not only to success in school but to getting along in life.

7.3 Language and Storytelling

As we have seen in the examples in the previous section, effective conversation often entails the telling of a story. But generally speaking, conversation involves mostly dialogue, and the narrative is essentially a monologue. As such, the full burden for telling the story and making oneself understood rests on the speaker. Just about all children love to hear stories, but learning to tell them is also important. "Telling stories helps children frame their thoughts, emotions, and social-cultural identity" (Curenton, 2006, p. 1). Learning how narratives are constructed is an extremely important prerequisite skill for reading comprehension, writing, and oral language development. Storytelling is a skill that begins to develop between the ages of 2 and 3 and continues into the 11th year.

Three Types of Narrative

Children have to learn the components of a narrative as well as how they all fit together. There are three basic types of narrative: the script, personal, and fiction or fantasy (Pan & Snow, 1999; Piper, 2007). **Scripts** are generalized accounts of procedures or recurring events—how to make a sandwich, what to say when answering the phone, or what happens when a plane lands. The dialogue between Shelby, age 3 years, 6 months, and her teacher illustrates:

> *Teacher: Do you know your address, Shelby?*
>
> *Shelby: My what?*
>
> *Teacher: Do you know where you live?*
>
> *Shelby: Yes. In my house. My house is at 3124 Camelia Court in Rosedale. My phone number is 211-555-4545, and my daddy is Mr. Frank Carson, and my mommy is Sheila Carson.*

Shelby has provided much more information than requested, using a script that she has learned from her parents as a safety precaution.

Personal narratives recount particular events that the individual has experienced—an account of a trip to Disneyland, what happened at a birthday party, or going to the movies with Nana. When Kam came home from preschool, he told his father a story about a significant event in his day, with only a little prompting:

> *Kam: We went on the bus. But the bus breaked down because no air in tires.*
>
> *Father: There was no air in the tires? You mean, the bus got a flat tire?*
>
> *Kam: Yes! There was air and then no air and the tire went down. So we had to get off the bus.*
>
> *Father: You did? Where did you stand?*
>
> *Kam: We stood on the sidewalk. Close, so I got to watch. Then a truck came and two men came and they put a new tire on the bus.*
>
> *Father: They did? How did they do that?*

Kam: First, they had to make the bus go higher. So the man got a thing—I don't know its name—and made the bus go up high in the air.

Father: It's called a jack.

Kam: Jack? Okay. So the bus went up high in the air, and we had to stay on the sidewalk 'cause the bus might fall. Then they taked the old tire off and put a new one on. Then they made the bus go down again and we could get on. But we couldn't go to the 'quarium then 'cause teacher said it was too late.

Kam used personal narrative to tell his father about the school bus incident. Have you ever heard a child tell a story using personal narrative? What do you remember about it?

iStockphoto/Thinkstock

Kam was recounting a specific event that had occurred in his life, a personal narrative.

Fiction or fantasy is the genre of narrative that children use during make-believe. When they engage in make-believe, whether it is by playing dress-up and pretending to be Mommy or in creating a wholly fictional role, children expand their use of language to include the projecting, or imaginative function. The following exchange between Lily and Guy shows them engaged in fantasy and using the language appropriate to their roles.

Lily: I am the princess Prissy and you are the princess Pearl.

Guy: I'm NOT a dumb princess. I'm Superman.

Lily: There's no Superman in this pretend.

Guy: Well, I'm no princess.

Lily: You can be a prince, then.

Guy: No.

Lily: Prince Superman?

Guy: Okay. I'm Prince Superman! [He starts zooming around the room.] I am a prince and you are my prisoner.

Lily: I am not. I am the princess and you have to save me.

Guy: Are the bad guys after you?

Lily: Yes, and I'm scared!

Guy: Don't be scared! Superman to the rescue!

Lily: PRINCE Superman!

Storytelling Abilities, Ages 3–5

Children as young as 2 to 2-and-a-half can, with assistance, recount recurring events as long as they are fairly brief—what happens every day when they get to daycare, how to get dressed, or what happens when Daddy comes home. At first, their accounts will sound more like a personal narrative, but gradually they learn how to construct a general rather than a specific narrative, as shown in the following three narratives. Here, Isabelle explains how to build a snowman at three different ages/abilities:

> *At 3 years, 3 months: Roll up snow. Make big balls. Then put on top of. And Mommy putted hat on snowman and then put carrot for nose. Gived him nose carrot [Laughs at her joke]. Mommy help me because I little girl . . .*

> *At 4 years, 7 months: First, we roll up one ball. Then you roll up another ball and another one, too. And you have to put one on top and then one on the other top. Then you put buttons, but not real buttons, and a nose but not a real nose. You put on hat and scarf, but real.*

> *At 5 years, 9 months: Well, you have to make three balls with snow, but not the same size. I make the little one first 'cause that's the head, but you don't have to. Then you build the snowman by putting one ball on the other one and then the little one on top. Then you put on his face. You can use a carrot for the nose and nuts—*

At age 3, this boy's ability to build a snowman likely exceeds his ability to recount the experience later. By next winter, he will be much better at explaining how it's done.

Associated Press

> *walnuts or maybe another kind—for his eyes. Mommy let me put my scarf on him, and we used Papa's hat but you could use a girl's hat.*

The first account sounds more like a personal narrative, but she is actually explaining the process of building a snowman after being asked by her father. In the second, we see not only more detail but we see her using the "timeless" present tense to indicate that this is not an account of a particular event but a recurring event. By the time she is nearing her sixth birthday, Isabelle has started to use the general pronoun *you* and her timeline is perfect. Like Isabelle, most children are able to construct an intelligible and accurate script by the time they are 5 or 6.

Well before they reach school age, children begin to create their own imaginative tales using the devices they have heard in stories and will later encounter in print. These devices include openings, such as *Once upon a time . . .* or *There once was a . . .* as well as connectors such as *And then he said . . .* or just *Then . . . .* One of the prerequisites to constructing a fantasy narrative is the ability to take alternative stances. Starting around the age of 2, children can engage in make-believe with older speakers, but at first they do not initiate or use the linguistic indicators of pretense (changes in pitch to indicate different characters, for example). They participate, but the language is much the same as the language they use for real life. By the time they are school age, however, children are able to initiate fantasy and use a variety of means to shift characters. They also are able to signal shifts between real-world and fantasy talk, usually by voice pitch. Fantasy talk is normally delivered in a higher pitched falsetto voice. By this time, they will also have mastered the narrative structure. An effective narrative includes background, which may include information about the setting, the location, the characters, and any other relevant information needed to set the stage. The second component is the episode, which is the heart of the narrative. The episode contains information about the event that caused the main character in the narrative to act, the nature of that action, and whether or not the character succeeded in carrying it out. It will also normally include information about the consequences of the plan and the character's own feelings about the action or the consequences. When a listener is unable to understand or is confused by a narrative, it is usually because critical elements of the episode are missing.

In the dominant North American culture, children begin to construct stories around the age of 3. Their first structures lack setting or much organization. They provide little information, and the timeline will seem to be random. Gradually, they begin to organize their narratives chronologically and tell stories with a discernible beginning, middle, and end; but the plot will likely be thin or nonexistent, particularly if the children have not been exposed to a lot of stories. Around the age of 5, a rudimentary plot structure begins to appear, and by age 6 or 7, children begin to acquire the linguistic devices for carrying the plot forward.

> *Princess Angelina wanted to go to the party, but her mommy said, "No, you have been a very bad girl!" So Angelina started to cry, and her mother said, "Stop crying and clean up your room." So Angelina stopped crying and picked up all her toys. "I'm done, Mommy. Now can I go to the party?" "Not until you hang up your clothes," said her mommy. Then Angelina hanged up her clothes. But she didn't hang up her pink tutu because she wanted to wear it to the party. The end. (Maria, age 5 years, 7 months)*

Notice that Maria's story, while light on background information, has a clear temporal structure that is signaled by words such as *so, but*, and *then*. She also used prosodic changes to indicate the different speakers—Angelina had a high-pitched voice, and her mother had a lower pitch than Maria's normal tone. She also used her own voice to deliver "The end," thus signaling in two ways that the story was over. It is important for children to hear many stories and to learn to tell them. Some children will be adept at telling a story by the time they are 3 or so; others will need encouragement (see *Activities to Encourage Storytelling*).

Activities to Encourage Storytelling

Nearly all children love stories, and teachers can take advantage of this fact to assist all children, and especially children who are learning English as an additional language, to develop their storytelling skills in order to facilitate cognitive, language, and academic growth. Some useful activities include:

Audio stories. Those read by the teacher are important, because they allow for comprehension checks and interaction. But prerecorded stories are useful, too, especially with different character voices, because children can play them over and over at listening stations or at home. In either case, hearing these stories helps to hone listening and visual imaging skills, and to expose children to the form of stories. Most of the prerecorded stories available in North America are in the traditional European/American structure (although there are some available in Spanish).

Ask children's parents or other family members to record their own stories. Hearing stories in their own language will hone their listening and visual imagining skills, skills that they will need in order to understand stories in English.

Take dictation. Teachers or older children can write down the stories that children tell. For children who do not know how or are just learning to write, it is helpful to have a scribe so that their stories are not constrained by their ability to write. Being able to dictate their stories greatly helps children develop oral fluency. Children who can read enjoy reading their stories aloud, and prereaders enjoy having their work read aloud to others in the class. If the stories are very short or incomplete, the scribe can prompt the child or ask others, "What do you think happened next?"

Encourage co-narration. By asking questions, and by inviting other children to ask questions, teachers encourage a kind of cooperative storytelling in which others contribute to the story by prompting more detail, by providing feedback, or by adding to the story. This assists all children in the group, not only as storytellers but to develop their conversational and social skills.

7.4 A Cross-Cultural Perspective

In general, the developmental milestones outlined in the previous chapter will be true of all children whatever the first language. Certainly, in terms of the order and rate in which children acquire the building blocks of language—words, syntax, the sound system—the patterns hold true across culture. When we get into the development of functions and the contexts in which these functions develop in children, namely conversation and constructing narrative uses of language outlined in this chapter, then culture may be more of a factor. For example, the uses to which young children put language—those functions identified earlier—are dependent on the kinds of interrelationships that exist between children and adults in a culture.

Using Language Appropriately

People in different cultures have different reactions to events or situations, and so the language that is appropriate will also be different. In Japan, for example, an expression roughly equivalent to *I'm sorry* in English is often used to express extreme thanks. A Japanese child using this structure, inappropriately in English, might be assumed not to have acquired the ability to express gratitude, and "thank you," is something that is learned almost from the cradle in the United States. But it would be a mistake to assume any kind of deficit when, in fact, the child might be attempting to express extreme gratitude. Mizne (1997) recounts the example of an Indonesian student who attempted to express concern for his professor's well-being by telling him to eat less fattening foods so that he would feel and look better. In his own country, the giving of unsolicited advice is a way of showing concern. If an Indonesian child were to inform her first grade teacher that she would look better with longer hair or that she should stop eating donuts, the child's concern might be misinterpreted. Being able to use language appropriately is as important as learning to use it correctly. For teachers, however, the problem is determining what has been learned. No, the language was not being used appropriately, but it is a cultural rather than a linguistic misunderstanding, and the teacher can infer little about the child's understanding of language function.

When considering how effectively a child has acquired a function, *understanding* it is just as important as producing it. Whether we are talking about structure or function, children cannot consistently and meaningfully produce a form they do not yet understand. Our inability to observe a child using a function does not mean that the child has not acquired it, but evidence that the child does not *understand* the function may mean just that.

Similarly, the fact that a non-English-speaking child does not initiate conversations or tell stories does not mean that she doesn't know how. Some children are shy; some children don't like to make mistakes and need to rehearse something internally until they are certain it is correct before producing it. Reluctance to engage in storytelling in a new language can be related to cultural differences.

Culture and Storytelling

All cultures engage in storytelling, though the form and type of story may differ from culture to culture. Here, an Alaskan Yupik native tells hunting stories to children.

Alaska Stock Images/National Geographic Stock

Storytelling is universal, and there is a great deal of similarity in the stories that are told across cultures and in the way they are structured. Since they tend to recount human experience, and because there is some degree of commonality in all human experience, this is not surprising. Nevertheless, there are culturally determined differences in both the stories that people choose to tell and in the structure of those stories. For example, Japanese children have a very succinct structure to their narratives that is usually told in sets of three episodes.

The organization of stories in the African American tradition is quite different from the organization in the classic European tradition. Rather than being topic-centered, African American stories are usually based around a theme, featuring several episodes or events that illustrate the theme. (Curenton, 2006, p. 1)

This structure is referred to as topic-associating (Hyon & Sulzby, 1994; Dickinson, Wolf, & Stotsky, 1993). Listeners who are unfamiliar with this approach to narrative (see *Culture and Story Structure*) will have difficulty following the story because the stories tend not to have the expected indicators of a change in time or character.

Another difference between the classic European storytelling tradition and other cultural traditions is the number of characters involved in the story. Stories from the European tradition tend to revolve around one main character, but African American and Latino American children's stories contain several main characters who all relate to the main story theme. (Curenton, 2006, p. 1)

The difference may be attributable to the fact that "Latino cultures highly value interdependence among family and friends and socialize children to think about the needs of others as much as—and perhaps even more than—their own needs" (Melzi, 2001). Researcher Qi Wang found that

. . . when Chinese children and adults remember things in the past, they tend to focus on social interactions and the roles of significant others in those events. European-Americans are more focused on their own roles, their feelings, their preferences and their thoughts in the events. They are the main characters of the story. (Dingfelder, 2008)

Culture and Story Structure

North Americans tend to judge whether a story is a good story based on criteria acquired in childhood, and for the most part these are related to the traditional European story structure. Many North Americans of European descent think a good story has a central character (the hero or heroine), a beginning, a middle, and an end, each consisting of certain properties. The beginning provides an introduction to the characters and setting and a background to the plot, the middle develops the plot to a climactic conclusion, which is the end of the story. But not every culture adheres to this structure. Some cultures use a structure of topic-association. The following story, told by an African American girl, is illustrative:

So we were going to the mall to the shoe store. But first we stopped at this other store that sells jewelry. I need some earrings to go with the bracelet I got for my birthday. Did you see that bracelet that Sonia's been wearing? Her boyfriend gave it to her. My mom says I'm too young for a boyfriend. But I'm old enough to get my ears pierced. So I got the earrings. They're silver and huge. And so I sat down in the shoe store and put them on. I didn't find the shoes I wanted, though.

This story seems rambling unless we understand how topic-association works: The first two sentences tell the story in simple chronological order, and the third gives the reason for stopping at the jewelry store, again in the traditional story frame. But when she introduces the bracelet into the   *(continued)*

> **Culture and Story Structure** *(continued)*
>
> story, the topic-association begins. She associates bracelet with another bracelet that Sonia has been wearing, a bracelet given to her by her boyfriend. This reminds the speaker that her mother won't let her have a boyfriend because she's too young. Being too young takes her to the notion of getting her ears pierced, which brings her back to the earrings she went to the jewelry store to get. She describes them and putting them on in the shoe store, which eventually brings us back to the starting point of going to the mall to get shoes. Ultimately, the story comes to its conclusion—she didn't get her shoes. How might the story be told using the traditional European story structure?
>
> As children grow older, their experiences at school and hearing other kinds of stories will influence the structures of the stories they tell.

Teachers run the risk of making the wrong assumptions about children whose stories do not conform to the classic European tradition. Teachers may think Asian children lack imagination because their stories tend to be succinct, with sparse detail, that African American children are rambling and disorganized or that Latino children lack focus because their stories have so many characters. In fact, all these cultures have rich traditions of storytelling, but the ways in which stories are told differ significantly. Researchers identified particular narrative traits used by African Americans in the Piedmont area of the Carolinas. They are far more likely to use rhyme, alliteration, repetition, and word-play because poetic language was a part of everyday language—the bantering, sermons, and songs that they hear regularly (Heath, 1983; Bardidge, 2009). The result can be a narrative structure that sounds more like poetry than prose. Listeners unfamiliar with this narrative structure may not know how to react or may assume that they are rambling or unfocused. Such assumptions are, of course, unfair, and they are dangerous because they mean that teachers are likely underestimating these children's language and cognitive abilities.

As teachers, it is incumbent on us to provide all children, whatever their language and cultural heritage, with a variety of experiences in English that will help them acquire the language they will need in order to engage in these activities. It is impossible for any child to engage in meaningful conversation or tell a story without the knowledge, experience, and language required to do so. Teachers must also be particularly sensitive to the kinds of assistance provided, such as paraphrasing. For example, if a child is trying to tell a story but is struggling with the words used for sequencing, an adult can repeat or paraphrase the child's utterance and provide the prompt for the next part:

> *Marie: My mommy put the, um, les oeufs in the . . . she put, um, in the—and then—and then . . .*
>
> *Teacher: She put the eggs in the bowl and then she mixed them up? [Miming the action of mixing]*
>
> *Marie: Yeah, she put the eggs in the bowl and then she . . . [Hesitates]*
>
> *Teacher: [Mimes the action of mixing again] She mixed?*

Marie: And then she mixed them up and put in flour and then, and then, we put cookies in, um . . .

Teacher: After she put in the flour, she put the cookies in the oven?

Marie: Yeah, in the oven. And then they come out and we eat.

Teachers of English as a second Language have long understood the importance of comprehension checks.

iStockphoto/Thinkstock

These kinds of paraphrasing and prompting that Marie's teacher did for her are characteristic of child-directed-speech (CDS) (Chapter 3) that adults often use with infants acquiring their first language, and since Marie, at age 4 years and 6 months, is within the critical period of language learning, they are also effective with her. Additional comprehension checks are another characteristic of CDS that can greatly assist young second language learners (see *Comprehension Checks*). These checks serve to ensure that the child understands the teacher but also that the teacher understands what the child is trying to communicate.

Comprehension Checks

The following classroom conversation illustrates how a comprehension check works and why it is important to the learner. Think about these questions as you read the following dialogue: How do the learners assist the teacher in making her message clear? How do adults use a similar strategy in talking with young children?

Teacher: [Handing out a form to class members] You should ask your mother or father to fill this out. Then bring it back tomorrow.
Learner #1: It is for me?
Teacher: No, you bring it back. Your mother fills it out.
Learner #2: [Hands the form back to the teacher]
Teacher: No, not now. Okay. You take this form home [She writes "Take form home" on the board.]. Understand? You put into your backpack [Taking the form and pretending to put it into a student's backpack]. And then you take it home [Motioning with her hand to indicate a distance].
Learner #1: To father?
Teacher: Yes. Father or mother. Okay?
Learner #2: Mother write on?
Teacher: Yes! See, it is in Spanish and in English.
Learner #1 and #2: Oh, si. Yes.

(continued)

Comprehension Checks *(continued)*

Teacher: [Writes on board "Fill-out" and mimes someone writing on the form] "Fill-out" means to answer questions on this paper. Then bring back tomorrow. When do you bring it back?
Learner #3: Tomorrow?
Teacher: Yes. [She points to a day on the calendar.] Tomorrow.

Notice the role the children play in helping the teacher to clarify her meaning. When Learner #1 says, "To Father?" he forces the teacher to be more precise. When Learner #2 says, "Mother write on?" he is doing his own comprehension check but also gives the teacher another opportunity to expand her utterance using different words. The learners' responses throughout the exchange encourage the teacher to rephrase, mime, and repeat to make herself understood. Adults talking to young children often use the same strategies as the teacher to ensure that children understand their meaning.

Conclusion

By the time they reach school age, most children are very proficient with the mechanics of language and are well on their way to acquiring the social aspects of language. They have developed some facility in all five of the basic functions of language and will continue to refine these throughout their school years. By the time they are 6, they have acquired many of the skills required to engage in conversation—being sensitive to the listener's perspective, turn-taking, making repairs when miscommunication occurs, becoming aware of relevance, understanding and making indirect requests, and acquiring the appropriate gender-based distinctions in language. They are able to tell simple stories, a skill that should be encouraged because storytelling helps children frame their thoughts and deal with emotions as well as giving them a head start on learning to read and to write. Children from all cultures engage in conversations and tell stories, but there are differences that can influence how these are shaped and how teachers respond. The teachers' task is to create environments that maximize all children to use language for all the purposes they need it to serve in their lives, academic *and* social.

Post-Test

1. The imaginative function is the same as the

   a. social function.
   b. controlling function.
   c. forecasting and reasoning function.
   d. projecting function.

2. One indication of a child's ability to take the perspective of others comes from their appropriate use of

   a. spatial relations.
   b. definite articles.
   c. indefinite articles.
   d. prepositions.

3. A _____ usually follows a procedural structure.

    a. script narrative
    b. personal narrative
    c. fictional narrative
    d. fantasy narrative

4. Stories featuring several related episodes or events, such as those used in the African-American culture, are classified as

    a. topic-centered.
    b. self-associated.
    c. self-centered.
    d. theme-based.

Answers

1. **d.** Projecting function. *The answer can be found in Section 7.1.*
2. **b.** Definite articles. *The answer can be found in Section 7.2.*
3. **a.** Script narrative. *The answer can be found in Section 7.3.*
4. **d.** Theme-based. *The answer can be found in Section 7.4.*

Key Ideas

- Children acquire language for social purposes—in order to participate in their families and the community.
- While children must learn the words and structure of their language, it is equally important that they learn to function effectively in it.
- Learning to be competent in conversation requires that children be sensitive to the listener's perspective, learn turn-taking and to make repairs when miscommunication occurs, be aware of relevance, understand and make indirect requests, and acquire the appropriate gender-based distinctions in language.
- Comprehension checks are important to ensure that conversations stay on track and for teachers in communicating with young children.
- Learning how to tell a story is important to learning to read because it teaches children how narrative is structured.
- Narrative structure, and thus how stories are told, may differ according to culture.
- Not understanding that culture influences how stories are structured and what kinds of stories are told may lead teachers to underestimate children's cognitive and linguistic abilities.

Critical Thinking Questions

1. Look at the following conversation between 4-year-old Sophie and 3-year-old Miguel. Identify all the functions of language used by each child. Remember that there may be overlapping functions.

   Sophie: We can play prince and princess.

   Miguel: No! What's that? [Pointing to a box on the floor]

   Sophie: I don't know. Let's play Sushi place.

   Miguel: What?

   Sophie: You know, like when we go to Sushi place for lunch? How the man rolls up the rice and stuff. And then cuts it.

   Miguel: No. What's that? [Pointing again to the box on the floor]

   Sophie: I already said. I don't know. Sushi is fun.

   Miguel: Is not!

   Sophie: Okay, maybe we can play outside on the swing or the playhouse.

   Miguel: No playhouse.

   Sophie: Why not?

   Miguel: Okay. Swings. I ask Mommy.

2. Refer to the dialogue between Sophie and Miguel. What does the dialogue reveal about what the children have learned about conversation? Is one child more proficient than the other?

3. Think about the social function and the informative function of language. Which would you expect to develop first, and why?

4. Boys and girls will eventually develop the same full range of language functions described earlier. Some evidence, however, suggests that the ways in which the functions are expressed may differ. Look at each of the following questions and try to determine whether an adult male or a female most likely asked the question.
   a. Do we have any bread?
   b. Where's the milk?
   c. Aren't you ready yet?
   d. Are you listening to that (radio program)?

Top Photo Group/Thinkstock

5. The boy in the photo is engaged in a telephone conversation with his father. They are talking about their plans to go to the park later in the day. What conversational skills will the boy have acquired in order to engage in this conversation? What language functions are likely to be involved?

6. There is a tradition in some cultures that when someone retells a story, the narrator attempts to improve on the story by adding details that make it more interesting. If the story is based in fantasy, this would likely cause no problem for the listener. But suppose that the story were the retelling of an actual event. If a child retells a story and adds details that were not present in earlier versions, what erroneous assumptions might a listener, particularly one from a different culture, make about the child?

7. Thinking back to what you read in Chapters 5, 6, and 7, why might a 4-year-old English speaking child, accustomed to hearing typical children's stories in English, tell stories that seem rambling and disjointed?

8. Look at the following dialogue and describe how topic association works in it.

> My papa rided his bike in Belgium. That's by France. We went to France for a whole month. But not my papa. He went to Belgium to ride his bike. He rides his bike a lot. He rode it in Toronto last year and I did too. I wore my orange tutu. I didn't winned, but I did get a ribbon. I think I was third. Nana said I should get a ribbon for my tutu. I like tutus a lot. (Isabelle, 5 years, 11months)

9. Comprehension checks are important to maintaining conversation. What strategies can preschool teachers use to ensure that children understand the intended communication?

Key Terms

comprehension checks Ways in which speakers find out whether the listener understands.

controlling function of language The language children use for controlling, or attempting to control, the self and others.

conversational competence The ability to engage in a meaningful conversation following the conventions of the culture.

fiction or fantasy narratives The genre of narrative that children use during make-believe.

forecasting and reasoning function of language The function that allows children to express their curiosity and to learn about the world.

informative function of language Those functions of language involved in conveying information, whether to the self or others.

language functions The general term for the practical purposes that language serves.

personal narratives Narratives that recount particular events that the individual has experienced.

projecting function of language The function of language that allows a child to enter into fantasy worlds and roles. Also referred to as the imaginative function.

scripts Narratives based on generalized accounts of procedures or recurring events.

social function of language The way in which children assert and maintain their social needs.

Weblinks

For information about effective adult conversations with preschoolers, see
http://www.education.com/reference/article/adult-conversations-preschoolers/

For further discussion of children's language functions, see
http://www.signosemio.com/jakobson/functions-of-language.asp

For hints on how to help preschool children develop conversational skills, see Denise Wang's (2011) article at
http://www.livestrong.com/article/93846-effective-communication-skills-children/

To learn how Chinese and Americans differ in the way they tell stories, see Dingfelder's article, Storytelling, American Style, at
http://www.apa.org/monitor/2008/11/storytelling.aspx

8

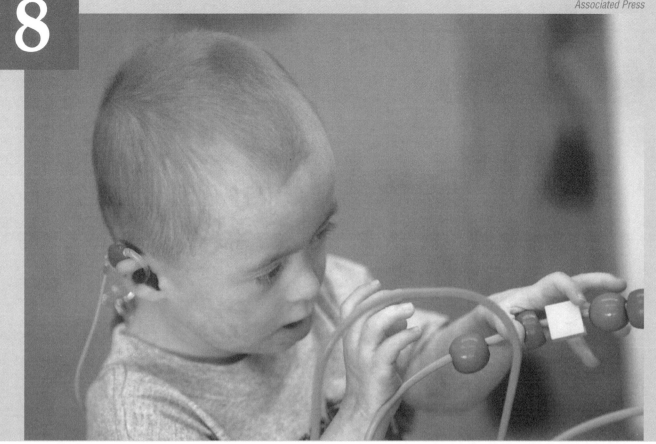

Bumps in the Road: Communication Disorders

Learning Objectives

By the end of this chapter, you will be able to accomplish the following objectives:

- Define communication disorder, and differentiate between speech and language disorders.

- Distinguish among articulation, fluency, and voice disorders.

- Differentiate between aphasia and other kinds of language disorder.

- Explain how culture can influence the perception of speech disorders.

- Explain why the early identification of speech and language disorders is important.

Introduction

Most children acquire language with little apparent effort. In fact, language acquisition seems so natural that we may not appreciate how truly complex it is until something goes wrong, until we encounter a child who has difficulty with some aspect of speech or language. As educators, we *will* encounter such children—children such as Kahlil. When he started to speak, Kahlil's speech appeared slow to develop. He had only a few words, when other children his age were quite fluent, and those he did speak were garbled and difficult to understand. Medical examinations showed him to have a normally developing vocal apparatus and good hearing, yet he clearly had some kind of communication disorder. In this chapter, we will take a closer look at communicative disorders, differentiating between speech and language disorders in children such as Kahlil, whom we will get to know better. We will also discuss the impact of culture on our perception of disorders and attempt to answer the practical question of when to refer.

Although it is impossible to get accurate figures on the prevalence of speech and language disorders in the population of U.S. school children, the American Speech-Language-Hearing Association (ASHA) reports that 24.1% of the school population (ages 3–21) with reported disabilities received services for speech or language disorders, an estimate that does not include children with speech or language problems secondary to other conditions (American Speech-Language-Hearing Association [ASHA], 2012a). This number almost certainly underestimates the actual number because it counts only those reported under the Individuals with Disabilities Education Act (IDEA), Part B. It is important that educators learn to recognize the possibility of a communication disorder in a child in order to seek early intervention.

Pre-Test

1. Hearing loss
   a. is classified as a language disorder.
   b. has decreased in the last 30 years.
   c. affects fewer than 40,000 children.
   d. can cause language disorders.

2. Stuttering
   a. usually begins during adolescence.
   b. usually self-corrects without intervention.
   c. affects about 10% of adults.
   d. leads to other linguistic problems.

3. Dyslexia involves
   a. about 2% of the population.
   b. intellectual difficulties.
   c. speech delays.
   d. no trouble retrieving words.

4. Evaluation of language disorders does NOT involve

   a. diagnosis by preschool teachers.
   b. use of toys to get specific types of language.
   c. testing proper word order usage.
   d. assessments created for children between 3 and 8 years.

5. One important consideration when using labels is to

   a. label the condition, not the child.
   b. use as many labels as potentially apply.
   c. include the term "deficit" to solidify the label.
   d. focus on changing the child.

Answers

1. d. Can cause language disorders. *The answer can be found in Section 8.1.*
2. b. Usually self-corrects without intervention. *The answer can be found in Section 8.2.*
3. c. Speech delays. *The answer can be found in Section 8.3.*
4. a. Diagnosis by preschool teachers. *The answer can be found in Section 8.4.*
5. a. Label the condition, not the child. *The answer can be found in Section 8.5.*

8.1 What Is a Communication Disorder?

In general, a **communication disorder** is any kind of impairment that adversely affects a person's ability to use language. There are two types of communication disorders—speech disorders and language disorders:

> When a person is unable to produce speech sounds correctly or fluently, or has problems with his or her voice, then he or she has a **speech disorder**. . . . When a person has trouble understanding others (receptive language), or sharing thoughts, ideas, and feelings completely (expressive language), then he or she has a **language disorder.** (ASHA, 2012a)

Speech and language professionals also distinguish between a language delay and a language disorder. A speech or language delay describes a child's language that is developing but at a slower rate than normal. A delay deserves attention because it may be indicative of a language or speech disorder or of more generalized delay that affects all aspects of cognitive development.

There are a myriad of causes and interventions for communication disorders, and it is beyond the scope of this book to examine all of the disorders, their causes, or possible therapeutic interventions. Our purpose here is to make teachers and future teachers aware of some of the more common disorders that may impede children's ability to acquire oral and written language so that they can make the necessary referrals. Because language and cognitive development are so closely linked, and because success in school depends on both, it is important to ensure that any potential problems are identified early. The earlier the intervention, the more likely it is to succeed, as we see in the story of Kahlil.

Diagnosing Kahlil

Kahlil was born in December 2003 on his mother's 36th birthday while his father was on active duty with the U.S. military. Kahlil was born one week past his due date and weighed almost 10 pounds. All neonatal tests were normal, and he went home with his mother when he was three days old. The first few months were a bit of a challenge for the new mother. Kahlil developed an unusually long list of infant ailments, including thrush, colic, severe diaper rash, several ear infections, and infant acne. From 4 months until the time he was 18 months old, he had seven ear infections. At 5 months, he developed Roseola. When he was 10 months old, he was sick for several weeks with an ear infection that turned into a bronchial infection and, eventually, pneumonia for which he was hospitalized for five days. Despite all his minor medical setbacks, Kahlil appeared to be developing normally and was a happy child.

Shortly after he was able to sit up, Kahlil began to scoot himself along the floor, propelling himself forward with his elbows and knees. At 10 months, he pulled himself up, holding onto furniture, and for the next 2 months, he walked around with support. A few weeks after his first birthday, Kahlil's mother noticed that he appeared to be walking on tiptoe. She had seen other children do this, so she was not particularly concerned. When it persisted for a year, the mother consulted her pediatrician at Kahlil's 2-year checkup. She also expressed her other concern about Kahlil, that he spoke only a few words and most of these unclearly. She had raised this before, but the doctor had explained that boys often developed language later than girls did. At this checkup, the doctor agreed that a hearing test was called for. The test showed that Kahlil had normal hearing.

Months passed. Kahlil still did very little talking, and the words he used were intelligible only to those who were closest to him and knew what he was trying to say. Kahlil and his mother were frustrated by his attempts to communicate. He would speak, but as his utterances got longer, he was increasingly unintelligible. Kahlil's mother took him to an audiologist who did a careful examination of his mouth and tongue, but his articulators appeared normal in every way. He appeared to listen attentively, but sometimes he did not follow his mother's instructions, although he always responded in some way. On one occasion, when she asked him to sit on the couch, he fetched his plastic toy cow from his toy box and took it to her. A few weeks before his 3rd birthday, the audiologist raised the possibility of **central auditory processing disorder (CAPD)**. CAPD is an umbrella term for various disorders that affect how the brain processes auditory information. Hearing is normal, but something causes the brain to distort the sound so that the brain does not get the same message that the ear does.

The audiologist explained to Kahlil's mother that she could not make a certain diagnosis of CAPD until Kahlil reached school age when it can be determined whether the written language is affected. A professional would look for any associated difficulty with reading and writing. The audiologist could tell from the testing and from recordings of his speech that Kahlil's speech was not developing normally. She explained that the problem might not be a speech disorder per se, but a language disorder.

In trying to determine the extent of Kahlil's speech and language problems, the doctor and the audiologist had begun with a hearing test. Because children cannot produce what they cannot hear, the first step in the diagnosis of virtually every language or speech disorder is a hearing test.

Hearing Loss

Hearing loss is neither a language nor a speech disorder, but it can be a cause of both. It is important to identify children with hearing loss early because "children who are hard of hearing will find it much

A hearing test is useful for diagnosing CAPD and many other speech and language problems. It is an important first step if any speech or language problem is suspected.

more difficult than children who have normal hearing to learn vocabulary, grammar, word order, idiomatic expressions, and other aspects of verbal communication" (ASHA, 2012b). The number of Americans with hearing loss has doubled in the past 30 years, according to ASHA, and government statistics show that more than 70,000 children a year receive treatment in public schools for hearing loss (ASHA, 2012b). That number almost certainly under-represents the actual number of children with hearing loss since many of these children have other disabilities as well and are reported in other categories.

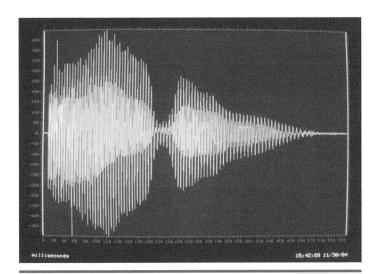

A computerized analysis of speech. Even though everyone has a unique "voice print," experts can pick out individual vowel sounds and some consonants from the patterns of time, frequency, and intensity.

In order to learn language, children need to hear language and have opportunities to use it. Children with hearing impairments are deprived of the sensory experience of language in varying degrees, depending on the severity of the loss. **Congenital hearing loss** means that an infant is born with a hearing impairment, either genetically inherited or because of health issues suffered by the mother during pregnancy or something that occurred during birth. If an infant is born with a hearing loss that limits perception of sounds to those exceeding 60 decibels (about the intensity of a baby's cry; see *Measuring Sound*), he or she is unlikely to develop oral language spontaneously. A baby born with a loss greater than 90 decibels is considered deaf and will not develop speech without therapeutic intervention.

Measuring Sound

The spectrum of sounds that the human ear can detect is very broad, ranging from the sound of a finger turning the page of a book to the sound made by a jet engine a few yards away. Although we commonly think of the differences in intensity as differences in volume, scientists use the **decibel (dB)** to measure the intensity of sound. Total silence would be 0 dB. "On the decibel scale, an increase of 10 means that a sound is 10 times more intense, or powerful. To your ears, it sounds twice as loud" (National Institute on Deafness and Other Communication Disorders [NIDCD] 2012). The decibel rating depends, of course, on how far away the origin of the sound is from the hearer. The following are some common sounds and their dB ratings:

A whisper	15 dB
Quiet bedroom at night	30 dB
A washer or dishwasher	40–55 dB
Average home	50 dB
Normal spoken language	60 dB
A baby crying	60 dB
A gas-powered lawnmower	90 dB
A diesel truck (10 yards away)	90 dB
A chain saw (1 yard away)	110 dB
A rock concert	120 dB
A jet engine (100 yards away)	110–140 dB
A gunshot or firecracker	140 dB
Stun grenade	170–180dB

A sound above 85 dB can cause hearing loss, depending on the strength and length of the sound. The louder the sound, the shorter the time before hearing loss can occur. Eight hours of 90 dB can cause damage to hearing, and the exposure does not have to be continuous. Any exposure to a 140 dB sound can cause immediate damage, sometimes temporary and sometimes permanent. Exposure of more than one minute to a 110 dB sound risks permanent hearing loss.

For further information, see Weblinks Noise-Induced Hearing Loss.
http://www.nidcd.nih.gov/health/hearing/pages/noise.aspx

A more common cause of hearing loss in young children is *otitis media*, or inflammation of the middle ear, which is also the most frequently diagnosed illness in infants and young children. Seventy-five percent of all children will experience one or more ear infections during the first 3 years of life (ASHA, 2012b). Many of these will lead to temporary hearing impairment, but children who experience many severe ear infections are at risk for permanent hearing loss and serious language disorders. Kahlil's medical history included a number of ear infections requiring medical attention, at least one severe enough to warrant hospitalization. While no clear causal relationship could be established between his ear infections and his eventual diagnosis of central auditory processing disorder, most children diagnosed with CAPD also have a history of chronic ear infections (Carter, 2000). Fortunately, most hearing loss can be effectively treated, the precise treatment depending on the cause and severity of the loss. Children diagnosed with speech disorders may also have experienced some degree of transitory or permanent hearing loss.

8.2 Speech Disorders

Speech disorders differ from language disorders in that they typically affect only a person's ability to produce normal sounding speech. There is no evidence of problems with language processing, oral or written. Speech disorders fall into three broad categories: **articulation disorders**, **fluency disorders**, and **voice disorders**.

Articulation Disorders

Articulation refers to the use of the tongue, lips, teeth, and mouth to produce speech sounds. Articulation disorders occur when sounds are added, omitted, substituted, or distorted. There is a broad spectrum of articulation disorders. At the low end of the spectrum is the problem in articulating a particular sound, a problem that can be very difficult to remediate. For example, Jorge, a 19-year-old who is bilingual (Spanish and English), has never learned to produce the "th" sound in either its voiced or unvoiced form in either of his languages. The sound is present in his dialect of Spanish, although not in all. In all other respects, his pronunciation is excellent. At the high end of the spectrum are disorders that are severe enough to render speech unintelligible.

Structural abnormalities, such as a cleft lip or palate, a tongue-tie, or other mouth deformity, cause many articulation disorders. Most of these can be corrected or improved, and generally, these conditions will have been addressed before children reach preschool. Missing teeth can also result in temporary pronunciation anomalies, which are corrected when the new teeth grow in. Some articulation disorders, however, do not have a visible cause. The audiologist can determine whether the child can hear the sounds correctly, since it is virtually impossible to replicate a sound if the child cannot hear it.

Missing front teeth will cause certain sounds to be produced differently. Which sounds are likely to be affected and how?

Exactostock/SuperStock

215

The American Speech-Language-Hearing Association identifies six speech disorders, four of which are articulation disorders. They include childhood apraxia, dysarthria, orofacial myofunctional disorders (OMD), and speech sound disorders.

Apraxia

Children with this disorder have trouble producing speech sounds correctly. They know what they want to say, but they cannot get the articulators to produce the sounds. Although apraxia is a motor speech disorder, it is not caused by muscular weakness; it originates in the brain, which is unable to "schedule" or coordinate the motor activities needed for speech. The result in young children is sometimes a failure to coo or babble, and in older children, leaving out sounds and greatly oversimplifying pronunciation. Children with apraxia may have difficulty imitating speech, but the speech they are able to imitate is more easily understood than speech they originate. Apraxia was considered a possible diagnosis for Kahlil. But children with apraxia (and no other speech or language problems) can normally distinguish between similar-sounding words. In Kahlil's case, he could not hear the difference between *Sam*, *jam*, and *dance* because, as the audiologist explained, his brain "jumbled up all the sounds." A child with apraxia would normally be able to hear the distinctions, but because the brain was imperfect in its communication with the articulators, would not be able to produce the differences.

Dysarthria

Children with dysarthria also have difficulty producing speech sounds correctly, but this condition is caused by weakening of the muscles of the mouth and face and sometimes the respiratory system. It is a condition that occurs after a stroke or other brain injury and also in children with muscular dystrophy (MD) or cerebral palsy (CP). It affects both children and adults, and the condition is associated with slurring and abnormal rate of speech—it may be very slow or it may be very rapid and sound like mumbling. The rhythm of speech is often distorted, and the voice quality may also be affected causing speech to sound overly nasal. Children with this disorder frequently have difficulty in chewing and swallowing and may have trouble controlling saliva. Since Kahlil had suffered no brain trauma and had neither MD nor CP, it was easy to rule out dysarthria as a cause for his speech problems. Apraxia and dysarthria are not mutually exclusive diagnoses—ASHA makes it clear that a person may have either or both conditions, and it takes a trained speech-language pathologist to make an accurate diagnosis and recommend the appropriate intervention.

Orofacial Myofunctional Disorders (OMD)

Children with OMD usually have difficulty with sounds such as /s/, /z/, "th," "ch" and "j." While it is normal for very young children to simplify some of these sounds (e.g., producing *sing* for *thing* or *dim* for *Jim*), these pronunciations do not normally persist beyond the age of 3 or so. The most recognizable symptom of OMD is a "tongue thrust," which causes the tongue to protrude between the teeth and to move forward in an exaggerated manner during speech. There are various causes of OMD, including heredity, but allergies, enlarged tonsils or adenoids, and excessive sucking of the fingers or thumb are a few of the other causes. Although a speech-language pathologist or a physician can usually reach a diagnosis, treatment of OMD usually requires a team of medical professionals,

This girl is practicing tongue movements during an OMD therapy session with her speech pathologist.

including a physician, an orthodontist, a dentist, and a speech-language pathologist.

Speech Sound Disorders

As we saw in Chapters 3 and 6, children often make developmental errors when producing certain sounds. By the time they are 5 or so, they are normally able to produce all the sounds of their first language correctly. Sometimes, however, a child will persist in an imperfect pronunciation beyond the period the correct one is normally acquired. When this happens systemically, or regularly, in the child's speech, then the child may have a speech sound disorder. Carmine and Thanos, both age 2, substituted a /d/ for "th" in words such as *thumb*, *three*, and *this*. By his third birthday, Carmine had mastered the /d/, except in rare instances—he would occasionally say *dat* for *that*, but it was common for the adults in his household to make the same substitution. Thanos, in contrast, was still unable to articulate the "th" sound at age 3. Thanos, it was later determined, had a speech sound disorder. He began to work with a speech-language pathologist at age 4, and by the time he entered kindergarten, he had good control over this and most of the other sounds he had struggled with.

Fluency Disorders

Fluency refers to the production of speech with the appropriate pauses or hesitations to keep speech clear and recognizable. A fluency disorder occurs when speech sounds are very rapid, have extra sounds inserted, or are repeated or blocked. Because children first learn to talk in a social setting, disruptions to fluency can have an adverse effect on their interactions with others. If the fluency disorder is mishandled, whether at home, school, or in public, a child may become withdrawn and reluctant to speak. Although fluency disorders are relatively easy to diagnose, it is often impossible to identify a cause. Fortunately, effective therapy is possible even when there is uncertainty about cause.

The most commonly recognized fluency disorder is **stuttering**. Stuttering is the involuntary repetition of speech sounds, particularly initial consonants. It is the most recognizable of all speech disorders. Approximately 5% of all children are affected, but for most of these, it does not persist for longer than 6 months. For about 1% of all children, however, the condition will continue into adulthood. Stuttering is not usually a pervasive condition, meaning that children who stutter do not stutter in all contexts or environments. It has long been noted, for example, that most stutterers become fluent when singing, reading, or speaking in unison with others, or when they whisper (Hulit & Howard, 1993), suggesting that when the speaker is saying something meaningless or has a limited audience (as with whispering), the stuttering ceases. Putting pressure on a child to "stop that stuttering" will simply make the problem worse, and teachers should consult with speech-language professionals. In general, children past the age of 4 and a half should be referred to a speech-language pathologist who will determine whether intervention is needed and what kind. See *Interesting Facts About Stuttering* for further information.

Interesting Facts About Stuttering

Stuttering is one of the most easily identified speech disorders. It is also responsive to therapy. Speech-language professionals have studied the disorder and its treatment for many years. The following are among the things they have learned:

- Children who begin stuttering before 3-and-a-half years are more likely to outgrow stuttering than if they begin later. If stuttering begins before the age of 3, the child is likely to outgrow it within 6 months.
- About 1% of the general population experience stuttering that persists into adulthood.
- For the onset of stuttering, girls and boys appear to be equally susceptible, but boys are three to four times more likely to continue to stutter into the school years (Felsenfeld, 1996).
- Family history plays a role. Children or siblings of stutterers are at greater risk for stuttering. If the family member outgrew the stuttering, chances are better that the child will also outgrow it.
- Between 75% and 80% of children who begin stuttering will stop within one to two years without intervention. Chances of the child stopping decrease the longer the stuttering persists.
- Other speech or language problems may influence whether or not stuttering persists. If a child otherwise speaks clearly and is easily understood, she is less likely to continue to stutter than if stuttering is one of several issues.
- In general, children who stutter do not have lesser linguistic abilities than children who do not stutter. In fact, according to the National Stuttering Association, children with advanced language skills are more at risk for persistent stuttering.

Source: The Stuttering Foundation, http://www.stutteringhelp.org/default.aspx?tabid=114

Stuttering is not the only type of fluency disorder. **Cluttering** is the name given to speech characterized by "a rapid and/or irregular speaking rate, excessive dysfluencies, and often other symptoms such as language or phonological errors and attention deficits." Speakers with a cluttering disorder seem not to be clear about what they want to say or how to say it and usually exhibit many interjections or revisions to their own speech. Isolating cluttering as the cause of nonfluent speech is complicated by the fact that stuttering and cluttering can co-occur (The Stuttering Foundation, 2012; Levy, 2011).

Voice Disorders

Voice is a result of the coordinated efforts of the lungs, larynx, vocal folds, and the oral and nasal cavities. Voice disorders are said to be present when the airstream or resonance are affected, creating speech that sounds breathy, whispery, or overly nasal, for example. Some voice disorders are caused by damage to the organs involved in articulation, but others can be caused by a speaker having developed inappropriate or improper voicing habits.

Most of us will experience some kind of voice disorder at sometime during our lives. Hoarseness and loss of voice due to a cold or other illness are common. A true voice disorder, however, is one that affects voice quality over an extended period and does not appear linked to a transitory illness. Voice disorders may affect the pitch of the voice, the loudness, or the quality. Pitch disorders can be manifested as pitch that is too high, too low, or flat (i.e., monotonous). Often, an abnormally high pitch is nothing more than a symptom of slow maturation, particularly in boys. Especially low pitch is much less common, and when it does occur, it may be because the speaker has a larynx that is larger than usual for his or her overall size. Older children can train themselves to speak in a lower pitch, but generally no intervention is required. Monotonic speech in speakers is often caused by a hearing loss, but it may also have a psychological basis, such as low self-esteem.

Loudness disorders occur when a voice is too loud, too weak, or very rarely, when there is no voice at all. Hearing loss may be the culprit with both overly loud and overly soft voices because the speaker cannot judge the volume of her own speech. There can be other causes, such as personality traits—some people are just more boisterous than others, and some people do not like to draw attention to themselves.

Voice quality refers to conditions such as hoarseness, hypernasality (meaning that the voice sounds like the speaker is speaking with a blocked nasal passage), a creaky or whispery voice, and extreme breathiness. Any of these conditions may indicate a voice quality disorder if they persist for an extended time. In extreme cases, there may be distortions to the pitch, volume, or quality of the voice to the extent that the speaker is unintelligible. In milder cases, the voice may simply sound inappropriate for the speaker's age or gender but intelligibility is only slightly impeded. There are a number of causes for vocal disorders, but only about a third of them have a physical basis—excessive breathiness and hoarseness, for example, might be caused by some abnormality in the vibration of the vocal folds. Most vocal disorders have other causes such as stress or abuse of the vocal apparatus. For example, this happens when singing too loudly for too long and will respond to rest or medical treatment.

A simple cold can lead to vocal hoarseness due to inflammation. This hoarseness is not a permanent voice disorder and should disappear with other cold symptoms or shortly thereafter.

iStockphoto/Thinkstock

8.3 Language Disorders

When a child fails to develop language normally, the potential consequences are severe because language is tied to cognitive development and school success (Chapters 5 and 6). Many professionals have attempted to describe and classify the multitude of language disorders, but despite many attempts, none has gained universal acceptance among physicians or speech-language professionals (Simms, 2007). For example, although speech-language therapists distinguish between speech and language disorders, there may be overlap in diagnoses. Also, a child may have both a language and a speech disorder. A widely accepted definition of language disorder is "any systematic deviation in the way people speak, listen, read, write, or sign that interferes with their ability to communicate with their peers" (Crystal, 1987, p. 264). This definition covers a broad spectrum of linguistic dysfunction; the structure, the content and the use of language can all be affected, singly or in combination. Usually, a language disorder is the result of a physical impairment such as brain damage or deafness and is identified by deficits in comprehension, production, or use of language in the absence of any general intellectual disability.

Despite their failure to agree on how language disorders are categorized, professionals do agree that language disorders may be broadly classified as receptive, expressive, or both. A child with a receptive disorder has difficulty in understanding speech sounds. A child with an expressive disorder has difficulty in appropriately putting sounds together to produce comprehensible speech. Kahlil, whom we met earlier in this chapter, appeared to have both. His speech was mostly incomprehensible, but his responses to simple directions indicated that what he heard was not what the speaker intended. In other words, the brain somehow "mistranslated" the sounds that the ear received, resulting in a garbled message.

CAPD is thus a language disorder rather than a speech disorder. Language disorders vary both in the aspect of language affected—sound, word, conversation, and so forth—and in severity. They also vary in cause, and with many, the causes are unknown. Most, however, are amenable to intervention, and the earlier a child is diagnosed, the more effective the intervention.

Specific Language Impairment

Specific language impairment (SLI) is the term language pathologists use for children whose language development is 12 months or more behind their chronological age and is not associated with other sensory or intellectual deficits or diagnosed cerebral damage. Estimates on the prevalence of SLI in preschool children vary from 7% to 10%, depending on the age at which it is diagnosed. The number is as high as 10% in 2-year-olds but drops to 7% two years later, suggesting that some of the developmental delays that prompted the early diagnosis have resolved themselves (NIDCD, 2012; ASHA, 2008a). The following traits characterize SLI:

- Slow progress in speech following normal onset time. In other words, children with SLI begin to speak at about the same time as other children, but over time, their development lags behind.
- Particular problems with morphology (Chapter 2), especially producing word endings such as -ing or -ed.

- Difficulty with picking up the meanings of new words from context.
- Problems with generalizing of forms, for example, that -ing is used on all verbs to indicate ongoing action. (Davidson & De Villers, 2012)

The general characterization of children with SLI is that even though they usually do not have any difficulty with social interaction, they have trouble picking up language incidentally as they play and interact with others. What appears to be at the root of the problem for these children is either an inability to perceive certain sound distinctions in speech or in their short-term phonological memory. They are not, however, hearing impaired. Some children with SLI may have "associated impairments in motor skills, cognitive function, attention, and reading," but these are not causal since many children with SLI exhibit no evidence of cognitive impairment. The causes are unknown, but there is some evidence that there may be a genetic component (Davidson & De Villers, 2012; ASHA, 2012a). What is known is that children with SLI are not afflicted with brain trauma nor is there any evidence of brain abnormality in these children.

Some disorders *do* result from specific brain damage, and they are collectively known as **aphasias**. Aphasias are classified according to the area of the brain affected, but the three general types recognized by most professionals are receptive, expressive, and global.

Aphasia

Aphasia occurs when there is damage to the language centers of the brain, usually in the left hemisphere. Both oral and written language are usually affected. The particular type of aphasia depends on the area of the brain that is damaged. **Wernicke's aphasia**, also called sensory or receptive aphasia, results from a lesion in Wernicke's area, the upper back part of the temporal lobe of the brain. As with all receptive disorders, those suffering from this type of aphasia generally exhibit no articulatory dysfunction, and may actually seem excessively fluent—talking rapidly and without hesitation, for example. The result may be garbled or even nonsensical to the hearer. Because this aphasia affects how well they comprehend speech, people with Wernicke's aphasia may repeat words or parts of words and phrases or rely heavily on formulaic expressions, repeating them often. People with receptive aphasia may also have difficulty in retrieving words from memory.

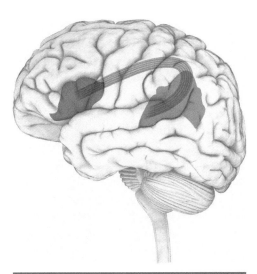

Wernicke's aphasia is associated with injury to Wernicke's area (orange), whereas Broca's aphasia occurs when there has been damage to Broca's area (purple).

Dorling Kindersley RF/Thinkstock

Broca's aphasia, also known as expressive aphasia or motor aphasia, occurs in people with damage to the lower back part of the frontal lobe. People suffering Broca's aphasia have severe articulation and fluency problems. In contrast to Wernicke's aphasia, this aphasia is characterized by slow, labored speech, with distortions in the individual sounds and the intonation pattern. Patients with this disorder speak in very short sentences, leaving out all but essential words and sometimes ignoring the rules of grammar. Unlike patients with receptive aphasia, however, they have little trouble with comprehension. **Global aphasia** refers to a disorder to both receptive and productive language ability. Those suffering from global aphasia will have minimal speech capability and limited comprehension. The prognosis for recovery or even significant improvement is poor for global aphasia.

Nobody is born with aphasia. The major cause is stroke, so it is more prevalent in adults than in children. But children with brain trauma due to accident or injury can suffer from aphasia as well. In general, the prognosis for recovery depends on the location and size of damage to the brain. Also, the younger the patient, the better the prognosis for recovery (Cheour, 2010).

Children with any of these aphasias would normally be diagnosed at an early age, so it would be unusual for an educator to encounter a child with untreated aphasia. If a child appears to exhibit symptoms of a mild aphasia, the first thing to rule out is hearing loss since it is far more common and can cause problems in both comprehension and speaking.

Central Auditory Processing Disorder (CAPD)

Toward the end of first grade, the professionals treating Kahlil confirmed the diagnosis of CAPD. His teachers in kindergarten and first grade had reported some of the same behaviors that his mother had observed—he appeared to have trouble following directions, he was easily distracted by loud noises, and the more noisy the environment, the more anxious he became. His anxiety level decreased and his behavior improved when he was in a quieter environment. Even though he could hear across the entire spectrum of speech sounds, Kahlil could not distinguish between certain pairs of speech sounds. He could not tell *cow* from *bow, chow,* or *now,* for example. He even had some problems differentiating vowels—remember from Chapter 2 that vowel sounds are more resonant and, thus, generally easier for children to hear and to discriminate. But for Kahlil, the vowels in *sit, seat,* and *set* were sometimes confused. Even though he was capable of hearing the different vowel and consonant sounds, something happened in the transfer of the sound into or out of the speech center of the brain, and the sounds became confused or garbled.

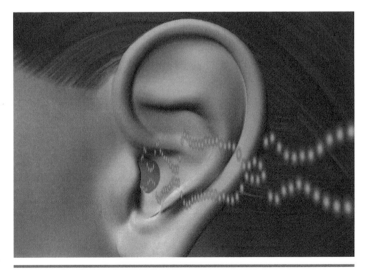

Although Kahlil's ears heard the sound waves just as everyone else did, his brain did not process them normally but scrambled them. This is a defining characteristic of CAPD.

Purestock/SuperStock

222

Kahlil had trouble learning letters and recognizing words as well, and it appeared to his teachers that he might have *dyslexia*, a condition affecting a person's ability to read and write. It is not surprising that Kahlil had difficulty with the printed language as well because a strong foundation in oral language is essential for success in reading. Moreover, there is likely a neurological connection. Just as dyslexics can see the words, but some letters get jumbled in their brains, those with CAPD can hear, but their brains aren't able to process some sounds (Carter, 2000). Eventually, the professionals working with Kahlil concluded that CAPD was the central diagnosis responsible for his oral and written language processing problems. A speech-language therapist had begun working with him at age 3, and once he was diagnosed with CAPD, he was referred to a clinic that dealt with CAPD and other serious language processing disorders. Initially, he spent most of the school day in the clinic, but gradually, he was able to go back into his class. Now 9 years old, Kahlil is finishing second grade, having repeated first grade when his family moved to be closer to the clinic he was attending. He says he likes school, and he is able to spend three fourths of every day in his class. His teacher coordinates her work with the other professional who care for him, and the prognosis for Kahlil is good.

Dyslexia

Although the term is not used by all school districts—some opt for the broader term *learning disability* instead—**dyslexia** refers to a category of reading disorders associated with impairment to the ability to interpret spatial relationships (in print) or to integrate auditory and visual information. The term is used to identify a broad spectrum of neurologically based language processing disorders and affects both reading fluency and comprehension. Symptoms may be mild to severe and include the following:

- Letter reversal or mirroring. This is the symptom most commonly associated with dyslexia, but it occurs only rarely. Letter reversal occurs among nondyslectic children and is, on its own, no cause for concern. Most children will reverse some letters when they are first learning, creating a "d" for a "b," for example. This behavior may persist until the age of 6 or 7. While children with dyslexia may experience written text as a jumble of letters, they only rarely see them as reversed or mirrored.
- Delays in speech. Many children who are subsequently diagnosed with dyslexia begin to speak later than their peers.
- Distractibility. Children with dyslexia are often easily distracted by background noise.
- Difficulty with sound segments. Sometimes, children with dyslexia have problems counting syllables in words, generating rhymes, and breaking words down into individual sounds, or "sounding out" words as they learn to read.
- Retrieval problems. Children with dyslexia often have difficulty in recalling words or the names of objects.
- Tendency to omit or add letters when reading, writing, or just copying words.
- Generally, writing that does not match their level of intelligence or general academic understanding.

Estimates of the incidence of dyslexia in the U.S. population range from 5% to 20%. There are no comparable data for CAPD, but although most clinicians rank the incidence much lower than dyslexia, they also acknowledge that it is not uncommon (ASHA, 2008b). While dyslexia and CAPD share many symptoms and some children have both CAPD and dyslexia, the two are different neurological disorders, and only trained professionals can determine the best intervention strategies.

Autism: Language or Cognitive Disorder?

In Chapters 5 and 6, we saw how language and cognitive development are interdependent. Even so, language disorders may exist in children who have no other cognitive impairment. But some children have language disorders rooted in or associated with a more generalized cognitive or learning disability. Especially in very young children, it is sometimes difficult to know whether an abnormality in some aspect of language development is indicative of a broader disorder, particularly a **social-cognitive disorder**. A social cognitive disorder is a result of a brain abnormality that interferes with infants' and children's abilities to develop normal social and cognitive skills. The medical profession has not been able to determine what causes the abnormalities to develop nor precisely how the brain is affected. The most commonly recognized of these disorders is **autism spectrum disorder (ASD)**.

These twin boys function at different ends of ASD. The fact that both have autism indicates there might be a genetic link, but a cause has not yet been established.

Jodi Cobb/National Geographic Stock

As the name suggests, autism admits of degrees of severity—the American Psychiatric Association recognizes three, not counting Asperger's syndrome (see *Asperger's Syndrome*). In making a diagnosis of ASD, the medical profession confirms that beginning in early childhood, a patient exhibits (a) persistent deficits in social interaction and communication in all contexts and (b) restricted and repetitive patterns of behavior and interests, which taken together impair everyday functioning (American Psychiatric Association [APA], 2011). Patients diagnosed with ASD will have both verbal and nonverbal communicative abnormalities including difficulty in using or interpreting facial expressions or body language. They may be either abnormally sensitive or insensitive to sensory input, for example, being oblivious to or extremely reactive to changes in temperature, light, or movement. Repetitive behaviors, vastly beyond the routines that most children develop, are also characteristic of children with ASD.

Asperger's Syndrome

At the high-functioning end of the autistic spectrum is **Asperger's syndrome**, which is not a language disorder, per se. Rather, it is social-cognitive disorder affecting children's ability to socialize and communicate effectively with others. Children with Asperger's syndrome typically exhibit social awkwardness and an all-absorbing interest in specific, sometimes arcane, subjects. They will develop language normally and may even demonstrate language ability in advance of their years. For example, Piper (2007) recounts the story of Kenny, who could read before he was 3 years old. The type of language problem typically exhibited by children with Asperger's is associated with their inability to engage in normal social interactions. That, coupled with their typically limited range of interests, means that they may have limited conversational competence (Chapter 7). Children with Asperger's may

- engage in long monologues, appearing to be unaware of whether or not others are listening or trying to take a turn;
- fail to make eye contact or exhibit few changes in facial expression while speaking;
- display awkward body posture or stances and gestures;
- show a near-obsessive interest in one or two very specific subjects such as snakes, weather, or a particular action hero;
- show little or no empathy or sensitivity to others' feelings or emotional states;
- have difficulty understanding humor;
- speak in a monotonous tone that may be unusually rapid;
- have poor coordination; and
- play alone or alongside rather than with other children.

The Viennese pediatrician Hans Asperger, who first described the condition, referred to his patients as "little professors" because they usually have very high intelligence, impressive vocabularies and facility with language (Osborne, 2000). Because they are so bright, they can sometimes be taught many of the "rules" for socializing and conversational turn-taking and how to interpret gestures, tone of voice, and sarcasm. They can also learn how to speak with a more natural rhythm. Speech-language professionals can assist such children, but the nonlinguistic aspects of the disorder will require other medical professionals.

For further information, see Weblinks at the end of the chapter.

Although autism is not a language disorder, even children with milder forms of autism will have difficulty with pragmatics, or using language appropriately in social settings. In fact, that may be the main symptom demonstrated by children who fall at the higher functioning end of the autism spectrum. Children with semantic-pragmatic-communication disorder (SPCD), for example, may play well with other children and exhibit no major problems in socializing, but they are likely to misinterpret the intent of messages. For example, they may not understand that when a teacher says, "Would you please sit down?" she neither expects nor welcomes an answer. Even as teenagers, ASD patients may not understand irony or sarcasm.

8.4 Issues of Cultural Diversity

Sometimes, a child will arrive in preschool or kindergarten with very little English. Estimates in Texas, for example, are that more than one third of children under the age of 5 speak Spanish as their first language (University of Texas at Austin, 2010). For these children, assessments of their language and speech ability in English will likely place them in an at-risk category, not because they are more likely to *have* a speech or language disability but because their English is insufficiently developed to get an accurate indication, most assessment tools were developed for use with English-speaking monolinguals and thus do not accurately gauge the language of bilinguals, or both. "In the early stages of bilingualism, children's language skills are in flux, so there's a huge range of proficiency in their second-language performance, which makes it difficult to distinguish between typical second-language differences and genuine language impairment" (University of Texas at Austin, 2010). As a result, it is difficult to determine with certainty whether children from linguistically diverse backgrounds have a disorder or whether they are simply exhibiting developmental errors.

Fortunately, early-childhood educators need not worry about making a precise or accurate diagnosis of a speech disorder. It is important, however, to recognize the *possibility* that one exists in order to make a referral to a professional audiologist or speech-language pathologist. One of the factors that teachers and language pathologists have to consider is cultural, because certain speech behaviors that may sound aberrant in one culture may be considered normal in another. Moreover, the fact that a child is learning two languages may have an impact both on the child's speech and on our perception of whether or not it is developmentally age-appropriate. In the case of articulation disorders, as we saw in Chapter 6, most first language learners have acquired the individual sounds of the language by the time they are 5 or 6 years old, but some children will still be working out certain distinctions—producing /l, r, y, w/, for example, may take a little longer. In almost all cases, these persistent substitutions are evidence only of a slight delay and not of a deviance; they do not require remediation. If, however, there are patterns of deviation that are markedly different from other children of the same age, referral to a speech-language professional is appropriate. But what if the child is bilingual and exhibits aberrant pronunciation?

Bilingual children may experience interference between the sound systems of their two languages. As we saw in Chapter 2, although there are many similarities, different languages have different sounds, and those sounds are distributed (or ordered) differently. These differences may contribute to the articulation problems experienced by second language learners. In Mandarin, for example, the only consonants that occur at the end of a word are nasals, /m, n, ŋ/, so it is not uncommon for Chinese children to omit any word-final consonant that is not a nasal. Words such as *bead* and *Mike* might be rendered as *bee* and *my*. The Arabic language does not permit word-initial consonant clusters, so Arabic-speaking children might say "fie" for fly or "gain" for grain. These deviations from English pronunciation are developmental errors of the type we saw in Chapters 3 and 4, and remediation is unnecessary. In fact, speech language therapies can be counter-productive for second language learners who need, instead, further exposure and practice with their new language.

The perception of fluency disorders is also culturally dependent, to a large degree. For example, one researcher has noted, "Asian Americans favour verbal hesitancy and ambiguity to avoid offence. . . . One should respect such a community's culture and thus the hesitancy should not be confused with a fluency disorder" (Kim, 1985; cited in Ndung'u & Kinyua, 2009). There is also a difference in what different cultures believe should be remediated. In North American Cowichan, for example, stuttering is seen by many as supernatural and remediation considered inappropriate. Similarly, there are some Native American communities in which the victim of a

Language differs from culture to culture. Care should be taken not to confuse culturally specific language traits with speech disorders. How would you evaluate a bilingual child's ability in both languages?

stroke is believed to have been "hit by the wind," because the person is out of harmony with nature (Westby & Begay, 2002; Ndung'u & Kinyua, 2009). Such beliefs would affect whether treatment was sought. Unfortunately, most treatments for speech and language disorders are most successful if they are begun early. The preschool years are well within the critical period for treatment since the brain retains its plasticity (Chapter 5), so children who arrive in preschool, kindergarten, or first grade with fluency problems can benefit from remediation.

With bilingual children, we must be extra careful to ensure that fluency orders actually exist since there is a possibility that what appears to be a dysfunction may be only a difference caused by limited proficiency in English. For example, a child who has not yet learned a vocabulary appropriate to her age level in English may hesitate or even stammer as she searches for the words to make herself understood. Similarly, a second language learner may make false starts and use frequent repetitions that impede the flow of speech. For these children, these impediments to fluency are developmental, and speech or language therapy is not recommended. On the other hand, teachers run the risk of not recognizing a speech disorder masked by an accent or a dialect that is markedly different from the teacher's own. The longer a disorder goes undetected, the more difficult it is to diagnose and treat (Guiberson, Barrett, Jancosek, & Yoshinaga-Itano, 2006). It is important, therefore, that someone who speaks their language or dialect assesses the children.

With regard to voice disorders, we know that ". . . voice quality is a language-specific property which may be different across different languages" (Yiu, Murdoch, Hird, Lau, & Ho, 2008) and that cultures vary in the amount of breathiness that is normal or acceptable in speech (Piper, 2007; Mattes & Omark, 1984). It is thus not surprising that the perception of voice disorders is largely culturally determined. For instance, in many African cultures masculinity and femininity are determined by paralinguistic features. A man who speaks in a low volume, a high pitch, or a smooth and slow voice, would be frowned upon and called upon to "speak like a man" (Ndung'u & Kinya, 2009).

Sometimes, the developmental errors that young bilingual learners make are a result of the normal process of learning English. Sometimes, they are indicative of a speech or language disorder. It is important to know which, because the intervention that works for one will not work for the other.

8.5 When to Refer

If a child seems to be significantly behind his or her peer group in language development, then parents or educators should consider the possibility of SLI. One diagnostic tool that professionals use for children between 24 and 36 months is to ask parents to complete a standardized questionnaire in which they identify the vocabulary the child knows and provide examples of two-word sentences that the child uses. "If the child's vocabulary contains fewer than 50 words and the child does not use any two-word sentences, that is an indication of SLI or another language disorder" (Davidson & De Villers, 2012).

Although the first person to suspect that a child might have a language or speech disorder is usually a parent or preschool teacher, it sometimes takes a number of speech-language professionals to confirm the diagnosis. Using assessment tools, often involving the use of puppets or toys to elicit specific language samples such as past tense or plural, they will test the child's speech and language skills. They will evaluate how well the child constructs sentences and whether or not she keeps words in the proper order. They will also estimate the number of words in the child's vocabulary and the quality of his or her speech. Tests are available for use with children between 3 and 8 years old and are best administered and interpreted by speech-language professionals.

Generally speaking, children might have a language disorder and should be referred if they exhibit the following conditions:

- They produce speech in combinations or patterns that are inconsistent with the language they are trying to speak and inappropriate for their age. For example, a 2- or 3-year-old child who says "gangershef" for *handkerchief* is no reason for concern, but a 6 year old might well be, unless it is an isolated instance and all other aspects of her pronunciation are normal.
- They appear not to understand certain words or categories of words that other children their age understand.
- They appear unable to follow directions or appear to be unaware of the "rules" of conversation by talking out of turn or failing to respond when it is their turn.
- They are significantly delayed in acquiring a number of speech sounds. For example, a child who cannot produce the entire spectrum of English consonants by school age might have a language disorder. Saying "do" for *shoe* or "delly" for *jelly* are perfectly normal substitutions in an 18-month old but not in a 4-year-old.
- They consistently produce shorter sentences than their peers.
- Parents or caregivers of bilingual children report irregularities in the child's first language.

By a child's 6th birthday, any potential speech or language disorders should have been diagnosed and treatment begun. Labels, despite their drawbacks, can help ensure success in school and life.

Hemera/Thinkstock

Why Labels Matter

Labels matter. Think about it. You are in a supermarket, and you read the label of a product—say a breakfast cereal. In addition to processed wheat and corn, you see a list of 17 ingredients, none of which has fewer than three syllables, most of which you have never heard of and one of which has received some negative press. What do you do? You probably put the box back on the shelf. What you do not do, usually, is to take the box home and have a closer look or even taste it. But suppose the label says *calciferol*. Never heard of that so it can't be good for you, right? In fact, *calciferol* is just another name for Vitamin D, which won't hurt you and might actually be good for you. What does this have to do with children?

While it is important to identify children with communication disorders and to identify them correctly, that is not the end-point but the beginning. In other words, labeling should not be confused with treatment. Although professionals use labels as a shorthand for talking about conditions and their treatments, there are dangers in labeling. The biggest one may be that it is the *child* who often gets labeled, rather than the *condition*. When it comes to dealing with children with communication disorders—or, indeed, any

learning or cognitive disorder—educators need to focus not on changing the child but on helping the child overcome or cope with the condition. With children, we have to look beyond the label.

Although it is important to identify communication disorders early, it is also important what happens next. Labeling a child as having a particular disorder does not make the disorder disappear, nor does it mark the child as deficient in some way—the child may have a condition that sets his learning on a different path. But the purpose of diagnosis and intervention is to help the child either work his way back to the more commonly traveled path or, if that is not possible, to smooth the way along his own path. In no way should the child with a communication disorder be viewed as deficient. Labeling a child in a particular way, while useful for professionals in understanding and discussing treatment, has inherent dangers (see *Advantages and Disadvantages to Labeling*).

Advantages and Disadvantages to Labeling

Labels are sometimes useful and almost always unavoidable. Educators need to ensure, however, that any labeling is done only to the child's benefit and, above all, that labeling is not harmful.

Advantages

- Labels enable professionals to communicate with one another because the diagnostic labels convey general information about the nature of the disorder. When we hear that a child has a fluency disorder, for example, we know that her stream of speech is affected in some way but that her comprehension is unaffected.
- The human mind seems to require some kind of categorical shorthand—a mental "hook" to think about and solve problems. It is easier for educators to think and talk about the causes and treatments for SLI than to use many sentences to describe the disorder. If the label did not exist, one would quickly be created to take its place.
- Labeling a disorder can raise social awareness and assist in advocacy efforts.

Disadvantages

- Labels may shape teacher expectations. If a child is labeled as language delayed, it may be tempting to assess all the child's behavior in that context when, in fact, all children have some troubling behaviors.
- Labels imply that the problem is with the child and may lead us to forget that the job of a teacher is to teach the child as is. Teaching and learning are interactive processes.
- Labels refer to categories of disorders and are abstract. Children are real and they are individual—no two children are the same even though they may have the same condition. No two stutterers are alike, and no two children with SLI will exhibit exactly the same behaviors.
- Diagnostic labels may be unreliable, but once they are in place they are hard to remove.

Conclusion

While the course of language learning is normally a seamless and seemingly effortless task, there are children who experience delays or deficits in the process. Communication disorders are among the most commonly reported conditions requiring intervention reported in the U.S. public school system, collectively affecting up to 20% of the population at some time during childhood. Speech disorders are those affecting the oral language a child produces, consistently and over time. Language disorders affect a child's ability to process language and may be either productive or receptive. The causes for communication are as varied as the disorders themselves—some have physical causes, some are associated with other cognitive disorders, and some have no known cause. For the early-childhood educator, it is important to recognize when children might have a communication disorder, not to put a label on them but to ensure that they get appropriate intervention that will help them improve or to overcome the disability. Fortunately, the prognosis for many children with communication disorders is excellent if the disorder is recognized and the appropriate intervention is begun early enough.

Post-Test

1. When there is evidence of a communication disorder, the first step is usually to
   a. check IQ.
   b. interview teachers and parents.
   c. test hearing.
   d. prescribe medications.

2. An example of an orofacial myofunctional disorder (OMD) would be a
   a. cleft palate influencing speech.
   b. tongue thrust.
   c. slurring.
   d. dysarthria.

3. Which of the following is NOT a type of aphasia?
   a. inventive
   b. receptive
   c. expressive
   d. global

4. Symptoms of diagnoses within the autism spectrum disorder include all of the following EXCEPT
   a. sensitivity to sensory input.
   b. preference for repetition and routine.
   c. excessive verbalization with others.
   d. difficulty reading social cues.

5. Which of the following is considered a disadvantage of labeling?
   a. Labels allow for communication among professionals.
   b. Teachers develop expectations based on labels.
   c. Labels provide brief mental "hooks" for understanding.
   d. Awareness and assistance can be increased with labels.

Answers

1. c. Test hearing. *The answer can be found in Section 8.1.*
2. b. Tongue thrust. *The answer can be found in Section 8.2.*
3. a. Inventive. *The answer can be found in Section 8.3.*
4. c. Excessive verbalization with others. *The answer can be found in Section 8.4.*
5. b. Teachers develop expectations based on labels. *The answer can be found in Section 8.5.*

Key Ideas

- Most children learn language without difficulty, but some will experience one or more communication disorders.
- The presence of a speech disorder does not necessarily indicate the presence of a language disorder, although some children may have both.
- Language delay, or the acquisition of language forms later than normal, is not in itself a disorder but should be monitored.
- Early identification and intervention is important because many conditions can be remediated.
- Culture can influence the perception of speech disorders.
- Assessment of communication disorders in bilingual children should involve both languages, if at all possible.

Critical Thinking Questions

1. According to *Interesting Facts About Stuttering*, girls are three to four times more likely than boys to outgrow stuttering. What are some of the factors that might contribute to this difference?
2. Many Romance languages, including Spanish, have fewer consonant phonemes than English. What kinds of articulation differences might result for a child of 5 or 6 who is a beginner in English? What should the teacher do to assist the child in learning the sounds of English?
3. How is stuttering different from other kinds of fluency disorders?
4. Charley is 5 years old. English is his only language. His kindergarten teacher has noticed the following pronunciations in his speech:

Table 8.1: Charley's pronunciations

Intended word	Charley's form
chair	sair
chip	sip
bubble	bobo
teacher	seeshur
cookie	kookoo
dog	gog
cat	cat

a. Should the teacher be concerned?
b. What should she do?
c. What are some of the possible causes for the irregularities in his pronunciation?

5. Carmelita is 5 and moved to Florida from Puerto Rico 8 months ago. Six months ago, she began kindergarten in an English-language school. Her teacher, Ms. Cook, speaks only English although there are Spanish/English bilinguals on the teaching staff. At first, Carmelita said little in English, but she learned the language quickly. Still, her teacher has noticed that Carmelita uses the following forms:
   a. She ride the car.
   b. It no red. It blue.
   c. Why she not go?
   d. Why he like me?

   Should Ms. Cook be concerned? What is the most likely cause of these "errors"? What should Ms. Cook do?

6. Why is the distinction between speech disorders and language disorders important?
7. Why is it important that teachers not think of second language learners in terms of deficits or deficiencies?
8. The box *Advantages and Disadvantages to Labeling* lists some of the advantages and disadvantages to attaching labels to communication disorders. Can you think of others?
9. Which of the disorders described in this chapter would you consider "bumps in the road," and which would be major barriers to success in school?

Key Terms

aphasia The name given to any language disorder resulting from specific brain damage.

articulation disorder One of the three broad categories of speech disorder, this is the name given to a spectrum of speech disorders characterized by speech with added, omitted, substituted, or distorted sounds.

Asperger's syndrome A pervasive developmental disorder characterized by severe difficulty with social relationships. Language problems associated with Asperger's are likely to be at the sociopragmatic level.

autism spectrum disorder (ASD) A category of developmental disorders that involve some degree of difficulty with communication and social relationships as well as obsessive and/or repetitive behaviors.

Broca's aphasia Also known as expressive aphasia or motor aphasia, a language disorder that occurs in people with damage to the lower back part of the frontal lobe. People suffering Broca's aphasia have severe articulation and fluency problems.

central auditory processing disorder (CAPD) This is an umbrella term for a variety of disorders that affect how the brain processes auditory information.

cluttering The name given to speech characterized by a rapid and/or irregular speaking rate, excessive dysfluencies, and often other symptoms such as language or phonological errors and attention deficits.

communication disorder Any kind of impairment that adversely affects a person's ability to use language.

congenital hearing loss A hearing impairment that is present at birth.

decibel (dB) Unit used to measure the intensity of sound.

dyslexia Refers to a category of reading disorders associated with impairment to the ability to interpret spatial relationships (in print) or to integrate auditory and visual information.

fluency disorder A speech disorder characterized by very rapid speech sounds that have additional sounds inserted or are repeated or blocked.

global aphasia A speech disorder characterized by impairment to comprehension and production of language.

language disorder Dysfunction characterized by difficulty in understanding others (receptive language), or sharing thoughts, ideas, and feelings completely (expressive language).

social-cognitive disorder A behavioral dysfunction resulting from a brain abnormality that interferes with infants' and children's abilities to develop normal social and cognitive skills.

specific language impairment (SLI) The term language pathologists use for children whose language development is 12 months or more behind their chronological age and is not associated with other sensory or intellectual deficits or diagnosed cerebral damage.

speech disorder The inability to produce speech sounds correctly or fluently, or problems with vocal quality.

stuttering The involuntary repetition of speech sounds, particularly initial consonants.

voice disorder One of the three broad categories of speech disorder, this is the term used to describe abnormalities in the voice when the airstream or resonance are affected.

Wernicke's aphasia Also called sensory or receptive aphasia, a language disorder resulting from a lesion in Wernicke's area, the upper back part of the temporal lobe of the brain. Patients with this aphasia typically exhibit no articulatory dysfunction and may actually seem excessively fluent—talking rapidly and without hesitation, for example.

Weblinks

To learn more about speech and language disorders, see the following:
http://www.asha.org/public/speech/disorders/
http://www.speechlanguage-resources.com/language-disorder.html

Two organizations provide excellent information about stuttering and cluttering. See The Stuttering Foundation at
http://www.stutteringhelp.org/default.aspx?tabid=114

and ASHA at
http://blog.asha.org/2011/01/13/stuttering-versus-cluttering-%E2%80%93-what%E2%80%99s-the-difference/

The Stuttering Foundation also has an excellent 30-minute video on stuttering in young children available at
http://www.youtube.com/watch?v=u2_mgt87g1Y

An informative article about culture and speech disorders can be found at
http://dsq-sds.org/article/view/986/1175

Examples of disordered speech and how they appear on sound spectrograms can be seen at
http://www.youtube.com/watch?v=CAyuDAUfUoE

To learn more about childhood aphasia, see
http://www.livestrong.com/article/182743-symptoms-of-child-aphasia/

To learn more about Asperger's syndrome, see
http://www.mayoclinic.com/health/aspergers-syndrome/DS00551

More information about central auditory processing disorder (CAPD) can be found at
http://dartmed.dartmouth.edu/summer00/pdf/Scrambled_Sounds.pdf

To learn more about specific language impairment (SLI), see

National Institutes of Health:
http://www.nidcd.nih.gov/health/voice/pages/specific-language-impairment.aspx

More information about CAPD is located at
http://kidshealth.org/parent/medical/ears/central_auditory.html
and http://www.asha.org/research/reports/hearing.htm

To learn more about the incidence of dyslexia, see
http://www.asha.org/Research/reports/literacy/

For information on issues surrounding the identification of speech problems in bilinguals, see
http://ehlt.flinders.edu.au/education/iej/articles/v5n4/tzivinikou/paper.pdf

For a good discussion on determining whether a disorder actually exists or is just a difference, see
http://www.utexas.edu/features/2010/09/27/language-2/

9

Language for Learning

Learning Objectives

By the end of this chapter, you will be able to accomplish the following objectives:

- Name and describe seven common-sense attributes of learning in early childhood.

- Explain the relationship between oral language and the acquisition of literacy.

- Describe the kinds of activities that foster language and arithmetic learning simultaneously.

Introduction

Lakeesha picked up a jar of jam from the breakfast table. She looked at the label, and the following exchange took place:

Lakeesha: What does it say?

Mother: What do you think it says?

Lakeesha: [Opening the jar and looking inside before answering] It says strawberry.

Mother: Why do you think that?

Lakeesha: [Shrugs] I don't know. Maybe because it tastes like strawberry.

Mother: That's a good guess, but actually, it is raspberry. See [Pointing to each word on the label], it says raspberry jam. You like raspberry jam, don't you?

Lakeesha: Yep. It says raspberry jam here [Pointing to the label].

Mother: That's right.

Lakeesha was not interested in learning per se—she was driven by curiosity about what the words on the label said and how they related to what she knew about the contents of the jar. She had already learned that print carries meaning and that the meaning of the words on the label was likely related to what was inside the jar. In the brief exchange with her mother, she began her journey along the path toward literacy. Understanding the written word is one of the academic skills that Lakeesha will develop more fully when she enters school. The language skills she possesses when she starts school will help her learn to read, learn to do math, and learn all the other subjects at school.

We learned in Chapter 6 that for most children, the foundations of language are well established by the time they reach first grade. This means that the foundations for academic success are also mostly in place when a child is 6 years old since language is the foundation for all learning. Therefore, what happens in the preschool years has a significant impact on children's ability to acquire the academic skills they need to succeed in school. Because language and cognition are interdependent processes, as we have seen in previous chapters, language is closely linked to the development of academic skills.

From birth onward, the child's job description consists of one word: *learn*. In this chapter, we will focus mainly on the academic learning, or, more specifically, the early learning that will provide a foundation for the academic subjects of the school curriculum, focusing as always on the role of language. But from children's perspective, all learning is pretty much the same, and it is all driven by their natural curiosity in the context of real problems or puzzles.

The purpose of this chapter is twofold. It is, first, to synthesize the content of previous chapters in a more practical context, and second to focus on the relationship among language, learning, and school success. The chapter begins with seven common-sense observations about children's early learning before we move on to examine more specifically children's early learning of arithmetic and literacy skills, skills that form the basis of the school curriculum.

Pre-Test

1. Language readiness is determined according to all of the following EXCEPT
   a. cognitive readiness.
   b. emotional readiness.
   c. relational readiness.
   d. physical readiness.

2. To facilitate play, adults should
   a. encourage children to make their own props.
   b. assume a role in the scenario.
   c. persuade children to use as many props as possible.
   d. redirect the play behaviors.

3. Two "best practices" for teaching math to young children include
   a. build on what children know and seize everyday teachable moments.
   b. use other children to teach each other and present information orally.
   c. encourage positive attitudes and be sure children know they're learning math.
   d. clearly correct mistakes and reward right answers.

Answers

1. c. Relational readiness. *The answer can be found in Section 9.1.*
2. a. Encourage children to make their own props. *The answer can be found in Section 9.2.*
3. a. Build on what children know and seize everyday teachable moments. *The answer can be found in Section 9.3.*

9.1 Seven Common-Sense Observations on Early Learning

Understanding how children learn makes it possible for teachers to plan activities that enhance that learning. Having a theoretical perspective from which to view how children learn language helps us create the environments that stimulate learning (Chapters 3 and 4). Over the centuries, philosophers, psychologists, and educators have concerned themselves with constructing theories of learning. They have put forward, refined, subcategorized, criticized, and ultimately found wanting hundreds of theories. There are perhaps a dozen theoretical perspectives (behaviorist, cognitivist, constructionist, post-modern, transformative, and neuro-educational, to name a few), and each one of these has several variations. These theories have all provided some insight into how children learn, but we do not need to review them all in order to make some common-sense observations about how children make sense of their worlds and learn how to learn.

Since our focus is on language and learning, our purpose here is to examine the characteristics of children's preschool learning that are especially important for teachers because whatever theoretical stance we might adopt, in the end, what matters is the circumstances and environment in which children learn. The following observations do not derive from any particular theoretical stance, but they are consistent with the positions taken earlier in the book. Specifically, they accord with the evidence supporting the position that children have a biological propensity to acquire language but do so within a community of speakers for purposes of socialization. As we saw in Chapters 3 and 4, innatist and social interaction theories are not mutually exclusive and are rooted in observation-based evidence of how young children learn language. From the experience of teachers and the observations of many researchers we have discussed in earlier chapters, we can extract these practical observations that are intended to help teachers of young children to replicate and create environments for children to continue and extend the learning they have already begun at home. In Chapter 5, we identified six characteristics of children's learning in the preschool years. Here, using examples, we expand and elaborate on those characteristics to focus more centrally on language and learning in the preschool.

Children Will Learn When They Are Ready

Trying to teach a 3-month-old baby to say *apple* or *cat* is an exercise in futility. The baby simply does not have the control of his articulators to form the sounds reliably and accurately. He does not yet have the memory capacity to remember the next time he sees the family feline that it is called a cat. Physically, he is not ready. The conversation we witnessed earlier between Lakeesha and her mother could not have taken place when Lakeesha was 2 and had yet to demonstrate any interest or "readiness" to find out about print. Now that she's 3, she has more interest in words, but this does not mean that she is ready to be handed *The New York Times*. In all likelihood, she is not yet ready to read at all. But soon she will be. When the baby has gained sufficient motor control over his articulators

and has developed the necessary memory capacity, he will be able to say *apple, cat*, and eventually thousands of other words. Lakeesha will learn to read but not until she is physically, cognitively, and emotionally ready.

Although children cannot learn until they are cognitively and physically ready, adults play an important role in helping children to reach and to take advantage of this readiness. Soviet psychologist Lev Vygotsky referred to the **zone of proximal development** as the distance between the child's actual physical and cognitive level of development and the level at which she can function with adult assistance (Vygotsky, 1934/1986).

Children learn when they are physically and mentally ready, but adults can help prepare them for learning. How does reading to this 3-year-old help prepare her to read?

Associated Press

Children Are in Charge

For the most part, young children are in charge of their own learning. They will determine what and when they will learn. Can the adult have some influence? Yes, but just as learning depends on readiness, it also depends on the child's desire to know. Had Lakeesha's mother held up flash cards with the words *raspberry* and *jam* printed on them and tried to teach Lakeesha to identify them, chances are that Lakeesha would have seen little point in the exercise and might have declined to participate. Two boys from the same family illustrate the point well. From the time he could sit up, Jurgen, the older brother, was passionately interested in puzzles. By the time he was a year old, he excelled at putting together wooden puzzles intended for children 1 or 2 years older. As he got older, his interest did not wane—he just became interested in more complex puzzles, and at age 6 was able to solve Rubik's Cube. His younger brother, Sven, never had the slightest interest in fitting together pieces of wood to form pictures, and his only interest in Rubik's Cube was to wonder aloud why whoever created the Cube hadn't used purple and orange (instead of red, blue, green, and yellow). His interest was numbers, and he insisted on counting everything in sight from the time he was 15 months old. Among his first 25 words were the numbers one to six. Not surprisingly, Sven learned to do simple addition and subtraction at age 4 while Jurgen waited until he got to school. Ultimately, both boys did well in all their school subjects, but in their preschool learning, they were clearly the ones in charge.

The transition from the relative independence of their learning in the early years to the more formal teacher-directed learning that occurs in the school years can be difficult for some children. One of the reasons is that when left to their own devices, children are inclined to tackle increasingly more challenging tasks. John Holt describes a boy learning to write who was not content to repeat his successes but kept pushing himself to more difficult tasks. He points out that when they get to school, the child's past experience of learning is sometimes incongruous with the expectation of the school, which are geared not to the individual child so much as the class. Some children will, thus, be less challenged than others or will find the school experience frustrating. Holt goes on to voice the concern that when children fall out of the habit of challenging themselves in school, they will gradually stop challenging themselves outside school, which will slow their learning (Holt, 1989, p. 17).

Play Matters

> As we learn more about how young children learn, it is becoming clear that we do not need to sacrifice play in order to meet academic requirements. On the contrary, only by supporting mature, high-quality play can we really help children fully develop their language and literacy skills. (Leong & Bodrova, 2012)

The job description of children might be to learn, but from infancy, every activity in the day is a learning activity. Play is especially important to young children's learning, and all kinds of play matter. Running around chasing or kicking a ball and swinging on monkey bars are just as important as make-believe or competitive games. We saw in Chapter 6 that physical activity helps children acquire gross motor skills and bodily coordination and that playing with smaller objects such as blocks or puzzle pieces helps them develop fine motor skills as well as eye-hand coordination. Language learning occurs during play, so play is important to academic learning. When playing with their infants, parents will instinctively label the objects they are playing with: "See the block? This one is red." Then, as they play games with their older children, parents and other adults routinely ask questions: "What is that you're playing with?" "Who did you invite to your tea-party?" "Where are you taking the wagon?" If the child does not know the answers, the adult will help out by labeling in a more indirect way, using commentary instead of questions to help the child learn the labels: "I like the red block best, do you?" or "This green car looks like Daddy's." This latter technique is especially helpful with children who have a developmental language delay (Chapter 8). Whether playing I Spy or making a game of counting the stairs while walking up or down, adults are helping toddlers to learn language and to learn categories, which is essential to concept development (Chapter 6).

Fantasy play helps children develop their imaginations and increase memory capabilities. What opportunities for language learning might also exist?

Tomas Rodriguez/Corbis

Almost all children enjoy playing make-believe or fantasy games, and they benefit in two important ways. First, this type of play helps develop the imagination by giving children the opportunity to think about the past and integrate it with the present and future, thus helping to increase memory capacity. Second, these games provide the opportunity for children to use language that is not bounded by the immediate environment or the present—they begin to decontextualize language (i.e., begin to use it for abstract representation). Vygotsky provides an often-quoted example about the importance of play. Suppose a child wants to ride a horse. If that child is under the age of 3, she may cry or stomp her feet in frustration, but around her 3rd birthday, her reaction might well be to grab a stick or broom and pretend to ride or to settle for a toy horse. Not only will she settle for the substitute, but she will enjoy doing so. Thus, play is the "imaginary, illusory realization of unrealizable desires" that fosters cognitive and linguistic growth and "represents a specifically human form of conscious activity. Like all functions of consciousness, it originally arises from action" (Vygotsky, 1978, pp. 79–91).

Adults Are Facilitators

If children had to rely on adult instruction in order to learn language, chances are they wouldn't learn nearly as much as they do on their own. Partly because they have an innate capacity for language and partly because they are in charge of their own learning, children benefit from facilitation more than instruction. As much as the parents might like to claim responsibility for teaching Jurgen to do puzzles or Sven to count, the fact is that their real roles were not as instructors but as facilitators. The difference is clear: An instructor is in charge of the content and the manner in which knowledge is supplied while a facilitator creates environments for knowledge to be acquired. With young children, the distinction is especially important.

Perhaps the most important role that these parents played in their sons' learning was as partners in daily interactions. Parents and other caregivers contribute significantly to children's language acquisition and to all learning by focusing their attention on and talking with them about things in their immediate environment and on the routines of the day. When parents talk in front of their infants, infants learn that the noises they hear are intentional and purposeful long before they are able to participate. Later, when children have learned to talk, adults engage with them in dialogues that do not constitute instruction but do constitute opportunities for learning more language. In these dialogues, adults typically take on more responsibility for ensuring that children understand (remember the comprehension checks from Chapter 7). Without completely taking charge of the conversation, adults can guide and assist in dialogues that further children's learning (see *Facilitating Dialogue with Toddlers*).

Facilitating Dialogue With Toddlers

Dialogues between adults and young children provide opportunities for language learning and many other kinds of learning as well. Children are not passive recipients of knowledge but are active participants in their own language. They are also in charge of what they learn, to a large degree. Adults can facilitate the learning that takes place in dialogues if they follow a few basic guidelines.

Follow the Child's Lead
Whether in the choice of topic or the level of sophistication of the language used, the wise adult follows the child's lead. There is no point in trying to engage 3-year-old Carolina in a conversation about space travel or how to make a pie if those are not things she knows or cares about. But if she goes with her father to the store to get paint for the garage door, there is an opportunity for a wide-ranging conversation—why the garage door needs painting, what color to choose, how the paints are mixed together to create a new color, and so forth.

Expand on the Child's Forms, Adding Information, but Don't Push!
At the paint store, Carolina says, "That paint red," when the paint is orange. Her father might respond, "No, that's orange," which will likely end the conversation. It is even more conducive to learning if he responds like this:

> Carolina: "That paint red."
> Father: "Yes, it is sort of like red. But it's different from this red, isn't it? [Pointing to a red paint] "The one you are looking at is the color orange."

Reinforce Positively or Not at All
At home, after leaving the paint store, Carolina says to her mother, "We buyed red paint."

Carolina's mother could correct the verb tense, but if Carolina were ready to produce the irregular past tense, she would be doing so. Carolina *might* remember the color orange after being corrected, but she will learn more if her father uses the opportunity to engage further.

> Father: "Remember, we talked about how this is kind of like red, but it's called orange?"
> Carolina: "Orange."
> Father: [Praises her] "Very good, Carolina."

Although children do not respond well to negative information, they do remember when they are praised for getting something right.

Interaction Is Essential to Learning

When John Donne wrote, "No man is an island. . . ." in the early 17th century, he wasn't likely thinking about how young children learn. We saw in Chapters 3 and 7 that language learning can only occur in the presence of speakers of that language, and so it is with almost all other learning. True, once they have had some experience in learning—learned *how* to learn, so to speak—children can learn some things on their own. But their first experiences with learning and much of their future learning occurs during and because of their interactions with others.

We have seen ample evidence throughout the previous chapters that children are not vessels into which knowledge is poured. They are not passive but active participants whose natural curiosity leads them to seek answers, test and retest hypotheses as they essentially reconstruct the world through their own experiences. They do this in the normal course of interaction with older children and adults. We have seen numerous times how adults' acting as conversational partners with children facilitates their language learning. Whether talking with children or participating in play with them, adults can encourage them and help them channel their curiosity. The quantity of interaction that children have with adults is not the only thing that matters. The way an adult interacts with children can play an important role in their learning and development. In fact, research suggests that the quality of the interactions occurring in classroom settings is even more significant for predicting the success of early childhood education than factors such as the education level or subject-area specialization of the teacher (Mashburn & Pianta, 2006). The kinds of interactions that help most are those in which adults provide feedback to children and encourage deeper thinking by asking "how" and "why" questions. In the following dialogue, we see a swimming teacher guiding her 6-year-old pupil to more advanced reasoning. They are in the family pool for Marta's swimming lesson.

> *Marta: I can touch the bottom!*
>
> *Teacher: Yes, you can.*
>
> *Marta: But yesterday, I couldn't.*
>
> *Teacher: That's true. What do you think happened?*
>
> *Marta: I growed?*
>
> *Teacher: You think you grew that much in one day? [Marta shrugs.] Look where the water comes on me today. It touches me here [Pointing at a place mid-abdomen]. Yesterday, it touched me here [Pointing to her waist]. Do you think I grew, too?*
>
> *Marta: [Tentatively] Maybe.*
>
> *Teacher: I don't think so. What else could have happened? [Marta thinks and the teacher leads her to the side of the pool.] Look where the water comes on the side. What would happen if we turned on the water and put more water in the pool?*
>
> *Marta: It would come up to here [She indicates a higher level on pool.].*

Teacher: Right. And then where would it be on you? [Marta stands closer to pool side and points to her nose.] Right! So what do you think happened last night?

Marta: Some of the water went away.

Teacher: Yes, it looks that way, doesn't it?

Encouragement Is More Important Than Praise

In their interaction with young children, adults often praise them. Praise is good when deserved, but in terms of helping children learn and grow, encouragement is even more important. Excessive praise will be meaningless to children after a while, but they never tire of encouragement. More importantly, they need encouragement. Whether trying to balance one block on top of another to build a high tower or learning to ride a bicycle, tie a bow, or name the letters of the alphabet, children need encouragement to try again.

A teacher's encouragement is more important than praise in helping young children learn new skills. How would you encourage young learners?

Associated Press

The following dialogue between Selena and her mother illustrates how praise and encouragement work together to advance the 4-year-old's learning. Selena wants to braid her doll's hair, but her mother is teaching her first to braid using three different colored ribbons pinned together at the top.

Selena: I can't do it.

Mom: Show me what you did. [Selena shows her a tangle of ribbons.]. Well, you have the right idea.

Selena: [Throwing the ribbons down] No, it's too hard. I can't.

Mom: It is hard, but you can do it. You just have to know the secret.

Selena: Secret?

Mom: Yep. Let me show you. [She picks up the ribbons and lays them down in front of Selena.] Okay. Three ribbons, right?

Selena: Yep.

Mom: The secret is that they all take turns being in the middle. Show me which one is in the middle. [Selena points to the blue ribbon.] Right. And the red one is on this side and the yellow one on the other side. All the ribbons are going to take turns being in the middle. It's a game for ribbons!

Selena: A game for ribbons? [She giggles.] That's silly.

Mom: Yes, kind of. But it works. Let me show you. First, let's put the red one over the blue one. Now which is in the middle?

Selena: The red one!

Mom: And whose turn is next?

Selena: The yellow one.

Mom: So we put the yellow one over the red one so that it is in the middle. Whose turn is it to be in the middle now?

Selena: Um. Red?

Mom: No. It had the last turn, didn't it?

Selena: Oh, right. Blue again!

Mom: Excellent! See we go back and forth, first on this side and then on the other side. You want to try? [Selena braids the ribbon slowly but correctly.]

If Selena's mother had simply praised her tangled attempt at braiding, Selena would not have made a great deal of progress. Notice that she didn't praise her at all until the end of the "lesson" when Selena had mastered the process. What she did, and very effectively, was to encourage her and integrate the new learning—braiding—into Selena's existing knowledge—turn-taking and games. The same principle works with language learning. Empty praise is ineffective, but encouragement motivates children to keep trying.

Learning Is Embedded in Socialization

We have seen throughout this book that language learning is qualitatively different from other learning, and not only because the infant brain comes hard-wired to learn language. Language learning is also the basis for all other language, and it occurs within and because of the process of socialization, of becoming part of the human community. So it is with all learning that young children do. It is in their job description, but from their perspective, learning about the world is a process of becoming part of the world.

When children begin formal schooling, the school day is usually broken down into units of time assigned to different activities in support of learning different subjects in the curriculum—reading, arithmetic, social studies, and so forth. But that is not how young children experience the world outside the classroom. In general, their days are not divided into segments—an hour for gross motor development, half an hour for fine motor skills,

This family is preparing dinner together. Although their goal is dinner, the talk that occurs is important to the children's language development.

Jodi Cobb/National Geographic Stock

40 minutes for social interaction, an hour for memory development, and so on. Learning for infants and toddlers is an unfragmented whole as they figure out what they need to know to achieve group membership, whether the group be the family, the extended family, or the neighborhood. Although their learning follows a kind of developmental schedule, as we saw in Chapter 6, children don't learn parts of language because their biological clock says it is time—they learn in order to communicate. From their perspective, their first years are not devoted to learning words, improving memory capacity, or learning categories and concepts, but in learning to become like the people around them. The important take-away for preschool teachers is that learning should be embedded in activities that are reflective of children's prior experience of learning and that are embedded in the process of socialization. Such activities need to be appropriate to children's stage of development and natural rather than instructional (see *Surreptitious Teaching*).

Surreptitious Teaching

Sometimes, well-meaning adults engage in **surreptitious teaching**, thinly disguised attempts to push children beyond their current stage of development into the next level. This dialogue between Liam, age 2, and his mother illustrates the effect of surreptitious teaching.

Mother: You want jelly on your sandwich?
Liam: No sandish.
Mother: It's not sandish. It's sandwich. Can you say "sandwich"?
Liam: No. No sandish!
Mother: So do you want jelly?
Liam: No sandish. No delly.
Mother: It's sandwich and jelly.
Liam: No! Want ronie and cheese.
Mother: Macaroni and cheese.
Liam: Yep.
Mother: Can you say "macaroni"?
Liam: Ronie.
Mother: MA-CA-RO-NI
Liam: I hungry.

(continued)

Surreptitious Teaching *(continued)*

We can see that the surreptitious teaching has no effect on Liam, at least not a positive effect. But is it potentially harmful? It could be if it were a regular occurrence, because it could discourage the child from talking with the adult at all. Clearly, though, it is a waste of everyone's time. The dialogue between Lincoln, age 3, and his mother illustrates a more effective tactic.

> *Lincoln: I be Pider-Man.*
> *Mother: You're Spider-Man?*
> *Lincoln: Yep, Pider-Man. But I no fly.*
> *Mother: You can't fly?*
> *Lincoln: No. I run really fast.*
> *Mother: Yes, you do run fast, and you can pretend-fly, right?*
> *Lincoln: Yep, I tend fly. Then I be Pider-Man.*

Notice that Lincoln's mother makes no attempt at all to correct his pronunciation, but focuses on the content and on repeating his utterances correctly. While the repetition could be construed as surreptitious teaching, the more likely effect is to show Lincoln that his mother is interested in what he has to say. In focusing on what he has to say and leaving how he says it alone, she provides strong motivation for further communication.

These general observations on the nature of early learning apply to all early learning, but they are especially important for literacy and arithmetic learning because they are so central to school success. Literacy is foundational to all learning, so we will take a closer look at how the foundations for literacy are built.

9.2 Language, Learning, and Literacy

Acquiring literacy is built on a foundation of oral language, but it is also interdependent with it. In other words, children continue to develop oral language skills as they begin to acquire literacy skills. We learned in Chapter 3 that exposure to language in a normal environment is the only requirement for children to acquire oral language. Whether learning to read can be accomplished as easily is the subject of some debate. In theory, it *should* be. After all, learning to speak and learning to read are both language skills, and we have seen that the human brain is uniquely wired for acquiring language. We have also seen that the brain is most flexible from birth to age 5.

Toddlers understand far more language than they can speak, and they also go through a period of rapid vocabulary expansion, which would seem to indicate that they are at a peak stage for language learning. Yet, in the American and many European education systems, children are not formally taught reading until age 5 or 6. Why? First, we need to differentiate between teaching and learning. Formal reading instruction as it is practiced in schools probably should not be started before that age, and we only have to review the observations about children's learning in the previous section to understand why. When it comes to learning, however, young children tend to be in charge, suggesting that if we create the optimal environments for learning to read and write, children will acquire the foundations before they begin school.

In this section, we look first at what constitutes preliteracy, or the knowledge and skills that help young children to become fluent readers and writers later. Then we examine three approaches that help them to acquire these skills.

What Are Preliteracy Skills?

Learning to read begins in infancy.

> We now know that learning to read is a process of brain building and brain training. Early experiences build the connections in the areas of the brain that deal with seeing and hearing, social connection and communication, basic information processing, and then language. (Bardige, 2009, p. 174)

Learning to read begins with comprehension. In a sense, that is where it ends, too, because the goal of reading is not the ability to identify printed words or to pronounce words correctly for reading aloud. The goal is to comprehend the writer's intended meaning. Comprehension, then, is not a stage of literacy development but a strand that is woven throughout all language learning, oral and written. Comprehension is dependent on three stages: phonological awareness, print and alphabet awareness, and early writing. These stages are not discrete but overlapping, and they are also developing parallel with oral language, although young children's oral language abilities will almost always exceed their literacy skills.

Phonologicial awareness refers to the knowledge and conscious understanding of the sound structure of language. This knowledge manifests itself in various ways including word and letter identification and the ability to rhyme and to spell. Why is it important to literacy? In general, phonological awareness helps children develop skills such as decoding, spelling, and ultimately, reading comprehension. Research has shown us the following:

- Children who are good at identifying syllable boundaries and rhyming learn to read better and faster than their peers (Lonigan, 2008).
- Children who are able to play with the sounds in words also tend to be better readers (Beauchat, Blamey, & Walpole, 2010).
- Children who do not have these kinds of phonological awareness tend to have difficulty making the connection between the written and spoken word (Lonigan, 2008).

Although phonological awareness is foundational to learning to read, it exists prior to learning to read and even in people who never learn to read. It is not the same as reading aloud, although it is required in order to read aloud, but phonological awareness can be developed "in the dark" (Beauchat et al., 2010, p. 71) so that parents and preschool teachers help children develop sensitivity to language sounds. Any vocal activity that allows children to experiment with and play with the sounds of words increases their phonological awareness. Sally was only a few months old, when her grandmother made up a story about Sally. The story was about Sally's silly sister singing songs to Sam the simple snake. The story ended with the words "Sally starts with ssssssss." As children grow older, they are able to participate in more advanced verbal play, so when they are confronted with letters, they are ready to extend to the printed page their knowledge about the sounds they hear. With an older child, saying a simple sentence such as, "I love bananas!" and asking her to count the words builds phonological awareness that will be especially important when she begins to identify words in print during the stage of print and alphabet awareness.

Print and alphabet awareness refers to a range of skills including the ability to recognize that the words on a page correspond to spoken words, that letters correspond to sounds (phonemes) and to their understanding of the purposes of print—to convey information or tell a story—and the fact that print serves many purposes in people's lives. Following are some of the reasons that print and alphabet awareness are important to success in learning to read and write:

- Knowing the correspondence between print and speech—for example, that the marks on a page represent particular sounds and words that tell a story—is a building block for comprehension because children know what to expect.
- Conversely, children who do not have a grasp of the functions of print are more likely to struggle with early literacy instruction (National Early Literacy Panel, 2007).
- The critical period for language learning (Chapters 3 and 5), which starts to atrophy after age 5 or so, applies to all language learning, including print. It is easier for a preschool child to learn sound-symbol correspondence during this period than later. Although, it is certainly possible to learn even as an adult since all literacy has oral language as its starting point.

It is unlikely that this infant can read the book. What preliteracy skills is he learning?

Print awareness begins in infancy, and if an infant is surrounded by print and by people who read, much of the awareness comes without direct intervention. An infant who is read to comes to understand that there is a story contained between the covers of a book and, eventually, that the story is told by the words, not the pictures. However, even though the interventions aren't direct, they do involve active interactions with adults, and the amount and quality of these indirect "print interventions" will determine the amount of print and alphabet awareness the preschooler brings to the classroom. Preschoolers will have had vast differences in their experiences with print. Some children may not know the front of the book from the back or how text is written left to right in English or even that it is the text that conveys the information and not the pictures.

Others will have all those skills and may be able to recognize certain letters or the letters in their own names. This means that the preschool teacher must provide an environment that makes it possible for children with less print awareness to catch up while continuing to grow the print awareness in other children.

Before they have gained the fine motor skills needed to print legibly, children demonstrate their awareness of writing and begin to engage in activities that are precursors to true writing. This **emergent writing** refers to the efforts that children make before they know the conventions of writing. Chinh and his father provide a good example of emergent writing. Three-year-old Chinh has a cold and had to stay at home with his mother while his father took his brothers and sisters to the ice skating rink. Chinh is very disappointed, and he resists his mother's attempts to mollify him by reading his favorite book. She tries to interest him in playing with his cars or a puzzle. He finally settles down with some crayons and begins to draw. When his father comes home, Chinh hurries to show him the picture he has drawn. His father sits down with Chinh on the couch and starts to put the drawing aside.

Chinh: No! You read.

Dad: You want me to read to you?

Chinh: Yes, please.

Dad: Okay, well, get me a book and I will. Which book do you want?

Chinh: Not book. This. [He retrieves the picture he has drawn—see Figure 9.1.] Read this!

Dad: [Unable to read the scribbles] It's your story. Why don't you read it to me?

Chinh: It says the boy got sick so couldn't go skating. Then another day, he felt better, and then he did go skating. And the sun shined and made the ice into water.

Dad: [Pointing to another person in the picture] Did the boy go alone? Who's that?

Chinh: That's you! And that's Mommy.

Dad: That's a good story, Chinh. Thank you for writing it. And for reading it to me, too.

Figure 9.1: Example of Chinh's early writing

Chinh's drawing and story show awareness of print.

The squiggles on the page in Figure 9.1 illustrate early writing. Not much of the print is decipherable, but there are a couple of letter-like symbols that suggest that Chinh is aware of sound-symbol correspondence and, thus, that this may be a genuine attempt by Chinh to express himself in print. A year earlier, Chinh might have told his story with pictures only, and the pictorial story is a very early kind of emergent writing. Chinh's scribbles are typical of the next stage of emergent writing, a transitional stage. His picture tells the story, but with his scribbles, he has demonstrated his awareness that print conveys meaning and has begun to show some understanding of the conventions of print. Recognizing the power of words to convey meaning and his ability to control those words, Chinh is exhibiting two ways in which children develop preliteracy and literacy skills.

How Do We Help Children Acquire Preliteracy Skills?

A full description of the approaches and the tools that teachers have available to help children acquire literacy skills is beyond the scope of this book. Acquiring literacy is an aspect of language learning, and it is interactive with oral language development. It is important, however, to help children to develop them in tandem. Three effective approaches for helping children integrate and expand oral and written language are independent literacy, literacy in play, and interactive reading.

Independent Literacy

Independent literacy refers to reading and writing, or prereading and prewriting, activities that children initiate themselves. But as we have seen, young children often rely on adults to facilitate that learning. Fostering independence is one way in which parents and preschool teachers facilitate literacy development at every stage. Other ways include linking literacy to play and engaging in interactive literacy. The ultimate goal of literacy instruction is independence, and it is wise to encourage independence at every stage of the process and to build on it. In fact, there are many opportunities to do so. As soon as an infant shows an interest in any print, whether on labels, in books, or on an electronic tablet, she has begun to take charge of her own learning. Parents and teachers can take advantage of the infant's natural curiosity by reading the words aloud, reinforcing that print has meaning. Eventually, the child's innate curiosity will cause her to ask or guess what the print says. At the point when the toddler is becoming aware that the print represents particular sounds and words, the adult points to the individual words. This is the stage when simple picture books with only a word or two on the page are most useful. They should not replace longer, text-rich story books, because the stages of learning to read overlap—while the child is figuring out sound-letter correspondence, she is also learning how stories are constructed (Chapter 6), which helps her comprehension and will later be important when she is learning to write.

We see in the dialogue between Chinh and his father a good illustration of literacy independence. Using art, Chinh has created the story he wants to tell even though he is not yet able to form the words. He has a grasp of narrative structure and is well aware that print conveys meaning. Although he is not yet able to create letters, we can see some level of phonological awareness—the story is about the sun and skating, and he has used a facsimile of the letter "s." Clearly, Chinh is taking charge of his own learning, but that is not what he intends. From his perspective, he's doing what the others in his family do: He is reading and writing to become part of the community of the literate. Chinh's father wisely acts as a facilitator; he offers encouragement—notice that he doesn't tell Chinh that he can't read his writing but instead encourages Chinh by asking him to read the story. This exchange reinforces the observations that young children's learning is interactive and that it occurs as part of socialization. We can also see how a child's interest in drawing can be used to integrate literacy awareness. See *Using Art to Foster Literacy* for other ideas.

Using Art to Foster Literacy

Most children love to draw, and there are many ways of integrating art and literacy. With very young children, you can ask their permission to label the elements of the picture, using sticky notes or printing directly on the page. With older children, one way of fostering early interest in reading is to ask the child to tell the story portrayed in the picture. The adult can take dictation on another page and then tape the pages together to form a book. Then the adult can read the book with the child and encourage the author to read the story to others. The child can also be encouraged to add to the story with new pictures and text. Can you think of other ways to integrate art and literacy?

Literacy in Play

We learned earlier in this chapter that play is essential to young children's learning. While it might seem that learning to read and write are less integrated with playtime, this *should not* be the case. Literacy-rich play environments provide children with valuable prereading experiences, including practice in storytelling (Christie & Roskos, 2003). The most effective play for developing literacy is dramatic play because it helps to develop a strong sense of narrative, imagination, and the oral language skills on which literacy is layered. But not all kinds of pretend play are equally effective. To be most effective in helping children develop their sense of narrative and in expanding their oral language abilities, pretend play should have three elements:

1. Pretend play should stretch the imagination by having children assume more than one character role or multiple aspects of a single character: *You can be the mommy, and the mommy is also a teacher.*
2. It should involve changing the functions of objects. For example, rather than using a telephone or a toy telephone, use a block or a ruler as a telephone. This stretches the imagination and helps teach children representation (i.e., that objects can be represented by other objects just as they can be represented by words).
3. This kind of play can involve a pretend scenario that has a problem or conflict to be solved: *Sadie invited four people to her party, but Mommy has only three cupcakes. . . .* This helps to develop the notion of character and plot in stories.

Books and stories can be a good starting place for these dramatic activities for prereaders. Children can take on the roles of characters they have heard about from the stories and then expand their experiences in their dramatic play. Depending on age, children can draw pictures to illustrate their expanded story, or they can dictate them to teachers or older children to write down for them.

Earlier in this chapter, we noted that adults are facilitators of learning but also that children are in charge. In the context of children's play, these observations are very important: Adults must be very careful about intervening in children's play. If we are to help children elevate the level of play as described in the preceding list, then we can't leave them entirely on their own. Some children may not be well socialized in play, and even those who are may be engaging in more reality-based than imaginative play. It is possible, however, to guide without directing (see *Facilitating Play for Preliteracy*).

Encouraging children to dress up as their favorite characters from books can help encourage literacy through dramatic play. How could you make this type of play even more effective?

Associated Press

Facilitating Play for Preliteracy

Do Not . . .

- Become a player in children's games by assuming a role, unless specifically invited. Even if invited, remember who is to benefit and play a low-key role.
- "Correct" or redirect their imaginative play (e.g., "Don't put that dress on the baby. It's too cold out!"). Doing so changes the play to a teacher-directed activity.
- Encourage the use of too many "real" props. Some real props, such as an apron or a crown, might help the child to stay in character. But too many real props stifle imagination. Remember, imagination is built by using objects for unusual purposes.

Do . . .

- Help children see alternate uses for props or create new ones. One way of doing this is by modeling the use of objects for unique purposes: "I don't have a microphone, but we can use this water bottle as a pretend microphone," or "We don't have a stethoscope, but what else can we use as a pretend stethoscope so Tammy can be a doctor?"
- Encourage children to make their own props—modeling clay, paper, and glue can create useful props for their plays. The talk that occurs as children work on the props is an added bonus.
- Expand their repertoire of pretend-play themes by exposing children to new stories and ideas. For example, if the children seem always to be pretending to be princesses, read them stories or use carefully chosen videos to introduce new themes such as jungle animals or space travel.
- Encourage children to retell the story of their play orally the following day.

Interactive Reading

As we learned in Chapter 5, infants begin to learn about books and what print is very early when they see parents or older siblings reading and when they are read to. We know that children's early learning is an interactive process that occurs within the context of socialization. One of the most effective ways that adults can act as facilitators of learning is to read interactively with children. "**Interactive reading** involves an extended, meaningful exchange between adults and children, during which both parties are actively engaged in the learning process" (Cabell, Justice, Vukelich, Buell, & Han, 2008, p. 199). The more that children participate in the reading, the better, whether that participation involves pointing to pictures or turning pages, as it might with very young toddlers. Or children can participate by asking and answering questions either about the story itself or something suggested by the story. But to get the most out of interactive reading, some advance planning and thought are required

Interactive reading engages children in the reading process by allowing them to take part as active participants.

Sven Hagolani/Corbis

in order to make the story come alive for toddlers and preschoolers. Children become engaged in reading when adults select stories that will expand children's experience or introduce new themes. Children also become engaged when adults, facilitate use of props, identify places in the story that will have particular relevance, or introducing new ideas to children.

The many advantages to interactive reading include the following:

- Reading becomes an active rather than a passive learning activity that provides opportunities for dialogue, which enhances vocabulary growth and expanded language forms.
- Children's level of engagement in the reading process correlates with accelerated gains in language and literacy development (Cabell et al., 2008; Wasik & Bond, 2001).
- At-risk children benefit especially from interactive reading. The gap between low-risk and high-risk children in all reading skills can be narrowed by increasing the amount and quality of their engagement during interactive reading (Chaney, 1994; Hart & Risley, 1995; Justice & Ezell, 2001).

Thoughts on "Accelerated" Literacy

Should we teach children to read before the usual age of 5 or 6 when reading instruction normally begins in school? Many parents are nervous about doing so, thinking they lack the skill. True, many parents are not formally "reading teachers," but this does not mean they cannot teach their children to read. Reading and writing are extensions of language, so the critical period for language learning discussed in Chapters 3, 4, and 5 constitutes a strong argument for early reading instruction, and some of this can be accomplished at home.

Maybe the most important factor in whether children should begin reading prior to first grade is readiness. Children who are ready for reading send strong signals—they point to a word or a sentence and ask what it says. They "read" out loud from familiar books mimicking what they remember hearing. They scribble, as Chinh did, on paper and ask someone else to read it. Children who show this level of readiness will benefit from more advanced interventions. These interventions might include letter and word identification, perhaps beginning with rhyming words such as *cat/bat/hat*. Another unobtrusive intervention is simply to label items in the child's environment with words on 3" x 5" cards or sticky notes. It is important to attend to children's signals—if they are preschoolers and are uninterested in or resist these early efforts, then abandon the efforts and wait. It is also crucial to remember that although the first 5 years are all about learning, from the perspective of the child, these years are about play, so any "teaching" needs to be invisible. Learning has to be fun.

9.3 Language, Learning, and Arithmetic

The most basic arithmetic concepts, such as learning to count, rely on language (Chapter 5). Further evidence for the importance of language for learning arithmetic comes from bilingual learners. If mathematical learning were independent of language—as theoretically it *could* be—then bilinguals would be expected to solve arithmetic problems equally well in either of their languages, assuming that they were equally proficient in their two languages. Research has shown, however, that when asked to solve simple arithmetic problems, adult bilinguals tend to revert to the language in which they were taught even if that language is not currently considered the stronger language (Moschkovich, 2007). This fact should not be interpreted to mean that bilinguals have any kind of a deficit—quite the contrary; since the preference is just that, a preference not a necessity, most bilinguals learn to calculate and compute in both languages. But the preference for the language in which they were taught points to the centrality of language in the learning process.

Although most bilingual learners will have a lifelong tendency to count and to calculate basic arithmetic problems in the language in which they first learned the concepts, that does not mean that parents should insist that their children learn to count in English instead of their mother tongue. Arithmetic concepts and mathematical reasoning *do* transfer to the other language. A bilingual child who learns basic arithmetic concepts in one language will be capable of acquiring more advanced math skills in either language. A bilingual preschool setting that introduced and reinforced basic numeric concepts in both languages would be ideal, but a monolingual environment works just as well. Bilingual children need exposure to integrated math and language in at least one of their two languages. The child will benefit from a strong linguistic foundation on which to build— *which* language is not terribly important. As we shall see in Chapter 10, bilingualism can be an advantage to children learning math in school.

Math Learning at Home

Like language acquisition, math learning begins at home, and it begins early. Research shows the following:

- Infants as young as 5 to 6 months appear to understand very small numbers, noticing that something is amiss when they witness simple errors in addition or subtraction (adding two blocks to two more but showing the infant only three blocks, for example).
- Preschool children have a great deal of potential to develop informal math knowledge, and this early knowledge helps them to learn formal mathematics later.
- Children who begin school with a strong sense of basic math concepts do better in school than those who do not. This benefit extends throughout the school years.
- Effort matters more than any perceived innate ability. Children who focus on effort and are made to believe that they *can* learn do better than those who do not.
- Attitude also matters. Children who develop a positive or neutral attitude toward numbers early are more likely to do well in math. (National Mathematics Advisory Panel, 2008)

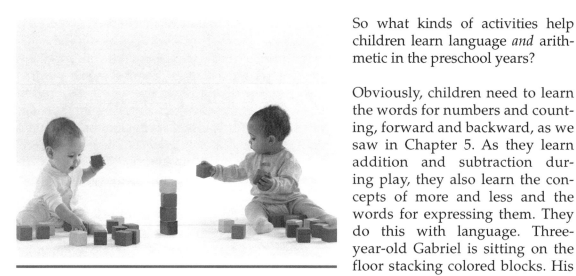

These babies are drawn to the color and shape of the blocks. Later, they will learn to manipulate them in ways that will aid their development of language and arithmetic skills.

Photodisc/Thinkstock

So what kinds of activities help children learn language *and* arithmetic in the preschool years?

Obviously, children need to learn the words for numbers and counting, forward and backward, as we saw in Chapter 5. As they learn addition and subtraction during play, they also learn the concepts of more and less and the words for expressing them. They do this with language. Three-year-old Gabriel is sitting on the floor stacking colored blocks. His 2-year-old sister, Sophia, is playing beside him. Gabriel reaches over and takes a block from the ones in front of Sophia.

Sophia: No! Mine!

Gabriel: I need it.

Sophia: [Taking a block from Gabriel's pile] Okay.

Gabriel: No, I need it. I'm making a house. [He takes another of Sophia's blocks.]

Sophia: No! Mine.

Gabriel: You don't need all the blocks. I need this one.

[At this point their mother intervenes.]

Mother: Gabriel, why did you take the block away from Sophia?

Gabriel: I'm building a house and I want it bigger.

Mother: So you need more blocks?

Gabriel: Yes.

Mother: I see. But that doesn't mean you can take Sophia's. You both get the same number of blocks.

Gabriel: The same?

Mother: Give me the block. [Gabriel hands her the block, reluctantly.] Okay, let's start with yours. Can you count them?

Gabriel: One, two, three, four, five, six, seven, eight, nine, ten, 'leven, twelve.

Mother: Right. And now, Sophie's blocks.

Sophia: One, two, three, six, four, um . . .

Mother: Let's start again and do it together. [The three of them count together.] Okay, Sophie has 12 blocks, too. Now, if we borrow one block from Sophie . . . [Sophie objects.] Just for a minute, Sophia. Just for a minute. Now, let's borrow one more. Now, who has more blocks?

Gabriel: Me! I have more blocks.

Mother: Now, we have to give them back to Sophie. But I have an idea. Why don't you and Sophia build a house together and then you'll have lots of blocks for a really big house.

There has been no formal math lesson going on in this exchange, yet the children have both advanced their understanding of basic mathematical concepts and acquired some of the language they will need to advance it even further. Later, when Gabriel had moved on to play with other toys, the children's mother took the opportunity to play with Sophia.

Mother: You have lots of blocks. Let's sort them by color, shall we?

Sophia: What?

Mother: Here, I'll show you. Can you get all the red ones? [Sophia picks up one red one and then another.] Good. Are there any more red ones? [Sophia finds another one and hands it to her mother.] Good. Now, let's put the red ones together over here. Can you count the red blocks, Sophia?

Sophia: One, two, three!

Mother: Right! Three red blocks. Do you think there are more red blocks or more yellow blocks?

Sophia: Red!

Mother: Well, let's see. Can you find all the yellow blocks, and we'll put them over here. [Sophia picks out four yellow blocks and her mother puts them together apart from the red blocks.] Okay, which pile is bigger? The red or the yellow?

Sophia: Lallo!

Mother: Right again! Can you count the yellow blocks for me?

Sophia: One, two, three, four!

Mother: That's right. Can you count the red ones?

Sophia: One, two, three.

Mother: Right! So which pile has more? [Sophia points to the yellow pile.] Yep, the yellow pile has more blocks!

The mother has engaged in a little surreptitious teaching here, but in this case, it seems to have worked because Sophia remained engaged. Notice how she has adjusted the task of counting and the concepts of more and less to make them appropriate to Sophia's stage of development. With both children, the mother has demonstrated two "best practices" for the teaching of early math: Build on what children already know, and seize on everyday teachable moments. Let's consider each in turn.

Finding Teachable Moments for Math

What knowledge did Gabriel and Sophia's mother build on in these two exchanges? First, with Gabriel, she built on the fact that he could already count forward to 12. She used concrete objects that he could see and touch to illustrate a basic subtraction problem as well as the concepts of *more* and *less*. At the end of the exchange, she also began to link the concept of *more* with *bigger*—with more blocks, Gabriel could build a bigger house. With Sophia, she worked from (and reinforced) the child's knowledge of color to work on her counting. Sophia knew the vocabulary for counting to four, but there is a difference between knowing the words for numbers and understanding the concept of counting. In this interaction, her mother helped to solidify her understanding of what those words mean. She also demonstrated the meaning of *more*, a word that Sophia also knew but for which she had not yet acquired a fully formed concept. Notice that while the mother guided both her children, she essentially followed their lead and used the opportunity of play to extend their learning. She built on what they already knew.

Counting coins before putting them into a piggy bank is an example of how opportunities for learning arithmetic concepts exist in everyday life. How would you extend learning with this activity?

Exactostock/SuperStock

The most obvious characteristic of both exchanges is that the mother seized on teachable moments. With arithmetic, there are many such moments since children like to count. For instance, when Gloria was walking well enough to climb steps while holding onto an adult, her mother counted the stairs going up and down. They counted the steps from the kitchen to the play-room, and the number of books on the shelf. They counted the eggs in the carton, and then when she got older, her mother would ask Gloria how many would be left in the carton after they took out two to make cookies. Then they would count again to confirm.

Building on what children know and seizing teachable moments in everyday situations are excellent practices for all teaching, particularly since they are firmly grounded in the observations about children's early learning. Gabriel and Sophia's mother embedded her lessons on counting and on the concepts of *more* or *less* in the children's ongoing play activity. She adjusted her language and the activities to match the developmental level of each child, and she facilitated rather than instructed them in basic arithmetic concepts. Language and arithmetic are learned in tandem as shown in *Activities to Develop Both Language and Arithmetic*.

Activities to Develop Both Language and Arithmetic

Children learn to use words before they acquire the full range of meanings behind them or the concepts embodied in them. Adults can engage in play activities that extend the meanings of the words the child already knows. This will help to develop the concepts essential to their learning arithmetic later in life.

Sorting. Categorizing objects according to their color, size, or function helps children to expand their understanding of and develop the concepts behind *alike* and *different*. Sorting helps them learn to categorize, which assists in conceptual development generally. It also affords opportunities for counting and comparison. Later, this will assist them in data management, which is important for applying arithmetic concepts.

Identification of shapes. Almost every object a child encounters in the day can be labeled with a shape. Encourage children to recognize and name different shapes. This develops a math skill related to geometry.

Recognizing patterns. Pattern recognition is a foundation for higher math. Children benefit from all kinds of pattern-recognition activities, including experiencing the repetition of sounds in rhymes or songs, pointing out the recurring patterns in the curtains, or stringing beads in particular patterns of color.

Measurement. Like counting, measuring is something that most children like to do. When they learn *more* and *less* and *bigger* and *smaller*, they are learning the elements of measuring. Later, they can use a plastic ruler, measuring cups, or a piece of string to determine measurements of many things in their everyday environment.

Conclusion

This chapter began with a description of seven common-sense observations about the nature of early learning, reminding us that early childhood is a time devoted to a great deal of learning, all of it interdependent with language and within the context of socialization. The learning of basic arithmetic concepts is intertwined with language and language learning. Many opportunities arise in children's everyday lives for developing both. Reading and writing, the other foundations of academic success in the school years, are also closely linked to oral language. It is both possible and desirable to create environments that foster their development in tandem. The components of preliteracy—phonological awareness, print awareness, and early, or emergent, writing—are effectively established when we encourage independent reading, literacy in play, and interactive reading. In helping children develop strong preliteracy skills, we help guide them toward the ultimate goal of reading comprehension and the ability to convey their thoughts in writing.

Post-Test

1. Children's interests and desires in learning remind us that

   a. they learn independent to their degree of readiness.
   b. play is unimportant.
   c. they learn more from requirement than praise.
   d. they are the ones in charge.

2. Which of the following is NOT an approach to helping students integrate and expand oral and written language?

   a. interactive reading
   b. independent literacy
   c. literacy in play
   d. dependent literacy

3. Which of the following is NOT listed as an activity for developing language and arithmetic?

   a. measuring
   b. recognizing patterns
   c. sorting
   d. reading math books

Answers

1. d. They are the ones in charge. *The answer can be found in Section 9.1.*
2. d. Dependent literacy. *The answer can be found in Section 9.2.*
3. d. Reading math books. *The answer can be found in Section 9.3.*

Key Ideas

- All of children's early learning is rooted in language and occurs as part of socialization.
- Both early arithmetic and literacy skills are built on a solid foundation in oral language.
- From the perspective of young children, learning and play are indistinguishable.
- Learning progresses according to children's degree of readiness and at a pace that is also dependent on their development.
- Adults can facilitate children's learning by interacting with them in meaningful ways.
- Phonological awareness, print awareness, and emergent writing are components of preliteracy, and this development begins in infancy.
- Approaches such as independent reading, literacy in play, and interactive reading foster literacy development.

Critical Thinking Questions

1. How is language learning different from other kinds of learning in early childhood?
2. How could you, as a preschool teacher, take advantage of what the 3-year-old child in the image is doing to

Corbis/SuperStock

   a. expand her vocabulary and
   b. develop basic arithmetic concepts? Be specific.
3. Read the first dialogue in the box entitled *Surreptitious Teaching*. What would have been a better approach for Liam's mother to take with him and why?
4. In the section on helping children to acquire preliteracy skills, the author discusses both independent literacy and interactive reading as useful tools. These appear to be near opposites. Are they? How do they work together?
5. Consider the following conversation between 5-year-old Gloria and her grandmother. Gloria is bilingual in Spanish and English and attends a Spanish-language kindergarten. Her grandmother speaks only English with her. They are decorating cupcakes for Gloria to take to school.

Gloria: Can we make pink ones and blue ones, too?

Grandmother: Yes. How many pink ones do you want?

Gloria: Lots!

Grandmother: What's lots?

Gloria: Um, I'm not sure.

Grandmother: Okay, let's start by counting all the cupcakes we have and then we can decide how many to put pink icing on and how many blue. Okay?

Gloria: Yep. [She begins counting.] One, two, three, four . . . (and on to 16). Is it okay if I count in Spanish now?

Grandmother: Of course it is!

Gloria: [Continues to count in Spanish until she gets to 24 and then switches back to English] 24! We have 24.

Grandmother: Seems that way. Now how many pink ones. Half?

Gloria: [Seems uncertain] How many is half?

Grandmother: Well, half would mean an equal number. Do you know how to divide?

Gloria: I don't think so.

Grandmother: I'll show you an easy way. We'll just separate these cupcakes into two sets of cupcakes, one for pink and one for blue. This one goes over here into the pink pile, and this one over here to the blue. [Gloria separates the cupcakes one at a time into two piles.] Now we count them.

Gloria: [This time, she counts both piles in English.] They're the same! We have 12 and 12.

Grandmother: Right. Now, do you want 12 pink and 12 blue?

Gloria: No, I want more pink.

Grandmother: How many pink do you want?

Gloria: 15!

Grandmother: So how many do we have to put on this side to have 15?

Gloria: [Taking one cupcake at a time from one side and moving it to the other.] That's 13. That's 14, and that's 15!

Grandmother: Okay, so now how many blue will we have?

Gloria: 12?

Grandmother: Do we? Didn't we take some away?

Gloria: Oh, right. [She starts to count the cupcakes again.]

Grandmother: Wait a minute, Gloria. Let's see if we can figure it out without counting. We had 12 cupcakes, right? How many did we take away and put in the other pile?

Gloria: Three.

Grandmother: Right. So let's count backward from 12. [She holds up three fingers.] We'll take away three.

Gloria: Eleven [Grandmother lowers one finger.]. Ten [Grandmother lowers a second finger]. Nine.

Grandmother: Okay. Now count them to see if you're right.

This real-life math lesson brings together many of the ideas introduced in this chapter.

a. Gloria first learned to count at home with her mother, using the stair steps up to her room (there were 16). She also began Spanish-only school at age 3. What effect of her bilingualism do you see in this conversation?
b. Which of the seven observations about how children learn do you see at work in this conversation?
c. Should the grandmother have taken advantage of the situation to teach Gloria the English numbers between 17 and 24?

4. What kinds of early literacy skills are being developed with the following activities?
a. Ask a 4-year-old child to count the syllables in words. Would you use the word *syllable?* If so, how would you explain it?
b. Begin with a word such as *cat*, and ask a 5-year-old what sound it begins with. Then ask, "What word would it be if you started with an 'm' sound?" Could you do this with print? If so, what additional skills is the child learning?

Key Terms

emergent writing The print efforts that children make before they know the conventions of writing.

independent literacy Reading and writing or prereading and prewriting activities that children initiate themselves.

interactive reading A shared reading experience in which adults and young learners work together to get meaning from text.

phonologicial awareness The knowledge and conscious understanding of the sound structure of language.

print and alphabet awareness A range of skills including the ability to recognize that the words on a page correspond to spoken words, that letters correspond to sounds (phonemes) and to their understanding of the purposes of print—to convey information or tell a story—and the fact that print serves many purposes in people's lives.

surreptitious teaching Thinly disguised attempts to push children beyond their current stage of development into the next level.

zone of proximal development Referring to readiness, Vygotsky's term for the distance between the child's actual physical and cognitive level of development and the level at which she can function with adult assistance.

Weblinks

An article by Mashburn and Pianta (referenced in this chapter) reporting research on the importance of physical environment in early childhood classrooms can be found here: http://www.earlychildhoodrc.org/events/presentations/mashburn.pdf

Visit this site for information on the importance of adult interaction with children: http://www.highscope.org/Content.asp?ContentId=180

For a review of the literature on the quality of caregiver-child interactions for young children, see
http://www.acf.hhs.gov/programs/opre/other_resrch/qcciit/quality_caregiver.pdf

For information on early arithmetic learning, go to the National Mathematics Advisory Panel's site:
www.ed.gov/mathpanel

Making Meaning, Making Sense: Putting It All Together

Learning Objectives

By the end of this chapter, you will be able to accomplish the following objectives:

- Articulate the major differences between the language children use at home and at school.

- Describe how early childhood educators can facilitate learning in culturally and linguistically diverse children.

- Identify best practices for dealing with individual differences in the early childhood classroom.

- Explain the impact past learning experience has on children's learning in the early childhood classroom, particularly as it affects the pace of their work.

- Explain how play is critical to language development.

- Explain the importance of teacher talk and what is meant by authentic language in talking with children.

Introduction

Acquiring language means acquiring all its component parts—the sounds, words, inflections, and the rules for putting them together. But the *purpose* is to make meaning. Children do not learn to talk only because they are born with the mechanism that makes it possible. They learn to talk in order to communicate. By the time most children start kindergarten or first grade, they are already very effective communicators. They have acquired most of the mechanics of language, they have well-established patterns and habits of learning, and they have made a good start toward becoming full participants in the community into which they were born. What has happened at home and in preschool has already had a profound impact on their future. When children leave these years behind and begin kindergarten or first grade, the learning environment changes and the linguistic and cognitive demands on them increase. In order to appreciate the differences and to ensure that we have done the best that we can to prepare children for more formal education, we begin this chapter with a broad description of the differences between the informal language and learning of the home and preschool and the more formal language and learning of the school. This will provide a context for us to synthesize what we learned in the previous chapters. From this synthesis, we will extract principles that early childhood educators can use in their practices. The remainder of the chapter is devoted to examining how some of those "best" practices are applied. Through a series of vignettes, some involving children that we met in earlier chapters, we will review the major concepts from the previous chapters. Each story will embody a number of different concepts about language and learning that we will discuss and evaluate.

Pre-Test

1. When looking at differences between home and school language, children

    a. primarily use casual language at home.
    b. use more purposeful language at home than they do at school.
    c. tend to display little difference in the two before first grade.
    d. tend to use concrete language in school.

2. The critical period for language

    a. applies only to the native language.
    b. applies only to the second language(s).
    c. begins around age 5.
    d. starts to wane after puberty.

3. A preschool child who shows no interest in words or letter identification but does have interest in readings and books should first be tested for

    a. language disorders.
    b. developmental delays.
    c. dyslexia.
    d. poor or low vision.

4. Which of the following would NOT be typical of the Montessori method?

    a. discovery, hands-on approach to learning
    b. attractive and interactive classroom
    c. teacher assigned tasks and assignments
    d. mixed-age groupings of students

5. Which of the following is true of using language for problem solving?

    a. It applies only to classroom conversations.
    b. It is a childhood task.
    c. It includes negotiation skills.
    d. It is distinguished from conversational skills.

6. An important characteristic of authentic language is that it

    a. involves concrete concepts.
    b. includes first-person references.
    c. does not insult or isolate the listener.
    d. closely resembles prior experience with language.

Answers

1. a. Primarily use casual language at home. *The answer can be found in Section 10.1.*
2. d. Starts to wane after puberty. *The answer can be found in Section 10.2.*
3. d. Poor or low vision. *The answer can be found in Section 10.3.*
4. c. Teacher assigned tasks and assignments. *The answer can be found in Section 10.4.*
5. c. It includes negotiation skills. *The answer can be found in Section 10.5.*
6. d. closely resembles prior experience with language. *The answer can be found in Section 10.6.*

10.1 Differences Between Home and School Language

School language (or school talk), which is the distinct pattern of language typically used in classrooms, can differ in many ways from home language. Families and cultures differ in their approaches to child rearing, and these differences can impact how the child adapts to school.

> For some families, learning may be accomplished more by demonstration and observation than by discussion, so verbal display of knowledge may also be quite rare. A quiet child may be valued and considered respectful and intelligent, while a talkative one might be considered self-centered, discourteous, undisciplined, and unintelligent. As a result, a child's participation in conversation, particularly with adults, may be discouraged in any number of ways. (van Kleeck, 2007)

Obviously, when a child speaks one language at home and another at school, that is a major difference. But even for children who speak the same language at home as at school, the talk happening in the home usually differs in significant ways from what happens in school. Even though we all know that school talk is critical to success, as Anne van Kleeck points out, ". . . school talk is rarely addressed directly as a possible reason that a child may be experiencing difficulty in school. A child with excellent academic potential may simply lack experience with this important pattern of language use" (2007, p. 1).

If their inability to understand the language of the school goes undetected, children may not become well socialized to the school, and their reading and overall academic achievement will be negatively affected as well (Cazden, 2001; Nystrand, 2006). If the language that children bring to school differs significantly from the language of the school, and if they do not adapt to the requirements of school talk fairly quickly, a teacher's perceptions of the child might also be affected. Therefore, examining how home and school language can differ is important so that we can better prepare preschool children for the language of the school.

At home, children learn the language appropriate for carrying out household routines.

Creatas/Thinkstock

Before we take a closer look at the different purposes for which talk is used at home and at school, we should note that the differences are not absolute but a matter of degree. In other words, families differ in the language they use as do schools, so the differences between the two are necessarily varied. In broad terms, though, talk in the home tends to be focused on meeting the social needs of the child—on participating in the family unit and on household routines. In contrast, school talk tends to be focused on accomplishing particular academic goals—learning to read, to add, to subtract—and on the more formal routines of the classroom. It also tends to be more abstract, meaning that it focuses less on the here and now. It is easy to see the distinctions by examining how, why, what, and when children talk.

How Children Talk

From the time children utter their first words, they talk about the things that are relevant to them. They name the members of their families, pets, and label familiar objects. Similarly, their first verbs tend to be action verbs, and their first adjectives describe familiar objects. So their first words are both familiar and concrete. Their talk may be more casual, or even marked by slang, and because of the social setting in which it occurs, is usually characterized by much turn-taking. Often, the conversation between children, family, and friends will share common experiences and knowledge, so there is not much need for explanation. A kind of verbal shorthand develops in families. Consider the following dialogue between Eleeshia and her father.

> *Father: [Holding up Eleeshia's lunch box] Same as yesterday?*

> *Eleeshia: Nope. I don't like red.*

> *Father: What do you like? Orange?*

Eleeshia: No, apple.

Father: I don't have apple.

Eleeshia: Cow, then.

Father: Right. Chocolate?

Eleeshia: Yep.

Father: Excuse me?

Eleeshia: Yes, please. And can I have jelly butter?

Father: No peanuts in school.

Eleeshia: No peanut butter, then. Just jelly.

Father: Not happenin'.

Focused on getting Eleeshia's lunch ready to take to school, this conversation is concrete and assumes common knowledge: Colors are used to indicate what kind of fruit juice, milk is cow juice, and what others may call peanut butter and jelly, or PB&J, is jelly butter in this family. The final utterance "Not happenin'" is slang and, while perfectly appropriate in the home, is less likely to be used in the school. Consider what a similar conversation might sound like in school, where the teacher and Eleeshia did not share the same knowledge. The first version of Eleeshia's response is the one she might give at home. The one in parentheses is the expected one in the school.

Teacher: Shall we have the same lunch as yesterday?

Eleeshia: No, I don't like red. (No, I don't like cranberry juice.)

Teacher: What do you mean, red?

Eleeshia: [Points to the juice]

Teacher: Oh, you don't like red juice. Okay, then, what kind do you think we should have? Orange?

Eleeshia: No, apple. (Could we please have apple?)

Teacher: I'm sorry, but we're all out of apple juice. Would you like something else?

Eleeshia: Cow, then. (Could I have milk, please?)

Teacher: Cow? You mean milk, don't you? White or chocolate?

Eleeshia: Yep. Chocolate.

Teacher: Yes, PLEASE.

Eleeshia: Yes, please. And can I have jelly butter?

Teacher: You want a butter and jelly sandwich? Or do you mean peanut butter? You know the school doesn't allow peanuts.

Eleeshia: No peanut butter, then. Just jelly.

On the playground, children learn the language they need to socialize with other children.

Associated Press

Teacher: I don't think that would be very good for you, Eleeshia. Chocolate milk and a jelly sandwich is not healthy.

From first grade, and sometimes kindergarten, onward, how children talk—how children *need* to talk—changes. At school, they will encounter new, unfamiliar words, and these words are more likely to be abstract. From the child's point of view, teachers can spend a lot of time talking about things that aren't there. To some degree that is necessarily true since the school curriculum becomes more abstract as children get older. As we learn history, for example, we have to rely on words to paint images of times past—the words may be concrete, but they have to convey meanings that are not. Also, at school, informal language and the slang of the playground get replaced with more formal words. Perhaps the biggest difference, however, is that at school children have to listen more while someone else tells them something they do not know. In school, more explanatory talk is needed since it is not safe to assume that listeners know what we are talking about. In school, teachers do more of the talking, and this is one of the reasons that the quality of teacher talk is so important.

What Children Talk About

At home, children talk about almost anything and everything. Relevance is the most important requirement for a subject of conversation. At home, families talk about personal experiences, about people they know, pets, favorite toys, food, or anything that is relevant to them. As children get older, the subjects expand as their interests grow, but generally, the topics of conversation are grounded in their own experience, past or present.

When they get to school, children find a big difference in what is talked about. Almost every child gets bored at some point during the school year, if not in the school day. If questioned, most will say that what they are learning is not relevant (Morin, 2012; Belton & Priyadharshini, 2007). Although what they are learning *may* be relevant, children may not immediately see the relevance, and talk that is not relevant tends not to be heard. Suddenly, in the school curriculum, they are thrust into print or oral descriptions of people and events they do not know, who are far away, or lived long ago. This is highly abstract for children. There is no concrete referent to help them understand and remember the new content or the language for talking about it.

Why Children Talk

Children learn to talk in order to participate in human society, to communicate. In order to learn to communicate effectively, they have learned a number of different functions of language (Chapter 7). They have learned to use language to get things done, to seek and to give information, and to establish social relationships with family and friends. They have already learned to use talk for play and to tell stories, some true and some imagined.

At school, talk becomes more purposeful and children begin to use language to think logically and analytically. Informative language is used in the classroom, but it is often one-sided—the teacher telling the children something they do not know. Children more often use language to demonstrate their own knowledge to the teacher (who usually already has it).

When Children Talk

Children who have attended pre-school may have a head start on adjusting to this difference between home and school talk. As any parent knows, children talk at home whenever they want to. Except for nap-time and time-outs, there are no boundaries put on talk. No one normally has to put up their hands to speak. Certainly, part of socialization during the school years is to learn to respect others' right to speak. Also, there is only one teacher in most classrooms, and in order for her to be effective, she will have to do more of the talking than any one child. Nevertheless, we must remember the close link between language acquisition and

Engaging children in familiar activities will promote language and cognitive growth while easing their transition from home into the preschool environment.

Associated Press

cognitive development (Chapters 5 and 6). Given the close association between language and thought, language can be thought of as a kind of operating system that supports cognition. A computer operating system is software that supports the computer's basic functions such as scheduling tasks, executing applications, and controlling peripheral programs or devices. In the brain, as we learned in earlier chapters, language is what accomplishes similar tasks. Children learn oral language by hearing it and by using it in a variety of contexts. That being the case, surely classrooms should be filled with talk and much of it children's.

The ways in which teachers fill classrooms with talk that helps children make the transition from home to school and facilitates learning is the subject of the remainder of this chapter. We will meet children and teachers in either prekindergarten or kindergarten. Each one exemplifies an important concept we have been discussing. As you read, look for examples of how children's experience of home and school language may be in conflict. Each example illustrates a language principle and is followed by an analysis of the principle and the best practices that can be extrapolated from the example.

10.2 Linguistic Diversity: Carlo and Chun Hei; Huang and Chen

Carlo and Chun Hei are acquiring more than one language simultaneously. We met Carlo in Chapter 4. Carlo is a simultaneous bilingual from a linguistically mixed family who began prekindergarten at age 4, fluent in Italian, Spanish, and English. After the Christmas vacation, a new girl joined the class, Chun Hei, a Korean girl who is 5. Chun Hei's parents have been in the United States for only a few months, and while they have enough English to function, they are by no means fluent. Chun Hei does not speak at all for the first few weeks in the preschool. The teacher, Ms. Malan, who does not speak any Korean, is uncertain about how much the girl understands, but notices that the child seems to function by watching the other children closely and following what they do. She often plays with Carlo, who appears to be her closest friend even though they have no language in common. The teacher learns from Carlo that he and Chun Hei attend the same Sunday school.

Ms. Malan: Does she speak there?

Carlo: Sometimes.

Ms. Malan: Do you speak Korean?

Carlo: What?

Ms. Malan: Do you speak the same language as Chun Hei?

Carlo: No. Well, sometimes.

Ms. Malan: What language does she speak to you?

Carlo: English, and sometimes Italian.

Ms. Malan: [Surprised] Carlo, are you saying that Chun Hei speaks two languages at Sunday school?

Carlo: Sometimes. I told her some Italian words. Mostly English, though.

Ms. Malan: Does she know a lot of words in English?

Carlo: [Shrugging] Maybe. She understands a lot. I'll show you. [He turns to Chun Hei.] Are you my friend? [The girl nods.] How old are you? [Chun Hei hesitates and then holds up five fingers.] See? She understands.

Following this exchange with Carlo, the teacher thought a great deal about what she could do to help Chun Hei. Once again, she sought Carlo's assistance.

Ms. Malan: Carlo, what do you talk about when you and Chun Hei talk?

Carlo: [Sighing and rolling his eyes] She's got this doll her noni gave her, and she talks about that. [Carlo clearly didn't think much of the doll.]

Ms. Malan: In English?

Carlo: Yep, 'cause we don't understand her language.

Ms. Malan: [After thinking for a minute] What's the doll's name?

Carlo: It's a funny name. Show Lee, I think.

Hearing this, Chun Hei looked up from the paper she was coloring. "Cho Lee!" she said firmly.

"Is that your doll's name?" the teacher asked. Chun Hei nodded. "That's a beautiful name. Would you bring Cho Lee to school tomorrow so I can meet her?" Chun Hei nodded again, a broad smile on her face.

Like Chun Hei, Huang and Chen do little talking at school. Huang was born in Taiwan and Chen was born in Shanghai. Although he is not nearly as talkative as Carlo, Huang has excellent English—his parents are bringing him up to speak both English and Cantonese. Chen appears to understand much of what is said, but so far, he has spoken little. Two kindergarten teachers, Ms. Collier and Ms. Browning, are getting ready to take the children to the outdoor playground a half a block away.

Ms. B: Boys and girls, we need to line up to walk to the playground. Just like we do every day. Chen, you should get your jacket. It's cold and it might rain.

Chen: Wain?

Ms. B: Yes, rain. [Chen turns and goes to the back of the room.] Huang, I'm not sure he understood me. Would you go and help him get his jacket? [Huang turns and follows.]

Ms. C: Okay, let's line up now. In pairs. Two at a time. [The children eventually line up, and Chen is left alone.] Okay, Chen, you can walk with me. [She reaches for his hand, but Chen pulls away.]

Chen: No.

Ms. C: You don't want to walk with me? It's not safe to walk alone. You want to walk with Mrs. Browning?

Ms. B: [Before Chen can respond.] Chen, would you be the leader with me? [Chen doesn't answer, and so she turns to Huang.] Huang, would you ask Chen if he will be the leader and walk with me?

Huang: Chen, would you be the leader? With Mrs. Browning?

Ms. B: Why didn't you ask him in your language?

Huang: I did.

Following this exchange, Ms. Collier took Ms. Browning aside and explained that it is possible that Chen speaks Mandarin, and not Cantonese, as Huang does.

What We've Learned About Linguistically Diverse Children

These two exchanges remind us that young children are capable of acquiring more than one language simultaneously and that whether they are acquiring one, two, or three, they do so without much apparent effort. They are able to acquire language without instruction in many different environments and under many different conditions. Carlo, for example, acquired three languages by the time he was 4 years old (Spanish, Italian, and English, as we learned in Chapter 4). Now, at age 5, and in kindergarten, his English is indistinguishable from that of his monolingual English peers. Huang has acquired two languages and has become quite proficient in English. These boys' accomplishments, as well as the progress Chun Hei and Chen are making, point to the importance of language learning during the critical period, which functions at its best in the first 5 or 6 years of life and begins to atrophy after puberty. Learning more than one language during the first 5 years means that the children are essentially acquiring two first languages.

These linguistically diverse children also remind us of a central theme that runs through the preceding chapters: Because we are born with innate capacity for language, human language does not need to be taught; children will acquire it given adequate exposure. Chun Hei has had only a few months of exposure to English, but she already understands much of what she hears, and when the subject is of sufficient interest, she will speak a little. Because first and second language are more alike than they are different, she reminds us that children's receptive ability is always greater than their productive ability. Like other children her age, monolingual and bilingual, she has learned a great deal about language and language structure, and she has done so in order to communicate what she wants to communicate. Her learning of her native Korean was embedded in the process of socialization, and to a large degree, so is her learning of English. We see this in the fact that her earliest words are devoted to talking about the doll that her grandmother gave her.

Although informal assessments of language can be very useful to a teacher, it is never safe to assume that we have correctly assessed the child's level of competence, or as in this case, what language the child speaks at home. With his answer to the teacher's question at the end of the second exchange, Huang reminds us of a central fact about language: It is not something that exists "out there" to be learned, but rather it is a part of who children are. What Huang implied was not only that English is his language, but that from his perspective any language he speaks is *his* language. In another kindergarten class, Lucy, who spoke both English and Portuguese, was asked which language she used when talking to her baby brother. Lucy answered, "Mine!" This tells us all we need to know about how Lucy perceives language. Whichever "code" she happens to be using, the language belongs to her.

Best Practice With Linguistically Diverse Children

Should the teacher push Chun Hei to speak more? We saw in Chapter 4 that children learning a second language sometimes go through a silent period before they begin to speak. They are working out the rules of the new language in their own way and in their own time because, as we saw in Chapter 8, children's learning progresses according to their own schedule. That schedule is governed by their degree of readiness and proceeds at a pace that depends on their level of development. The teacher can do much to encourage Chun Hei, as she is doing by encouraging her to bring her doll to school for "show and tell." She will also be wise to remember that for young children, learning and play should be seamless activities, and that Chun Hei will learn English as she plays with the other children, as she has clearly done with Carlo. But the teacher should resist any attempts to "instruct" her in English or to correct her usage. What are other ways the teacher can create an environment that facilitates English development while also benefitting the rest of the children in the class? Some suggestions are offered in *How to Facilitate English Language Learning in the Classroom.*

Bright, colorful, literacy-rich environments will help promote language learning in classrooms.

How to Facilitate English Language Learning in the Classroom

Early childhood educators can do much to facilitate English language learning in their classrooms, including some of the following suggestions:

- Create an emotionally positive environment where all children feel safe and valued, because language learning is embedded in socialization.
- Encourage activities in which other children take the lead and can participate, even if they choose not to speak.
- Create a literacy-rich classroom where common objects are labeled in large, brightly colored letters to provide another mode of language. In Chun Hei's case, such labels would give her a second memory hook for remembering words and also give her a head start on literacy.
- Resist the urge to correct. Chun Hei is well within the critical period for language learning, and she will eventually learn English with no foreign accent. But at this point in her development, she may simplify the English sound system to something that is easier for her to manage—she does not yet know all the rules. She may also simplify the morphological structure by leaving off word endings. The teacher can continue modeling correct forms, but that is the only intervention she should attempt. If other children correct her, as they sometimes will, the teacher should still not intervene unless the correction is unkind or mocking.
- Read aloud to children and encourage their participation. Ask questions such as, "Why do you think he did that?" or "Why do you think he looks sad?" After a reading activity, use hand puppets or stick puppets and invite children to retell the story.
- Encourage parents to read to their child in their native language, if they prefer that language. Also encourage use of their native language at home. Assure parents that this will not interfere with English language development, oral or written.

Keep in mind that these practices will benefit all children in the class, regardless of their level of English language development.

During the course of this conversation with Chun Hei and in other interactions with her, Ms. Malan noticed that the child would not look directly at her, even when Ms. Malan was speaking only to her. Ms. Malan was puzzled by this since the child appeared otherwise respectful, and there was no evidence that she could not see properly. Fortunately, she did not make an issue of this before she learned in conversation with another teacher that in Korean and many Asian cultures, it is considered rude for a child to stare directly at a person in authority. Throughout her teaching career, Ms. Malan will encounter a diverse population of children representing many cultures and many languages. She has learned an important lesson from Chun Hei that will help her: Do not assume that you know why a child does or does not do something, especially when the child is from a culture different from your own. *Becoming Culturally Aware* offers some advice for beginning teachers striving to understand the impact of cultural differences on our beliefs and expectation of others.

Becoming Culturally Aware

Communication is fraught with misunderstandings, even when speakers share a language and culture. When different cultures communicate, the possibility for miscommunication is greatly multiplied. It is not possible to understand every nuance of every culture of every child we will encounter, so these general suggestions are intended as guidelines for what will likely be a lifetime of study.

- Become a student of the world. If you don't enjoy history, read current events and take the time to find out where the countries you are reading about are located.
- Conduct research. Once a day, do an Internet search about the country and customs of one of the children in your class. Make it a point to learn one new thing.
- Contemplate your own beliefs. Whenever you encounter a belief that is different from your own, take a few minutes to reflect on your belief and how you came to hold it. To what degree does your culture shape your belief?
- Don't make assumptions. People who come from the same region of the world may have little in common except for geography. They may have different languages, cultures, politics, beliefs, religions, and so forth.
- Read fiction, even in translation, from other countries. It is a valuable source of information and insights about a culture.
- Make an attempt to learn a foreign language. It will give you empathy and insight, and if you persist, many new people to communicate with.
- Become an advocate for the rights and needs of bilingual children.
- Be open minded about ways of life other than your own.
- Finally, remember the words of Aldous Huxley: "To travel is to discover that everyone is wrong about other countries."

Approximately 5 and a half million children (roughly the population of Arizona, Maryland, or Tennessee) in the United States are learning English as their second—or third or fourth—language (Spellings, 2005). That number represents many languages and many cultures. The teachers and children in these examples remind us how important it is not to forget about culture in the classroom. "If teachers are to become effective cross-cultural communicators, it is essential to understand the role that culture plays within the multi-cultural school setting" (Pratt-Johnson, 2006).

The United States is home to a diverse population. As a teacher of English learners, you must learn to be culturally aware and incorporate that awareness into your classroom.

iStockphoto/Thinkstock

10.3 Individual Differences: Matilda

Matilda is 5 years old and has just begun kindergarten in Boston. Her parents both hold PhDs and are professors at a local university. At the first meeting with the kindergarten teacher, Matilda's mother expresses her concern that Matilda's language development is delayed. When questioned about her reasons for saying this, the mother admits that she has taken her for an assessment and that the speech-language professional found no evidence of delay in Matilda's oral language ability. When pressed about why she believes her daughter's language is "behind schedule," as the mother put it, she responds, "Well, she can't read yet, and she won't even try to identify letters." The mother goes on to explain that Matilda's older sister, Julie, had been reading by the time she was 4, and she does not understand why Matilda is so slow, especially since she likes having stories read to her. The teacher assures Matilda's mother that many children do not learn to read before first grade, and that this is not abnormal. The mother is skeptical but leaves Matilda in her care.

The teacher requests a copy of the speech-language professional's report but also decides to observe Matilda carefully. At first, Matilda is shy and has little to say, but soon she joins in play with the other children, and after the second day in kindergarten, the teacher observes her talking with the other children, and she appears to engage normally in conversation with them. She follows the teacher's directions well and usually offers more than minimal responses to questions. For example:

Teacher: Matilda, did you ride the bus this morning?

Matilda: No, my mother brought me. She always brings me in the car. Julie rides the bus.

Teacher: Is Julie your sister?

Matilda: Yes. She's in the third grade but she goes to a different school. Julie is very smart.

Teacher: I think you're pretty smart, too!

Matilda: Maybe. I don't know. Maybe.

Teacher: Would you like to pick the story for me to read today?

Matilda: Okay. "Dog and Bear."

Teacher: I don't think we have that one. Do you have it at home?

Matilda: Yes, my mom reads it to me.

Teacher: Since we don't have that, why don't I pick a book about another dog? Would that be okay?

The teacher can tell after this conversation that Matilda has excellent oral language skills. She also notices that Matilda pays close attention when the teacher is reading aloud and appears to enjoy the story. Later, when the children sit down to draw, the teacher notices that Matilda's drawings are colorful but resemble those made by a much younger child.

If a child shows little interest in learning to read or seems frustrated at trying to identify letters or words, he may need corrective lenses.

Design Pics/SuperStock

When the teacher asks her to tell her about the picture, Matilda tells a good story with a lot of detail about the characters and with a beginning, middle, and end. She clearly understands story structure and has a vivid imagination. The teacher also notes that Matilda appears to have a very good productive vocabulary, using words such as *scarlet* and *pumpkin-colored* when other children her age would more likely use *red* and *orange*. Matilda's pronunciation is excellent, and she has control of most inflections. On one occasion when she said "she gots," she immediately self-corrected to "she's got." There is obviously nothing wrong with Matilda's oral language development, but the teacher makes a note to herself to pay close attention to her preliteracy development.

The other children in the class can write their names, read them, and recognize the letters in their names when they see them in other contexts. Matilda is able to write her name, although her printing resembles that of a child a year or two younger. She manipulates objects and is able to count and to do addition and subtraction activities with blocks or other objects. After a few weeks, the teacher notices that Matilda has begun to show more interest in books. She carries around two of her favorite books, including "Dog and Bear," and when the teacher offers to read it to her, Matilda says, "I'll do it." She then begins to read the story. She skips some words and improvises with others, but this is not unusual with 5-year-olds, and the teacher does not think too much about it until she sees that Matilda does not turn the pages corresponding with the words. She has memorized the story! Again, this is not unusual in young children, but coupled with the fact that she still does not show much interest in words or letter identification, the teacher concludes that there may be a rather simple cause. She calls Matilda's mother and recommends what she thinks she should have thought of from the beginning, namely to recommend a vision test.

What We've Learned About Individual Differences

Matilda's ability to communicate, the size of her vocabulary, her knowledge of complex structure, her command of English pronunciation and inflections serve as potent reminders of the amount and complexity of language children acquire during the first 5 years of life. The speech-language professional who met with Matilda just before her 5th birthday judged her productive vocabulary to be 6,000 and her receptive vocabulary to be several times that. Her conversational ability, as shown in the preceding exchange and with others with her teacher, showed that she was using language for the social and interactive purposes for which it is intended. She also demonstrated another language skill that children begin to acquire before the age of 5—she was able to tell a story. The ability to construct a narrative will help her to comprehend the stories she encounters when she begins to read independently and to construct her own stories as an emergent writer.

Even though her mother has expressed concern about her apparent disinterest in reading, Matilda had acquired preliteracy skills with her oral language as well as an interest in reading and clear understanding of how stories are structured. We did not witness what occurred in her first years, but we know that she did not need to be "instructed" in the ways of language. Once Matilda had had her vision tested and corrected with lenses, she showed more interest in books and began to ask her mother to point to the words as she read them. Before, they had been a blur to her, so it wasn't surprising that she had shown little interest. At school, she began reading almost immediately. There is another lesson to be learned from Matilda. The fact that Matilda was not as interested in reading as her sister is not itself a cause for concern. It is perfectly normal, as we saw in Chapters 3 and 6, for children to develop at different rates and to have different levels of interest in reading.

Best Practice for Individual Differences

Matilda's teacher, and indirectly, her mother, offer insights about language learning that help us to build on children's oral language ability when they begin kindergarten. Most children begin kindergarten able to write their names and with some letter-identification ability. The fact that Matilda had such excellent oral language but little interest in reading, was, from the mother's perspective, a cause for worry. The teacher, on the other hand, with more awareness of more variation in children, was not initially concerned. Within a few weeks, they both reached the same conclusion, and Matilda began to thrive. What have we learned from Matilda, her mother, and teacher to help as we plan for kindergarten-aged children?

The most important lesson they have taught us is that as teachers we need to delve more deeply if a child seems to lag behind in some aspect of language development for no apparent reason. A child with very good oral skills and a large vocabulary who loves to hear stories but has no apparent interest in reading should cause us to think broadly about the possible causes.

Colorful large-print books will help preschool and kindergarten children transition from prereaders to readers.

Associated Press

A child who appears to enjoy reading silently and is able to demonstrate understanding of text but struggles to read aloud requires further evaluation, as well. Another child may stutter in the classroom but not at home. The underlying issues are likely different for the three children, but the teacher's response is the same: Investigate further. Some suggestions are included in *How to Address Individual Differences in the Classroom.*

How to Address Individual Differences in the Classroom

- Children learn according to their level of readiness, but if some aspect of their learning seems to lag behind others their age, investigate further.
- All children should have a vision test, at school or arranged by a parent.
- Request a hearing test for a child who appears consistently inattentive or ignores spoken directions.
- Fill the classroom with print: books, posters, brightly colored labels.
- Encourage vocabulary development, attending to the wide range of skill levels in the classroom. When Matilda used the word *scarlet*, for example, the teacher could have responded, "Matilda said that Henry's jacket is scarlet. What's another name for scarlet? Red? Yes, and what other things are red?" When a child identifies a tomato, the teacher can respond, "Yes, so we could say that Henry's jacket is tomato red, couldn't we?"
- Encourage interactive reading by asking questions about the stories and inviting children to retell the story.
- Take dictation as one child tells the story. Print the story on large paper for everyone to read. This permits children who are skilled and those who are less skilled at storytelling to participate.
- Treat everyone like readers, but be watchful for any child who seems to be having more trouble than others.

10.4 The Impact of Prior Learning Experience: Kerry

Kerry is a year older than Matilda, but the two children know each other because their families are friends. Kerry attended preschool and kindergarten at a private Montessori school (see *Characteristics of Montessori Education*) and has transferred to the same public school that Matilda attends. In November of Kerry's first grade year, the teacher requests a conference with Kerry's mother. She began the conference by stating, "Kerry is a bright little boy, but I am very concerned because he seems to have no interest in learning to read." Kerry's mother was surprised to hear this. If the teacher had said that he didn't want to paint or to play with clay, she wouldn't have been surprised, but at home, he always had his nose in a book. She asked on what basis the teacher had reached this conclusion. The teacher took out an accordion folder filled with Kerry's work. She extracted some worksheets of the kind shown in Figure 10.1.

Figure 10.1: Kerry's phonics worksheet

Kerry circled only the dog on this worksheet.

"What's the problem?" Kerry's mother asked.

"He doesn't complete his work." Kerry's mother looked at the worksheet on which Kerry had only circled one object, the dog. The teacher continued. "He doesn't seem at all interested in any of the reading activities."

"You mean like these worksheets?"

"Well, yes, that is one thing. It wouldn't worry me quite so much except that he doesn't pay much attention to the stories that we use in class, either." The teacher indicated a popular basal reading series.

"Have you asked him why he doesn't complete the worksheets?"

"I did once, yes," the teacher said. "He didn't really give me an answer. He just stared at me."

Kerry's mother promised to look into the matter with her son. That night, she showed him the worksheet with the letter "D" and asked why he hadn't finished it.

Kerry answered, as though it were the most obvious thing in the world, "Because I know how to do that." Then he went back to the book he was reading, a mystery novel written for pre-teens. Kerry was 6.

Characteristics of Montessori Education

The Montessori approach recognizes and embodies the belief that children control their own learning. Emphasizing independence, freedom within certain limits, and respect for children's natural psychological development, Montessori education is an individualized approach based on the work of Italian educator Maria Montessori. Although Montessori is a general approach to education, it is very well suited to language learners and to meeting the needs of culturally diverse learners. Some schools in the United States include Spanish Immersion in their curricula (see Weblinks). According to the Association Montessori Internationale and the American Montessori Society, the following traits characterize the approach:

- Appropriate technological advancements are used. Montessori schools, for example, were among the first to introduce computer workstations into the preschool classroom.
- "Family" or mixed-age groupings are utilized so that, for example, children between 2 or 3 and 6 share a classroom. This fosters language skills by allowing younger children to learn from older children the language that is relevant to them and the classroom environment.
- Children have uninterrupted blocks of work time, as opposed to the fragmentation of the day into assigned tasks.
- Students are permitted to choose activities from within a prescribed range of options.
- Children are encouraged to follow their own interests, thereby fostering independence in learning.
- A discovery approach is employed in which children learn concepts from working with objects and materials rather than by direct instruction. Concrete, hands-on learning is encouraged.
- Specialized educational materials have been developed by Montessori and associates. These include materials for teaching the structure of language.
- Classrooms have an inviting and attractive environment that invites exploration and discovery.

For further information, see Weblinks at the end of the chapter.

What We've Learned About the Impact of Prior Learning

Kerry's teacher assumed that he had little interest in reading because he only circled the dog. But Kerry clearly liked to read and was extremely good at it. The problem was that the teacher reached the wrong conclusion based on the behavior she observed. Had she probed a little further with Kerry, she might have found another answer. There might have been reason, for example, to suspect a mild form of Asperger's syndrome (Chapter 8). Had she discovered that he could stay focused on an activity that interested him for significantly longer times than the others in his class, she might have probed into the type of schooling he had before coming to her. If she knew that he had a relatively narrow range of interests but was keen to learn about those he had, she might have guessed that he was intellectually gifted. But the point here is not to blame the teacher but to remind ourselves once again the extent to which children are in charge of their own learning and that their prior experience has a profound impact on what and how they learn. Children vary in the speed at which they acquire language, oral *and* written. It is important to look beneath the surface of what we think we know about children.

Best Practice for Dealing With Differences in Prior Learning Experience

Kerry had attended Montessori school, and he was accustomed to the individualized attention that characterizes that educational approach. In the Montessori classroom, once he discovered that he was able to do an activity, he moved on to something else that he wanted to learn. As it happened, that approach was especially effective for him. Kerry was fascinated by how things work and could happily spend time taking them apart and putting them back together. He was also able to focus for long periods of time, exploring all aspects of an object or an activity. In Montessori school, he had more control over how he learned.

Montessori schools offer more individualized attention, which some children find more engaging than traditional schools.

Associated Press

When Kerry's mother returned to the school, she had a long discussion with the teacher, explaining that Kerry could read and the kinds of stories that interested him. She even brought him in for a demonstration. She also explained that he had been accustomed to the Montessori school, and so he was having a little trouble adapting to the new routines and expectations. A year later, his sister Patricia was in the same teacher's class. At the first parent conference, the teacher used several minutes telling the mother how having Kerry in her class had changed her approach. In particular, she had augmented the basal reader (that her school district required her to use) with books that the children were allowed to choose, bringing from home if they wished. She would invite the child who chose it to read it aloud, or if it was too difficult, would read it to them. She spent a lot more time having children tell stories, which she would transcribe and use as texts. And most important, she learned to be more flexible about letting children work at their own pace. "I've learned to pay attention to what the children tell me about their own learning," she explained. Patricia did very well in her class.

10.5 Learning Language During Play: A Kindergarten Class

Alinah is a girl and Ahmad is a boy from Malaysia, but they are unrelated and do not know each other outside the kindergarten class where they have just begun. They have both grown up with English as one of their two languages. Alinah and Ahmad also speak Malay, but different dialects. Lakisha is a 5-year-old English-speaker and knows Alinah from the neighborhood where they both live. The kindergarten is a private kindergarten in urban Orlando, Florida. The teacher is nearby, monitoring the children as they play on the playground. Alinah has brought a soccer ball outside.

Ahmad: I want to play, too. [Alinah does not respond.] Alinah!

Alinah: [Ignoring Ahmad] Lakisha, do you want to play?

Ahmad: I said I want to play!

Alinah: Lakisha, we can play the game we played with your sister. Okay?

Lakisha: I guess. Ahmad wants to play, too.

Alinah: You don't know how, Ahmad.

Ahmad: I know how to play soccer.

Alinah: This is a special game. It's called Puddle.

Ahmad: Puddle? That's a stupid name. That's a soccer ball. It's for soccer.

Lakisha: We can play soccer, Alinah.

Alinah: Okay. So you can be on my team, Lakisha.

Ahmad: Who will be on my team?

Alinah: I don't know. Why don't you play with them? [She indicates another group of children.]

Ahmad: No, I want to play soccer. It's my favorite.

Lakisha: [To Ahmad] I can be on your team, I guess.

Alinah: No! That's not fair. Then I will be by myself.

Lakisha: So what do we do?

Alinah: He can play something else.

Lakisha: I know! He can keep score!

Ahmad: I don't want to keep score. I want to kick the ball.

Alinah: But we can't have three teams.

[At this point the teacher comes over bringing a portable soccer net.]

Teacher: I have an idea. We can set up the net here, and you can all take turns kicking the ball into it. That way you can have three teams if you want to.

Ahmad: Yeah! We can do that.

A few minutes later, Carson, Melinda, and Kee are sitting on a mat on the floor playing with a wooden train. The train has seven brightly colored wooden cars that they are trying to attach together. Bao-Zhi watches from the edge of the group.

Carson: M'inda! You can't do it that way.

Melinda: Yes, I can.

Carson: No! You can't have two blue ones.

Kee: Put yellow one there.

Carson: Yeah, put yellow next.

Melinda: I want two blue. [Turning to Bao-Zhi] You want two blue, don't you?

Bao-Zhi: No.

Carson: See? You want yellow, right?

Bao-Zhi: No. Wed.

Kee: Me too. Red. Then we put yellow. Right, Bao-Zhi?

Bao-Zhi: [Comes to join the group] Bu, den wed and yayyo.

Carson: Okay. That's okay, right M'inda?

Melinda: I guess, but then another blue!

Carson: [Getting all seven train cars hooked together] Now, we can go. Let's go to Disney! [The children all agree that this is a good idea.] And I can be the driver!

Kee: No, it's my turn.

Carson: Why? You can drive next time.

Melinda: Nobody needs to drive.

[At this point, Ms. Cameron intervenes.]

Ms. Cameron: Do you know what the driver of the train is called?

Melinda: Train doesn't have driver.

Ms. Cameron: Yes, it does!

Carson: Train driver?

Mrs. Cameron: That's one name. Another name is engineer.

Kee: My daddy's an engineer.

Melinda: Does he drive a train?

Kee: No, he fixes bridges and stuff.

Ms. Cameron: That's another kind of engineer. Now, where are we taking this train?

Carson: I'm going to play with the robots now.

Melinda: Me too. [She and Kee follow Carson.]

Ms. Cameron: Bao-Zhi, do you want to play with the train?

Bao-Zhi: No. [He follows the others to the robot.]

What We've Learned About Play and Language Learning

The language learning that occurs during the school years involves more than academic language and teacher talk. Part of the task of learning during these years, as we learned in Chapter 7, is expanding the uses of languages to include problem solving using the forecasting and reasoning function of language. Not all problem solving happens in the classroom. In fact, it is through play, as we saw in Chapter 8, that much language learning takes place. In the first example, Ahmad, Alinah, and Lakisha need help, but they recognize that they have a problem and begin to talk their way through it. Lakisha's suggestion that Ahmad keep score is a good solution, but since Ahmad does not want to keep score, the children have to keep negotiating. In doing so, they are developing their conversational skills.

Looking more closely at the interaction among these three children, we see evidence that the children are using more than forecasting and reasoning language that they use when they confront the matter of how to play soccer with three people. Alinah and Ahmad both use controlling language to assert their wishes, and there is evidence of the projecting function in Alinah's suggestion that Ahmad serve as timekeeper, and the entire conversation is contextualized within the social purpose of play. We see that the children are each aware of the other's perspective. The girls understand that Ahmad does not have the same knowledge that they have about a game they play in their neighborhood, and in this case they solve the potential conflict by agreeing to play a game they all know. With Alinah, Ahmad, and Lakisha, we see three children learning to negotiate and doing it within the play environment.

In the second exchange, we see children using language to fulfill a number of functions of language. When Carson takes charge of the play situation, he uses controlling language as he attempts to direct the behavior of the other children, but we also see language that is used for social purposes when he seeks Melinda's agreement. What other functions of language do you see in this exchange?

Children learn while playing. A wise teacher will offer guidance only when it is needed and with a very light hand.

Associated Press

Best Practices for Developing Language During Play

The younger the child, the fuzzier the boundary between play and learning. Preschool and kindergarten teachers know that important learning takes place during play, learning that is invisible to the children. The teacher in this situation has wisely intervened only minimally, offering a solution only when the children get stuck. In similar situations, teachers often pose questions to guide children toward a solution, and that is also good practice. What is important is that the problems engage the children's interest, and nothing will be more compelling than when children face and resolve real problems. Giving children the chance to talk through possible solutions to problems that they identify themselves is a good way to encourage authentic language in an authentic situation.

In the first interaction, the teacher could have engaged in a series of questions to guide the children to a solution of their own. She might, for example, have asked one of the girls to explain the rules of the game, Puddle, thus providing an authentic opportunity for them to use informative language. But to do so would also have taken a great deal more time and diverted the children's attention from their goal—it would have effectively meant hijacking the play situation for her own instructional purposes and would no longer have been authentic. If she wished to pursue the matter, she could have done so once the children were inside by asking one of the girls to explain the rules of Puddle to the class so that perhaps they could all play later. In this way, she would not appropriate the activity itself and would provide opportunities for language growth for the larger group.

In the second interaction, the teacher exemplified best practice by not correcting Bao Zhi's pronunciation. Kindergarten-aged bilingual learners will acquire the appropriate pronunciation in time, and they will not respond to correction anyway. Mrs. Cameron twice intervened in other ways, however. The first time, she attempted to expand their knowledge and vocabulary by introducing the word *engineer*. The result was less than successful—one child knew a different meaning of the word already, and her attempt to appropriate the children's play failed. They abandoned her and the trains to play with the robots. Ms. Cameron did not exemplify best practice in this scenario; it is always risky to interfere in children's play. A better strategy would have been for Ms. Cameron not to have intervened but to have observed and then extracted "teachable moments" to use later. For example, she could have asked Kee if he could help them build a railroad bridge for the train and ask where the bridge would go. Or she could read a story about a train, or ask the students to help her write a story about a train, or ask them to draw a picture of their train later in the day.

The Impact of Technology on Play

Throughout the previous chapters, there has been little mention of technology in the lives of preschool children because our attention has been focused on children learning language. Smartphones, television, and computers are a part of most children's lives, however, and teachers often express concern about the amount of technology in children's lives (National Association for the Education of Young Children [NAEYC]; Downey, Hayes, & O'Neill, 2008). Although technology affects young children through the content it offers and through the different kinds of interactive media it makes possible, our primary concern here is the other activities that it replaces. Research in Australia showed that preschool children who had televisions in their rooms were more likely to be obese than children who did not, suggesting that these children do not engage in as much physical play as others (Pitman, 2008). Researchers in Ireland studied the impact of technologies on the play preferences of children between 4 and 12. For their studies, "technologies" referred to television, console games, computers, and phones (the electronic tablet was not yet available).

> The findings on how children like to spend time with their friends suggest that, given the opportunity, children will make their own fun. Sports and other outdoor activities are very popular. However, when alone, children often turn to technology for entertainment and most of them have quite a high degree of access to technology. (Downey et al., 2008)

Since play is critical to development, we also need to think about the overall developmental impact of growing up in a technological culture, as most of today's children are.

> Such a culture will influence the language and concepts that children learn. The concepts of space and time have been altered by technology. Elkind (2003) suggests that the focus on speed that the developing technologies have brought to education and other aspects of society has created a hurried society where children may feel guilty about taking time off to play. (Downey et al., 2007)

Professionals stress the importance of monitoring both content and the total time young children spend viewing screens. How would you balance a child's use of educational technology with these recommendations?

Associated Press

The Irish researchers conclude that parents and teachers have to strive to create a balance of opportunities for different kinds of play. Because children will usually prefer to play with their friends if given the choice, it is important to ensure that they have many opportunities to do so. It is also important to limit screen time for young children. The National Association for the Education of Young Children (NAEYC) recommends no more than two hours per day *total* screen time—computer, tablet, phone, television—for preschool children over the age of 2. Given the ample access most children have at home, they go on to recommend, that teachers restrict the time children spend viewing screens to fewer than 30 minutes for half-day programs and less than one hour for full-day programs (NAEYC, 2012).

10.6 Teacher Talk

Examples in the previous sections focused on language from the perspective of children. We looked at early childhood language through the lens of the demands of school language. The biggest single difference between home and school language has to do with teacher talk. One of the differences is in the quantity of time accorded to each child for talk. At home, unless the family is very large, children don't have to share their speaking time with as many people as they do at school. Since the teacher is the one in charge of what happens in school, it is not surprising that in most situations, it is the teacher's talk that dominates (see *Evaluating Teacher Talk*). Research on teacher talk during the past three decades has focused on second language classrooms. The conclusion often reached was that

Teachers do most of the talking in most classrooms. Therefore, the quality of their talk is especially important.

Associated Press

teacher talk was undesirable because when the teacher is talking, the learner can't be, and it is the learner who needs the practice (Corden, 2000; Edwards & Westgate, 1987). At best, this is an overly simple assessment. At worst, this is poor educational practice, especially when applied to young children. True, children need to talk. True, when the teacher is talking, children can't also be talking. But teacher talk is not necessarily bad. On the contrary, that adult interaction is important to young children's learning, and the teacher's thoughtful participation in and guiding of talk in the classroom is essential. It is the *quality* of the teacher talk that is important. Let's conclude, then, with two transcripts of classroom interaction in which we pay particular attention to teacher talk. The first is between a first-grade teacher and one of her students and illustrates less-effective teacher talk than the second between Mrs. Cobb and two of her kindergarten students.

Using Inauthentic Language: Ms. Fitz and Jimmy

Sometimes teachers engage in language that, from the child's perspective, has little purpose or has a purpose that is alien to the child's perspective. Inauthentic language is "teacher talk" that is geared to a particular teaching goal and that would not take place in other settings. English is Jimmy's second language, but he has a good vocabulary and is fluent. He has some pronunciation problems, but they are not unusual for speakers of his language.

Ms. Fitz: [Holding up an apple] Jimmy, what is this?

Jimmy: [Puzzled by the question] Apo?

Ms. Fitz: Yes, apple. Can you say ap-puhl?

Jimmy: Apo.

Ms. Fitz: Apple. [Jimmy nods.] Can you say apple? [Jimmy nods again.] Say it after me. AP-PUHL.

Jimmy: Ap-puhl.

Ms. Fitz: Excellent! Now, what is this?

Jimmy: Apo.

Ms. Fitz: What color is it?

Jimmy: Don't know.

Jimmy knows the color of the apple, but he has given up on talking to Ms. Fitz. Why? Because there is a mismatch between Jimmy's understanding of what language is used for and what the teacher is trying to accomplish. What makes it worse is that Ms. Fitz is not being honest in her interaction with him, so Jimmy has decided that talking to her is unproductive. It's not that she's lying. She is attempting to use language to try to accomplish her goal to "teach" Jimmy to pronounce a word correctly. Jimmy, however, is not used to talk used for this purpose. He knows the name of the fruit, probably knows that that the teacher does as well, and he doesn't understand what she is trying to accomplish. He does not understand that Ms. Fitz is trying to correct his pronunciation, and although he can produce the sequence of sounds correctly, as he shows when he mimics the form, when he is left to his own devices, he reverts to his developmental form (Chapter 3). This is an extreme example of bad classroom talk. The next example, also from first grade, provides another glimpse into the nature of school talk.

Using Authentic Language: Ms. Cobb, Ileana, and Harmon

The teacher is engaged in a conversation with two children. Ileana is from Romania and has been in the United States just over a year. She was adopted along with her baby sister by American parents. The other child is Harmon, who is an English speaker.

Ms. Cobb: Ileana, would you help Harmon spread out the plastic on the table? We're going to paint.

Ileana: [Looking confused] Pastic?

Ms. Cobb: Yes, plastic. You know, the yellow cover that we use when we paint.

Ileana: Oh, okay.

Harmon: I can do it.

Ms. Cobb: I know, but let Ileana help you. It's easier that way. Okay?

Harmon: Okay. Can I fill the water cups?

Ms. Cobb: No. Thank you, Harmon, but we're not doing water colors today. We're going to use special paints. They're called acrylics. They don't need water.

Harmon: No water?

Ms. Cobb: No. Acrylic paints don't have to be mixed.

Harmon: 'Crylic?

Ms. Cobb: That's right. Acrylic. Ileana, do you see those tubes over there? [She points to a box of paint tubes on a low shelf.]

Ileana: Tube?

Ms. Cobb: Yes, there, in the box. See?

Ileana: Okay.

Ms. Cobb: Could you bring them to me?

Ileana: [She goes over, picks up one tube and brings it back to her teacher.] Wed.

Ms. Cobb: That's right. That's red acrylic paint. What would you like to paint red, Ileana?

Ileana: F'ower.

Ms. Cobb: That's a good idea. A red flower. What other color would we need—for the stem?

Ileana: Gween.

Harmon: She said "gween" instead of "green."

Ms. Cobb: That's okay. Harmon, would you mind getting the rest of the paints for me? You can bring the whole box.

The talk between the teacher and these two children is purposeful, and she accomplishes the goal of getting the painting activity started, but she also does a little language teaching at the same time. Notice how she expands Ileana's single word, *wed*, to a full sentence using the new word *acrylic* within a context that is not at all artificial. Notice, too, that she ignores the child's problem with the "r" sound and moves Harmon off the topic skillfully. This teacher engages in honest dialogue in a way that the teacher in the first example does not. She has engaged the children in a real activity, has taken advantage of the situation to expand their language and their understandings, and focused on the meaning rather than the form of Ileana's speech. In doing so, she has used **authentic language** that more closely resembles the children's prior experience of language. In this particular instance, the differences between home and school language are not great, which means that the children will learn more naturally.

As we saw with Ms. Fitz and Jimmy, teacher talk is sometimes dishonest in that it is unnatural and transparently calculated. This is not to imply that teachers cannot or should not adjust their speech to children's level of comprehension. We learned in Chapter 3 that child-directed speech (CDS) is natural and useful for adults talking with children. But there is a difference between CDS and dishonest or manipulative language. In the first example, the purpose of every one of the teacher's utterances was to teach the child something. In the second example, her words had the effect of teaching them something new, but her purpose was to get a painting activity underway; therefore, the language she used served a dual purpose. She taught the children something new, and she accomplished a practical classroom chore. This teacher was effective because the way she talked to the children was genuine, and in that regard, was like their previous experience with language.

Evaluating Teacher Talk

Read the following transcript of a second grade teacher preparing her children for a reading activity.

Mrs. T.: Today, we're going to read a story. [She holds up the book.] What do you think it's going to be about?

Jesse: A garden? I don't want to read about a garden.

Mrs. T.: Not a garden. What's growing in the garden?

Karim: Punkins.

Mrs. T.: PUMPkins. Yes.

Claudia: Oh, I know. Like in Cinderella.

Jesse: No! Like in Halloween. My daddy carved a scary face in one.

Mrs. T: That's nice, Jesse. Do you think this pumpkin looks scary?

Claudia: No, it's still growing.

Jesse: I would make it scary. I'd get a big knife.

Karim: No, you wouldn't. Your mommy wouldn't let you use a knife.

Mrs. T.: We're not talking about knives today, boys and girls. Look at the picture on the book. What do you think the story is about?

All: Punkins!

Mrs. T.: That's right. PUMPkins. What are some of the words that we can use to describe pumpkins?

Claudia: Round. Big.

Mrs. T.: Those are good. [She writes them on a flip chart.] Karim, can you think of another one?

Karim: No.

Jesse: I can. Scary!

Mrs. T.: No, this pumpkin isn't scary. What color is it?

Jesse: Same as all pumpkins.

Mrs. T.: What color is it, Claudia?

Claudia: Orange?

Mrs. T.: Right! Now, what do you think will happen in this story?

Jesse: Nothing. It's a pumpkin.

Looking carefully at this exchange, evaluate the quantity and quality of the teacher's language. First, was it purposeful? Mrs. T. clearly had a purpose, and she was unwavering in her efforts to achieve it. For the most part, however, the children did not share the goal. They were excited to talk about pumpkins, but since their responses were not what she had planned for, the exchange did not accomplish any purpose and undoubtedly left Mrs. T. frustrated. Was it honest? No. While Mrs. T. didn't lie to the children or misrepresent anything, she did attempt repeatedly to engage them in a conversation that was awkward and did not accomplish her goals. What would you have done differently?

Conclusion

We have come a long way toward understanding and appreciating the wonder of what children accomplish in their first 5 years of life. As we have seen, language is comprised of layer upon layer of complex structure and is populated with thousands of words including many words for the same thing, words that sound the same but have very different meanings, and meanings that can change with the addition or deletion of a syllable. Because children are born with the predisposition to learn language—the dedicated hardware, so to speak—they acquire one or more languages with apparent ease. Language is the "operating system" of thought, and the two develop in tandem. Even children with significant impairments are able to learn to communicate with language under the right circumstances. If adults had to teach children language, they would surely fail—the subject is too big and too complicated, and most of us are not that gifted as teachers. But adults do play a significant role as facilitators and guides in children's language learning, and indeed, in all their learning.

The first 5 years are especially important because the language that children have acquired during this period—whether one language, two, or more—will have given them a very solid grounding on which to grow additional language and academic skills. Nevertheless, the language of the school can differ significantly from the language children are accustomed to using in the home. For second language learners, this may be particularly true. For all learners, school language differs in functional ways from the language of the home. Yet, there is still much language left to be learned during the years a child is in the school environment, and, indeed, throughout life. The teacher who is able to find and build on the many opportunities that exist throughout the school day, to build on the scaffolding that is already in place, will set children on a good course.

Post-Test

1. Children's first words tend to be all of the following EXCEPT

    a. relevant to them.
    b. familiar.
    c. concrete.
    d. abstract.

2. The case of Chun Hei and Carlo demonstrate that bilingual children are capable of each of the following EXCEPT

    a. befriending children who speak other native languages.
    b. acquiring the productive ability to speak a second language immediately.
    c. acquiring multiple languages without much obvious effort.
    d. learning new languages under many conditions.

3. The case of Matilda illustrates that

   a. children can have strong oral skills while struggling with literacy.
   b. poor drawing skills are an indication of language problems.
   c. the development of one sibling predicts the development of later siblings.
   d. starting kindergarten can be particularly difficult for children with disabilities.

4. One method Kerry's teacher implemented to encourage students to work at their own pace was to have students

   a. bring their own stories to school for reading time.
   b. choose the assignments that they wanted to complete.
   c. explain their interests to her so she could use them in curriculum.
   d. be "student of the day" and dictate the classroom activities that day.

5. Ms. Cameron's questions about the engineer were most likely viewed by the children as

   a. teachable moments.
   b. learning opportunities.
   c. excitements.
   d. interruptions.

6. One of the biggest differences between children's language use at home and at school is that children

   a. use less formal language at school.
   b. tell more stories at school.
   c. talk more overall at home.
   d. wait longer to answer questions at school.

Answers

1. d. Abstract. *The answer can be found in Section 10.1.*
2. b. Acquiring the productive ability to speak a second language immediately. *The answer can be found in Section 10.2.*
3. a. Children can have strong oral skills while struggling with literacy. *The answer can be found in Section 10.3.*
4. a. Bring their own stories to school for reading time. *The answer can be found in Section 10.4.*
5. d. Interruptions. *The answer can be found in Section 10.5.*
6. c. Talk more overall at home. *The answer can be found in Section 10.6.*

Key Ideas

- The language children learn at home may differ from the language of the school in many ways, but the teacher's job is to minimize the effect of those differences.
- Differences between home and school language may be evident in how, when, and why children talk.
- School talk may be more abstract than the language children use at home.
- Children with more than one language bring dimensions of experience and learning to the classroom that the teacher can build upon to encourage further learning.

- When people of different cultures communicate, the possibility for miscommunication is greatly multiplied.
- All children bring some prior learning experience to the classroom. It is the teacher's task to recognize the potential conflicts that can arise and to ease each child into the new learning experience.
- Teachers should monitor their own talk, both for amount and for authenticity.

Critical Thinking Questions

1. Notice that in the two hypothetical dialogues with Eleeshia (one with her father and one with her teacher), the teacher uses far more words than the father, yet they both accomplish the same end. If this is typical of an interaction between the teacher and one child, what does it tell you about the likely proportion of teacher talk with the entire class?

2. Review the dialogue between Jimmy and his teacher.
   a. Should the teacher use another approach for correcting Jimmy's pronunciation? Should she not correct his pronunciation at all? Provide reasons for your answer.
   b. What does it tell you about Jimmy's language learning that he can mimic the teacher's pronunciation of *apple* correctly, but later reverts to his own?
   c. What does "developmental form" mean?

3. When the child Lucy answers the question, "Which language do you speak to your baby brother?" by saying "Mine," she reminds us that language is central to our identity. If that is the case, what does that tell you about how to go about correcting errors with non-native speakers? Do you see appropriate examples of correction in any of the vignettes in the chapter?

4. *There is a certain age at which a child looks at you in all earnestness and delivers a long, pleased speech in all the true inflections of spoken English, but with not one recognizable syllable. There is no way you can tell the child that if language had been a melody, he had mastered it and done well, but that since it was in fact a sense, he had botched it utterly (Annie Dillard, Pilgrim at Tinker Creek).*
   To what stage in language acquisition does this quotation refer? What does it tell you about the nature of the child's capacity to acquire language?

5. Read the article on the benefits to bilingualism at
   http://news.bbc.co.uk/2/hi/uk_news/education/6447427.stm
   Of what relevance are these findings to teachers in American preschools or primary schools?

6. With their apparent disinterest in reading, Matilda and Kerry appear to be similar, yet their underlying issues are very different. What do their stories tell you about how to assess children with an apparent disinterest in reading?

Key Terms

authentic language Oral or written language that is used for an actual purpose.

inauthentic language Teacher talk geared to a particular teaching goal and that would not take place in another setting.

school language (or school talk) The distinct pattern of language typically used in classrooms.

Weblinks

For a description of the Montessori approach, see
http://home.earthlink.net/~aletaledendecker/newhorizonmontessorischool/id1.html
and
http://livingmontessorinow.com/2011/03/08/top-10-montessori-principles-for-natural-learning/

Some of the schools using Montessori to teach second language immersion describe their approach at
http://www.leportschools.com/spanish-immersion/why-montessori-spanish-immersion/
and
http://www.interculturalmontessori.org/index.php?option=com_content&view=article&id=11&Itemid=62/
and
http://www.misolmontessori.org/

For tips on integrating play into the preschool, see
http://www.pbs.org/teachers/earlychildhood/articles/dramaticplay.html

For a bibliography including weblinks to articles addressing the impact of technology on young children, see
http://www.techandyoungchildren.org/research.html

For the position statement of the National Association for the Education of Young Children on the use of technology in preschool, see
http://www.naeyc.org/files/naeyc/file/positions/PS_technology_WEB2.pdf

A general discussion of some of the best practices in kindergarten can be found at
http://www.kindergarten-lessons.com/best-teaching-methods-kindergarten.html

Glossary

active construction of a grammar theory A theory that contends that children use the speech they hear around them to construct the rules of the language by listening for and discovering patterns, hypothesizing about the rules that create those patterns, and then testing those rules in their own usage.

affect Feelings or emotion.

analytic language A strictly analytic language would have one morpheme per word.

aphasia The name given to any language disorder resulting from specific brain damage.

arbitrariness One of the four attributes of human language, referring to the fact that words are not predictable from their meanings. The animal known in English as *pig* is represented by other words in other languages.

articulation disorder One of the three broad categories of speech disorder, this is the name given to a spectrum of speech disorders characterized by speech with added, omitted, substituted, or distorted sounds.

Asperger's syndrome A pervasive developmental disorder characterized by severe difficulty with social relationships. Language problems associated with Asperger's are likely to be at the sociopragmatic level.

assimilation Making the sounds in a word more like each other (*yellow* becomes *lalo*).

authentic language Oral or written language that is used for an actual purpose.

autism spectrum disorder (ASD) A category of developmental disorders that involve some degree of difficulty with communication and social relationships as well as obsessive and/or repetitive behaviors.

bilingualism The ability to function in an age-appropriate manner in more than one language.

bilingual programs Language programs designed to maintain children's first language while adding a second language, usually English in the United States. There are two types: maintenance programs are intended to preserve children's first language in the school setting, and transitional programs are intended to assist them in coping with English as a medium of instruction.

Broca's aphasia Also known as expressive aphasia or motor aphasia, a language disorder that occurs in people with damage to the lower back part of the frontal lobe. People suffering Broca's aphasia have severe articulation and fluency problems.

category Essential to the formation of concepts, a grouping of similar attributes—things with wheels, words that begin with *r*, vegetables that grow underground, etc.

central auditory processing disorder (CAPD) This is an umbrella term for a variety of disorders that affect how the brain processes auditory information.

child-directed speech (CDS) Language that adults use in talking with a young child, adapted to the child's level of comprehension and featuring simplified structure and changes in pitch and rate of speech.

cluttering The name given to speech characterized by a rapid and/or irregular speaking rate, excessive dysfluencies, and often other symptoms such as language or phonological errors and attention deficits.

cognition The mental process of knowing, which involves awareness, perception, reasoning, memory, and conceptualization.

cognitive development The process of acquiring intelligence and increasingly advanced thought and problem-solving ability from infancy to adulthood.

communication The activity of a sender conveying a message to a listener.

communication disorder Any kind of impairment that adversely affects a person's ability to use language.

comprehension check Involves the speaker finding out whether the listener understands.

concept A general idea derived or inferred from specific instances or occurrences.

congenital hearing loss A hearing impairment that is present at birth.

consonant A speech sound produced by impeding the airflow in the vocal tract.

consonant reduction Reducing the number of consonants in a syllable (*stop* becomes *top*).

context-specific words In first words, those that refer only to a particular person, object, or action.

contextually flexible words In first words, those that are used generically or with several referents.

controlling function of language The language children use for controlling, or attempting to control, the self and others.

convergent thinking The ability to bring together different kinds of information to arrive at a solution to a problem.

conversational competence The ability to engage in a meaningful conversation following the conventions of the culture.

creole A language with more of the properties of natural language that has its origins in a pidgin; sometimes referred to as "second-generation" pidgin.

critical period (for brain development): The period before plasticity ends and the brain is at its most opportune time for development.

critical period hypothesis With regard to the first language, the first 5 years or so of life during which the child's brain is most receptive to language learning.

crossing the midline The point at which an infant learns to pass an object from one hand to another, indicating a significant neurological development.

decibel (dB) Unit used to measure the intensity of sound.

developmental forms Imperfect forms (i.e., pronunciations, past-tenses, etc.) that young children produce during the process of learning a language.

dialect A variety of language defined by either geographical factors or social factors, such as class, religion, and ethnicity.

diphthong A vowel sound created by one vowel "gliding" into another as in the word *eye*.

displacement An attribute of human language, referring to the fact that language is capable of generating meaningful utterances not tied to the immediate environment.

divergent thinking Ability to come up with multiple solutions to problems.

dyslexia Refers to a category of reading disorders associated with impairment to the ability to interpret spatial relationships (in print) or to integrate auditory and visual information.

early second language acquisition Used to describe children who acquire a second language before the onset of puberty.

emergent writing The print efforts that children make before they know the conventions of writing.

ESL resource center A drop-in center in a school where second language learners can go for language materials or other supplemental assistance in English.

expressive strategy The approach used by children whose first words are action words or people's names.

feral children Children who have lived in relative isolation, apart from or only marginally exposed to human society.

fiction or fantasy narratives The genre of narrative that children use during make-believe.

fluency disorder A speech disorder characterized by very rapid speech sounds that have additional sounds inserted or are repeated or blocked.

forecasting and reasoning function of language The function that allows children to express their curiosity and to learn about the world.

functional morpheme A morpheme, either a word or an inflection, that has minimal content meaning but serves a grammatical purpose in the sentence.

function words Stand alone as words, but unlike other words in the language, they cannot usually have other morphemes attached.

global aphasia A speech disorder characterized by impairment to comprehension and production of language.

homesigns A rudimentary sign language that nonhearing people develop themselves to communicate within their own communities.

idiolect The idiosyncratic speech of individuals.

immersion A carefully planned instructional approach for children to learn a language that is not the dominant one of the community. Children are taught school subjects in an unfamiliar language for half the school day or more. (Compare to *submersion*.)

inauthentic language Teacher talk geared to a particular teaching goal and that would not take place in another setting.

independent literacy Reading and writing or prereading and prewriting activities that children initiate themselves.

inflectional morphemes Types of function morphemes; they carry grammatical information.

informative function of language Those functions of language involved in conveying information, whether to the self or others.

innateness hypothesis The belief, first put forth by Noam Chomsky, that humans are predisposed to learn language.

interactive reading A shared reading experience in which adults and young learners work together to get meaning from text.

intonation The rise and fall and rhythm, or cadence, of language.

jargon Language associated with a particular occupation, hobby, or sport.

language delay Language that is developing in the normal sequence but slower than would be expected.

language disorder Dysfunction characterized by difficulty in understanding others (receptive language), or sharing thoughts, ideas, and feelings completely (expressive language).

language functions The general term for the practical purposes that language serves.

language variety A term linguists use to refer to different languages (e.g., Mandarin and English) as well as to the way a specific group of speakers within a language speak (e.g., Appalachian English or Boston English) and sometimes to differences among individuals.

lexical morpheme A morpheme with substantive content meaning.

memory strategies Those conscious activities we employ in the hope of improving our chances of remembering.

metalinguistic awareness Refers to a person's ability to reflect on and ponder over language (i.e., to objectify it).

metamemory The knowledge or awareness we have *about* how memory works that assists us in improving our ability to remember.

minimal pair Two words that differ by only one sound.

morpheme The smallest unit of language that carries meaning.

morphology The branch of linguistics concerned with how words are structured.

neurons Brain cells.

nonstandard dialect Any language variety that does not conform substantially to the standard.

personal narratives Narratives that recount particular events that the individual has experienced.

phoneme The smallest unit of sound that has meaning to a native speaker.

phonologicial awareness The knowledge and conscious understanding of the sound structure of language.

phonology The branch of linguistics concerned with the description of the sound system.

pidgin A simplified language with elements taken from local languages, used for communication between people who do not share a common language.

plasticity Refers to the ability of the human brain to change in response to environmental experiences.

pragmatics The study of language as it is used in real-life context.

precursory language behavior Infant vocalization such as crying and cooing, more related to emotional state than to intention to communicate.

print and alphabet awareness A range of skills including the ability to recognize that the words on a page correspond to spoken words, that letters correspond to sounds (phonemes) and to their understanding of the purposes of print—to convey information or tell a story—and the fact that print serves many purposes in people's lives.

productive vocabulary The words that a child speaks, as opposed to those he understands but may not be heard to speak.

productivity An attribute of human language, referring to the capacity of language to create an infinite number of new and unique utterances.

projecting function of language The function of language that allows a child to enter into fantasy worlds and roles. Also referred to as the imaginative function.

pull-out program Language program in which second language learners attend mainstream classes but are withdrawn for specialized English language classes for part of the day.

receptive vocabulary The words a child understands but may not necessarily produce in speech.

recursion An aspect of language productivity that allows a speaker to add infinitely to a sentence.

referential strategy The approach used by children whose first words refer mostly to objects.

school language (or school talk) The distinct pattern of language typically used in classrooms.

scripts Narratives based on generalized accounts of procedures or recurring events.

second language acquisition (SLA) The more general term referring to all second language acquisition, but particularly that which occurs after the onset of puberty.

selective attention The ability to focus on a particular aspect of a task and ignore others.

self-monitoring Children's ability to compare their utterances with some mental representation of what they know about language.

semanticity One of the four attributes of human language, referring to the capacity of language to represent ideas, objects, or events with symbols.

semantics The branch of linguistics concerned with the study of meaning.

semiotics The study of signs and symbols and how they are used or interpreted.

sheltered English programs Language programs that may have students from a single language background or may group together students from different language backgrounds and focus on content, with teaching methods resembling those used in immersion.

simplification processes The processes by which children simplify pronunciation to forms their immature articulators can manage. These include consonant reduction, assimilation, and substitution.

simultaneous bilinguals Children who learn two languages from birth or before the age of 2 to 3 years.

slang Language used in informal settings, often indicative of the relationship between the speakers.

social-cognitive disorder A behavioral dysfunction resulting from a brain abnormality that interferes with infants' and children's abilities to develop normal social and cognitive skills.

social function of language The way in which children assert and maintain their social needs.

specific language impairment (SLI) The term language pathologists use for children whose language development is 12 months or more behind their chronological age and is not associated with other sensory or intellectual deficits or diagnosed cerebral damage.

speech delay A delay caused by a developmental problem with the speech mechanism—lungs, vocal cords, tongue, teeth, lips.

speech disorder The inability to produce speech sounds correctly or fluently, or problems with vocal quality.

standard dialect A term used to refer to the variety of language used by the media, by political leaders, and the one taught in school, and sometimes considered to be the "prestige" variation of a language.

stress The force with which a syllable is articulated.

stuttering The involuntary repetition of speech sounds, particularly initial consonants.

submersion A "sink or swim" approach, essentially doing nothing. Submersion is not a formal program but rather the default when educators do nothing but place second-language learners in mainstream classes without providing any supplemental instruction. (Compare to *immersion.*)

substitution Replacing a difficult sound with an easier one (*juice* becomes *du* or *dus*).

successive approximation The process by which children move progressively closer to the adult forms in certain aspects of their language learning. For example, a child learning the past tense of sing might progress from singed to sanged to sang.

successive (or consecutive) bilinguals Those who add a second language after the first is largely established.

surreptitious teaching Thinly disguised attempts to push children beyond their current stage of development into the next level.

syllable A unit of pronunciation consisting of a single vowel and any consonants that cluster around it.

synapse The junction between two nerve cells, consisting of a minute gap across which impulses pass.

syntax The branch of linguistics concerned with sentence structure.

synthetic languages A strictly synthetic language would combine all the morphemes needed to make the meaning of a sentence.

two-way immersion Language programs that integrate English-speaking children with language-minority children in an effort to promote academic achievement in both languages.

vocabulary spurt Sudden surge in the number of words a child knows and uses, typically occurring a little later in boys than in girls.

voice disorder One of the three broad categories of speech disorder, this is the term used to describe abnormalities in the voice when the airstream or resonance are affected.

vowel A highly resonant speech sound made when air passes through the vocal tract with little obstruction.

Wernicke's aphasia Also called sensory or receptive aphasia, a language disorder resulting from a lesion in Wernicke's area, the upper back part of the temporal lobe of the brain. Patients with this aphasia typically exhibit no articulatory dysfunction and may actually seem excessively fluent—talking rapidly and without hesitation, for example.

word A unit of language consisting of one or more spoken sounds, or their written representation, that is a principal carrier of meaning. A word must contain at least one morpheme but may have more.

zone of proximal development Referring to readiness, Vygotsky's term for the distance between the child's actual physical and cognitive level of development and the level at which she can function with adult assistance.

References

American Psychiatric Association (APA). (2011). A 05 autism spectrum disorder. Retrieved from http://www.dsm5.org/proposedrevision/pages/proposed revision.aspx?rid=94

American Speech-Language-Hearing Association (ASHA). (2008a). Incidence and prevalence of communication disorders and hearing loss in children—2008 edition. Retrieved from http://www.asha.org/research/reports/children.htm

American Speech-Language-Hearing Association (ASHA). (2008b). Communication facts: Special populations: Literacy—2008 edition. Retrieved from http://www.asha.org/Research/reports/literacy/

American Speech-Language-Hearing Association (ASHA). (2012a). Speech and language disorders and diseases. Retrieved from http://www.asha.org/public/speech/disorders/

American Speech-Language-Hearing Association (ASHA). (2012b). The prevalence and incidence of hearing loss in children. Retrieved from http://www.asha.org/public/hearing/disorders/children.htm

Anderson, S. (n.d.). The number of languages in the world. Linguistic Society of America. Retrieved August 12, 2011, from http://www.danielburke.com/files/howmany.pdf

Apel, K., & Masterson, J. (2009). *Beyond baby talk: From sounds to sentences—A parent's complete guide to language development*. New York: Random House Digital, Inc.

Arterberry, M. E., & Bornstein, M. H. (2001). Three-month-old infants' categorization of animals and vehicles based on static dynamic attributes. *Journal of Experimental Child Psychology, 80*(4), 333–346.

Atkinson, D. (2011). A sociocognitive approach to second language acquisition: How mind, body, and world work together in learning additional languages. In Atkinson, D. (Ed.), *Alternative approaches to second language acquisition* (pp. 143–166). *Oxford, UK and New York*: Routledge.

Bardige, B. S. (2009). *Talk to me, baby!: How you can support young children's language development*. Baltimore: Paul H. Brookes.

Bates, E., Bretherton, I., & Snyder, L. (1988). *From first words to grammar: Individual differences and dissociable mechanisms*. Cambridge, UK: Cambridge University Press.

Bauer, L., & Trudgill, P., Eds. (1998). *Language Myths*. New York: Penguin.

Beauchat, K. A., Blamey, K. L, & Walpole, S. (2010). *The building blocks of preschool success*. New York: The Guilford Press.

Belton, T., & Priyadharshini, E. (2007). Boredom and schooling: A cross-disciplinary exploration. *Cambridge Journal of Education, 37*(4), 579–595.

Bereiter, C., & Scardamalia, M. (1982). From conversation to composition: The role of instruction in a developmental process. In R. Glaser (Ed.), *Advances in instructional psychology*. Hillsdale, NJ: Lawrence Erlbaum.

Bialystok, E. (2001). *Bilingualism in development: Language, literacy and cognition*. Cambridge: Cambridge University Press.

Bialystok, E., Craik, F. I. M., & Freedman, M. (2007). Bilingualism as a protection against the onset of symptoms of dementia. *Neuropsychologia, 45*, 459–464.

Black, B. (1989). Interactive pretense: Social and symbolic skills in preschool play groups. *Merrill-Palmer Quarterly, 35*, 379–397.

Bloom, L. (1973). *One word at a time*. The Hague: Mouton.

Boeree, C. G. (2004). Dialects of English. Retrieved from http://webspace.ship.edu/cgboer/dialectsofenglish.html

Bomba, P. C., & Siqueland, E. R. (1983). The nature and structure of infant form categories. *Journal of Experimental Child Psychology, 35*, 294–328.

British Broadcasting Corporation (BBC). (2007, March 15). Bilingual classes "raise results." Retrieved April 1, 2012, from http://news.bbc.co.uk/2/hi/uk_news/education/6447427.stm

Brown, R. (1973). *A first language*. Cambridge, MA: Harvard University Press.

Burman, D. D., Bitan, T., & Booth, J. R. (2008). Sex differences in neural processing of language among children. *Neuropsychologia, 46*(5), 1349–1362. Retrieved February 2012, from http://www.sciencedirect.com/science/article/pii/S0028393207004460

Byers-Heinlein, K., Burns, T. C., & Werker, J. F. (2010). The roots of bilingualism in newborns. *Psychological Science, 21*(3), 343–348.

Cabell, S. Q., Justice, L. M., Vukelich, C., Buell, M. J., & Han, M. (2008). Strategic and intentional shared storybook reading. In L. M. Justice & C. Vukelich (Eds.), *Achieving excellence in preschool literacy instruction* (chap. 11). New York: Guilford.

Carmichael, L., Hogan, H. P., & Walter, A. A. (1932). An experimental study of the effect of language on the reproduction of visually perceived form. *Journal of Experimental Psychology, 15*(1), 73–86.

Carter, L. S. (2000). Everybody's talkin' at me. Can't hear a word they're sayin'. . . . Dartmouth Medicine. Retrieved from http://dartmed.dartmouth.edu/summer00/pdf/Scrambled_Sounds.pdf

Cazden, C. (2001). *Classroom discourse: The language of teaching and learning* (2nd ed.). Portsmouth, NH: Heinemann.

Center for Applied Linguistics (CAL). (2011). Directory of two-way bilingual immersion programs in the U.S. Retrieved from http://www.cal.org/twi/directory

Chaney, C. (1994). Language development, metalinguistic awareness, and emergent literacy skills of 3-year-old children in relation to social class. *Applied Psycholinguistics, 15*, 371–394.

Cheour, M. (2010, July 23). Symptoms of child aphasia. Livestrong.com. Retrieved from http://www.livestrong.com/article/182743-symptoms-of-child-aphasia/

Chisolm, K. (1995). A three-year follow-up on attachment and indiscriminate friendliness in children adopted from Romanian orphanages. *Child Development, 69*(4), 1092–1106.

Chomsky, N. (1959). Review of verbal behavior. *Language, 35*, 26–58.

Chomsky, N. (2006). *Language and mind* (reprint with additional chapters). New York: Harcourt Brace Jovanovich. (Original work published 1968)

Christie, J., & Roskos, K. (2003). Literacy in play. In B. Guzzetti (Ed.), *Literacy in America: An encyclopedia of history, theory and practice* (pp. 318–323). Denver, CO: ABC-CLIO.

Cincotta, M. S. (1978). Textbooks and their influence on sex-role stereotype formation. *Babel: Journal of the Australian Federation of Modern Language Teachers' Associations, 14*(3), 24–29.

Clark, E. V. (2003). *First language acquisition.* Cambridge, UK: Cambridge University Press.

Clark, E. V. (2004). Strategies for communicating. In B. C. Lust & C. Foley (Eds.), *First language acquisition* (pp. 423–431). Oxford, UK: Blackwell.

Cook, A. S., Fritz, J. J., McCormack, B. L., & Visperas, C. (1985). Early gender difference in the functional usage of language. *Sex Roles, 12*, 909–915.

Corden, R. (2000). *Literacy and learning through talk: Strategies for the primary classroom.* Philadelphia: Open University Press.

Corder, S. P. (2009, November). The significance of learner's errors. *International Review of Applied Linguistics in Language Teaching, 5,* 161–170.

Craik, F. I. M., Bialystok, E., & Freedman, M. (2010). Delaying the onset of Alzheimer's disease: Bilingualism as a form if cognitive reserve. *Neurology, 75,* 1726–1729.

Cross, I. (2009). Communicative development: Neonate crying reflects patterns of native-language speech. *Current Biology, 19*(23), R1078-R1079. Retrieved from http://www.sciencedirect.com/science/article/pii/S0960982209018557

Crystal, D. (1987). *The Cambridge encyclopedia of language.* Cambridge, UK: Cambridge University Press.

Curenton, S. M. (2006). Oral storytelling: A cultural art that promotes school readiness. *Young Children, 61*(5), 78–89.

Davidson, T., & De Villers, l. (2006). Specific language impairment. Gale encyclopedia of children's health: Infancy through adolescence. Encyclopedia.com. Retrieved April 29, 2012, from http://www.encyclopedia.com/topic/Specific_Language_Impairment.aspx#1-1G2:3447200530-full

DeCasper, A. J., & Spence, M. J. (1986). Prenatal maternal speech influences newborns' perception of speech sounds. *Infant Behavior and Development, 9,* 133–150.

DeHirsch, K., Jansky, J., & Langford, W. (1966). *Predicting reading failure.* New York: Harper & Row.

DeVilliers, J., & DeVilliers, P. (1973). A cross-sectional study of the acquisition of grammatical morphemes in child speech. *Journal of Psycholinguistic Research, 2,* 267–278.

Dickinson, D., Wolf, M., & Stotsky, S. (1993). Words move: The interwoven development of oral and written language. In J. B. Gleason (Ed.), *The development of language* (3rd ed.) (pp. 369–420). Upper Saddle River, NJ: Merrill/Prentice Hall.

Dingfelder, S. (2008, November). Storytelling, American style. American Psychological Association. *Monitor on Psychology, 39*(10), 24.

Downey, S., Hayes, N., & O'Neill, B. (2007). *Play and technology for children aged 4–12.* Dublin, Ireland: Office of the Minister for Children. Retrieved from http://www.dcya.gov.ie/documents/research/Play_and_Technology.pdf

Dromi, E. (1987). *Early lexical development.* Cambridge, UK: Cambridge University Press.

Dromi, E. (1993). The mysteries of early lexical development. In E. Dromi (Ed.), *Language and cognition: A developmental perspective* (pp. 32–60). Norwood, NJ: Ablex.

Dromi, E. (1999). Early lexical development. In M. Barrett (Ed.), *The development of language* (pp. 99–131). Hove, UK: Psychology Press.

Dulay, H. C., & Burt, K. (1974). Natural sequences in child second language acquisition. *Language Learning, 24*, 37–54.

Edwards, A. D., & Westgate, D. P. G. (1987). *Investigating classroom talk*. London: The Falmer Press.

Eimas, P. D., Siqueland, E. R., Jusczyk, P., & Vigorito, J. (1971). Speech perception in infants. *Science 22, 171*(3968), 303–306.

Eliot, L. (1999). *What's going on in there? How the brain and mind develop in the first five years of life*. New York: Bantam.

Elkind, D. (2003, Fall/Winter). The reality of virtual stress. *CIO Magazine*.

Ellis, R. (2012). *Language teaching research and pedagogy* [Kindle for iPad version]. Chichester, UK: John Wiley & Sons.

Elman, J. A. (2001). Connectionism and language acquisition. In M. Tomasello & E. Bates (Eds.), *Essential readings in language acquisition* (pp. 295–306). Oxford: Basil Blackwell. Retrieved from http://crl.ucsd.edu/courses/commdis/pdf/elman-chapter.pdf

Fantz, R. L. (1963). Pattern vision in newborn infants. *Science, 140*(3564), 206–215.

Felsenfeld, S. (1996). Epidemiology and genetics of stuttering. In R. Curlee & G. Siegel (Eds.), *Nature and treatment of stuttering: New directions* (pp. 3–23). Boston: Allyn & Bacon.

Gaff, R. (1978). Sex stereotyping in modern language teaching—An aspect of the hidden curriculum. *British Journal of Language Teaching, 20*(2), 71–78.

Garcia-Sierra, A., Rivera-Gaxiola, M., Percassio, C. R., Romo, H., Klarman, L., Oritz, S., & Kuhl, P. K. (2011). Bilingual language learning: An ERP study relating brain responses to speech, language input, and later word production. *Journal of Phonetics, 39*(4), 546–557. Retrieved from http://www.elsevier.com/locate/phonetics doi:10.1016/j.wocn.2011.07.002

Garvey, C., & Kramer, T. L. (1989). The language of social pretend play. *Developmental Review, 9*, 364–382.

Graham, J., & Forstadt, L. A. (2000, 2011). Children and brain development: What we know about how children learn. University of Maine: Cooperative Extension Publications #4356. Retrieved from http://umaine.edu/publications/4356e/

Guiberson, M., Barrett, K. C., Jancosek, E. G., & Yoshinaga-Itano, C. (2006). Language maintenance and loss in young preschool age children of Mexican immigrants: Longitudinal study. *Communication Disorders Quarterly, 28*, 4–14.

Halliday, M. A. K. (1975). *Learning how to mean.* London: Edward Arnold.

Harris, M. (2004). First words. In J. Oates & A. Grayson (Eds), *Cognitive and language development in children* (pp. 61–112). Oxford, UK: The Open University/Blackwell Publishing.

Harris, M., Jones, D., & Brookes, S. (1988). Linguistic input and early word meaning. *Journal of Child Language, 15,* 77–94.

Harris, M., Jones, D., & Grant, J. (1983). The nonverbal context of mothers' speech to infants. *First Language, 4,* 21–30.

Hart, B., & Risley, T. (1995). *Meaningful differences in the everyday experience of young American children.* Baltimore: Paul H. Brookes.

Hawley, T. (2000). Starting smart: How early experiences affect brain development. Retrieved from http://www.ounceofprevention.org/news/pdfs/Starting_Smart.pdf

Heath, S. B. (1983). *Ways with words: Language, life, and work in communities and classrooms.* Cambridge, UK: Cambridge University Press.

Heath, S. B. (1986). Separating "things of imagination" from life: Learning to read and write. In W. H. Teale & E. Sulzby (Eds.), *Emergent literacy: Writing and reading.* Norwood, NJ: Ablex.

Hepper, P. (1988). Fetal soap addiction. *The Lancet, 331*(8598), 1347–1348. Retrieved from http://www.lancet.com/journals/lancet/article/PIIS0140-6736(88)92170-8/fulltext

Hitti, M. (2004). Being bilingual boosts brain power. Retrieved December 1, 2011, from http://www.bbc.co.uk/news/health-17892521

Holt, J. (1989). *Learning all the time.* Reading, MA: Addison-Wesley.

Howard, E. R., & Sugarman, J. (2001). Two-way immersion programs: Features and statistics. ERIC Digest EDO-FL-01-01. Washington, DC: ERIC Clearinghouse on Languages and Linguistics. Retrieved November 2011, from http://www.cal.org/resources/digest/0101twi.html

Hoyt, A. (2008, September 24). How propaganda works. HowStuffWorks.com. Retrieved July 8, 2012, from http://history.howstuffworks.com/historians/propaganda.htm

Hulit, L. M., & Howard, M. R. (1993). *Born to talk.* Upper Saddle River, NJ: Merrill/Prentice-Hall.

Hyon, S., & Sulzby, E. (1994). African American kindergartners' spoken narratives: Topic associating and topic centered styles. *Linguistics and Education, 6,* 121–152. Retrieved April 2012, from http://deepblue.lib.umich.edu/bittream/2027.42/31890/1/0000842.pdf

Jakobson, R. (1960). Linguistics and poetics. In T. Sebeok (Ed.), *Style in language* (pp. 350–377). Cambridge, MA: MIT Press.

Johnson, E. K., & Jusczyk, P. W. (2001). Word segmentation by 8-month-olds: When speech cues count for more than statistics. *Journal of Memory and Language, 44,* 548–567.

Justice, L. M., & Ezell, H. K. (2001). Written language awareness in preschool children from low-income households: A descriptive analysis. *Communication Disorders Quarterly, 22,* 123–134.

Kim, S. C. (1985). Family therapy for Asian Americans: A strategic-structural framework. *Psychotherapy, 22,* 726–734.

Kirk, E. W. (1999). Dictation and dramatization of children's own stories: The effects on frequency of children's writing activity and development of children's print awareness. Retrieved February 2012, from http://cardinalscholar.bsu.edu/handle/handle/177378

Klass, P. (2011, October 10). Hearing bilingual: How babies sort out language. *The New York Times,* p. B10. Retrieved from http://www.nytimes.com/2011/10/11/health/views/11klass.html

Kormi-Nouri, R., Moniri, S., & Nilsson, L. (2003). Episodic and semantic memory in bilingual and monolingual children. *Scandinavian Journal of Psychology, 44*(1), 47–54.

Krashen, S. (1977). Some issues relating to the monitor model. In Brown, H. D., Yorio, C., & R. Crymes (Eds.), *On TESOL '77.* Washington, DC: TESOL.

Krashen, S. (1981). *Second language acquisition and second language learning.* Oxford: Pergamon.

Leong, D. J., & Bodrova, E. (2012). Building language & literacy through play. Scholastic. Retrieved from http://www.scholastic.com/teachers/article/building-language-literacy-through-play

Levy, G. (2011, January 13). Stuttering versus cluttering—What's the difference? American Speech-Language-Hearing Association (ASHA). Retrieved from http://blog.asha.org/2011/01/13/stuttering-versus-cluttering-%E2%80%93-what%E2%80%99s-the-difference/

Lieberman, A. F., & Zeanah, H. (1995). Disorders of attachment in infancy. *Infant Psychiatry, 4,* 571–587.

Lightbown, P. M., & Spada, N. (2006). *How languages are learned.* Oxford: Oxford University Press.

Lonigan, C. J. (2008). *(Almost) everything you wanted to know about phonological awareness and were afraid to ask.* Paper presented at the Early Reading First Grantee Meeting, New Orleans.

Mampe, B., Friederici, A. D., Christophe, A., & Wermke, K. (2009). Newborns' cry melody is shaped by their native language. *Current Biology, 19*(23), 1994–1997.

Mashburn, A. J., & Pianta, R. (2010). Opportunity in early education: Improving teacher-child interactions and child outcomes. In A. Reynolds, A. Rolnick, M. Englund, & J. Temple (Eds.), *Childhood programs and practices in the first decade of life: A human capital integration* (pp. 243–265). New York: Cambridge University Press.

Mattes, L. J., & Omark, D. R. (1984). *Speech and language assessment for the bilingual handicapped.* Sand Diego, DA: College-Hill Press.

Meisel, J. M. (2007). The weaker language in early child bilingualism: Acquiring a first language as a second language? *Applied Psycholinguistics, 28,* 495–514.

Meisel, J. M. (2011). *First and second language acquisition.* Cambridge, UK: Cambridge University Press.

Melzi, G. (2001). Cultural variations in the construction of personal narratives: Central American and European American mothers' elicitation styles. *Discourse Processes, 30*(2), 153–177.

Mihalicek, V., & Wilson C. (Eds.). (2011). *Language files: Materials for an introduction to language and linguistics* (11th ed.). Columbus, OH: The Ohio State University Press.

Mizne, C. A. (1997). Teaching sociolinguistic competence in the ESL classroom. (Senior thesis projects, 1993–2002). Tennessee Research and Creative Exchange. Retrieved from http://trace.tennessee.edu/utk_interstp2/20

Morin, A. (2012). *Is your kid bored at school?* Retrieved from http://childparenting.about.com/od/schoollearning/a/Is-your-kid-bored-in-school.htm

Moschkovich, J. (2007, February). Using two languages when learning mathematics. *Educational Studies in Mathematics, 64*(2), 121–144.

Muthukrishna, N., & Sokoya, G. O. (2008). Gender differences in pretend play amongst school children in Durban, Kwazulu-Natal, South Africa. *Gender and Behavior, 6*(1), 1577–1590.

National Association for the Education of Young Children (NAEYC). (2012). Technology and interactive media as tools in early childhood programs serving children from birth through age 8. Fred Rogers Center for Early Learning and Children's Media at Saint Vincent College. Retrieved from http://www.naeyc.org/files/naeyc/file/positions/PS_technology_WEB2.pdf

National Early Literacy Panel. (2007). *Developing early literacy: Report of the National Early Literacy Panel.* Washington, DC: National Institute for Literacy.

National Institute on Deafness and Other Communication Disorders (NIDCD). (2012). Specific language impairment. National Institutes of Health. Retrieved from http://www.nidcd.nih.gov/health/voice/pages/specific-language-impairment.aspx

Ndung'u, R., & Kinyua, M. (2009). Cultural perspectives in language and speech disorders. *Disability Studies Quarterly, 29*(4). Retrieved from http://dsq-sds.org/article/view/986/1175

Nystrand, M. (2006). Research on the role of classroom discourse as it affects reading comprehension. *Research in the Teaching of English, 40,* 392–412.

Osborne, L. (2000, June 18). The little professor syndrome. *The New York Times Magazine.* Retrieved from http://www.nytimes.com/library/magazine/home/20000618 mag-asperger.html

Painter, C. (2005). Researching first language development in children. In L. Unsworth (Ed.), *Researching language in schools and communities* (pp. 65–87). London & Washington: Cassell.

Pan, B. A., & Snow, C. E. (1999). The development of conversational and discourse skills. In M. Barrett (Ed.), *The development of language* (pp. 229–249). Hove, UK: Psychology Press.

Pearson, B. Z. (2008). *Raising a bilingual child: A step-by-step guide for parents.* New York: Living Language (Random House).

Pinker, S. (2007). *The stuff of thought: Language as a window into human nature.* New York: Penguin Books.

Pinker, S. (2010). *The language instinct: How the mind creates language.* New York: Harper Collins.

Piper, T. (2007). *Language and learning: The home and school years.* Upper Saddle River, NJ: Pearson.

Pitman, S. (2008). The impact of media technologies on child development and wellbeing. OzChild. Retrieved from http://www.ozchild.org.au/userfiles/docs/ozchild/research-papers/ImpactOfElectronicMedia.pdf

Plunkett, K., & Schafer, G. (1999). Early speech perception and word learning. In M. Barrett (Ed.), *The development of language.* Hove, Sussex, UK: Psychology Press Ltd.

Pratt-Johnson, Y. (2006). Communicating cross-culturally: What teachers should know. *Internet TESL Journal, 12*(2). Retrieved from http://iteslj.org/

Prieto, M. D., Parra, J., Ferrando, M., Ferrandiz, C., Bermejo, M. R., & Sanchez, C. (2006). Creativity in early childhood. *Journal of Early Childhood Research, 4*(3), 277–290. Retrieved from http://www.sagepub.com/eis2study/articles/Prieto%20Parra%20Ferrando%20Ferrandiz%20Bermejo%20and%20Sanchez.pdf

Quinn, P. C., & Oates, J. (2004). Early category representation and concepts. In J. Oates & A. Grayson (Eds.), *Cognitive and language development in children* (pp. 21–60). Oxford: Blackwell Publishing Ltd.

Ramey, C., Campbell, F., & Blair, C. (1998). Enhancing the life course for high-risk children. In J. Crane (Ed.), *Social programs that work* (pp. 184–199). New York: Russel Sage Foundation.

Reber, P. (2010, May). What is the memory capacity of the human brain? Scientific American. Retrieved from http://www.scientificamerican.com/article.cfm?id= what-is-the-memory-capacity

Rennie, J. (1993). ESL and bilingual program models. Retrieved from http://www.cal .org/resources/digest/rennie01.html

Rhodes, R. L., D'Amato, R. C., & Rothlisberg, B. A. (2010). Utilizing a neuropsychological paradigm for understanding common educational and psychological tests. In C. R. Reynolds & E. Fletcher-Jantzen (Eds.), *Handbook of clinical child neuropsychology* (3rd ed.). New York: Springer.

Ricciardelli, L. A. (1992). Creativity and bilingualism. *Journal of Creative Behavior, 26*(4), 242–256.

Ronjat, J. (1913). *Le développement du language observé chez un enfant bilingue.* Paris: Champion.

Rutter, M., & the English and Romanian adoptees study team. (1998). Romanian orphans investigation. Retrieved from http://www.integratedsociopsychology.net/ romanian_orphans_investigation.html

Segalowitz, S. J. (1983). *Language function and brain organization.* New York: Academic Press.

Shafer, R. E., Staab, C., & Smith, K. (1983). *Language functions and school success.* Glenview, IL: Scott, Foresman.

Simms, M. D. (2007). Language disorders in children: Classification and clinical syndromes. *Pediatric Clinics of North America, 54*(3), 437–467. Retrieved from http:// www.sciencedirect.com/science/article/pii/S0031395507000442

Skinner, B. F. (1957). *Verbal behavior.* New York: Appleton-Century-Crofts.

Spellings, M. (2005, December 1). From essential elements to effective practice. Address at the fourth annual "Celebrate Our Rising Stars Summit." Sponsored by the Department's Office of English Language Acquisition (OELA). Washington, DC. Retrieved from http://www.ed.gov/news/speeches/2005/12/12012005.html

Stennes, L., Burch, M., Sen, M., & Bauer, P. (2005). A longitudinal study of gendered vocabulary and communicative action in young children. *Developmental Psychology, 41*(1), 75–88.

Stuttering Foundation, The. (2012). Retrieved from http://www.stutteringhelp.org/ prevalence

Swoyer, C. (2003). Relativism. In E. N. Zalta (Ed.), *Stanford encyclopedia of philosophy* (2010, Winter). Retrieved from http://plato.stanford.edu/archives/win2010/ entries/relativism/

Tannen, D. (2001). *You just don't understand: Women and men in conversation.* New York: William Morrow.

Tannen, D. (2011). *That's not what I meant! How conversational style makes or breaks relationships.* New York: Harper Perennial.

Tardif, C., & Weber, S. (1987). French immersion research: A call for new perspectives. *Canadian Modern Language Review, 44,* 67–78.

United States Census Bureau. (2010). Language use. United States Department of Commerce. Retrieved from http://www.census.gov/hhes/socdemo/language/

United States Department of Education. (2008). Foundations for Success: The final report of the National Mathematics Advisory Panel. Retrieved from http://www2.ed .gov/about/bdscomm/list/mathpanel/report/final-report.pdf

University of Texas at Austin. (2010, September 27). Difference or disorder? Retrieved from http://www.utexas.edu/features/2010/09/27/language-2/

Van Kleeck, A. (2007, September 25). Home talk and school talk: Helping teachers recognize cultural mismatch. *The ASHA Leader.* Retrieved from http://www.asha.org/ Publications/leader/2007/070925/070925c.htm

Vygotsky, L. S. (1978). *Mind in society: The development of higher psychological processes.* Cambridge, MA: Harvard University Press.

Vygotsky, L. S. (1986). *Thought and language* (A. Kozulin, Trans.). Cambridge, MA: MIT Press. (Original work published 1934)

Walsh, D. J., Price, G. G., & Gillingham, M. (1988, Winter). The critical but transitory importance of letter naming. *Reading Research Quarterly, 23*(8), 108–122.

Wasik, B. A., & Bond, M. A. (2001). Beyond the pages of a book: Interactive book reading and language development in preschool classrooms. *Journal of Educational Psychology, 93,* 243–250.

Weikum, W. M., Vouloumanos, A., Navarra, J., Soto-Faraco, S., Sebastián-Gallés, N., & Werker, J. F. (2007, May). Visual language discrimination in infancy. *Science 25, 316*(5828), 1159.

Welton, R. (2010). Early childhood writing development. Livestrong.com. Retrieved from http://www.livestrong.com/article/88414-early-childhood-writing-development/

Westby, C., & Begay, V. (2002). Living in harmony: Providing services to Native American children and families. In D. E. Battle (Ed.), *Communication disorder in multicultural population* (3rd ed.). Boston: Butterworth-Heinemann.

Williamson, G. (2011). Child-directed speech. Speech Therapy Information and Resources. Retrieved from http://www.speech-therapy-information-and-resources.com/child-directed-speech.html

Yardley, A. (1973). *Young children thinking*. London: Evans Brothers.

Yiu, E. M., Murdoch, B., Hird, K., Lau, P., & Ho, E. M. (2008). Cultural and language differences in vocal quality perception: A preliminary investigation using synthesized signals. *Folia Phoniatr Logop, 60*(3), 107–119.